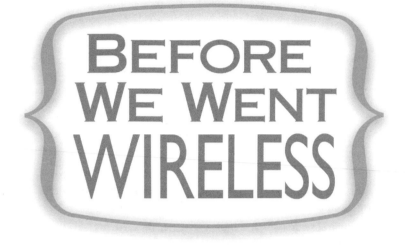

BEFORE WE WENT WIRELESS

Library of Congress Cataloging-in-Publication Data

Hughes, Ivor, 1940–

 Before we went wireless : David Edward Hughes, FRS : his life, inventions, and discoveries   (1829–1900) / Ivor Hughes & David Ellis Evans. — 1st ed.

   p. cm.

 Summary: "The first biography of the brilliant inventor and practical experimenter in late 19th century telegraphy, telephony, metal detection, and audiology, British-born David Edward Hughes"—Provided by publisher.

 Includes bibliographical references and index.

 ISBN 978-1-884592-54-6 (hardcover) — ISBN 978-1-884592-53-9 (pbk.)

 1. Hughes, David Edward, 1829-1900. 2. Inventors--United States--Biography. 3. Inventors—Great Britain--Biography. 4. Telegraph—History. 5. Telephone systems—History. 6. Metal detectors—History. 7. Electromagnets—History. I. Evans, David Ellis, 1943- II. Title.

 TK140.H84H84 2011

 609.2—dc22

 [B]

2010042978

ISBN 9781884592546 hardcover   9781884592539 paperback

Copyright ©2011 Ivor Hughes

First edition, First printing

Published by Images from the Past, Inc.
www.imagesfromthepast.com
PO Box 137, Bennington VT 05201
Tordis Ilg Isselhardt, Publisher

Printed in the USA

Design and Production: Toelke Associates, Chatham, NY

Printer: Versa Press, Inc., East Peoria, IL

BEFORE WE WENT WIRELESS

DAVID EDWARD HUGHES FRS

HIS LIFE, INVENTIONS AND DISCOVERIES

(1829–1900)

IVOR HUGHES & DAVID ELLIS EVANS

IMAGES FROM THE PAST

Bennington, Vermont
www.imagesfromthepast.com

Professor Hughes with the upgraded version of his telegraph instrument, which had been a success all across Europe.

CONTENTS

THE HUGHES PROJECT

This book is an invitation to stop for a moment—to stop the endless stream of cell phone calls, the search for Wi-Fi hotspots, Google queries, text messages, and emails—to consider and appreciate one of the scientific pioneers who helped build the technological foundations of today's pervasive 24/7 connectivity. It is a book about David Edward Hughes, who was an accomplished musician and composer, an adventurer, a self-educated inventor, a decorated scientist, a successful business man, and a philanthropist, who showed how we could make important use of the two invisible forces called electricity and magnetism.

When we started this biography neither of us had any idea of the fantastic journey of discovery it would take us on. For my part, the project got its start because of my interest in the history of the electric telegraph and the evolution of wireless. In my research I often came across references to the Victorian scientist Professor David Edward Hughes, and wondered whether I might be related to him, as we shared a surname and also Welsh roots (in fact we are not related). The more I learned about him and the wide range of his discoveries, the more he fascinated me.

My co-author David Ellis Evans became interested in Hughes when he returned to live in the cottage of his childhood in the tiny village of Druid between Corwen and Bala in North Wales, UK. He soon discovered that the village was thought to be Hughes's birthplace. Like any good historian he had to find out more.

David's and my paths crossed when we were introduced to each other by Mr. Donald M. Smith, a descendant of the family of Hughes's wife Anna Chadbourne. Don was the custodian of Hughes's papers, and when I contacted him I found a man who shared my enthusiasm for Hughes. Don was living near Chicago at the time, had taken a great interest in Hughes's life, and was very proud of his heritage; his father had met Hughes on a number of occasions. David's and my friendship with Don grew, and before we knew it he had persuaded us to write Hughes's biography—and he generously gave us full access to Hughes's papers, as well as sharing with us the fruits of his own investigations.

Researching David Edward Hughes has been a glorious chase across Europe and America. I have walked the dusty red earth lanes of Buckingham, Virginia, where he farmed, mined gold, and played music with his family on the veranda in the evenings. I have visited the splendid home that was once Roseland Academy in Bardstown, Kentucky, where Hughes taught philosophy and music, have sat in the square in Bowling Green, and have visited the town of Springfield where he developed his first telegraph instruments. I have walked up and down Great Portland Street in London imagining him doing the same with his first-of-a-kind portable wireless receiver. I have strolled the streets in Paris where he lived, an area that Ernest Hemingway would later describe in his short novel *A Movable Feast*, and visited the opulent area of Rue de la Paix where Hughes's future wife Anna had lived and where Hughes must have been struck by her beauty and *vivacité*. I have held his first model telegraph at the Smithsonian and his wireless apparatus in the Science Museum of London.

The fact that I lived in America and David lived in the UK turned out to be an advantage, as Hughes's life had spanned both continents. David's knowledge of the Welsh language proved invaluable in our research, particularly as he was able to translate some of the early accounts of the family's life.

Don has since passed away, but would have been very pleased to learn that David Edward Hughes's biography has now been published. This book is dedicated to Don's memory. We hope that you enjoy reading this book as much as we did researching and writing it.

Ivor Hughes
David Ellis Evans

ACKNOWLEDGMENTS

This book would not have been possible without the kind and most gracious help of Donald M. Smith, whose infectious enthusiasm was the inspiration and impetus behind the project. Unfortunately, Donald passed away before he could see the final result. His cause, however, was taken up by other members of the family, and we would like to thank them for their continued encouragement and support, specifically Diane Mather, Donna D'Andrea, and William B. Michaels in America, and Joan Lloyd (née Hughes) in North Wales.

The authors are indebted to numerous other people who made this book possible. Research over a ten year period and spanning two continents has obviously brought us into contact with many interesting and knowledgeable people who have selflessly given of their time, provided information, and offered advice.

We are indebted to the researchers, historians, and technical reviewers for their input and constructive comments during the book's formative phase. Their comments and advice on specific chapters have, I hope, kept us on track and objective in our views. These include Paul Israel, Director and General Editor of the Thomas Edison Papers Project; Bernard Finn, Curator Emeritus of Electricity Collections, Smithsonian Institution; Paul J. Nahin, University of New Hampshire; Bill Burns, John Casale, Dixie Hibbs, Anton A. Huurdeman, Dr. Vivian J. Phillips, Steven Roberts, and Eric P. Wenaas.

Hughes's first telegraph instrument is preserved in the Smithsonian Institution, Washington DC, and thanks go to Harold Wallace, Associate Curator, Electricity Collections, for his time and assistance in our research. Another valuable collection of Hughes's instruments has been carefully preserved at the Science Museum, London, and we appreciate the time and assistance of John Liffin, Curator of Communications, during our research and his support during the filming of the British Broadcasting Corporation's mini-documentary on Prof. David Edward Hughes.

In Europe we had invaluable assistance from a number of people. In France, where Prof. Hughes spent many years of his life, I would like to thank Maria Malanchuk, my guide and translator, who took the time to educate herself about Professor Hughes so that she could converse with various experts and translate French technical jargon of the Victorian era. We would also like to thank for their help Michel Atten, Patrice Battison, Pascal Lesourd, and the staff at the France Telecom Archives, Paris; as well as Roger Taylor and Kathleen Carney for their help and friendship in Paris.

In London, we received valuable assistance from the helpful staff at the British Library Department of Manuscripts, the Institution of Engineering and Technology archivist Anne Locker, and Raymond Martine of the British Telecommunications Archives; and support and encouragement from Aosaf Afzal and Julie Hodgkinson of the Royal Society. We are also grateful to Phillip Boyes, Operational Director, University College London Hospitals Charity for his background research and for providing information on the current status of Hughes's charitable gift to the London hospitals.

Special thanks to Ralph Barrett who kept the spirit of Prof. Hughes alive through his lectures and who was instrumental in seeing that 94 Great Portland Street, Hughes's home and the site of many of his experiments, received a commemorative English Heritage "Blue Plaque" site marker.

We are also grateful to Neil Johannesson and John White who helped early on and provided research and reference material. John, who sadly has since passed away, was one of the few people who could still repair a Hughes printing telegraph instrument. Thanks also to Alan Renton, Porthcurno Telegraph Museum, Cornwall; and to Peter Rowlands, University of Liverpool, an Oliver Lodge researcher, for providing inspiration in the early stages of the project.

The list would not be complete without mentioning the contribution made by Dr. R. Glyn Roberts and Dr. J. O. Marsh through their original research and publication of material on Prof. Hughes in 1980.

In Wales, Prof. Hughes is celebrated as a Welsh hero and still has a following, as exemplified by the Wireless in Wales Museum in Denbigh, the dream of David Jones who brought it to fruition and whose wife Vesi Jones now continues his work. We would also like to thank Pegi Talfryn and Bethan Gwanas and the late Ivor Wynne Jones, journalist, author, and historian, who gave us the advice and push "to get on with it and write."

Every so often we came across someone who was passionate about preserving historic telegraph instruments and took the time to share his or her knowledge and collection with others. One such a person is Fons Vanden Berghen, telegraph collector extraordinaire, and we thank him for maintaining and preserving telegraph treasures and freely sharing his knowledge and photographic material with us.

Thanks go to the following libraries; in Europe: the National Library of Wales, Aberystwyth; Flintshire Library and Information Service; Gwynedd Archives Service; Tunbridge Wells Library; and Merseyside Maritime Museum, Liverpool; and in the US: the Nelson County Public Library, Bardstown, Clarksville Public Library, Clarksville, Tennessee; the Logan County Public Library, Russellville, Kentucky; and the Department of Library Special Collections, Western Kentucky University Library, Bowling Green, Kentucky. Special thanks to Linda Braginton, Bixby Library, Vergennes, Vermont, who dealt with my many requests for difficult-to-obtain books.

Our thanks also to others who helped in various ways: Tom Cuff, Dan Worrall, Darrel Emerson, Janice B. Edwards, Mrs. Booker Noe, Marilyn (Green) Day, and to Nina and Jason Bacon for their kind help and interest and for providing a place to stay during my London research. To Historic Buckingham, Inc. in Virginia; to William B. Jones in Springfield, Tennessee; and to Lloyd Raymer and Roger G. Ward in Kentucky. Also to Edwin Gladding Burrows and Edwin Gwynne Burrows. And for his support and companionship on the Newfoundland road trip, to my cousin Richard W. Jones, and for his help on the Washington trip, to Donald Sharp, Christy and Joel. Also the interest and encouragement greatly appreciated from the "Wednesday Night Crew."

All of this research and writing would have been to no avail if it was not for our publisher Tordis Ilg Isselhardt's belief that this was a story worth telling, and for her enthusiasm which equaled our own. After our submission of the manuscript it was gratifying to see this enthusiasm rub off onto the publishing team as they went to work to turn it into a publication I am sure David Hughes would have been proud of. Thanks go to our editor Chet Van Duzer for his patience, immeasurable labors and invaluable suggestions over many months to hone and polish the text into a presentable form. Also, to Ron Toelke, our designer, for giving the book its own special visual impact both inside and out, for capturing the spirit of "Hughes the great experimenter," and for remaining flexible to accommodate the many changes and requests we presented him with; and to illustrator Carole Ruzicka for producing the technical illustrations.

Finally, to our indexer Helen Passey, who had to wait and wait patiently until we were all finished before she could start her exacting task.

Throughout the project we have had the unwavering support and encouragement of our families and close friends, particularly of Brenda my wife and of David's wife Joan, who have had to put up with David Edward Hughes as a long-term guest. Thanks also to my daughter Jill for her sympathetic ear and encouragement, and to my journalist son Trevor who early on tried to steer me away from engineer-style writing (read boring) and to teach me the importance of keeping the story moving along—easier said than done when there were so many side trails to explore. To my mother who has been patiently waiting for the book: here it is.

INTRODUCTION

Two young women in their early twenties made their way along Great Portland Street in London on a blustery gray November day. Deep in conversation as they headed for the shops in Oxford Street, they were abruptly interrupted by the muffled sounds of music from somewhere within their clothing.

"It's mine," Jill said, as she rummaged around and pulled out her cell phone. "Hi Dad."

"Hi, Jill, just calling to say I've finally arrived in Beijing."

"Oh good."

"I'm heading over to the hotel, sure am tired after the flight."

"Ah, I bet you are. Catherine is here with me. Hang on, and I'll send you something."

Jill held the phone at arm's length, pulled Catherine over, and recorded a short video of them with their heads together, their hair blowing across their faces while they laughed. Within seconds it popped up on her father's phone, and for a moment he felt as if he was right there with them, instead of several thousand miles away. Smiling, he saved the video and pocketed his phone.

Jill was about to put the phone away when it beeped with a new message. A picture appeared of a busy Victorian street full of horse drawn carriages and carts, ladies in long dresses, and men in unfamiliar-looking overcoats and hats. The women looked at each other in puzzlement.

A note popped up on the screen: "Historic Site, 94 Great Portland Street, 1879." The street scene changed, and now among the hustle and bustle one person stood out; passers-by were gazing at him. The screen zoomed in. He was holding something in his hand and walking slowly down the street. He was concentrating intently, apparently listening to a device clasped to his ear. Wires descended from the device into a leather satchel slung across his chest.

The scene faded and another note scrolled up on the display:

Professor David Edward Hughes, FRS, scientist and inventor (1829–1900) carried out the first mobile wireless experiment in November of 1879 here on Great Portland Street.

They looked at each other, bemused. "Wow, that was quite a while back and right here," Catherine remarked. Jill looked at the dinky device in her hand. "I wonder what the dear professor would think of it now," she said, flipping it closed.

Like many mobile phone users, they would be the first to plead ignorance of how the "dinky device" actually worked. How can it pluck signals right out of thin air? How does it know which ones are just for me? And how is it that its signals can reach almost anyone at any time at any place in the world?

Human civilization has been developing and advancing for thousands of years, but our methods of communications had hardly changed at all until quite recently in historic terms. Messages were passed by word of mouth or by notes and traveled no faster than a human could go on foot or a horse gallop. It could take days, weeks or even months to pass messages any distance, and this was reflected in the slower pace of life and commerce—hard to imagine in today's world of instant messages and instant responses. Up until the mid-1800s, it had always been that way, but then it all changed. Suddenly people could communicate over vast distances almost instantaneously. This was due to the introduction of the electric telegraph. Its arrival had profound implications on society, just as the introduction of the cell phone has had on modern culture.

These technologies, which we take for granted and on which we are so dependent, can be traced back to the pioneering work of Victorian scientists. One of these was Professor David Edward Hughes. Hughes was a brilliant inventor as well as a gifted musician, ever inquisitive and a true lover of science. He was born when Michael Faraday and Joseph Henry were still unlocking the mysteries of electricity, and when they and others were wrestling with the observations that electricity could create magnetism and magnetism could be used to create electricity. He lived through a period rich in famous names that are still familiar today, such as Charles Dickens, George Stephenson, Samuel Morse, Charles Darwin, Louis Pasteur, Albert Nobel, Thomas Edison, and Alexander Graham Bell.

Hughes left his mark through his inventions in the fields of telegraphy, telephony, wireless, metal detection, and audiology. He invented a telegraph instrument which was much more efficient and sophisticated than that of Samuel Morse, and which thanks to Hughes's great entrepreneurial energies, was adopted in America, and was used throughout Europe, in some areas for almost a hundred years. He was involved in an early attempt to communicate over a transatlantic telegraph cable from Britain, where he had been born, to America, where he had become a naturalized citizen. He discovered the carbon microphone, which became essential to the success of the telephone; derivatives of his microphone were in use in telephone systems until the 1980s—and in some parts of the world they are still in use! He discovered methods to transmit and receive radio waves about a decade before Heinrich Hertz did so, and with equipment far superior to Hertz's, though Hughes was unable to understand what he created, and unable to convince senior scientists that it was a legitimate discovery.

His telegraph instrument brought Hughes financial success, and partly as a result he did not patent his later inventions, but gave them freely to the world. His inventions also made him one of the most decorated scientists of his era: he received high honors from no fewer than nine countries, starting with the Imperial Order of the Legion of Honor from France in 1862. His life was one of high adventure, travel, and innovation; he was blessed with a knack for being in the right place at the right time with the right product. He was also involved in his share of controversy, including a dispute with Thomas Edison over the discovery of the microphone, and an extended debate with theoreticians about how high-frequency signals traveled on telegraph and telephone lines.

Hughes was a brilliant experimenter who was said to have "thought with his hands." Many other contemporary electricians were experimenters too; what set Hughes apart was his instinct for finding the right approach or combination of electrical components that brought about success, and for seeing opportunities or possibilities where others saw problems. He was one of the "practical men" as they were called to distinguish them from academics and theoreticians. Early in his career the practical men ruled: they wired the world for instant communications first with the electrical pulses of the telegraph, and then with the telephone, all without the aid of any theory or formula. But times were changing, and during the latter part of Hughes's career he and the other practical men were coming to the limit of their knowledge as electrical technology became more and more complex and they found themselves at a loss to explain the new mysteries of electricity and magnetism. The theoreticians gained credibility by showing that theory could predict the outcome of experiments. In fact it was the discussion of some of Hughes's experiments which most dramatically marked the new ascendancy of the theoreticians. This episode near the end of Hughes's career confirmed his status as one of the most influential electricians of his age.

It is the story of this man, one of the great inventors of the nineteenth century, and a man who helped usher in the Communications Age, which is told in the following pages.

WELSH ROOTS

LONDON, 1838

Everyone was talking about the show, insisting that you had to go see it. With all the hullabaloo, it was no wonder that there was such a large crowd piling into the theater.

The warm air spilling out from the doorways only served to draw them in out of the evening chill. My goodness! What a squash, the foyers an absolute zoo. Which way to go? Which door? Which stairway? The ears were assaulted by the noise of a hundred simultaneous conversations. Onward into the theater, jostle, shuffle down the aisles, there are our seats. Oh! Those large ladies' hats and the suffocating scent of "Eau de Cologne."

The atmosphere was alive with anticipation and excitement.

> "Ladies and gentlemen, your attention please. Ladies and gentlemen please."

The master of ceremonies, a ruddy faced, barrel-chested man with a voice that rattled the rafters, had appeared on stage, his arms outstretched appealing for quiet.

"Ladies and gentlemen please, I beg your indulgence," he entreated.

The footlights did their job, casting a greatly enlarged shadow onto the curtains behind him which made him appear ogre-like. The audience tailed off into silence. He continued his bellow:

> "We have for you tonight for your sheer delight and pleasure an act of musical brilliance. An amazing performance to titillate your fancy. A performance by the Masters Hughes as patronized by her most gracious Majesty. The extraordinary performances of these gifted children have been universally acknowledged as the most astonishing instance of instrumental precocity ever yet beheld. Master Joseph Hughes, ten years of age and a celebrated harpist known as the Welsh Paganini, and his brothers Master David Hughes six years of age and infant brother John Hughes four years of age."

He continued the introduction, building up the audience's anticipation in true Victorian music hall fashion.

> "And now, without further ado, I give you the Masters Hughes."

The curtains drew back to thunderous applause. And there they were, three small boys, like miniature porcelain figures, in their matching frock coats, lace collars, pantaloons and buckled shoes; the child prodigies dwarfed by their harps. The audience fell silent, startled by their small size. They started playing, the notes sweeping out over the audience, and the quality of their performance was that of much more mature musicians. The audience was enraptured with their renditions of favorite melodies and moving Welsh airs such as "Ar hyd y nos" ("All Through the Night") and "Men of Harlech." The two younger brothers played standing on pedestals to give them more presence on the stage. The older brothers Joseph and David played solos and duets on the harps while the younger brother John played the violin. They played a duet on one harp, followed by a solo concerto played by one of them on two harps. The program ended with a rendition of "Rule Britannia" followed by "God Save the Queen" that brought the audience to their feet with thunderous applause and shouts of "Bravo, bravo!" as the performers took their bows and the curtains closed.

This music hall performance in London in 1838 by the "Child Prodigies" may have been how David Edward Hughes first came to the attention of the world. According to the press reports, the "Child Prodigies" gave many concerts throughout the length and breadth of the country.[1] Certainly, the success of these concerts had propelled the family into the limelight. These gifted young musicians, who had inherited their father's musical talent, had turned their family's life upside down. Show business was far more lucrative than the boot-making business in which David Hughes's father had been working. He had given this up to become their fulltime manager and promoter. Their rise to fame had brought an increase in income, and that, together with their celebrity status, was moving them up the social ladder—which was the goal of all of the lower classes in the very class-conscious society of the Victorian period. Their popularity eventually brought them requests from royalty for private concerts, which only increased their fame and reputation.

It had not always been this way, of course; David Hughes's father, Dafydd Hughes had made his way to London from Wales some years earlier, around 1821–22, with little to his name.[2] Were the streets of London really paved with gold? There was only one way to find out. When he arrived, all he had to show was empty pockets, his boot-making skills and his music. But he had many inner strengths: he was extremely resourceful, an adventurer, an opportunist, and a gifted musician, and these traits were bound to propel him to better things. As will be seen later, his son David Edward Hughes had inherited these valuable characteristics.

Dafydd Hughes's family had its roots in the Bala and Corwen area of North Wales (UK),[3] a picturesque rural valley through which the River Dee slowly wound its way from Llyn Tegid (Bala Lake) past the town of Corwen on its way to the Irish Sea.[4] This was an area rich in Welsh tradition and myth, and a stronghold in the fifteenth century

The musical concerts by the "Child Prodigies" lifted the Hughes family to celebrity status and brought them financial security.

of Owain Glyndŵr, the Welsh prince who fought gallantly to end the English occupation of Wales.

Dafydd Hughes was born in Bala in 1803, the eldest child of Robert and Margaret Hughes, whose family had lived in the area since the early 1700s.[5] Robert Hughes operated a boot and shoemaking business there. Like many who lived in Wales, he had music, poetry and song in his veins, and these activities formed a large part of his social life. Robert performed the duty of bandleader of the local militia, with the young Dafydd often joining in with the band.[6] As Dafydd grew older he followed in his father's footsteps, learning the boot and shoemaking trade and also showing a talent for music. He tried to learn to play any instrument that he could lay his hands on, but was mostly drawn to the traditional instrument of Wales, the harp.

By the time Dafydd was seventeen, he had probably become fascinated by the stories and talk he heard from customers in the boot shop, especially from those who had traveled beyond the valley, stories of towns and cities, ships and the sea, factories and machines—a whole different world. He was ready for some adventure, a rite of passage, an opportunity to prove himself. Home was becoming crowded as the family grew, and this appeared to add to his restlessness. This all led to his making a bold decision:[7]

The Hughes family roots were in the market town of Bala, situated in the area now known as Snowdonia National Park.

He went to Liverpool at quite an early age to ply his trade, and every spare hour he got he spent practicing and perfecting himself on some musical instrument or other. He was in Liverpool, he says, when news arrived of Bonaparte's death—and he remembers he was there at the time of George III's death and the ascension of George IV to the throne.

Around 1820, times were tough for the lower class in Britain. The majority of the male population was still employed as farm laborers or in related trades, earning meager wages. Women and children, as soon as they were old enough, worked long hours in domestic service or as laborers to help put food on the table. It was, however, a time of social transformation. Britain's industrial heart was starting to beat faster, set in motion by mechanization and industrialization as Herculean steam-powered engines made use of the abundant coal and iron to turn Britain into the workshop of the world.

It was indeed the time of the "Industrial Revolution," and the mold for the future character of the country was being cast. Innovations were coming from self-made men who had had little formal education rather than from aristocrats, and these men's new-found money propelled them into a world previously occupied only by the upper class.

Leading the charge to mechanization in the north of England were the cotton mills of Lancashire. These were like a magnet, drawing people from the surrounding countryside to the mill town factories, a migration motivated by the poor conditions in the countryside and by the perceived greater opportunities in the cities.

Dafydd Hughes's world up to that time probably only extended to the rural valleys surrounding Corwen and Bala, with the occasional excursion to Dolgellau and Barmouth. He probably knew most of the people in the town, where Welsh was almost exclusively spoken. When he left home he embarked on a journey literally into the unknown as far as he was concerned, a village teenager who spoke no English but who obviously had plenty of spunk! His family would have little or no knowledge of his whereabouts or well being. News took days, weeks, or months to reach the outlying areas, traveling only at the speed of a horse or foot traveler.

Dafydd Hughes struck out for Liverpool, the largest city and a major port in the region. It had grown in importance since cotton had become king, funneling raw materials from North America to the Lancashire cotton mills.

As his family had little money he would have set out on foot to travel the seventy or so miles from Bala to Liverpool, no doubt wearing a good pair of boots of his own making. Any money he had would have been used for food and for ferry crossings of the rivers Dee and Mersey. Walking was how the majority of people traveled in those times, and they covered vast distances. Welsh drovers routinely walked their herds of cattle or sheep one to two hundred miles to markets in the Midlands of England or down to London and then walked back, as did the "merched y gerddi," the Welsh garden girls who walked to the London area for the fruit-picking season and to work in the market gardens.

When Dafydd arrived in Liverpool it must have been an eye-opener for him. It was big, crowded with people and busy like market day in Bala, but perhaps a thousand times greater. He was seeing foreigners for the first time, and even black men. There were grand buildings and there were slums. There were well-dressed merchants and poverty-stricken multitudes, street vendors and peddlers. Then there was what it was all about, the wharves, beautiful sailing ships and the smell of the sea wafting in with the tide. It must have been overwhelming and he must have wondered if he had done the right thing, especially as all of the people there spoke a different language.

During his stay in Liverpool, Dafydd Hughes's attention must have been drawn to the throngs of people heading out for a new life in America, weary of the low wages, poverty and slum conditions in England. He was adjusting to his move from the countryside to the city, whereas these people were moving to another country. Was there really a land of new opportunities out there? Why would these people risk all, traveling thousands of miles via a long and perilous sea journey? Possibly this was when the seed was first planted in his mind which would lead him to the same course of action some years later.

Liverpool had grown to be the most important port in Britain, but there was a dark side to its growth. Vast numbers of Liverpool ships were involved in the slave trade, the so-called "African Trade" or "Triangular Trade," and it was precisely this trade that had been fuelling Liverpool's growth and prosperity. Yet the city's involvement in the slave trade was largely invisible, as few slaves ever appeared in Liverpool. The trade route was to carry cloth, pots, pans, muskets, gunpowder, knives, beads, brandy and salt as well as other commodities to West Africa. Here, slaves would be picked up and packed into the ships like sardines in a can and transported to the British colonies in the West Indies and to the American South, and sold to work on the cotton plantations.[8] On the return leg of the voyage the ships carried rum, sugar, tobacco, and cotton from the New World back to Liverpool—at a big profit. Little did Dafydd know during this fleeting brush with the slavers that he would later find out for himself what the slave business was all about.

He stayed in Liverpool for a year or so before once more becoming restless and moving on:[9]

> He moved from there to London and went to work with an uncle who lived in Charterhouse Lane. Whilst working with his uncle, he fell in love with a young girl who was in service with a family of oil merchants by the name Higgins who lived at No. 3 Charterhouse Square. She was from Ware in Hertfordshire and before he was yet twenty years of age he married her. (He did quite right.) By this time he was quite an accomplished harpist and spent some time most evenings entertaining his wife and himself and any friends who might be with them, with a tune on the harp.

Very little is known about how Dafydd actually met his wife Catherine who was in service at a residence in Charterhouse Square, not far from where he resided. Catherine, who was some five years his senior, may well have taken him under her wing when he arrived in London and was no doubt responsible for helping him learn English. Up to this time he had had a limited command of the language, having managed to get by in his native Welsh even in Liverpool, where there was a large Welsh population. Dafydd's and Catherine's friendship led to marriage on August 7, 1823 at St. Giles, Cripplegate, London.[10] It is possible that Dafydd at some time after his marriage returned home to the Bala and Corwen area so that his parents could meet his wife, but little is known of this period of his life. Their first child was a son, Joseph Tudor Hughes, said to have been born on October 27, 1827, possibly in Bala.[11]

As regards the birth of David Edward Hughes, there seem to be as many different birth dates quoted and suggested as there are authors who address the matter. In a letter that he wrote to his sister Margaret later in his life, it is apparent that David himself was uncertain when or where he was born, and also that the matter did not greatly concern him.[12] The inscription on his tomb indicates that he was born on May 16, 1830, exactly a year earlier than the date usually quoted in most references; no official source can be found to corroborate either date.[13] However, in the pages of the baptismal register of St. Andrew's Church, Holborn, London, the handwritten entries reveal:

September 9th. 1829. Reference No. 2130. David Edward, Born 18th. June 1829. Parents: David and Catherine Hughes of Suffolk Street, St. Pancras, Boot maker. Ceremony performed by R. Black.

The church of St. Andrews, London, held a special significance for Hughes: he had been baptized there and later returned from the continent to marry at the same church.

The child's given names, together with the names of the parents and the father's occupation, all tally, and although there is no corroboration of the Suffolk Street address, it is in the right area of London, and this must be our David Edward Hughes.[14] Unfortunately the place of birth is not recorded, and there is an interval of almost three months between the birth and the baptism, unusual in those days of high infant mortality, when it was customary for children to be baptized as soon as practicable. Perhaps the family was visiting relatives in Bala or Corwen at the time of the birth, and deferred baptism until their return to London, which would explain the claims that he was born near Corwen, at the cottage called Green-y-Ddwyryd.[15] It is certainly highly significant that when he decided to get married, he and his bride traveled from Paris to London, to marry at his baptismal church, St. Andrew's, Holborn.

Besides Joseph, David Edward Hughes had two other siblings, a younger brother and a sister. John Arthur Hughes was born on March 10, 1832,[16] and Margaret on October 17, 1837.[17]

Shortly after marrying, Dafydd Hughes set up in business in the boot and shoe trade in South Audley Street, near Oxford Street, London. Soon there was plenty of hammering mingled with the rich smell of leather. Boots and shoes were individually made to order in this period, and there were plenty of ordinary customers as well as higher paying gentry to take care of in the city. The business grew as word got around and additional workers were taken on until he was keeping a dozen of them busy—a good start considering that he had arrived in London with little more than his skills. In his leisure time he loved to play the harp and spent some time in the evenings entertaining himself and his wife and friends. When their eldest son Joseph was about two and a half years of age, he started to take an interest in the harp. Whenever he saw his father playing, he would run to him, and nothing would satisfy him except to be allowed to try his hand at it. His father had a small harp made for him. By the time he was three and a half years of age, he could accurately play "All Through the Night," "New Year's Eve," and one or two other old Welsh airs, and his reputation soon spread throughout the neighborhood.[18]

The parents were encouraged to allow their son to play in public and eventually some of Dafydd's acquaintances managed to obtain permission for him to perform at a concert in the New Strand Theatre. A clipping from an unnamed newspaper of the time ran as follows:

> Master Hughes has a just claim to the title "Infant Prodigy" with which he is announced if he be really no older than he seems, and is said to be in his fifth year. The son of Maia himself in his fifth year scarcely drew sweeter or more skilful notes from the lyre which he fashioned out of tortoise-shell than this extraordinary little Welshman managed to bring from harp strings that seem to be nearly as thick as the fingers of the tiny musician. His playing is not mere mechanical, or the result of drilling, but bold, free and expressive, far beyond anything of which so young a child could be thought capable of producing.

David Hughes's elder brother Joseph, seen publicized in this poster, paved the way for his siblings, leading to the formation of the "Child Prodigies" musical group.

The *Times* (London) of February 18, 1832, was a little more objective:

> At the end of it, a little boy of the name of Hughes, apparently about 5 years of age, performed some airs and variations on the single-action harp, among which was God Save the King. What he can do on that instrument is certainly surprising in a child of his age. We observed that he plays the principal part with his left hand and the bass with his right hand, though holding the instrument on his left shoulder. His teachers would do well to accustom him to the proper position.

Of course the critic was more familiar with the Continental method of playing the harp, which was influenced by the piano keyboard where the right hand played the high notes, rather than the Welsh tradition which was followed by the young Hughes.[19] However his father seems to have heeded this advice, since a later poster for his concerts shows him with the harp on his right shoulder. This same poster, which was printed in Caernarfon, North Wales, mentions that his tutors were Messrs. Weippert, Chatterton and Bochsa.[20] The first two named were competent harpists, while the third, Robert Nicholas Charles Bochsa, was a brilliant French harpist of Czech extraction and a composer of some note. The price of admission to these concerts given by "Master Hughes," as Joseph became known, was three shillings a head, with children half price, while a family ticket to admit four was ten shillings. This was a considerable amount of money in those days, in excess of what an average working man would earn in a week.[21]

Although he had established a successful boot and shoe business, Dafydd Hughes soon found that he could earn far more in a month holding concerts with his children than he could in a year in his shop. So he turned his business over to his foreman, with the proviso that he could take it back if he should decide to return. By now Joseph's siblings David and John were demonstrating that they were also musically gifted, so they joined their elder brother on the concert stage, playing the harp and violin respectively.

David Hughes's specialty was described in a poster announcing a concert to be held in Tunbridge Wells on May 31, 1839.[22]

MASTER DAVID E. HUGHES
(Only Six Years of Age)

> Who will perform, at sight, any piece of Music arranged for the Harp, which may be introduced by the Company during the Concert. A note being sounded on any instrument, he will name it (blind-folded) at a moment's notice. A person singing, or playing on an instrument, in any key, he will write in their presence every note; also transpose it to any other key the party may request, and play it on the Harp.

As can be readily calculated from David E. Hughes's date of birth in 1829, he was a little older than six in 1839—he was in fact ten! However his small physique and some added skullduggery surrounding the ages of all the "Child Prodigies" seems to have allowed them to continue to pull off the ruse.

The Welsh magazine *Y Ddolen* listed the towns and cities in England, Wales and Ireland, which they had visited on their concert tour and provided the details of the musical program under the following introduction:[23]

> As performed by them at Windsor Castle, on the 10th November, 1838, before HER MAJESTY and the ROYAL COURT.

Dafydd Hughes and his wife must have been very proud of their children at this point, as playing for royalty was considered a great honor. On one occasion David and his brother Joseph had been forced to cancel an evening concert at Kingston-upon-Thames after Joseph received a royal command to play before Queen Victoria at Windsor on very short notice.[24]

However, the family was probably well aware that the "Child Prodigies" act could not go on forever. The children would eventually grow up and they would lose their novelty. They had by now completed the rounds of the United Kingdom with their act and the parents were no doubt considering what to do next. A tour of the Continent? Or perhaps America?

It may have been thoughts of expanding their horizons as performers, or the lure of additional wealth,[25] or it may have been the idea of escaping the poor economic

St. Katharine Docks, London, a gateway to the world, with the infamous Tower of London in the background.

conditions in Britain; but whatever the reasons, the Hughes family began thinking of America.[26] And so plans were made and they embarked from St. Katherine's Dock in London on the sailing vessel *Catharine* of 499 tons, which cleared the Port of London on Friday, August 28, 1840, under the command of her master, Michael Berry, bound for New York and Charleston.[27] Little did they know when they set out on what was possibly a concert tour that only one member of the family was destined to return to the old country.

They would have set sail with the high tide, moving down the Thames, passing the Isle of Dogs and Greenwich Observatory, passing Gravesend and the Nore as they left the Thames estuary behind and sailed out into the North Sea. More canvas would have been added and the ship would have taken on a heel that they would learn to live with, off and on, for the rest of the voyage. A turn to the west through the Straits of Dover would have seen them saying farewell to the white cliffs. From the English Channel they entered the broad reaches of the Atlantic Ocean, which would be their home for some weeks.

THE ADVENTURE BEGINS

AMERICA, 1840

America at long last—maybe only one more day's sailing to New York. The news sent an excited ripple through the passengers, and the children reverted to their mischievous selves. An end was in sight to the nine long cold weeks of Atlantic punishment, with its penetrating dampness and nauseating pitching and rolling. Color and hope was creeping back into the stark white faces of the landlubbers.

Having spent weeks without seeing another ship, the passengers now seemed to see them everywhere, and one came alongside and a sailor from the *Catharine* tossed bundles of British newspapers to the other ship. Sandy Hook, the well-known lighthouse that marks the entrance to New York harbor, passed by on the port side. The semaphore telegraph could be seen on shore, looking like a large stick doll with flailing arms that would soon be signaling the arrival of the *Catharine*. The message would be picked up by the lookouts on Staten Island and relayed to the Battery at the southern tip of Manhattan.[1] Another ship approached to transfer the pilot aboard to navigate them into the busy port.

Sailing more slowly now, the ship pitched uneasily on the swell. The passengers crowded the rail as they strained to see

Before the electric telegraph, signaling was done visually by semaphores such as this one on Staten Island that relayed ship arrivals to the Battery on the southern tip of Manhattan.

for the first time the details of the land most of them had chosen to be their home. The Atlantic cold had now given way to a warm October sun that seemed to be welcoming them.[2] Sailing up to the island of Manhattan with its hundreds of wharves, chock-a-block full of sailing ships with their forests of masts and confusion of ropes, the *Catharine* found its place and edged in among them. The Hughes family climbed down the gangplank on wobbly legs, glad to be back on firm ground.[3] Their celebrity had evidently preceded them, as we are told that "They were given a princely reception by the Mayor and Corporation of New York in the City Hall."[4]

When the Hughes family set off for America, they were probably planning to stay for a few months, enough time for a concert tour. However, given their wanderlust, they likely had in the back of their minds the possibility of making the New World their home. Like Europe's many emigrants, the Hugheses saw America as the land of opportunity. It was a vast land that had only gained its independence some sixty-odd years earlier and whose frontier was still only as far west as St. Louis and the Mississippi. But it was a nation that was growing rapidly through the influx of immigrants.

By 1840, New Yorkers were in the mood for a good dose of laughter and fun. They had just endured the "Economic Panic of 1837" and were hoping for better times.[5] P.T. Barnum was starting on his great career as an impresario and was wooing the masses with acts that included minstrels, displays of freaks and the "Believe It or Not" exhibitions. The Hugheses could not have timed their arrival in the New World, or their concert tour, any better. People flocked to see the young performers and were fascinated by their mastery of music and instruments. David's younger sister Margaret (now three years of age) made her debut and thus all of the Hughes children were performing. The little players coaxed their harps alive, playing popular tunes and their own compositions and variations. The "Child Prodigies" looked as young as the audience anticipated. Resplendent in their frock coats, lace collars, and pantaloons, they thrilled the audiences, with Joseph at times playing two harps simultaneously or playing a duet with David on a single harp, and John and Margaret making up a quartet with John on the violin and Margaret on the concertina.

Of course there was always some mystery surrounding the "Child Prodigies." People often asked whether they were really as young as was claimed. The truth was that a pinch of theatrical liberty had been used to create their stage image (not an uncommon practice). The Hughes boys were portrayed as a few years younger than they actually were.[6] Over time, their true ages became blurred even to themselves and they came to live this illusion. They toured extensively, visiting many cities and towns including Baltimore and Richmond. Their visit to Philadelphia must have reminded them of home, as many Welsh immigrants lived there and had named one of its outlying towns Bala-Cynwyd after a town and village in the area where David's father had grown up in Wales. Their fame even led to the honor of a reception at the White House late in 1840 with President Martin Van Buren, whose term was just expiring, and the new President-elect, General William H. Harrison. After their busy tour, they returned to New York City where they stayed for a while before their next engagements.

Immigrants to America faced many new experiences, and often there was no way of knowing how a new situation would play out, or what course it might take. And so it was with the Hugheses. Their next engagement was in Albany in upstate New York, to which they set out by steamship up the Hudson River. What started out as a light-hearted adventure ended in dire consequences and the accidental death by drowning of young Joseph. [7]

Sailing ships in New York harbor, the Hughes family's point of entry to America.

Up to now the Hugheses had the wind behind and the sun always shining on them. Now a black cloud came over the horizon, and a storm broke over their pavilion. After traveling for about a year in America, they were on a journey from New York to Albany, and staying a day or two in Newburg, on the banks of the Hudson, about sixty miles upstream of New York. On Tuesday night they held a concert in that town and intended to hold another the next day. In the morning, there happened to be an old lady selling fish in the inn where they were staying—*shadfish*, which were completely unknown in Britain. The children happened to be around at the time; they saw the fish, and started to question the landlord about them, where they were caught, by what means, and so on. "If you wish," he replied, "I will take you out in the boat this afternoon to see the fishermen hoisting their nets." The offer was gratefully accepted. The afternoon came. Hughes and his three boys, Joseph Tudor, David and John together with two others, went out in the boat. After sailing some distance, there was a sudden squall—the boat capsized—he kept hold of the two youngest, but poor Joseph Tudor went down and was drowned. It was a fortnight before his body was found. He was taken to New York and was buried in the graveyard of the Welsh Baptist chapel in Enmity Street [*sic*] where they used to meet at that time. The news of the drowning of the young harpist caused deep sorrow, not only in New York but throughout the whole country.

Joseph's death hit the close-knit family hard, and they suspended their concert tour, mourning their loss.[8] Many years later David Hughes's father broke down in tears when recalling the loss of his eldest son when interviewed by a reporter.[9]

In order to see for myself what coverage there was in the New York papers at the time, it occurred to me to visit the office of the *Tribune*—Horace Greeley's paper, and one of the foremost and respected New York newspapers. Old Hughes came with me. We made our way to the editor's room and asked to see the file for 1841. Directly, one of the boys came with us to an adjacent room and it was handed to us. We turned to May, and on the 18th—three or four days after Joseph Tudor's drowning, we found a report of about half a column on the incident. Whilst I was copying the report the old man was turning the pages of the Tribune, and soon, I saw that he had struck on something—and with that, lord help him, he started to weep! He wept loudly, whatever I did, and lest the office boys should think us both demented, I took him out, with the intention of returning on my own to see which paragraph had so upset our old friend's feelings. And so it was; and I went there at the first opportunity. It was a letter, together with a piece of poetry composed by a gentleman from Philadelphia who had taken a great liking to the little lads.

The weeks that followed Joseph's death brought the family another scare as David contracted scarlet fever, but luckily he recovered.[10] As the months slipped by, the family tried to come to terms with events, even contemplating returning home. But they were persuaded to restart their concerts, the first of which was held in Boston. An article about the event appeared in the American Welsh-language paper *Cyfaill Americanaidd* (American Friend) in October, 1841, and reported that the Hugheses received inscribed pocket-watches from members of the gentry, who were impressed with their playing at the Lee Grand Theater. As the family eased back into performing concerts, they appeared with other artists, such as Ole Bull, one of the great nineteenth-century European violinists.[11]

While they were on tour, another British celebrity swept into America in the form of Charles Dickens. Dickens and his stories enjoyed unprecedented popularity on both sides of the Atlantic. He toured extensively, although it is not known whether he crossed paths with the Hughes family. When he returned home Dickens recorded his experiences in his book *American Notes for General Circulation*. He appeared to have been disappointed in his visit and revolted by the slavery he witnessed.[12]

The Hugheses' concerts took them the length and breadth of the eastern part of North America, from Canada down to New Orleans. They were still giving concerts in 1845, including a series in Charleston, South Carolina, in May of that year.[13] The three Hughes children, billed as the Hughes family, appeared before large audiences of well-to-do planters and town folk in the city's Hibernian Hall. The price of admission was fifty cents, and the little group performed four times over the course of a week. The reviews were enthusiastic: Margaret, at seven years old, was said to sing operatic airs and play the harp "with great originality of genius." John played the violin in a manner "creditable to old and experienced masters, not excepting Paganini himself." Of David, who was fourteen, it was said that "his flying fingers swept the lyre." David also played the English concertina, which a reviewer called "a most pleasing instrument."

Being constantly on the move brought its own challenges, not the least of which was the lack of space and the necessity of continuing the children's education. They traveled around in their own carriage and four, which was cramped. All of the available space was probably taken up by bodies, valises, trunks, musical instruments, books and sundry boxes. The four horses must have strained under the load but always seemed to get them to where they were going. We know very little about David's mother during this period. She surely had an important role managing the family, providing emotional stability during what must have been a very challenging period, and seeing to their education.

Between concerts there were suitable intervals to allow for finding suitable lodging at an inn or other hostelry and for sight-seeing. During these periods the children received their education from a private tutor who traveled with them, as well as from David's father, an accomplished harpist who orchestrated their musical training.[14] They probably all looked forward to their performances as a break from their studies, as it was an enjoyment that they could all share. David Hughes had now become fluent in French and had also learned Welsh from his father, besides taking a keen interest in the sciences, as his father had introduced him to chemistry, or alchemy, as it was often called then.

Alchemy, which can be thought of as chemistry with an admixture of philosophy and magic, often conjures up an image of someone in flowing robes tending bubbling retorts and searching for the elusive formula for turning base metals into gold. Perhaps David's interest in alchemy can be seen as a sign, as in a few years the search for gold would become the Hugheses' major preoccupation. Nevertheless, chemistry was becoming an accepted discipline in its own right, and David Hughes later recalled producing many different salts of mercury as well as alloys and various gases while experimenting with his chemistry set, enduring the occasional explosion along the way. Even at this early age, David suffered from a common ailment experienced by scientists and experimenters: mercury exposure.[15] He records that:[16]

> having injured my health by the fumes of sulfur & mercury, I was not allowed to study or experiment further, but I did continue the study of music.

Even as the family traveled, David continued his investigations into the world of science, experimenting with electricity and with model steam engines. An entry in his notes reads:[17]

> Attempted to produce perpetual motion by a pump acting upon an overshoot water wheel, did not succeed.

He was presumably referring to a water wheel driving a water pump that pumped water back to drive the water wheel, which drove the pump and so on in the pursuit of perpetual motion. He was certainly not the first to seek to create the ultimate machine; the Patent Office had seen its share of purported designs for such machines, and had finally stopped accepting applications for patents on them.

David Hughes's father had taken a particular interest in geology, and David too became interested in rocks, minerals and their formation. This was to lead to what became a shared fascination with gold. By now, the Hugheses were financially independent, and their direction and priorities in life shifted from show business to traveling for enjoyment and pursuing their growing interest in gold mining. They still gave occasional concerts, but they had outgrown their "Child Prodigy" image. So, with more leisure time, they set off on their travels, heading up to New Brunswick, Nova Scotia, Newfoundland, and Labrador, and then back south to the West Indies, sailing on the brig *Champion* from Newfoundland to Jamaica. From there they returned to America and the southern states. To satisfy their curiosity about gold and its mining they visited gold mines in North Carolina, Georgia, Alabama, and Virginia.

It is at this point that we get our first real glimpse of David Hughes's emerging scientific interests, as his father relates in this interview some years later (in this quotation the name Dafydd refers to David Edward Hughes):[18]

The old man says of Dafydd that since he was a lad, he was remarkably inquisitive, and would notice and want to know about everything, particularly machines and mechanisms of all kinds. When touring England and Wales, Dafydd, when visiting a city or town, would, before departing, have had a look at every mill and factory there. He could relate what kind of machinery was used in one, and what kind in another; and if there was anything remarkable about one or the other—some more recent invention or another—or an improvement of any kind, Dafydd was sure to study it carefully, and would ensure that he understood it fairly comprehensively. That is how Dafydd went through life. It was unusual for him to visit anywhere without learning something before leaving. Not only machines and mills either; he was also a keen student of chemistry, mineralogy, geology, &c.

Around 1845–6 David, now a teenager, records that he was studying natural philosophy, as physics was known at the time.[19] He also continued studying chemistry and his beloved music. His interest in geology became more concentrated as he and his father started analyzing various ores, specifically copper, lead, and gold ores from mines that they had visited. By the time David was fifteen he was using a portable laboratory to chemically analyze mineral samples.[20]

Finally, with all of this amassed knowledge of gold mining, their thoughts turned to putting down roots and investing their capital in a gold venture. It was natural to head for Virginia, as this state was the predominant producer of gold in America at the time (prior to the discovery of gold in California in 1848 that resulted in the famous California Gold Rush).[21]

Around 1847 the family settled on a plantation (or farm) that was located in the Virginia gold belt. The plantation was located near the village of Maysville, later to be renamed Buckingham, in Buckingham County.[22] Like many of the early settled areas, the town was believed to have taken its name from England, specifically from Buckinghamshire. Buckingham County had also attracted other Welsh immigrants from the quarries of Caernarvonshire to work in its slate quarries.

The farm was some sixty miles west of Richmond, the state capital, and five miles southeast of Maysville, located on both sides of the high road that ran between them.[23] The countryside was one of red earth and rolling hills with the Blue Ridge Mountains off to the west, and Willis Mountain overlooking the area. Thomas Jefferson's estate Monticello was thirty-five miles to the north, from which Willis Mountain was visible. The farm came to be known as "St. David's Farm," a little corner of Wales in the new country.[24] It included an orchard of peaches, apples, and cherry trees, as well as fields and woodland. They built a sawmill, as well as a laboratory for David, next to the house. As for gold mining, they were encouraged by the fact that a number of commercial mines, including the Booker and Seay mines, operated close by.[25] They had located gold veins on their property and began sinking shafts and erecting machinery for crushing the rock and separating out the gold. Having previously surveyed the machinery in many mines, they saw that there was much room for improvement. David noted that they:[26]

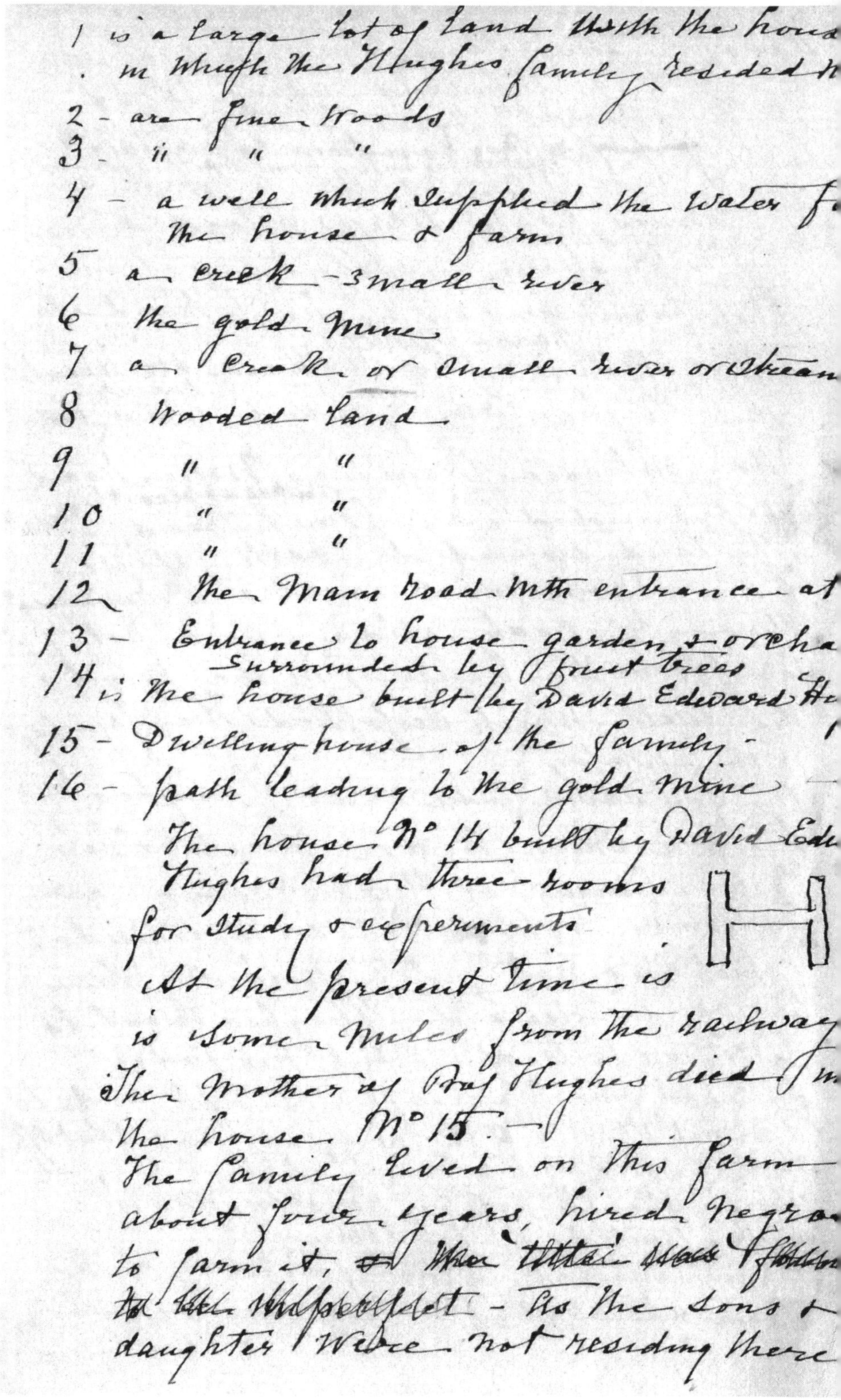

1   is a large lot of land with the house
.   in which the Hughes family resided n

2   - are fine woods

3   - "   "   "

4   - a well which supplied the water f
        the house & farm

5   a creek - small river

6   the gold mine

7   a creek or small river or stream

8   wooded land

9   "   "

10   "   "

11   "   "

12   the Main road with entrance at

13 - Entrance to house garden & orcha
        Surrounded by fruit trees
14 is the house built by David Edward He

15 - Dwelling house of the family -

16 - path leading to the gold mine -

The house No 14 built by David Ed
Hughes had three rooms
for study & experiments

At the present time is
is some miles from the railway
The Mother of Prof Hughes died in
the house No 15 -
The family lived on this farm
about four years, hired negro
to farm it, the tttttt stees fttttt
th ttt tttpttttt - As the sons &
daughter were not residing there

Gold mining fever seized the Hughes family, so they settled in the Virginia gold belt and started mining for it on their farm in Buckingham.

commenced sinking shafts and erecting machinery of my invention, which was adopted by the other mines in the state.

Even at seventeen, he was creating models of his ideas for machinery to take to Pittsburgh so that full-size wooden patterns could be made for casting parts for an improved rock-crusher.

However it was not smooth sailing as they experienced a host of "start-up" problems with the mine, including flooding, machinery malfunctions, labor and financing.[27]

We determined to suspend operations until we could get steam power having already expended over $15,000 without any return whatever.

This was quite a significant sum of money at that time, but rather than let this situation get them down, they used it as an excuse to go exploring again. Off they set for a tour of the Southern and Western states, while waiting for the delivery of the steam engine. A piece of land in the neighboring state of Tennessee, at Dover on the Cumberland River between Memphis and Nashville, must have appeared attractive and to have potential, as they purchased 5,000 acres there.[28] It was about this time that the great California gold rush started and many pioneers headed out west to seek their fortune. The Hugheses may have thought about pulling up stakes and joining in the fever, but they stayed put and persevered with their own mine.

Sinking shafts, working the mine, and operating the farm—clearing the land, felling, transporting and sawing trees, tending animals, planting and harvesting the crops—required a significant amount of manual labor, and these tasks were performed by black slave labor.[29] The Southern States had been built on black slave labor, and their economy depended upon it. Although he may not have made the connection, this was Dafydd Hughes's second encounter with slavery: as a youth he had stayed for a while in the port of Liverpool, a city that had prospered from its part in the slave trade, transporting slaves from Africa to America, and now here he was, a slave owner himself.

Virginia was caught between the Northern States, which were against slavery, and the Southern States, which condoned it. Tensions between them would eventually flare into the Civil War in 1860. At the time, however, Virginia struggled with the conflicting philosophies: on the one hand, Virginia was a slave state, but on the other, Buckingham's representative to state government was warning that the system of slavery was a great evil and that these oppressed and degraded people could not be held forever in this way.[30] This warning was not heeded, and later the Hughes family was trapped in the middle as the Civil War wreaked havoc on the country.

By 1849 the Hugheses were working hard on the farm to install a large steam engine to drain water from the mine and to crush the gold-bearing ore. Their situation seemed to improve at least for a short while, as they entered into a contract to supply the nearby Booker Mine with machinery. David records that they:[31]

entered into a contract with the Booker Gold Mine Company to supply them with machinery of my invention, did so, and was cheated out of the whole, having not been careful enough in making an agreement, trusting to words more than paper.

But there was more disturbing news to come. The family soon learned that the 5,000 acres purchased in Tennessee had been sold to them fraudulently and they lost everything that they had invested in the deal.

While the Hugheses may have had problems with and doubts about their business ventures, nobody could take away their music, and they probably spent many a warm evening out on the veranda, playing their instruments and competing with the chirping crickets. David was becoming an accomplished musician and was beginning to consider it as a career; he was now composing and writing an opera and his passion for music was a common theme in his personal notes.[32] However, he had not abandoned his interest in the natural sciences and continued his studies. Using his scientific knowledge he was able to solve one of the frustrating problems with the gut strings used on the musical instruments that went out of tune due to the high humidity that prevailed in the summer in Virginia. His answer was to coat the strings in a solution of shellac dissolved in ether.

He was coming to the end of his teenage years, and it was at this time that the first hint of his restlessness and dissatisfaction with farm life surfaced. It appears that while on a family trip through Oxford, Mississippi, he saw something that was not only to draw him away from the farm but also to set the direction for the rest of his life. What he saw was one of the newest inventions that was sweeping the country, namely the electric telegraph. Since its introduction in 1844, the telegraph had seen rapid expansion and adoption. Wires and poles were popping up everywhere, driven by businesses and newspapers that constantly strived for more up-to-date news and reports. There were many individual telegraph companies, but at this point all made use of the system invented by Samuel Morse and Alfred Vail. The following is an account of David Hughes's first encounter with the telegraph (in this citation the name Dafydd refers to David Edward Hughes):[33]

It was whilst traveling through the state of Mississippi, in the city of Oxford that the young man had his first opportunity to see the electric telegraph in operation. He was at that time about eighteen years of age and the telegraph was then new to the country. He had thoroughly understood the principle before leaving the telegraph office and also the workings of the instrument that was actually being employed. When leaving Oxford, he explained to his parents, his brother and his sister, everything about the telegraph, and furthermore, he said he believed that he could make an improvement to the instrument that he had seen in Oxford.

In one of the towns that they were staying in later, Dafydd went into a second-hand store and purchased an old clock with the intention of working out with it his improvement to the telegraph. He worked away at the clock during every spare moment he had. And after getting it to work, he bought another and another after that.

What David Hughes had observed in the telegraph office was a means of sending and receiving messages from distant cities almost instantaneously.[34] News, that only yesterday had taken days or weeks to reach its destination, now took only minutes: it was a revolutionary system that changed how people communicated and did business. He grasped the potential immediately, and his mind raced ahead to ponder how he could implement a new telegraph system, not by adding bells and whistles to the Morse system, but by an entirely different approach. He could see the limitations of the current system, which was prone to human and electrical errors, and required operators to know the special Morse code for converting the words, spaces, and punctuation of a message into dots and dashes. They then had to be able to tap out this code on an electrical key at a reasonable speed. The operator at the receiving end had to be able to decode the message and write it out again in English. Hughes must have mulled over questions such as, Why use a complicated code? Why not have a keyboard and enter the letters directly and print them out at the other end? With all of these new ideas for an improved telegraph buzzing around in his head, David found life in rural Virginia less and less appealing: he was coming of age and was ready to spread his wings. In a letter to his sister Maggie, written later in his life, David explains his decision to leave the farm and head west for Kentucky:[35]

Seeing the Morse telegraph for the first time inspired David with the conviction that he could

On the farm I could do nothing and I longed to get away so as to pursue my musical studies, according to my heart. I then wrote to Mr. Cosby the President of the College in Bardstown and received a favorable reply—which resulted in my going to Bardstown—where I taught and studied music to my heart's content and soon afterwards returned to take you to Bardstown for you to be educated in the College I was teaching at.

In David's personal notes he made the following entry for the years 1849 and 1850:[36]

Received the appointment of Professor of Natural Sciences, Music &c. to the Protestant Female College Bardstown and contrary to the wishes of my Father accepted the appointment.

   At the age of twenty I commenced teaching at the Female college of Bardstown. Was also appointed Teacher of the Teachers of Music in the Catholic College of Nazareth in same place.

invent a better instrument. Left: Morse key; right: Morse register.

So, with his teenage years behind him, he packed up his belongings, said his good-byes to a saddened family, and headed out for new horizons in Kentucky. Was his father seeing a reflection of himself in David? After all, had he not done the same in his youth when he packed up and left Wales? In this case at least they could keep in touch through the telegraph.

3

Go West Young Man and Seek Your Fortune

KENTUCKY, 1850

When David Hughes left Virginia for Kentucky he embarked on a new chapter of his life. He intended to become independent and earn his own living, but was to wrestle with this latter issue for a couple of years. He had become torn between his love of music and his scientific creativity, which was constantly tugging at him to pursue his telegraph interests.

Bardstown, Kentucky, turned out to be a good place for him to begin his independence, as it was a pleasant town of some 2000 citizens which had established itself as a center for education, the medical and legal professions, and religious institutions.[1] While Hughes made some notes about his time in Bardstown, he omitted the early days, and therefore it is left to the historian to piece together the events of that period.

Hughes could have traveled from Virginia to Kentucky via two different routes. One would have been to head west to catch a steamboat and travel down the Ohio River to Louisville, followed by a stagecoach to Bardstown. Alternatively, he could have traveled by stagecoach over the mountains by way of the Cumberland Gap. Either way, he would have finally been put down outside the Hynes House Tavern, after several uncomfortable days of travel.

David Hughes's first glimpse of Bardstown; he would have arrived by stagecoach at the Hynes House Tavern..

Was he filled with apprehension and excitement? Probably. His enquiries for the Female Academy would have led him up Main Street and across Chestnut Street, past large houses set back on their lots. He would not have been disappointed when he saw the Academy, a striking two-story brick building with an inviting entrance and balustrade roof, a neat walkway up to the front door bordered by carefully clipped hedges, and large shade trees offering a cool retreat from the heat.[2] Upon entering the Academy and standing in the entrance hall he certainly would have been struck by its architecture: a grand spiral staircase that appeared to climb to the sky, an illusion created by the domed stained glass skylight at the apex that dramatically bathed the stairs in sunlight; the spacious rooms separated by glass fan archways, the fine woodwork and elaborate fireplaces and mantels.

While he was still standing there admiring the splendor of the decor he may well have been brought back to earth by a greeting from the Reverend Jouett Vernon Cosby, the principal, and his wife Mary.[3] "Welcome, Professor Hughes, to Bardstown and Roseland Academy." That title probably made him feel pretty proud.[4]

The Rev. Cosby would no doubt have introduced him to the other staff members and shown him around the classrooms and dormitories which were housed in two large wings off the main building. During his tour, he would have been introduced to the students, who numbered about thirty-five young ladies in their teens.

Teaching young "Southern Ladies" philosophy and music was certainly going to be a different calling from farming and digging for gold; were any of his rough edges going to show through? He need not have worried, as, at twenty-one, he had already experienced more than many others would encounter in their whole lifetimes, and his experiences would have provided him with the necessary confidence. He had become a fine musician who captivated his listeners, for many of whom even hearing a harp would have been a novelty. His knowledge of the sciences had become remarkably comprehensive, due to his studies, inquisitiveness and experimentation, which had

Hughes was a professor at Roseland Academy where he taught philosophy and music.

involved plenty of "rolled-up sleeve" action. From this foundation, he would eventually become one of the great scientific experimenters—and famous for his achievements in this area.

He soon settled into his teaching career, and had the opportunity to socialize and enjoy the company of other musicians.[5] He must have been glad that his move was working out, for he certainly did not relish the thought of failing and returning to Virginia with his tail between his legs to receive a chiding from his parents. They had made it clear they were not happy with his leaving.

While engaged in his new-found profession he hoped that he could also find the time to pursue his idea of building a better telegraph instrument. Telegraphy had certainly taken off since Samuel Morse and Albert Vail had carried out their demonstration between Washington and Baltimore six years earlier in 1844. It is difficult to imagine that those who watched that first instrument click-clacking realized that they were seeing history unfold, or understood what was about to be unleashed on the world. The huddled bodies craned to see the message as the paper ribbon shuffled out of the machine marked with its dots and dashes; the code was deciphered and hurriedly written out: "WHAT HATH GOD WROUGHT?" These words were appropriate, for the transmission of this message was to start a social and technological revolution that continues unabated to this day.

By 1850, telegraph fever had swept America: telegraph wire was being strung at a tremendous pace and competition was keen. Wires were spreading out like spokes of a wheel from that initial Washington-Baltimore line to New York, Philadelphia, Harrisburg, Pittsburgh, Buffalo and Boston, then south to New Orleans, west to St. Louis, and north into Canada. It seemed that everyone wanted to get in on the act, and speedy communications became very much in vogue. The telegraph was already having a significant effect on commerce and industry, and was even changing social interaction. It changed the face of newspapers, as current news from far and wide became available even in the most remote towns, and the news industry soon became a driving force behind the spread of the telegraph network. The advent of the telegraph was truly a milestone in history, and the beginning of an important cultural shift.

It seems that after Hughes saw the Morse telegraph in operation for the first time, thoughts about how he could improve it were always in the back of his mind. There had to be a better system than the cipher of dots and dashes that only the operators could understand. It was during this time that his ideas for an improved telegraph instrument seem to have started coming together. His idea was to send the letters of the alphabet directly over the telegraph wire, and to print them at the receiving end without any need for deciphering.[6]

Hughes, of course, was not alone in recognizing that there was room for improvement. Both in Europe and America, new telegraphic inventions were appearing. But Morse and his associates were exerting considerable efforts to maintain a monopoly on the telegraph business in America. He prevailed in a court case in 1848, and the judge, as part of his ruling, said that Morse had the "exclusive right" to use "electro-magnetism" for telegraphic purposes. This was tantamount to giving someone exclusive rights to the use of steam power or electricity! This ruling led to outcries of monopoly, and a firestorm in the press. The Supreme Court overturned this decision the following year (1849).[7] After this ruling, competing telegraph companies were able to use other inventors' telegraph instruments on their lines (that is, other than the Morse system), such as the Bain and House instruments.[8] It is not known whether Hughes had read the newspapers accounts of the strife and court battles fought between Morse and his competitors, or whether he knew of these other telegraph instruments. If he did read about them, the accounts certainly did not deter him, and he proceeded to develop his own ideas for a telegraph system.

Having left the security and home life of the farm, Hughes was now experiencing the "time vs. earnings" conundrum of a young independent person with entrepreneurial ambitions. That is, he had to decide whether it was better to work longer hours to earn money to eat and have a place to sleep, or work less and starve, but have time for the development of his invention. Initially, earnings and eating won out, as he decided to take on additional private students and to teach music to some of the staff at the nearby Catholic College of Nazareth.

He continued teaching in Bardstown for about two years, and at the same time made some progress on his invention. During the summer recess, he returned home to the farm in Virginia where the biggest change he must have seen was in his sister Margaret or Maggie, as she had become known, and who was now a teenager. It was probably during this period that he suggested she attend Roseland Academy where he was teaching; an idea that was no doubt very upsetting to his mother, who was faced with the prospect of seeing another of her children leave the farm. However, it was an opportunity for Maggie to receive an excellent education, an opportunity that her mother must have felt she could not deny her. So at the end of August she packed up her belongings, and after tearful farewells, accompanied her brother when he returned to

Bardstown. The school opened on the first Monday of September with the cost of each five-month term ranging between $12 and $18. Board was $2 per week and included washing, lights, and fuel for heating the bedrooms. Extra courses could be taken in the harp, piano or guitar, ranging between $14 and $30. Charges for the use of books in the Academy library and use of chemicals and philosophical apparatus could add on another $3.50 per term. Extra courses were also offered in languages, art, and needlework, only the last of these being free of charge.[9]

David Hughes was probably able to exchange some of his teaching time to offset the cost of his sister's tuition. Even so, it sounds as if it was hard going financially, as he recalls in a letter to Maggie later in his life:[10]

> Well without going into details, I may say the year or two was a rather hard struggle for me—for my whole receipts for teaching etc. did not average more than 4 to 600 dollars per year—out of which I had to keep myself—and you, at the college, but I managed it well and never got in debt for a single cent.
>
> I worked hard on my music, knowing that my only chance in life was to become a real famous musical artist, but just midway in these studies my mind again became haunted with my old idea of a Telegraph—I could not resist it so I again bought old clocks and again went to work, dividing my time as near as possible between the practise and composing of music and tinkering on my Telegraph.

While he was engrossed in his teaching and Maggie was attending to her studies, a scourge of the times suddenly flared up: a cholera epidemic hit the town and all of the colleges closed. We assume that he sent Maggie home out of harm's way, but he remained in the town and took the opportunity to continue his studies in electricity and to compose some 400 pages of music, of which half was published in Louisville.[11] Hughes reports that by the time the epidemic was over, one sixth of the town's inhabitants had died. It seems that he made good use of these weeks without teaching, as he relates the following in connection with his telegraph experiments:[12]

> At last I got one Instrument to work tolerably well alone—but I could not make a distant Instrument or a Second Instrument work with the first—still, I could see it in the clouds, and felt sure with time I should finally succeed.... Suddenly a very serious thought came over me—It was this—you are neglecting your musical studies upon which depends your whole successful career—for a Will o' Wisp invention, which can only lead to your ruin, this nightmare persued [sic] me for a few days when I suddenly resolved to send a specimen of the printing done on a single instrument, and speak of it as if it had been finally resolved for two or more instruments working together, I wrote June 1852 and sent this to Mr. Woodward—who was then a telegraph agent in New York which I learnt from an advertisement. I asked if such an instrument would be of any value—and could he manage to bring it out etc.—He sent a long reply dated June 9th. 1852 telling me that there was a great demand for such an Instrument and that whenever I was ready to demonstrate its

practicability he could easily get up a company to buy the patent—This letter decided me
to continue my work until I succeeded.

Once the epidemic was over Maggie returned and he settled back into teaching.
Then, one day, they were surprised by the appearance of their brother John:[13]

> his brother John had run to him from the farm having fired a gun at some one which had
> not caused any harm but feared it had, so John ran to Bardstown to his brother.

Perhaps John had shot at a trespasser at their gold mine to frighten him off, and
then, concerned about the injuries he might have caused, and reprisals that might
result, decided that the best course of action was to get out of town. This was probably a wise choice, as in those days differences of opinion and feuds were often settled
frontier-style. We can imagine that John arrived somewhat white-faced, bedraggled and
constantly looking over his shoulder. David Hughes and his sister were probably able
to settle their brother down and put his mind at rest, reassuring him that the distance
between Virginia and Kentucky conferred safety.

In the days that followed, however, David Hughes began to view the problem of his
brother's arrival in practical terms of dollars and cents, concerned about the additional
strain it placed on their already tight budget. It was imperative that they should find
some employment for him, and it was decided that there would be more opportunity in
a larger town such as Bowling Green, ninety miles southwest of Bardstown.

Bowling Green was at that time one of Kentucky's largest and wealthiest towns.[14]
Situated at the head of the slack water of the Big Barren River, a tributary of the Green
River, it provided a route to New Orleans via four to six weeks' travel by flat boat.[15]
With the advent of steamboats had come a regular service, which established the town
as an important center for commerce. It was also on the stagecoach line that ran from
Louisville to Nashville in Tennessee. With connections in Bowling Green, the 170-mile
bone-shaking trip took three days and cost $12.

David and John Hughes were able to recruit a large number of private music students in Bowling Green as well as in the nearby town of Franklin. Once they were established and John had settled in, David Hughes moved on to Russellville where he took a
post at the Female Academy (thirty miles west of Bowling Green).[16] Here, he was able
to enroll his sister as a student, probably again bartering some of his time for her tuition
costs. Of course, all of this movement from one town to another must have been quite
time-consuming, leaving little time to devote to his telegraph invention.

It was while teaching private pupils in Russellville that he made the acquaintance
of a Dr. Brodnax, whose family he tutored.[17] During Hughes's visits to his home, Dr.
Brodnax came to learn of Hughes's idea of developing a new type of telegraph instrument that would be a significant improvement over the current Morse telegraph. With
the telegraph's popularity growing, Dr. Brodnax saw an opportunity to get in on the
ground floor and invest in an instrument that could bring him a nice monetary return.

He therefore made an offer to invest in the instrument. Hughes, however, declined, considering the instrument still too rudimentary, and suggested that Dr. Brodnax wait until he had a working prototype.

In 1853 a letter arrived from the young Hugheses' mother in Virginia, saying that she was not well.[18] They became quite concerned and felt helpless, being so far away. Shortly thereafter, another letter arrived saying that her situation had worsened and that she had become very ill, and feared that she would not live to see them if they did not come home at once. This letter spurred the three of them to head back to Virginia. When they arrived at the farm, they found their mother was not at all well, and it appeared that she had become broken-hearted after they had all left home. It was as if she had been holding on, waiting to see them just one more time—and after she had seen them, she slipped away.[19]

The farm must have seemed empty without her, and all the memories of the adventures they had shared would most likely have flooded back, one after another. London, the Queen, the concerts, the sea voyages, the travels, the smell of baking from the kitchen, singing to the harp in the evening: and now another member of the family, and one of the important participants in all of these events, was gone. As they mourned, their next concern would have been for their father, who would be alone and would have to manage the farm by himself. Now that they had started to establish their own lives in Kentucky, they were unlikely to return to Virginia. They also realized that being so far away, they missed seeing him. So he was persuaded to sell the farm and to move down to Kentucky with them.[20] As David Hughes was on friendly terms with the owners of a music store in Louisville called Peters and Webb, he was able to secure employment there for his father, who put his musical skills to good use, demonstrating and selling their pianos, as well as providing instruction to the customers who purchased them. Now that he had moved to Louisville, it would be much easier for the family members to get together.

Having taken care of their father, the three siblings returned to Bowling Green. It is at this time that David Hughes is believed to have become an American citizen, as when he later traveled abroad, he traveled on an American passport. It is also likely that the other members of the family became citizens around the same time.[21]

When David Hughes finally returned to Russellville he found that many of his students and their parents were disgruntled by his long absence. Also, he learned that Dr. Brodnax had come into an inheritance and had moved away and purchased a farm on the outskirts of Louisville. By now Hughes had come to the realization that he would never complete his telegraph instrument unless he devoted himself to it full time. He would have to knuckle down and find a place where he could work undisturbed. Leaving Margaret with his brother in Bowling Green, he moved to Springfield, just across the border in Tennessee, a small town of only about 200 people (twenty-five miles south of Bowling Green).

Small communities like Springfield were often very close-knit: everyone knew everyone, as well as everyone's business. Gossip circulated quickly, especially if a newcomer came to town. So when young Hughes showed up, rumors circulated about the mysterious character who shut himself away in his room, keeping to himself. A candle was always burning late into the night at his window. It was rumored that he was building something very secret, but what? Speculation ran amok, and soon it was about town that he was building a counterfeiting machine and was busy printing money! David Hughes relates in his notes that he:[22]

> Became very unpopular with the inhabitants because I did not mix with them, they then thought I was making counterfeit money. Was forced to keep a loaded pistol to keep them from breaking my instrument.

This was an interesting misconception about his telegraph instrument. He stayed in Springfield for about six months, working long hours, vowing that if he did not succeed in making two of the instruments communicate with each other, he would give up and return to his music full time. These first prototype telegraph instruments were made from an assortment of parts that he scrounged up, made himself, or improvised. The construction left a lot to be desired, owing to the lack of a workshop and suitable tools. However, at the time this was the only way to experiment for people with few resources except an idea and determination. His instrument was quite ingenious, and to be able to obtain parts manufactured with the necessary precision, it was only natural that he started with the most precise mechanism of the day: clocks. He disassembled many clocks to obtain the right components such as gears, springs, escapements etc., and writes in his notes:[23]

> Used Yankee clocks for wheels—knitting needles for vibratory springs. Bonnet wire for insulated wire. Writing apparatus of Piano wire. Fly wheels of Copper coins.—Keys for Writing Apparatus of vest buttons. Battery of Daguerreotype plates.

A colorful account in a newspaper clipping which Hughes saved paints the scene for us:[24]

> ...this pale faced young man, night after night, illuminated by tallow candles and the unflickering flames of immortal genius, working and studying and inventing, fixing a battery here changing another yonder, intensifying electric currents....

The question arises as to how he was supporting himself financially during this period, as he was living in a hotel located in the Public Square; perhaps this was why the local people were suspicious that he was actually printing his own money. It is possible that he had received money from the sale of the farm, or from the sale of gold that had been mined. He did however continue to teach music to private students, which would have provided a modest income.

While Hughes portrayed his stay in Springfield as somewhat "monastic," it appears that this was not the full story. A newspaper article on Hughes and his inventions appeared in the *Robertson County Times* many years later, written by a local historian.[25]

The article discussed Hughes's inventions and gave an account of a romance that blossomed between Hughes and a local young lady called Miss Virginia Manlove (who may have been one of his music students), the daughter of a Dr. Manlove. Smitten by the young lady, he courted her. However, Miss Manlove's mother, who was of a noted Virginian family, thought a poor music teacher did not offer much of a prospect for their daughter, and made the couple break off their relationship. This was probably to the good, as our story might otherwise have ended right here.

Helped by the romance or not, Hughes made significant progress on his telegraph. He knew what he wanted the instrument to do: the sender would type in the words to be sent via letters on a keyboard, these would be transmitted electrically over a telegraph wire to a distant town or city, where a comparable instrument would receive the electrical signals and print out the message, reproducing what had been typed, without the need to use ciphers of dots and dashes. However, there were many challenges involved in the implementation of this scheme, not the least of which was the need to build two identical instruments that could synchronize and communicate with each other at a distance of tens or hundreds of miles.

The "eureka" moment, which came when he was able to type a message on one instrument and transmit it over a telegraph wire to a second instrument which then printed the message out, finally arrived in the last week of the six months he had given himself; he must have been ecstatic that after years of thinking and experimenting, his dream had come true. He wasted no time in contacting Dr. Brodnax in Louisville to see if he was still interested in investing in his telegraph instrument. Brodnax shared Hughes's excitement, once again visualizing his own future wealth and prosperity, and was swept up by telegraph euphoria. They struck an agreement whereby Dr. Brodnax would receive a one-quarter share of the income generated by the invention. In return, he would provide the funds to take out American and European patents, pay for refinements and improved parts for the prototype instruments, and supply money that would enable Hughes to build two brand new instruments.

Now that he and Dr. Brodnax were business partners, David Hughes, who had moved to Louisville, became a frequent visitor at Dr. Brodnax's house. He had also brought Maggie back to live in Louisville so that they could be with their father. On his frequent visits to Peters & Webb, where his father was employed, Hughes had become friendly with one of their salesmen by the name of Robert S. Millar. Often, David Hughes, Robert Millar and Maggie would visit Dr. Brodnax, where David would relate his progress. However, it seems that there was something else afoot with Robert:[26]

> I thought then, that he visited Dr. Brodnax, simply to see my progress, but I am afraid now, that there was a double attraction, and that he came more to see my sister, than to listen to my dreary talk on my hobby.

Robert and Maggie's friendship continued to blossom and they were married in 1859.

With Brodnax's funding Hughes was now able to employ some professional help to make the necessary improvements to the prototype telegraph instrument. He indicated that the first thing to be done was to repair the instruments and remake all of the parts that were badly made. A clockmaker located on Third Street by the name of Mr. Hirschbuhl was employed to do the work. [27] Like Hughes, Hirschbuhl was an immigrant, but from Germany. German clockmakers had brought with them to America their remarkably advanced skills, and together with the Swiss they were producing the most precise mechanisms at that time. They were, in fact, master craftsmen, able to make parts from scratch, cut gears whose teeth meshed precisely, and make springs of the right temper. They made their own tools to manufacture these parts, and were mechanically astute, having come from the technical tradition that had created some of the famous clockwork writing robots of the late 1700s and early 1800s.

Hirschbuhl set to work to remake and replace some of the parts that had been crudely fashioned by Hughes. When he had finished, the instruments worked better, but still suffered from a number of defects. He suggested that it would be better for him to make a new instrument rather than patching up the prototypes, so it was determined to make an entirely new instrument, with new parts that were more precise and robust. This time, accurate drawings were made so that all of the parts would be correct from the beginning; precise gear mounting plates were drilled, and gears cut. A brief account of this instrument

The 1856 patent model of Hughes's first telegraph instrument, which is now in the Smithsonian Institution. Clearly visible are the keyboard, the rotating helix plus finger contacts also known as the comb and pin barrel, the clockwork mechanism, and the print wheel. Unfortunately the Hughes relay to the left is missing some components, as is the weight drive mechanism.

appeared some years later when a letter was published in the technical press in connection with an article about David Hughes. The letter was written by a Mr. Louis Schaefer, a technician for the Eastern Telegraph Company who appeared to have made the instrument for Professor Hughes in 1854 when he was working in Louisville for Mr. Hirschbuhl:[28]

> The telegraph instrument in question was the first Hughes' printer.... only 13 inch square by 7 inch high, consisting of clockwork of arched design, with revolving type-wheel, vibrating regulator and keyboard and alphabet, was finished by me in three months and exhibited at a ladies' fair held in Louisville in midsummer 1855.

By this time, David Hughes must have been feeling more confident in his design, as the prototype worked, and he also had a set of accurate drawings and a description of its operation—in other words, he had everything necessary for proceeding with a patent application. Dr. Brodnax continued to monitor his investment, and he and Hughes went to Washington to meet with a patent agent by the name of Mr. Joseph Camp Griffith Kennedy, and applied to the Patent Office for a "caveat," a preliminary step prior to filing for a full patent.[29] They then returned to Louisville, intending to have a second instrument made by Mr. Hirschbuhl.

Their plans, however, were suddenly overturned by an unexpected telegraph message from New York; a sequence of events was about to unfold that would start them on the roller coaster ride of their lives.[30] The telegraph message was from a Mr. D. H. Craig, and he requested that they come to New York "immediately" with their new printing telegraph instrument, which he had just learned about.

This episode was eloquently described in James Reid's book *The Telegraph in America* (1886):[31]

> Just at this period D. H. Craig, the agent of the Associated Press of New York, unearthed from one of the towns of central Kentucky, David E. Hughes a professor of music, who had been attracted by the power of vibration upon isolated tuning forks, and who had invented, down among the blue grass of that gallant state, a telegraphic printing instrument of great apparent merit. It required only a single electric wave to produce a letter.... It was called "The Compound Magnetic and Vibrating Printing Instrument." The name was euphonious and suggestive of high art.

Daniel Craig was an astute businessman who was the driving force behind the Associated Press, and must have heard about Hughes's invention from one of his many contacts. Craig was a master at keeping ahead of his competition, having constantly outmaneuvered rival companies in securing the much sought-after European news, expertly extracting it from in-bound ships before they arrived in port. Craig was also aware that this news was of limited value unless there was a reliable and economic method of quickly distributing it—hence his keen interest in the telegraph, the fastest way for disseminating his news.

His summons to the Kentucky duo presented them with a dilemma, their plan had been for David Hughes to go to Europe to obtain patents, and then return to complete the American patent application, as otherwise they would have no legal protection of his invention.[32] However, Dr. Brodnax had other ideas: he smelled money, and impulsively proclaimed that they would go directly to New York City.

Before they left Kentucky, however, Hughes did manage to persuade Dr. Brodnax to arrange for patents to be filed in Europe. As Hughes could no longer go himself, he and Brodnax sent their Washington patent agent, Mr. Joseph Kennedy, to England to start the filing process by submitting the provisional specification for a patent.[33]

And so Professor David Hughes and Dr. Brodnax, with their telegraph instrument, headed post haste for New York City.

The following paragraphs provide information for readers who would like to understand the basics principles of an electrical telegraph system, including David Hughes's instrument.

Readers who wish to delve into the specific technical development of David Hughes's first printing telegraph and its operation may refer to Appendix 1.

HOW AN ELECTRICAL TELEGRAPH SYSTEM WORKS

To understand how an electrical telegraph system works, it is best to start with the Morse system, as this represents a basic and simple system that was widely used at the time Hughes was developing and introducing his instrument.

The Morse Telegraph System

The Morse telegraph was the predominant telegraph system used in America following its introduction in 1844, while in Britain, a different system was used, called the Cooke and Wheatstone.

The state of electrical knowledge in the mid-1800s was still very crude, with technical books still devoting much of their attention to static electricity.[34] Simple batteries could be made, based on Galvani's voltaic pile, using multiple copper and zinc discs separated by cloth moistened with a saline solution. This principle was further developed and improved into what were called "Constant Batteries" such as the Daniell cell (approximately one volt) and Grove cell (approximately two volts).[35] Passing an electrical current through a coil of wire had been shown to create a magnetic field (electromagnet). It was also known that electricity could travel long distances on wires made of iron or copper. If a battery was connected to such a wire and it was switched on and off, a pulse of electrical current was created which would appear instantaneously at the other end of the wire. Thus, on/off signals could be sent and received over a distance of five, ten, fifty, or a hundred miles in what appeared an instant. This formed the basis of a system for sending information over long distances at a much greater speed than a horse or carrier pigeon could travel, which were the fastest methods of information transmission prior to the advent of the telegraph.

Samuel Morse and Albert Vail came up with a method to transmit information in just this way by inventing an instrument and a code of electrical pulses to represent each letter of the alphabet. They could have used a single pulse of electricity to signify the letter "A," two pulses for the letter "B," and so on to twenty-six pulses to represent "Z." However, this would have been cumbersome as well as time consuming, so they came up with a better method. They did this by adding a second dimension to the on/off pulse—that is, they varied the length of the "on" pulse. A short pulse was known as a "dot" (•) and a longer pulse as a "dash" (▬). A dash remained on for a period equal to the time of three dots. By using a combination of dots and dashes, they could represent any letter of the alphabet with four or fewer pulses, as we see in this excerpt from the Morse code:[36]

"A"   • ▬
"B"   ▬ • • •
"C"   ▬ • ▬ •

To transmit a message, each letter was first converted into the Morse code of dots and dashes. These codes were then sent electrically over a telegraph wire by an operator switching on and off an electrical current from a battery with a switch known as a telegraph key. At the receiving telegraph station the electrical pulses were passed through a coil of wire wrapped around an iron core (an electromagnet). Each electrical pulse caused the coil to act as a magnet and attract an iron armature, which thus oscillated back and forth in sympathy with the received pulses. The armature, in turn, inscribed the short and long pulses corresponding to dots and dashes on a moving paper strip. This instrument was known as a Morse Register. The telegraph operator then translated them back into their corresponding letters, and wrote the message out on a telegraph form which was given to the recipient. Later, particularly in America, the receiving stations would dispense with the Morse Register, and the operators would instead listen to the sound made by the oscillating armature. It was found that as the armature responded to the electrical pulses, it emitted a click-clacking sound that could be interpreted as dots or dashes. The receiver then became known as a "sounder." By listening to the sound the operator could directly decode the message. The Morse sending key and receiving instrument were separate instruments.

The electrical pulses were transmitted over telegraph wires strung between insulators mounted on poles, and could be sent over many miles between towns and cities. Only one wire was needed, as the earth itself was used for the return path instead of a second wire, saving significant cost. Initially, only one operator at a time was allowed

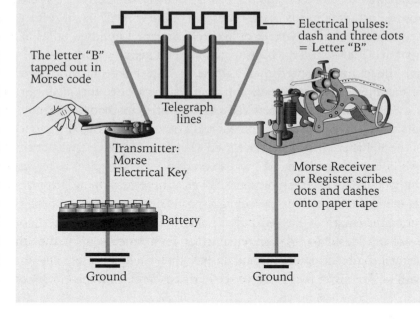

Typical Morse telegraph system showing the operator who transmitted short and long coded electrical pulses and the receiver or register whose electromagnetic relay responded to the pulses and scribed or inked them on a moving paper tape.

The letter "B" tapped out in Morse code

Electrical pulses: dash and three dots = Letter "B"

Telegraph lines

Transmitter: Morse Electrical Key

Morse Receiver or Register scribes dots and dashes onto paper tape

Battery

Ground

Ground

to send on a telegraph line. Towns and villages along a telegraph route could simply be added to the line by connecting on to the telegraph wire, so everyone could hear all of the messages being sent. To send a message an operator had to wait until the wire was not in use by someone else.

In summary, in the Morse system:

1. Only telegraph operators could send and receive messages, owing to the need to be familiar with the code used.
2. Operators had to be skillful, accurate and fast in encoding and sending the message, and also in decoding the received message.
3. Up to four electrical pulses were required to send letters, and six to send numbers and letters.
4. Messages could only be sent in one direction at a time (later this changed).
5. The system required batteries of twenty-five to fifty Grove cells. Later the addition of an intermediate relay in conjunction with a local battery reduced the number of main batteries needed.
6. Messages could be sent at a speed of fifteen to twenty-five words per minute.

The Hughes Printing Telegraph System

David Hughes wanted a telegraph system in which a keyboard could be used to type in a message in plain English— no codes, just Roman letters. At the receiving telegraph station, the message would be directly printed out letter for letter (in the style of the much later teletype machines and electric typewriters). Thus, Hughes's telegraph both looked different and operated differently from Morse's telegraph. While simple in concept, it was a sophisticated and ingenious device.

As each telegraph office needed to be able to both send and receive messages, each needed to have a transmitting instrument as well as a receiving instrument. Unlike the Morse system, however, Hughes's system combined these two functions into one instrument. These identical instruments were then installed in each telegraph office. A keyboard with all of the letters of the alphabet arranged in alphabetical order (the QWERTY keyboard was developed much later) was used for typing in the message to be transmitted. A mechanical device repeatedly scanned the keys to determine which letter had been pressed so that this information could be sent over the telegraph line to the receiving station. When it detected that a key had been pressed, it transmitted a single electrical pulse over the telegraph line. More precisely, this action occurred as follows: when a key was pressed it pushed a lever forward that was in turn struck by a pin on a spinning drum. There were twenty-six such pins arranged in a spiral around the drum, one for each letter.

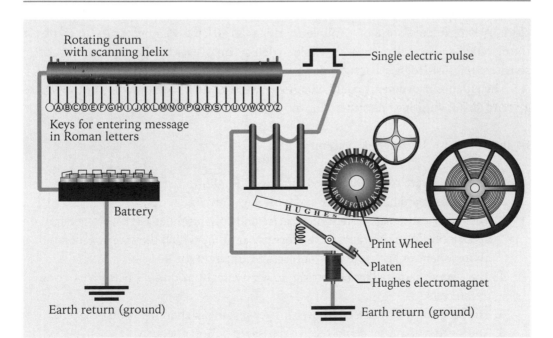

The Hughes telegraph system showing the keys and scanning rotating helix of the transmitter. Pressing any key resulted in the transmission of a single electrical pulse which activated a Hughes relay in the (synchronized) receiving instrument, causing the rapid release of the platen and the printing of the letter on a moving paper tape.

If the drum made one revolution in twenty-six seconds, for example, and the letter "A" key was pressed, it would be struck by the first pin in the 1st second, and if the letter "B" was pressed it would be struck by the second pin in the 2nd second. As the pins were in a spiral formation, they followed each other in succession to Z in the 26th second, each pin in the spiral being displaced in time by one second. This gave each letter a precise place in time for each rotation of the drum. If the word "HUGHES" was typed in, the drum in its six revolutions (one for each letter) would make contact at different times in each revolution as follows: 8th second, 21st second, 7th second, 8th second, 5th second, and 19th second.

The receiver had a printing wheel with the letters embossed on its surface spinning at the same speed as the transmitter's scanning drum. Thus when the transmitter sent out the letter "H" pulse to the receiving instrument, its type wheel was in the same position and would print the letter "H," and so on. The letters were printed on a moving paper strip.

In Hughes's instrument the scanning drum and print wheel typically made a complete revolution each half second, much faster than the speed of one revolution every twenty-six seconds cited above in the interest of making the operating principles clear.

The operation of the instrument involved a number of clockwork-type mechanisms. First, each instrument had to have a precise timing device, and second, the transmitting and receiving instruments had to be synchronized with each other, and Hughes had worked out an innovative method of meeting both of these requirements using temperature compensated vibrating steel spring strips. The power to drive the mechanisms was provided by a wind-up weight drive similar to that in a grandfather or long-case clock. A battery consisting of a couple of cells was all that was necessary to transmit the electrical pulse. The receiver was able to detect the pulses by the use of a fast-acting sensitive relay of Hughes's design.

The Hughes instruments could operate over the same telegraph wires as the Morse system, so substituting one system for the other was easy.

In summary, in the Hughes system:

1. Messages were sent and printed directly in English.
2. Messages could be sent faster and with fewer errors.
3. The electrical signals were more precise and consistent as they were generated automatically, in contrast to the Morse system, in which they were generated by the operator and were thus subject to human error.
4. The system required less electrical power, typically requiring batteries of one to ten cells.
5. The Hughes system operated over longer distances than the Morse system.
6. The system could send and receive messages simultaneously.
7. The Hughes instruments were more expensive than the Morse instruments.
8. The average speed of transmission was forty words per minute.

4

INTO THE BIG LEAGUE
WITH BOTH FEET

NEW YORK, 1855

The New York City in which Professor David Hughes and
Dr. Brodnax arrived had become the country's most
populous city, as well as its foremost center of commerce and industry. It was the busiest port, and had become
the gateway to the country. The Hudson River had become a
major trade artery with the opening of the Erie and Champlain
Canals, which connected the city with the Great Lakes and the
resources of the North. Californian gold and European capital
flowed in, to be invested in all manner of industries—mining,
shipbuilding, railways, and of course, telegraph companies.
Hundreds and thousands of immigrants landed in the city:
some stayed, some moved on; it was as if the country had an
insatiable appetite for them.

David Hughes would have seen many changes from what
he remembered from his stay in the city nearly ten years earlier.
The city had grown and the streets had become clogged with
every conceivable horse-drawn conveyance: hacks, cabs, omnibuses, carts, carriages, and wagons, all clattering on their steel-rimmed wheels over the cobblestones. He would no doubt have
been musing about what to expect from their impending meeting with Mr. Craig. A letter he had received three years earlier
from another telegraph man, Mr. Woodward, indicating that

Hughes's telegraph invention "would be much in demand and he could get up a company to buy it" would have heightened his expectations.

His hopes for success were not without foundation, as it was a dynamic time of wheeling and dealing which saw the rise of the self-made millionaire. Businessmen

New York had become the nation's premier port, business, banking and manufacturing center.

had been seduced by the power of the telegraph and its all-but-instantaneous transmission of information; it had become one of the tools necessary to their success. The telegraph service had expanded to support not only businesses, but also newspapers. A network of wires now covered the eastern states, penetrating into the interior of the

Daniel H. Craig, the powerhouse behind the Associated Press and an early supporter of Hughes's telegraph instrument.

country and down to the South, but it was far from a homogeneous or harmonious business, as the telegraph lines were administered by innumerable, and in many cases competing telegraph companies. Fortunes had already been made and lost: court cases abounded as Samuel Morse and his associates continued to fight to protect the monopoly that their system enjoyed.[1] However, from this combination of networks of wires and dynamic business conditions emerged new thinkers with a vision for the future of communications.

Among the movers and shakers of the day was the man who had summoned them to New York: Daniel H. Craig.[2] Craig was an exceedingly resourceful person who seemed to be always ahead of the game, and whose ambition was always to be the first with the news. His specialty had been obtaining the all-important European news and getting it to Boston and New York and onto the wire first. His competitors, the New York Associated Press (an association of New York newspaper editors), found themselves always two steps behind Craig's slick and often innovative operation. They finally decided that if they could not beat him, they should employ him. So Daniel Craig joined the Associated Press in New York and started his drive to build the company into a news service powerhouse.

Under Craig's guidance, the Associated Press (AP) developed their business to supply foreign and market news to newspapers all over the country. This scheme, of course, relied completely on the telegraph, and to be successful, needed cheap rates, priority, and fast service. Many of the telegraph companies were under the control of Samuel Morse, F.O.J. Smith and Amos Kendall,[3] who were often at odds with the AP, especially over rates. Consequently, Craig's relationship with the telegraph companies was not an easy one. He tried various ways to break free of their control, such as switching some of his news services to competing telegraph lines that used the Bain or House telegraph instruments (instruments outside the control of the Morse patents). However, these were only partial solutions, and did not really get to the heart of the problems of priority and rising costs. At this time, early in 1854, another visionary appeared on the scene who would do much to move communications forward. This was Cyrus West Field, who had made his fortune in the newspaper industry by the time he was thirty-five years of age. He had established his family and household in the upscale area of Gramercy Park in New York City.[4]

Field was casting around for a new venture, and as is often the case, timing, connections, and coincidences played a large part in the development of that venture, although when it was all played out, the term "ad-venture" would have seemed more appropriate.

Cyrus Field's brother, Matthew, an engineer, happened to meet a fellow engineer by the name of Frederick Newton Gisborne at the Astor House Hotel in New York City. Gisborne was down from Canada, and related a fascinating story concerning his telegraph enterprise there to Matthew, who thought this might be just the thing to interest his brother. Gisborne had been working on a project to speed up the communications between Britain and America, specifically from London to New York. To achieve this goal he had attempted to establish a telegraph line from New York to St. John's, Newfoundland, and the remaining gap between the continents was to be serviced by steamships. Unfortunately, the hostile wilderness of Newfoundland had defeated Gisborne's attempt to construct a telegraph line, and he had run out of money.

Cyrus Field must have been struck by the boldness of this project and recognized its potential; inspired by this project, he conceived one even bolder, which was to lay a telegraph cable from St. John's to Ireland and dispense with the steamships. He was taken with the possibility of connecting America with Europe via an undersea telegraph cable. As he knew nothing about telegraphy, he sought advice on the feasibility of laying a 2000-mile long cable on the bottom of the Atlantic (which many thought an impossible task). He also wanted to know if an electrical telegraph signal could actually travel that far. The answers came back that it was all feasible. Field also investigated the ins and outs of the telegraph industry to gain an understanding of its workings and operations. He was surprised at how disjointed they were. His assessment was that if a transatlantic cable was to be successful, messages would have to be able to flow to and from it easily. For this to happen, there would need to be some control over the existing telegraph network and companies so that some order could be brought to the situation.

Cyrus Field's vision and Daniel Craig's goals were on intersecting paths, and they were about to join forces—the catalyst was to be Hughes's new invention. Daniel Craig's discontent at being at the mercy of the telegraph companies had prompted him to look for alternative solutions. The ideal would be to locate a new telegraph instrument that could compete with the Morse system and bring it to heel, as it were. As if on cue, Hughes appeared on the horizon with his telegraph instrument.

David Hughes, accompanied by Dr. David W. Brodnax, made his way through the city to meet Daniel Craig, who had been described as:[5]

Cyrus W. Field, one of the great visionaries and organizers of the telegraph era, and the principal planner of the Atlantic telegraph cable.

...a cool, shrewd, indefatigable man, to whom processes were valuable only as they secured success. His manners were peculiar and unique. He preserved at all times the placidity of a summer's morning. His speech was as gentle and suave and courtly as if the world had made him its exceptional favorite, and he was its benignant son. Beneath this calm exterior there was a fertility of resource, a capacity of terse Saxon, especially with his pen, and an energy and force of will, which for a time, made him a very prominent factor in the telegraphic enterprises of the period.

The meeting was to take place at the grand palace of New York, situated on Broadway: the Astor House Hotel. This grand edifice had become a center for commercial activity. Craig appeared to have been impressed by Hughes's instrument, and requested him to set it up for a demonstration to his business associates and various investors who might be interested in forming a new company. What he did not tell Hughes or Brodnax was that they were about to become unsuspecting players in a giant telegraph poker game. At the table were two not-so-well-off players from Kentucky and several savvy, shrewd businessmen. When the game was over, one of the Kentuckians would emerge richer, the other poorer.

The Astor House on Broadway, one of the most prestigious hotels in New York, was where Hughes and Brodnax had been invited for their meeting with Daniel Craig—the site alone must have conjured up visions of success for them.

Hughes demonstrated his instrument to many visitors, including Cyrus Field, Peter Cooper, James Eddy, Abraham Hewitt, Moses Taylor, H.O. Alden, Wilson Hunt and Hyram Hyde.[6] As Hughes recalls, "I had worked the Instrument day and night to crowds of visitors, until I was so tired of explaining that I thought I should drop."[7]

It was now time for Daniel Craig to put his plans into action. He was aware of Cyrus Field's desire to span the Atlantic with a telegraph cable and of his formation of a company called the "New York, Newfoundland and London Telegraph Company" the previous year in order to pursue this venture.[8] At the same time, Field and his partner, the industrialist Peter Cooper, were concerned that their link between the New and Old Worlds would be worthless if the messages could not flow smoothly to and from the cable. To this end, they had already made overtures to some of the telegraph companies with an eye to unifying them. Some companies had shown interest, while others were suspicious or hostile to the offer.

Daniel Craig saw a way forward that would both benefit the AP and solve Cyrus Field's problem. While he needed lower rates and priority to send his dispatches, he also wanted to ensure that once the transatlantic cable was in operation, the AP was in a commanding position in the distribution of European news. Craig had brought together Cyrus Field and other members of the "New York, Newfoundland and London Telegraph Company" to see the Hughes telegraph instrument in action at the Astor House for a specific purpose: to recommend that they purchase the rights to the instrument as a means of pursuing their common goals. The time was right, and all the pieces were coming together, so Cyrus Field and his business associates decided to move forward boldly and to form a new company to be called the "American Telegraph Company." They would purchase the rights to the Hughes instrument so that they could either set up their own telegraph lines using Hughes's instrument, or use it to obtain better rates from the Morse companies by threatening competition if better rates were not forthcoming. They apparently believed that the Hughes instrument was different enough from the Morse instrument that there would not be any problems with patent infringement.

The importance of Professor David Edward Hughes and his invention now becomes apparent: Hughes was in the right place at the right time with the right product, which had become the key to the business strategy of this new company. The American Telegraph Company and Daniel Craig had a winning hand, and as Craig had put it, they "could now bring the Morse companies to heel."[9]

On November 1, 1855, the "American Telegraph Company" (ATC) was formed. Even though Hughes's telegraph instrument was not perfect, Craig had recognized its merits and recommended its immediate purchase. The company made a provisional agreement to purchase the North American rights to the instruments for $100,000.[10] Hughes and Brodnax must have fallen out of their chairs when they heard this offer, as it was a considerable sum of money, approximately $2,000,000 in today's dollars. The terms of the agreement were that the payment would be made at the end of two years if the instrument was found to fulfill all expectations and work practically and absolutely perfectly—and not infringe the Morse patents, of course. Hughes and Brodnax received a down payment of $5000 for the option of buying the North American rights to the instrument in two years.

Had the ATC gone out on a limb with this offer? On one hand, they made this agreement before the instrument had received patent protection or really been tested in operational use. But on the other, this was a real instrument that the AP could promote in the press to create alarm among other telegraph companies. The ATC had also limited their liability to the initial payment of $5000, as a lot could happen in two years—and it did!

Hughes's contract with the American Telegraph Company; his telegraph instrument had been the catalyst for the formation of the Company, which became one of the first monopolies.

Cyrus Field, upon organizing the company, told Samuel Morse that he had purchased the Hughes telegraph instrument to keep it out of the hands of other competitors. However, as time passed, his real motive became apparent, which was to hold it over the heads of the Morse companies to force them to reduce their telegraph rates or to join the ATC; otherwise he threatened to go into competition with them using the Hughes telegraph. This move, of course, was to sour his relationship with Samuel Morse for a time.

Once the deal was struck with Hughes and Brodnax, the company needed to get the instruments ready for manufacture. Their assessment was that the instrument, in its current state, was not ready for the rigors it would experience in service. Also, as Hughes had only one instrument available, there was an immediate need for at least one more so that they could conduct trials over various telegraph lines. Hughes himself was aware of these factors and they had been a concern of his:[11]

> ...for I know that my instrument then, was not fit for actual work on a line but I was in hopes and saw clearly that when I could get a second Instrument that by experiments I could make work together, then I should feel sure of my ground.

To carry out the work, the ATC engaged Mr. George M. Phelps, a first-class telegraph instrument maker, to make two new instruments. George Phelps has been described as a quite genial person who was thoughtful and reserved in manner, with a strong sense of humor, and a good teacher. He was an accomplished musician who enjoyed playing the organ in church.[12] Given his personality it might seem that he would have had much in common with Hughes and that they would have gotten along well, but unfortunately this did not turn out to be the case.

The company gave Phelps (described in the words of the period as an "electro-mechanician") carte blanche to make or alter Hughes's model as he thought fit. Phelps was ten years Hughes's senior, and already a recognized skilled machinist who had been manufacturing the Royal E. House telegraph instrument for about four years at his workshop in Troy, New York.[13] He must have had some interesting thoughts when he first saw Hughes's instrument, probably considering the mechanism fairly rudimentary. Hughes, of course, was not a machinist but an experimenter, an idea man who used parts and components that were readily available or could be adapted. The author James Reid, writing later in the 1800s, provides the following description of Hughes's instrument:[14]

> The Hughes instrument, as first constructed, was meritorious chiefly in what it showed itself capable of accomplishing. But its workmanship was imperfect, and its parts unequally adjusted. Its action was irregular. To accomplish speed, it was made so light as to be incapable of steady and reliable movement. It had to be re-made on a more consistent adjustment of the parts to the work they had to perform. This required long experience in mechanical detail.

Hughes explained the principles of operation and the component parts to Phelps, who was easily able to grasp it all. Hughes had assumed that he would remain in Troy with Phelps, to be on hand to watch over the construction of the instrument and instruct him in the details that he wanted to improve.[15] However, Dr. Brodnax, who had become ecstatic over the financial deal, and whose mind raced ahead to visions of untold wealth, especially if he could pull off similar deals in Europe, had other plans for Hughes. He urged him to leave at once for Europe while he stayed in Troy to keep an eye on things. Phelps agreed with this arrangement, indicating that it was unnecessary for Hughes to stay, as he could manage the new instruments. Brodnax had already sent Mr. Kennedy to Europe to start the patent filing process, to ensure that they secured patents in England and France in preparation for selling or licensing the instrument there. Hughes lost the argument, and though reluctant to leave "my instrument to be worked on by a stranger," headed to London and then on to France. He was to be away for three months.

While Hughes was in Troy, an anonymous person with the *nom de plume* of Mother Goose evidently wrote a poem for Hughes, as a handwritten copy is among his papers. The characters mentioned are Daniel Craig from the AP; Eddy is James Eddy, who was the treasurer and general superintendent for the new American Telegraph Company; House is Royal Earl House, the inventor of the House telegraph instrument which would be eventually phased out in favor of the Hughes instrument; and Morse is Samuel Morse. The poem is a take on the nursery rhyme "Four and Twenty Blackbirds Baked in a Pie."[16]

Sing a Song of Telegraph
Pockets Full of Gold

For the four & twenty patents are already sold
When the line is open wont Craig begin to crow
That all the other telegraphs he will overthrow

While Eddy's in the parlor counting out the money
Poor House!!! is in the kitchen not thinking it so funny
And Morse is over the country stretching out his wires
Along comes Hughes the monster and puts out all his fires

Then this song of Telegraph we'll all unite to sing
For throughout every nation the Inventers name will sing

During this period Cyrus Field also traveled to London on business related to his Atlantic telegraph cable project. One of the purposes of his trip was to order a new undersea telegraph cable to span the Gulf of St. Lawrence. This would connect the mainland with the island of Newfoundland and would form part of the link that would eventually

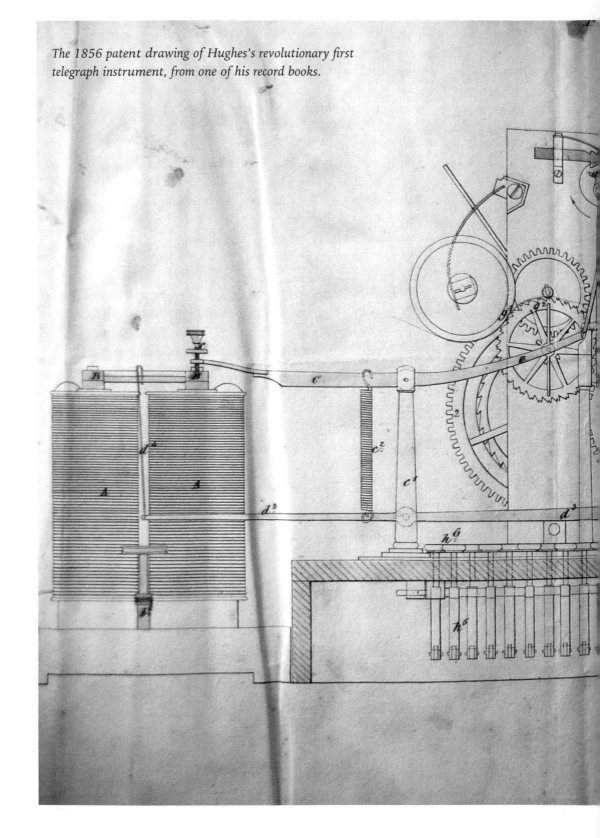

The 1856 patent drawing of Hughes's revolutionary first telegraph instrument, from one of his record books.

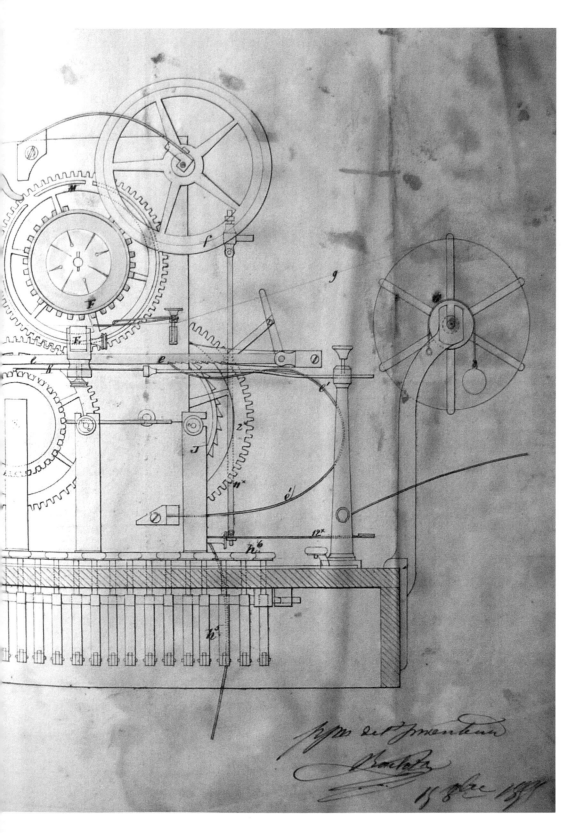

connect up with the transatlantic cable when it was landed in Newfoundland.[17] Field traveled on to Paris, where he met up with Hughes, who was there filing for a French patent. Hughes was some ten years Field's junior, and in the short time he had known him had become impressed by his business acumen. Charles Bright, with whom Field was to work in London, and who was an engineer for the Magnetic Telegraph Company, wrote that Cyrus Field,[18]

> besides being a man of sanguine temperament and intense business energy, also possessed shrewdness and foresight.... He was a man of destiny... you could not escape him... rapid in thinking and acting, and endowed with courage and perseverance under difficulties—qualities which are rarely met with.

Hughes seems to have looked to Field as a mentor, as later in life he remarked that of all the people who had been involved in his success, Cyrus Field had been particularly helpful in his early years. Unfortunately, when they met in Paris, Hughes heard from Field:[19]

> ...that Phelps had found that my model would not work, so had made one that would under a new patent, that he had taken out in his own name—thus my whole patent and claims on the American Telegraph Company were lost.

It is not clear how Field came by this information; it turned out that he had been misinformed, but this news was most upsetting to Hughes—all of his work and his financial future suddenly seemed to be on the rocks. The fact that he had not filed for an American patent, and the thought that Phelps and the ATC might secure for themselves a patent on his invention, must have caused him great anxiety. He could not understand why Dr. Brodnax would have allowed this to happen, as he was supposed to be keeping an eye on things. Field advised Hughes to return with him at once to see what could be done, and they returned together on the steamship *Baltic*.[20] Of course, during the whole voyage back to America Hughes could only stew in anger in his cabin over the catastrophe that he thought was befalling him. When he arrived in New York he reported: "I found matters in a deplorable condition."[21]

He found that Dr. Brodnax, instead of staying in Troy to take care of business, had returned to Louisville, his head in the clouds as he dreamed of how he was going to spend his future wealth. This only made Hughes angrier, and he set off at once by steamer up the Hudson River for Troy to see what Phelps was up to. And to use a New England colloquialism, he was probably "loaded for bear"! When he arrived he found that:[22]

> Phelps had made two new instruments after my model with his modifications and he said they would not work at all—the directors of the company believed him and told him to work out a new patent on his own account and throw mine overboard.

This resulted in an instrument with a modified timing mechanism:[23]

> The Am Tele's Machinist adopted not withstanding my protest a Centrifugal Governor in place of the Vibrating Spring—Tried them on the New York & Boston line, they worked very well with the exception of the Governor—Determined to have two instruments made in my own plan.

If this was the situation, and we have no evidence besides Hughes's word, it would only have increased his anger about what was transpiring. It would have brought into question his contract with the ATC: they had bought the rights to his invention but had so far paid him a mere 5 percent of the total they owed him. How could he claim the rest of the payment if the ATC stole the design and came up with their own instrument and patent? Had he and Brodnax, in their naivety, been duped?

Hughes must have felt very vulnerable and alone at this point as he considered his position in relation to the powerful businessmen of the ATC. He had believed, rightly or wrongly, that he was still to be involved with the design and improvements in making the instrument ready to enter service, and that Phelps was there to assist him (just like the clockmaker Mr. Hirschbuhl in Louisville). As far as Hughes was concerned, to collect his payments from the ATC, the instrument had *to fulfill all expectations and fulfill the guarantee that it should work practically and absolutely perfectly.* Like any inventor, he must have had difficulty letting go of his baby.

The ATC obviously viewed their contract with Hughes rather differently. Hughes had sold them the rights to his instrument, and their objective was to make it robust and bring it up to a production standard as quickly as possible, so that it could be put to good use. Phelps, as a skilled and knowledgeable instrument maker, was now their man to whip Hughes's instrument into shape, and the directors of the ATC were probably less interested in the subtleties of the design than in getting a working instrument. Their motive, of which Hughes was unaware, was to use the instruments as leverage to show the Morse companies that they were in a position to go into competition with them.

The ATC presumably expected Hughes to leave the instrument in their capable hands and for him to complete the application for the American patent. There appears to be no evidence of the ATC or Phelps taking steps to patent the instrument themselves. Besides, Hughes had already filed a caveat, which provided him with some protection, as patents were awarded to the first to invent, not the first to file. Had the ATC filed for a patent, the Patent Office would have conducted interference proceedings to determine which inventor had had the idea first. Hughes, of course, may not have been aware of these procedures.

Given this background, it can be understood why Hughes took his next step. Presumably still believing there was some truth in what Field had told him in Paris, and upset over Phelps's modifications, he had become very suspicious of both Phelps and the motives of the ATC. He was desperate not to lose out financially, so he approached the company's directors (he was still a corporate executive of the ATC) and pleaded his case with them, though he did not have much leverage, only persuasion and tenacity:[24]

> I implored the Directors to listen to me, which they would not—I then asked them, if they would give me 1000 dollars if I went away and had made at my own expense two perfect working instruments which they should buy and judge on their own line in practical use (1856). This they consented to, and I left New York for Louisville to have them made, telling the Directors that they would never see me again if I did not succeed and that in less than six months.

The directors, by this time, had read Phelps's assessment of Hughes's instrument and of how much work and time was required to bring it up to production standard. This was probably more than they had anticipated. However, as neither Hughes's original instrument nor Phelps's modified version appeared to be ready to go into service at that point, paying Hughes a thousand dollars (probably hoping he would spend some of it to get the patent that ATC needed to fend off any challengers) was cheap insurance. This payment also represented a hedging of their bets: certainly either Phelps or Hughes would be able to produce a set of working instruments.

Hughes returned to Louisville and Phelps carried on in Troy. The relationship between the two appears to have soured from this experience, and it seems that they both held the resultant grudge throughout their careers.[25]

It is at this point that "who did what" becomes rather gray. There is no doubt that the end product was a better, more robust instrument, but who was responsible for the various improvements is not so clear. Hughes would have us believe that he alone was responsible, which is plausible, as he had come up with the original invention himself, and while he was not a skilled machinist, he could certainly employ others who were. Hughes's notes on this period, however, may be biased, as some of these were written at a later date, by which time he would have learned how he had been manipulated by the ATC, and thus might have been less likely to give them credit.

The ATC's and Phelps's account of events, which is repeated in a number of books on the history of American telegraphy, including those of George Prescott, Robert L. Thompson and James D. Reid, gives the main credit to them. There is no doubt that Phelps was a good machinist with a number of years' experience in making telegraph instruments. He was certainly capable of turning Hughes's initial rudimentary model into a production version, and no doubt contributed the piano-type keyboard and the changes to the weight drive mechanism. But he favored a different timing mechanism based on a rotating governor that was not a feature of the first Hughes models to go into service. Phelps would also soon start work on a new model telegraph instrument called the "Combination Instrument" which certainly drew his attention away from the instrument that had been designed by Hughes. This combination instrument functioned in the same way as Hughes's instrument but was powered by an air pump from the House instrument and incorporated Phelps's rotating speed governor.[26]

As best as can be gathered, there were contributions from both of these innovative gentlemen. Hughes's version (which included some recommendations from Phelps) probably entered service first; then as Hughes became less and less involved with the ATC, there was a transition to a Phelps version, though the press did not distinguish between the versions and referred to them all as Hughes instruments. Eventually these telegraph instruments were superseded by Phelps's combination instrument.

Hughes's story picks up again with his return to Louisville in the spring of 1856 to start work on a set of upgraded telegraph instruments. Here, he found Dr. Brodnax making the most of his new found wealth, and not nearly as upset as he himself was over the whole affair; Brodnax probably had every confidence that Hughes would prevail in the end. Hughes was now in a race against time, and decided that he needed someone faster than Mr. Hirschbuhl, whom he had used last time to make his instruments. He was able to find another German instrument maker by the name of Mr. Tiensch who promised to let him have workmen at three dollars per day.

While Hughes had stated that he had his own ideas for improving his instrument, there is no doubt that he had benefited from his time with Phelps in Troy. He had certainly seen the House instruments that Phelps manufactured in his workshop, and thus the standard of workmanship required for a production instrument. It is not clear what other changes Phelps made in the short three month period, or what other ideas Hughes might have shared with Phelps. What is clear is that the instrument had started its transformation into a more professional production instrument. While its basic functions remained the same, the way those functions were implemented mechanically was to change.

While Hughes was engaged in Kentucky, the scene in New York City was far from quiet. Daniel Craig of the AP was keeping up his efforts to discredit the Morse companies, and though he was considered to be a mouthpiece of the ATC, the company denied it. The Morse companies started fighting back and threatening to sue the ATC on the pretext that the Hughes instrument infringed their patents in order to forestall the new competing telegraph lines the ATC was planning from New York to Washington. The feisty Craig, with his ever-sharp pen, fired back the following in a letter to Amos Kendall:[27]

> The friends and projectors of this new Line are well aware that you in connection with Messrs, Morse, Swain and others are threatening injunctions, prosecutions, &c., against them, should they attempt to put the Hughes instrument in practical use. But your blustering threats thus far have not deterred them from proceeding steadily onward with their enterprise; nor, if I do not greatly mistake the men who have the matter in hand will any thing which you may hereafter say or do prevent them from carrying out their project to its fullest consummation. The fact is neither you nor any of your associates

know anything of the matter upon which you and they have presumed to sit in judgment. Neither you nor they, nor any of the persons upon whose statements you rely, have ever seen the Hughes instrument; and consequently none of you are competent to decide whether it is an infringement upon your rights or not. I do not, however propose to discuss the legal question of the patent. The proprietors of the new Line have a responsible guarantee that the patent will be defended, if it at all becomes necessary and resting on that guarantee, and strong in the belief that there is no infringement of the rights of the party they will, as I have already said, finish the enterprise they have begun. If, in doing so, they should happen to deal a death-blow to the unprincipled parties who have recently combined to swindle the Press and the Public by extortionary tolls, they will receive, as they will deserve, the thanks of every business community over which the lines may pass.

Craig went on to predict:

I will state further, that at the expiration of three years from this date, you will see a Hughes Line extending from Halifax to New Orleans, on the seaboard and from New York to Buffalo, in this State; and I do not hesitate to add still further that whenever and wherever these Lines go into operation the House and Morse Lines will be *crushed out*.

Craig also stated that this competition could be avoided if only the Morse companies would agree to sell or lease their lines to the new company—the ATC. Just to make sure the Morse companies understood that the ATC meant business, as if the message was not already clear enough, Craig went on to detail on how formidable Hughes's instrument was, and how it was capable of sending up to 3000 words per hour. As it could transmit in both directions simultaneously, that was the equivalent of 6000 words per hour over a single wire using two operators, whereas the slower Morse system would require two wires and four operators for transmission in both directions. The Hughes system could also operate over much longer distances and under much more adverse weather conditions.

Several of the machines intended for immediate use are now completed. They have been thoroughly tested and on every point, by practical telegraphists, who declare unequivocally that they fully answer every expectation they had formed of them from the inventor's claims. These machines will soon be put into use upon the new line above referred to between this City and Philadelphia.

This was a bit of a bluff by Craig regarding the ready availability of several instruments in March, as it is unlikely that Phelps had produced this many, and Hughes, of course, was in Kentucky and had not completed his new models, which would not be ready for some months.

The ATC, however, was pushing ahead with their plans, and in the same month there was a report in the *New York Tribune* that Hughes's printing telegraph system was to go into service, first along the Harlem Railroad from New York to Albany:[28]

> We understand the Harlem Railroad Company have just concluded a contract this Spring of a very substantial telegraph line upon their road between this city and Albany.... The Directors, after full and careful scrutiny as to the merits of various systems of telegraph, have decided in favor of this invention of Prof. Hughes for simplicity, cheapness, rapidity of execution and reliability in storms and bad weather, has been pronounced by competent judges to be vastly superior to all other systems.

Meanwhile, down in Kentucky, some good news had arrived for Hughes and Brodnax from their patent agent Kennedy in England, to the effect that a patent had been granted for their Printing Telegraph on March 11, 1856.[29] This report jolted them into action to complete the filing for an American patent, which had taken a back seat to all of the business transactions. Hughes and Brodnax went to Washington in May and met with Kennedy, who by that time had returned from England. They were informed that due to the backlog of patent applications to be processed, they could not expect a patent to be granted in less than three months. This was a major setback, for they could ill afford to wait, as they were still suspicious of Phelps and the ATC, who might be trying to beat them to a patent.

David Hughes had with him one of his telegraph instruments (identical to the one patented in England), knowing that he would have to demonstrate it to the patent officer. Kennedy, understanding the gravity of their situation, went to see Professor Joseph Henry at the Smithsonian Institution to tell him about Hughes's telegraph instrument and its innovative method of operation, as well as its practicality in permitting the direct typing in and printing out of Roman letters.[30] Henry must have been intrigued, as he agreed to see a demonstration of Hughes's telegraph. Here is how the interview went, in David Hughes's words:[31]

> Professor Henry sent word for me asking me to bring the Instrument to the Smithsonian Institute, and explain its theory and working to him. This I did, and he was so much struck with the beauty of the theory, and its probable successful application when worked out in the future that he at once went to the Government Officials and begged them to make an exception in my case and examine and grant a patent in the shortest possible time—His influence was so great the Patent Office the next day examined my patent claims etc. and in a few days granted the full patent.

When Hughes demonstrated his telegraph system in Kennedy's office there was so much interest that there was a constant stream of visitors, in addition to the newspaper reporters covering the event.[32] Getting an endorsement by a scientist as prominent as

Prof. Joseph Henry was akin to being blessed by God at that time. The patent was granted on May 20, 1856.[33] It is interesting that the patent was issued in Hughes's name, and not assigned to the ATC; this may indicate Hughes's dissatisfaction with the ATC. However, the contract that he had signed specified that the drawings and specification on file in Washington belonged to the ATC.

After their successful but hectic visit to Washington, Brodnax and Hughes returned to Louisville. The new instruments were coming along fine, and Hughes busied himself with the final adjustments and testing. Dr. Brodnax, in the meantime, had begun to slip from being a financial supporter of the invention to a liability for Hughes. He had been spending money as if there were no tomorrow, buying a steam engine when he was in New York to cut up trees on his plantation so he could create a vineyard. He was now out of money, having spent the anticipated income from the telegraph before it had appeared, and had resorted to taking out loans. Desperate, he was now pestering Hughes to hurry and perfect the telegraph instruments so they could sell them as quickly as possible, as he was already in debt to numerous creditors. Hughes himself was down to his last few dollars, as he had to pay the workmen for the new telegraph models himself. Finally, two identical instruments were completed, and Hughes was pleased with the results and noted:[34]

> Well I made new drawings, studied on paper every detail—and the workmen worked with a will, sharing in a great measure my own enthusiasm—It was a proud day for my feelings when those two instruments entirely of my own model, and entirely my own invention, worked together very perfect in deed—there being no evident fault in them.

Brodnax wasted no time in sending Hughes back to New York City, probably around the end of May. He decided that before he presented the new instruments to the ATC, he wanted first to test them on various telegraph lines. This was to ensure that they worked over long distances and also to see how they functioned in ordinary use by telegraph operators. He installed them on the New York to Boston line, and while they worked well, he found that they were not standing up to the wear and tear. In Hughes's words the instruments:[35]

> ...worked perfectly but found the machinery too slight for constant use—had it strengthened. Tried again and it was still too slight for stupid operators.

While it would be easy to blame the operators' heavy-handedness, from which they had earned the nickname of "brass pounders" for pounding out Morse code on Morse keys, it appears that the instruments were still too delicate, and had to be made more robust to survive continuous usage. Hughes also seemed a bit insensitive to the needs of the operators, probably hoping they would adapt to his instrument and that he would not have to adapt the instrument to them. This was a learning experience for him as an inventor, and later, when he went to Europe, he realized that paying more attention to customer needs was important in order to be successful.

To carry out the necessary changes to the instrument Hughes used an instrument maker in New York City named Richards. The instruments were then tested again on the New York to Boston line and then on the New York to Bangor (Maine) line, a distance of 600 miles. The new instruments were found to work well and they were now more reliable, he notes:[36]

> Found them to work perfectly and reliable—transmitting messages at the rate of 40 words a minute during a heavy storm whilst the Morse would send but 150 miles on the same line.

The instrument had now gone through a transformation which had not only strengthened all of the components, but had also changed the way some of the functions were implemented. The rotating drum that scanned to see which letter had been pressed was replaced by a horizontally mounted disc that was swept by a rotating contact arm. Into the disc were set twenty-eight contacts. Each contact was linked to a key on the keyboard that raised the contact when depressed, thus making a momentary electrical contact with the rotating arm. Hughes retained the basic idea of his timing device, which had consisted of a vibrating spring and escapement, but substituted a vibrating metal rod for the vibrating spring strip. An innovative new feature was added which enabled multiple instruments to maintain synchronism with each other over extended periods of time. Each time a letter was transmitted, the receiver compared its actual arrival time against its expected arrival time. The receiver then made a micro-adjustment to its own timing, either advancing or retarding it, to maintain synchronism with the transmitting instrument. The Hughes electromagnet and printing mechanism was retained, and as already mentioned, the weight drive was consolidated to use only one weight instead of two, and incorporated a mechanism to wind the weights up via a treadle without interrupting the telegraph operation. The keyboard had been redesigned in the style of piano keys, something that would be more familiar to telegraph operators and which they would therefore be more ready to adopt.[37]

Hughes was finally satisfied with the instrument's performance, and decided that he and Brodnax were ready to go back to the directors. His reception was not what he had hoped for:[38]

> I found the Directors of the American telegraph Co. not very glad to see me, as they had abandoned the idea of working under my patent as the Morse party had made overtures to them to amalgamate with them.

The board probably believed there had been little chance of ever seeing Hughes again, and were not overjoyed when he showed up. Hughes sensed that the ATC

The earliest photograph (1857) of Professor David Edward Hughes with the upgraded model of his telegraph instrument.

was angling to get out of the contract, and he was beginning to understand what the game plan really was. While he had been busy in Kentucky, the ATC had been making progress towards their goal of consolidation. They were like a magnet that was slowly pulling in the Morse-affiliated companies. Craig, of course, had been fanning the flames on behalf of the AP and ATC, and his threat of using Hughes's instrument in competition with the Morse companies was having an effect.

Hughes's relationship with the ATC, which had started a couple of years earlier with so much promise, had now deteriorated. Hughes believed that with his upgraded instrument, he was now meeting the requirements of the contract. However, the ATC appeared to think that he was not, and they continued to spend their own money to improve his instrument in Troy under the direction of Phelps.[39]

Hughes and Brodnax had to walk a fine line in their negotiations with the ATC if they were to salvage anything. It can be imagined that Dr. Brodnax was in quite a state and probably wringing his hands in desperation. David Hughes, having been burnt a few times in previous business dealings, was becoming more experienced and patient in his negotiations. He had a role model in Cyrus Field, whose successful business style he had been carefully observing. Unfortunately, Field was not present, having left in April to go back to England to prepare for the laying of the Atlantic Telegraph cable. Negotiations between the American Telegraph Company and Hughes ebbed and flowed, but Hughes felt he could still rely on Daniel Craig to support him, and it was Craig who finally came to his rescue.[40]

> Mr. Craig thought I had been badly treated—and told them if they did not make me some reasonable offer he would again assist me to get up a new company.

The ATC knew they would have to pay Hughes, as they still had to buy his patent rights, and although their ploy of using Hughes's telegraph as a stick to prod the Morse companies appeared to be having the desired effect, they knew that they had to continue moving forward with Hughes if this strategy was to continue to be successful. Further, the ATC had figured out a way of not having to come up with all of the money that they would finally offer to Hughes and Brodnax: they planned to extract it from the other telegraph companies they were corralling into their unification plan.

The ATC offered to settle for $50,000, to be paid in four annual installments of $12,500 each, with the contract to be dated July 16 and the first payment to be made on July 15, 1857. Hughes and Brodnax accepted this offer, and it was not too bad a deal after all.[41]

But unknown to Hughes and Brodnax, while they were negotiating with the company, the company was in separate negotiations with a number of telegraph companies. The ATC, though it had been in operation for less than a year, had already become a formidable competitor, as it controlled lines from Newfoundland to Boston and New York, and its power would increase once the Atlantic cable was laid. Its ambitious plans and competitive stance were starting to frighten many of the established telegraph companies. At a meeting on July 1, 1857, the ATC offered these companies a business deal which would involve them amalgamating all of their lines into one company and also purchasing the Hughes patent rights.[42] The companies initially rejected the deal, but on August 10 some of the companies broke rank and pledged to unite with the ATC in an agreement known as "The Treaty of Six Nations."[43] In the contract, the five companies agreed to purchase the patent of David E. Hughes, and together with the ATC, to subscribe $50,000 plus a sum of $6,000 for the expenses the ATC would incur in improving and perfecting the invention, for a total of $56,000.[44]

> The American Telegraph Company along the Atlantic Seaboard was now believed to be almost impenetrable.... Stretching virtually unopposed from Newfoundland to New Orleans, the vigorous young Titan of the East gave promise to a bright future.

Cyrus Field's plan was coming together, and everything was now in place for the moment when the Atlantic cable came ashore to tie into their vast telegraph network that stretched from Newfoundland down to the Gulf of Mexico and west to the Mississippi. Daniel Craig of the AP had fully supported this move towards a monopoly that gave him preferential treatment on their telegraph lines. There was an unwritten law between the AP and the various telegraph companies in the ATC fold that none of them should do anything to prejudice the others' interests.[45]

Dr. Brodnax received his portion of the $12,500 in cash and company notes, but was so over his ears in debt for his plantation and the expensive tastes of his family that he had to sell his notes at once in order to raise cash. The "bankers" and "note shavers" severely discounted the notes' face value, so he did not receive the full amount that he had hoped for. His financial situation was such that he could no longer fulfill the terms of his agreement with Hughes with regard to the European patents, so he sold his rights to a Mr. Hyram Hyde, a friend of Mr. Craig. Hyde was rumored to be a moneyed man, and bought these rights for a mere $1000. Dr. Brodnax returned to Louisville to try and sort out his estate, and David Hughes remained in New York.[46]

The remainder of 1857 was a tumultuous period, as the business climate suddenly went sour in what would later be called the "Panic of 1857."[47] It turned out that Brodnax and Hughes had made their agreement with the ATC in the nick of time, for by August, a series of bank failures and other problems sent the economy into a tailspin, and the stock market plummeted. The economic malaise spread throughout the country and then overseas. On top of this, the first attempt to lay an Atlantic telegraph cable that summer failed, and Cyrus Field returned home to find the business world in disarray.

Hughes, however, had now come to understand how he and Brodnax had been used by the ATC and what was actually going on in the telegraph world. The ATC was becoming a monopoly. Acquisition seemed to be the name of the game, as another company that had its roots in Rochester, New York, was also rising and expanding westwards; it became known as Western Union. It was to be Western Union that in 1861 constructed a line connecting the East and West Coasts, and the company marched on to become another telegraph monopoly, overwhelming and absorbing even the ATC by 1866.

In January of 1858 the Hughes printing telegraph instrument was installed in the American Telegraph offices on Wall Street and shown off to the press. Some were fascinated by the fact that an operator could send messages to Philadelphia and Boston while at the same time receiving incoming messages from these cities.[48] This feature, known as "duplex" operation, was not thought to be of much value in some technical circles, and the author George Prescott scoffed at it, proclaiming that little use would be made of it.[49] But in fact it was a feature that anticipated a need that arose in just a few years when telegraph lines became overcrowded with messages. At that later date all kinds of duplex, quadruplex, etc. schemes were invented in order to fit more messages on the wires.

An account in the *New York Daily Tribune* gave an extensive review of the technical operation of the instrument. The instrument described in the article was the Hughes version with which he had returned from Kentucky, as its timing mechanism was described as consisting of a vibrating rod. The article provides some interesting additional facts. The weight drive, which employed a treadle to wind it up, used a weight of 75 pounds that descended 2½ feet in 15 minutes. A comparison of the number of battery cells required per hundred miles is also given as four for the Hughes system to work in both directions, 200 for the House system, and 50 for the Morse.[50] It appears that the instruments were being produced by a number of manufacturers at a cost of $130.[51]

HUGHES' INSTRUMENT.

Engraving of the Hughes telegraph instrument with cosmetic improvements, showing the popular scroll design of the period to its framework.

With the ATC's amalgamation of many telegraph companies, everything was ready to integrate the next link: the Atlantic telegraph cable. Field's and Craig's plan was falling into place nicely. Craig, however, had never lost sight of what it was all about for him, and that was to gather and distribute the news as quickly and efficiently as possible. His faith in Hughes's printing telegraph had never wavered, and now that they had control of the network, he lost no time in making use of it. It appears that the instrument was ideal for their purpose of moving large quantities of data speedily and accurately. Newspapers would often start lead stories or breaking news with the line "By American Printing Telegraph Lines—Hughes Instrument." The instrument greatly increased the capacity of single wire lines by its duplex mode of operation and also decreased telegraph prices, and it looked as if the success of the printing telegraph was assured.

The *Albany (Morning) Express* newspaper reported that the Hughes instrument was being substituted for the House instrument, and the instruments had just been installed on the Albany to Springfield (Mass.) lines. The article also indicated how dependable the instrument was in rain, wet weather and thunderstorms, the bugaboos of other telegraph systems.[52] The Hughes instrument had also been used on a New York to New Orleans line, using six repeaters.

Some additional light is shed on this period by a letter from the ATC to Hughes written in May of 1859, in response to some questions he had asked.[53] The letter indicates that the Hughes instruments were in use on the New York to Washington line (230 miles), the New York to Boston line (250 miles), the Washington to Richmond line (150 miles), and the Albany/Troy railroad line. They had also run the instruments from Boston to Richmond (700 miles). About thirty instruments were in use, with some having been in service for two years, and were being manufactured at the rate of four per month. It was said that they were performing well and were being run at 2000 words per hour and could be run up to 2500 words per hour if needed. Any youth or man of ordinary capability was able to learn to use the instrument and to keep it in good working order within one to two months. Repair costs were estimated to average six dollars per instrument per year. The estimate for the cost of new instruments was under $200. Some of the more recently manufactured instruments were combinations of the Hughes patent with some portion of the House (that is, the Phelps combination instrument). This is corroborated by the authors Reid and Prescott who indicated that the combination instrument entered service in 1859 after four years of development.[54] It is also believed that there were some Hughes instruments manufactured by Phelps which incorporated his rotating governor for the timing mechanism instead of the Hughes vibrating rod, but unfortunately, no drawing or image of this variant has survived.

It was now becoming obvious that there was little else for Hughes to accomplish in America. The business climate did not look as if it would recover for some time, and since he had sold his telegraph instrument rights to the ATC, there was no additional market in America. The ATC did not require any further technical support from him as they had their own man, George Phelps up in Troy. However, Europe was still wide open, and it looked as if there were better prospects there. Mr. Hyram Hyde, Hughes's new financial backer, was also eager to make good on his new investment and explore the opportunities in Europe.

Cyrus Field had decided to make another attempt to lay a telegraph cable across the Atlantic. But he was far from happy with the transmission speed (number of words per minute) that could be sent over the cable. Samuel Morse and the Atlantic cable's electrician had performed some tests in England which showed that they could send ten words a minute, and saw no reason why they could not get up to twenty words per minute, although so far it seemed that the electrician was struggling to meet this goal. If Field was to make any money, he needed to be able to send lots of messages, and that meant that they had to be sent faster.

It occurred to Field to see whether he could solve the problem by using Hughes's telegraph instrument. He knew that it was capable of sending thirty to forty words per minute on landlines, so perhaps it could be adapted to work on the Atlantic cable. After all, the ATC had paid for it and the development was complete. It was known that on submarine cables, the speed of transmission was reduced, typically by a factor of two-thirds. If a telegraph system could be used on the cable which required fewer pulses to produce each letter, then the lost speed would be gained back. As Hughes's instrument did exactly this, that is, required only one electrical pulse per letter, while the Morse instrument required several, it was reasoned that Hughes's instrument might be better suited to the job. Field gave Hughes a report that had been prepared by his electrician to see what he thought. Hughes had only worked on landlines and was not familiar with undersea cable operation, but read that electrical signals traveled much slower on undersea cables, and concluded that he would have to slow his instruments down considerably if they were to be adapted to the transatlantic cable. In their naivety, Hughes and Field probably thought that this conversion was feasible; no doubt Hughes was pushed along by his new financial partner Hyram Hyde, who was not about to let any opportunity slip away. Hughes, therefore, had two instruments modified to run at a slower rate.

In April of 1858 he packed up his possessions along with the two modified telegraph instruments and shipped out to England on the steamship *Persia*, accompanied by two assistant electricians, Chas. P. Craig and Henry Bishop. Hyde had already gone ahead to arrange various business meetings.

It should be noted that it is doubtful whether Hughes ever received all the money due to him from the ATC. In letters first to Daniel Craig and then to Cyrus Field written in November 1858 from England, he says he has been waiting most anxiously for a letter with the money due to him for his printing telegraph. Hughes also appears to have entrusted Field with some ATC stock to be cashed in, and was waiting for the proceeds. The letter also mentions a new proposal to the ATC that Hughes and Hyde had made which had not even been acknowledged. Craig thought that the tone of the letter was appalling and believed that Hyde was behind it:[55]

The truth is that Hughes is wholly under the influence of Hyde, and Hyde is like a <u>raging bull</u>. I have found it necessary to give him on two or three occasions pretty emphatic expressions of my disgust at his management, and as a matter of course, he is greatly enraged and visits his spleen upon every body with whom he is in any degree associated upon this side of the water.

5

CAN YOU READ ME NOW? RETURN TO BRITAIN AND THE ATLANTIC TELEGRAPH CABLE 1858

David Hughes was never at ease sailing on the high seas. No doubt the ship's crew told many a tale of how bad the weather could be and how high the waves could reach: this was not much consolation for the poor passengers. The steamship *Persia* which he was traveling on from America finally entered the Irish Sea, heading for the port of Liverpool. Now she was done thrashing the Atlantic with her great side-wheel paddles. During the voyage, Hughes would have had time to contemplate just how far it was between the two continents, and to begin to appreciate the magnitude of the task that Cyrus Field was attempting in laying a telegraph cable over such a vast distance and at such a great depth—and thus to gain a firsthand perspective of what he was about to be drawn into.

A shout of "Land ahoy!" would inevitably have drawn passengers from their tiny cabins out on deck, Hughes probably amongst them, hanging over the rail while bathed by the warm eddies of smoke and steam and heckled by gulls. He would have seen the Welsh coast and the South Stack lighthouse flashing in the distance. Was it sending out a sentimental message? "Welcome home David Hughes," or "Croeso" as his father would have said in Welsh? It was likely that the telegraph station at Holyhead was already chattering away, alerting Liverpool of the inbound ship's passing.[1]

The steamship Persia *was one of the many hybrid ships of the period, with steam-powered, 40-foot-diameter side paddle wheels augmented by sails. Ships of this type crossed the Atlantic in twelve to fifteen days.*

After rounding the Isle of Anglesey they would have set a course for the River Mersey and made ready to pick up the harbor pilot at the Mersey Bar.[2] It would have been time to pack up and prepare for disembarkation. It was to be the first time in England for his traveling companions, Henry Bishop and Chas. P. Craig, electricians who were along to assist him with his telegraph tests.

In Liverpool they were met by Hughes's new partner, Mr. Hyram Hyde, who had bought out Dr. Brodnax's interests in Hughes's invention. He had preceded them in order to set up appointments. It seemed that he had been successful, for he rattled off a series of meetings and events they were to attend. It was a hectic schedule: first to London, and then to Plymouth, then meet with this and that telegraph or railway company. Hyde, all business, was eager to cash in on his investment. He was intent on striking a deal with the Atlantic Telegraph Company as well as weaning the British off their Cooke and Wheatstone or Henley's needle telegraph in favor of Hughes's printing instruments.

It was April, and Cyrus Field was back in England once again; it was hard to keep track of him with his constant shuttling back and forth between the two continents. He had requested that Hughes and his associates meet him in London to arrange the testing of Hughes's telegraph on the Atlantic cable. While he was in London, Hughes took the opportunity to file for an additional patent to protect the latest version of his telegraph instrument.[3] At the Atlantic Telegraph Company offices in Old Bond Street they met with company officials and were briefed on the submarine cable project and the current situation. It was probably here that Hughes and Hyde became aware of the full extent of the massive undertaking.[4]

The island nation of Britain had pioneered the art of submarine telegraphy to connect to the European Continent and Ireland, and also to send and receive dispatches during the Crimean War via a Black Sea submarine cable. Its future goals included connecting to the far-flung colonies of its growing Empire, especially India. The most advanced knowledge of undersea telegraphy, including familiarity with the special cables required, techniques for laying the cables at sea, and specific telegraph instruments, resided in Britain. An important development which had made undersea cables practical had been the recent discovery of "gutta-percha," an electrical insulator derived from the sap of a tree from Southeast Asia.[5] Although British entrepreneurs had already put several undersea cables into operation, they were all much shorter than the one the Atlantic Telegraph Company would soon lay. While the Atlantic Telegraph Company was a British company, financed by British capital and staffed by British technical experts, it was Cyrus Field, the American, who was the entrepreneur and driving force behind the venture. For its day it was a very bold and enormously complex project that was being orchestrated by a relatively small cadre of people. It was pushing the state of the art in several areas, and many tasks necessary to the success of the project had quite simply never been attempted before.

Hughes must have been impressed with the team Cyrus Field had assembled. Its members together possessed practically all current knowledge of submarine telegraphy: John Watkins Brett, Charles Tilston Bright, Professor William Thomson, Dr. Edward Orange Wildman Whitehouse, and Charles Victor de Sauty; even Michael Faraday and Samuel Morse had provided guidance.[6]

During the meeting, Hughes and Hyde learned about the previous year's failed attempt to lay a cable and about the renewed efforts and preparations currently underway, which fully occupied the attention of the company's leaders.[7] Originally Hughes had believed that he was there to participate in tests to determine whether his printing telegraph could increase productivity on the transatlantic cable with respect to the Morse-type instruments that the company had developed. He had conducted such tests on land lines many times and had done so by simply substituting one instrument (his) for the other (Morse's). It must have been during these meetings that Hughes and Hyde became aware that all was not as they had assumed. There was some uncertainty about the readiness of the company's own telegraph instruments as well as frustration with the company electrician, Dr. Whitehouse. There were also stories of Professor William Thomson's philosophical differences with Whitehouse over the electrical operation of the cable. Hughes and Hyde must have been left with the impression that there was much more to the project than they had thought.

Hughes was told that time was short for carrying out tests on the cable, which was currently in storage at the docks in Plymouth, as it was soon to be reloaded aboard the ships which would depart in late May or early June to mount a new attempt to lay it across the Atlantic. Field wanted Hughes to go down to Plymouth and begin his tests right away, before the opportunity was lost. He particularly wanted to know at what speed Hughes could transmit (in number of words per minute) through the 2,000 mile cable.

Hughes and Hyde must have realized that if the company was experiencing trouble with their own instruments, it opened up a whole new opportunity for them and one that could lead to a lucrative contract. Hyde must have sensed the opportunity and enthusiastically supported Field. He offered Hughes's telegraph instruments along with their supervision of the necessary tests and indicated their willingness to carry out further modifications of the instruments, if necessary, on an unpaid basis, gambling that Hughes would be successful and that they could then secure an exclusive contract. It is unlikely, though, that they were fully prepared for the extent of the challenges that they would face—and for that matter, neither were many of the board members. A successful laying of the cable was only the first step. The second step was to be able to send messages through the cable at a reasonable speed, a factor on which the viability and economics of the enterprise depended absolutely.

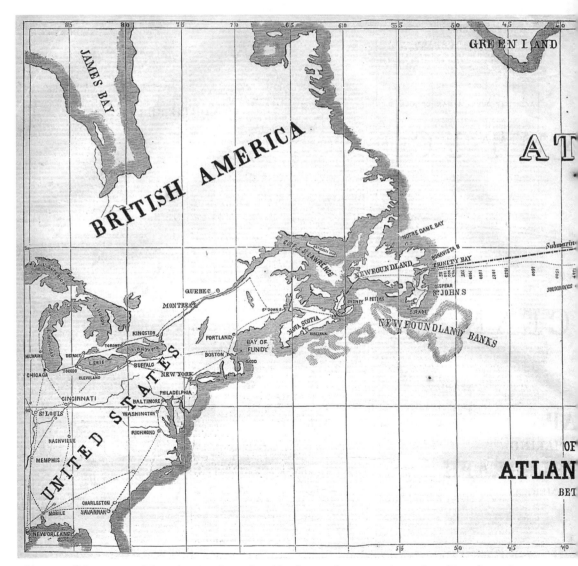

This map of the route of the Atlantic telegraph cable shows what a massive undertaking the project

Cyrus Field appeared to have taken the previous year's transatlantic telegraph cable failure in stride, and was forging ahead with the next attempt. The previous August the two cable-laying ships, *HMS Agamemnon* and *USNS Niagara*, heavy with the weight of 2,500 miles of cable between them, and accompanied by a squadron of support ships, had set out to connect the two continents.[8] The chief engineer Mr. Bright had favored proceeding to the mid-Atlantic, splicing the cable and then having the two ships steam towards their respective shores. This would have halved the time needed to lay the cable and reduced the chances of encountering bad weather. However, the company electrician, Dr. Whitehouse, insisted that they should start at the Irish coast, make a mid-Atlantic splice, and proceed on to Newfoundland. That way, the ships could stay

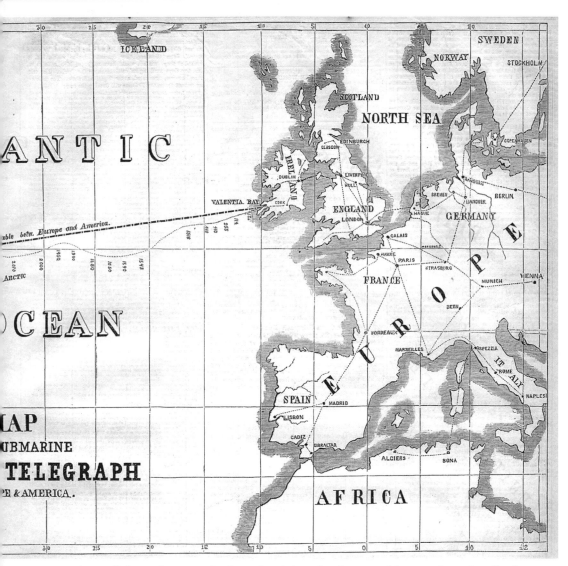

was: it entailed crossing not only the Atlantic but also the vast wilderness of Newfoundland.

Dr. Edward Orange Wildman Whitehouse, Electrician for the Atlantic Telegraph Company. His relationship with Hughes was strained right from the start.

in constant contact with Plymouth via the telegraph cable. It all started out well, but at a distance of 380 miles from Ireland, after they had entered the deep waters of the Atlantic, the cable broke and sank to 12,000 feet. Disappointed, the squadron returned to Plymouth as there was insufficient cable to complete the crossing. The whole telegraph cable was unloaded and put into storage and coiled in four large roofed tanks at Keyham dockyard in Plymouth, Devon.

Despite this failure, Field, deservedly known as the main "Projector of the Atlantic Telegraph Cable," was able to maintain the support of the board and the investors with his boundless enthusiasm and confidence. More importantly, he was able to raise the necessary capital for a renewed effort. With the new financing he purchased 700 miles of new cable to replace the lost section, plus some extra.

Hughes was joining this massive undertaking as a relative novice with regards to operating a telegraph system over submarine cables. He must, however, have felt honored to have the opportunity to meet and work with Cyrus Field's colleagues. He was probably looking forward to their assistance, given the challenge he faced, since at best he had three or four weeks to get up to speed and conduct his tests. At the end of April he traveled to Plymouth, where he met the company's electrician Dr. Edward Orange Wildman Whitehouse. While he had found the other members of the company to be cordial, Hughes found Whitehouse to be far from friendly. He treated Hughes with contempt, doubtful that this novice whom Field had unearthed in America could contribute anything, while he himself had been working for the last three years on submarine telegraphy. Whitehouse, some ten years older than Hughes, did not welcome this interference into his world.

Hughes, though, had apparently done some homework before he left America, reading through material that Cyrus Field had provided about Whitehouse's experiments.[9] It was already known that submarine cables performed very differently from landlines: signals not only became much weaker after traveling through 2,000 miles of cable, but also slowed down and became smeared together. Clean pulses sent into the cable emerged stretched out and jumbled together, a phenomenon the Victorians aptly termed the "embarrassment of the cable," which also became known as the retardation effect.[10] To counter this effect, and to enable the message to be read, pulses had to be sent very slowly and spaced well apart so that they did not interfere with each other. Hughes had realized that he needed to modify his instruments to operate under these conditions. He had therefore modified two instruments while in America so that they would run at a slower speed of ten words per minute (a speed that he obtained from Whitehouse's report) instead of the thirty-five to forty words per minute they normally achieved on landlines.[11] Also, to address the problem of the feeble signals, he devised a new more sensitive detector to add to the receiver of his instrument. To protect these new modifications he took out a further patent on May 5, about a week after he had filed his previous one.[12]

Hughes believed that the crux of the problem was in the detection of the very weak signals at the receiving end of the cable. His telegraph instrument had been designed from its inception with a sensitive detector built into the receiver.[13] This choice had been brought about by a number of considerations, one of which was the fact that as he had to make his own batteries (Daniell cells), so the fewer of them needed, the better. He had also wanted a quick-acting device, which resulted in his unique sensitive electromagnetic relay. He thus had ample experience in working with weak signals, which was to come in useful in his work on the Atlantic cable.

To be able to operate with the "feeble or attenuated currents" experienced on submarine cables he proposed to work his instrument through "the agency of a galvanometer," as he stated in his patent. What this amounted to was the addition of a new very

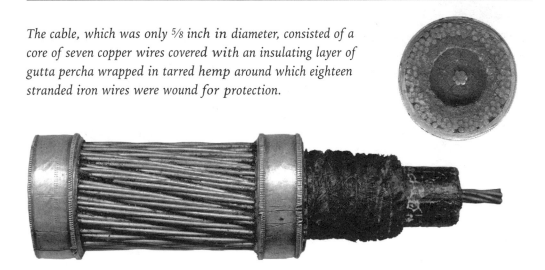

The cable, which was only ⅝ inch in diameter, consisted of a core of seven copper wires covered with an insulating layer of gutta percha wrapped in tarred hemp around which eighteen stranded iron wires were wound for protection.

sensitive detector to his telegraph receiver. A galvanometer was the most sensitive electrical measuring device of the day, so it was only natural that he should turn to it for ideas.[14] In the galvanometer a magnetized pointer (similar to a compass needle) was suspended inside a coil of wire of many turns. When an electrical current flowed through the coil it set up its own magnetic field with a north and south pole. The magnetic pointer would then rotate as it reacted to this field, much as a magnetic compass needle rotates when subjected to the earth's magnetic field. The degree and direction of its deflection were indications of the electrical current's strength and polarity.

Hughes made use of this principle by having the rotation of the pointer or armature trigger a much stronger electrical pulse that would then operate the telegraph receiver. By this means he determined the sensitivity would be significantly increased, as he stated:[15]

Invented a new local circuit which increased the sensitivity of the magnet 500 percent.

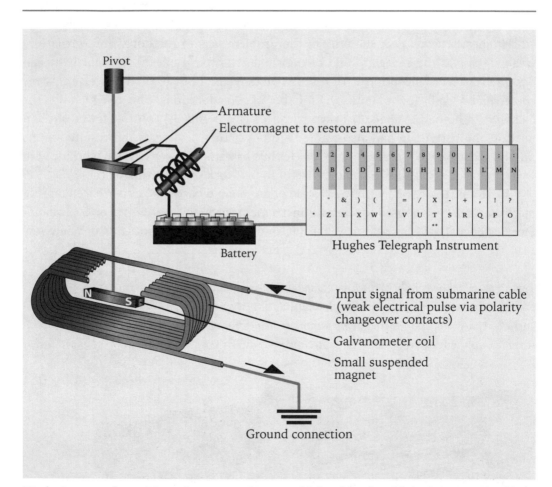

Hughes's patented sensitive galvanometer detector added to his telegraph instrument to enable it to operate with the Atlantic cable.

He designed the circuit with a coil of wire of many turns, in the center of which he mounted a magnetic needle. The needle was fixed on an arbor which was free to rotate. On the same arbor was mounted a small armature that could rotate and make electrical contact with a fixed contact. Passing the weak electrical signal from the submarine cable through the coil caused the armature to rotate and close this electrical contact. The armature only had to rotate through a small angle (20 degrees or less) to make the contact, and as a result the device was very sensitive. When the contact closed it connected a stronger voltage to the telegraph instrument from a local battery. The instrument then operated in its normal way. To restore the detector so that it would be ready for the next pulse Hughes added a feedback feature. When the contact was closed it activated a separate small electromagnet that attracted the armature back to its neutral position, thus breaking the contact and disconnecting the local battery. Hughes's addition of this very sensitive galvanometer to his instrument would probably have ensured the detection of the electrical signals over the full length of the cable.

When operating on a submarine cable Morse type instruments used alternative positive and negative electrical pulses (known as the cable code) so as to maintain the cable at a neutral potential state, as this had been shown to speed up the transmission. Hughes normally used single polarity pulses on landlines, but to operate on the submarine cable he added a device to alternate the polarity of the pulses transmitted, and a corresponding device at the receiver to restore the signal polarity ahead of his galvanometer device. This ensured that all the pulses fed to the galvanometer would be of the same polarity.

It appeared from the start that Hughes's relationship with Whitehouse was going to be a strained one as Whitehouse considered himself an expert on undersea cable operation and instrumentation and was not tolerant of the opinions of others. He already had to contend with Professor William Thomson from Glasgow suggesting contrary ideas, and now a new source of differing opinions had arrived, just as the company was about to make a new attempt to lay the cable.

Dr. Whitehouse's rise to the important position of company electrician was remarkable as he was actually a surgeon by profession. He had become interested in electrical technology in the early 1850s and had come to focus his attentions on the telegraph.[16] He subsequently met John Watkins Brett, head of the Magnetic Telegraph Company. Brett was studying undersea telegraph cables and their problems, such as retardation; Whitehouse found the topic intriguing, and he proceeded to investigate and carry out experiments of his own. In 1855 he had presented the results of experiments he performed on a 1,125 mile cable to the British Association meeting in Glasgow.[17] For these tests Whitehouse had devised his own apparatus for investigating the characteristics of such cables. Although the cable he used was designed as a submarine cable, it was not submerged in water but was stored on land, and thus his results were only partially relevant to submerged cables.[18] Whitehouse constructed a number of other instruments to conduct further tests, one of which he called a "magneto-electrometer."[19] He also made a relay receiver of his own design for detecting signals sent over a cable. For transmitting the pulses into the cable he used an induction coil which provided a much higher transmitting voltage than a battery alone. The power to excite the induction coil came from a battery he had devised which he called a perpetual maintenance battery. With this apparatus he claimed that he could transmit pulses faster than other instruments. He patented the induction coil and receiving relay in 1855.[20]

Whitehouse made a bold deduction from his experiments and proclaimed that retardation would not be a problem for submarine telegraphy: good news indeed for the proponents of the transatlantic telegraph. But his steadfast belief in this unfortunate and incorrect conclusion caused him to ignore the advice of colleagues which could have corrected this error, and to stick to a course of action and instruments that would prove to be poorly matched for operation with the Atlantic cable. His conclusion, however, only seemed to be corroborated by tests that he made with Charles Bright using some 2,000 miles of subterranean telegraph cables belonging to the English and Irish Magnetic Telegraph Company.[21] These tests were witnessed by none other than Samuel Morse, the veteran telegrapher and advising electrician to the New York, Newfoundland and London Telegraph Company, who was in England at the time. Upon completion of the tests Morse declared them a success and summarized the results in a letter to Field on October 3, 1856:[22]

> This result had been thrown in some doubt by the discovery, more than two years since, of certain phenomena upon subterranean and submarine conductors, and had attracted the attention of electricians, particularly of that eminent philosopher, Professor Faraday, and that clearsighted investigator of electrical phenomena, Dr. Whitehouse; and one of these phenomena to wit, the perceptible retardation of electrical current, threatened to perplex our operations, and required careful investigation before we could pronounce with certainty the commercial practicality of the Ocean Telegraph. I am most happy to inform you that, as a crowning result of a long series of experimental investigations and inductive reasoning upon this subject, the experiments under the direction of Dr. Whitehouse and Mr. Bright, which I witnessed this morning—in which the induction coils and receiving magnets as modified by these gentlemen, were made to actuate one of my recording instruments—have most satisfactorily resolved all doubts of the practicability as well as the practicality of operating the telegraph from Newfoundland to Ireland.

In another letter Morse stated that the cable could carry 14,400 words every twenty-four hours, or ten words per minute. Field thought this was a good start as there were indications that this speed could be doubled.[23] Of course, speed was important if the cable was to be an economic success; the higher the transmission speed the more messages could be sent each day and the more revenue generated. The company felt relatively confident of success with Samuel Morse's endorsement, and believed that the problem had now shifted from one of getting a signal through such a long cable to one of improving the speed of transmitting and receiving.

The encouraging information that retardation was no longer a problem was included in the Atlantic Telegraph Company's prospectus issued in England on November 1, 1856, by Cyrus Field as vice president of the New York, Newfoundland and London Telegraph Company.[24]

It was the results of these experiments, together with Morse's endorsement and an introduction to Cyrus Field from John W. Brett, that had led to Whitehouse being added as one of the four "projectors" of the Atlantic Telegraph Company and appointed their chief electrician. The company prospectus indicated that the appointment of these two gentlemen (Whitehouse and Brett) would entail the rights to use their patents. In addition, Whitehouse's experiments, in which he determined that retardation was not going to be a problem, provided a powerful argument that the venture was likely to succeed.

All of this good news was exactly what the projectors and subsequently the investors wanted to hear and helped propel the project forward. This view of the problem of retardation, however, was not shared by all, and in particular not by the young scientist Professor William Thomson, whose conclusion on retardation effects was very different from Whitehouse's. Thomson had brilliantly worked out the physics involved in sending electrical signals through a submarine cable earlier in 1854, and had determined that electrical pulses would suffer much more degradation in their passage through a long submerged submarine cable, and that as a result, retardation was going to be a significant problem. Thomson theorized that pulses would be delayed in proportion to the square of the cable length rather than in direct proportion to its length as had been supposed, and his law became known as the "Law of Squares." This meant that if the retardation in a 200 mile cable was $1/10$ second, then for a 2,000 mile cable it would be 100 times greater or 10 seconds.[25] Thomson's theoretical approach to the problem was not well received by the electricians and telegraph men, whose faith lay in solving problems by experimentation and practical means. Besides, it is unlikely that any of them understood the theory or its underlying mathematics.

Thomson's view was obviously not popular, as it cast doubt on the viability of the cable project. This was not Thomson's intent, though, as he was very much a proponent of the project and was actually trying to point out the practical problems that had to be overcome. Whitehouse, as chief electrician, was able to override Thomson's objections and he persevered with his solution.

Thomson realized that his counsel was falling on deaf ears. In his opinion, if the project was to succeed it should be based on scientific principles rather than Whitehouse's dubious beliefs. Thomson had, of course, stated that he was skeptical of Whitehouse's approach which was based on the premise that if he used high voltages generated by his induction coils, then enough would arrive at the end of the 2,000 mile cable to operate his relay device with its heavy electromagnetic components.[26] Thomson saw the problem differently, believing that electrical pulses derived from battery power alone coupled with a sensitive receiver would work. He therefore took it upon himself to investigate a receiving instrument of his own design, also based on the galvanometer principle.[27] What Thomson went on to invent was to be called the "mirror galvanometer."[28] Instead of a moving pointer he used a ray of light reflected off a mirror, which cast a spot onto a graduated scale. The tiny mirror was attached to a magnet that was delicately suspended by a silk filament and surrounded by a wire coil. Passing an electrical current through the coil caused the suspended magnet to rotate, and the light beam from the lamp focused onto the mirror was then reflected onto the graduated screen. Through a law of optics, the rotation of the mirror doubled the angle through which the reflected beam moved, and by moving the screen further away, the spot's movement was further increased and thus the instrument's sensitivity improved. In operation, the light spot was adjusted to mid scale, and its movement to the left or right of this position signaled the reception of a dot or dash. It was a simple but elegant instrument that he patented.[29]

Whitehouse disparaged Thomson's approach and his mirror galvanometer, and even criticized his methods in a pamphlet published in July of 1857; although the pamphlet was not authored by Whitehouse, it is believed that he had a significant influence on its content.[30] Thomson appeared to take Whitehouse's criticism in stride, diplomatically minimizing the differences between their views, possibly so as not to cause too much concern to the projectors and backers of the project.

Field thrust Hughes into the midst of this jousting between Whitehouse and Thomson. It appeared that Hughes and Hyde's observations had been correct with regard to the readiness of the company's instruments. The newspaper journalists, especially the American ones, had been closely following the progress of the Atlantic telegraph cable, which was of great interest to their readers, and they had sniffed out a story:[31]

> To the month of January last it was believed that the chief electrician would be able to fulfill the terms of his contract with the company; and the directors or at least a majority of them entertained no doubt of his ability to send messages through the whole length of the cable. Their confidence was sustained by a report which Dr. Whitehouse made to the company on the 4th of January last, in which he said he had at that time attained a gratifying speed of four words per minute and that by the aid of improvements which he was then making, he believed he would attain a still more satisfactory result. This statement and the promise of still better things so far from being supported by actual experiments and tests were proved, however, to be wholly incorrect and without foundation. One of the directors desirous of satisfying himself in regards to the rate of speed went down from London to Plymouth, where the cable then was and where Dr. Whitehouse had been for several months engaged in his experiments. He told the Doctor the object of his visit, said that he would remain in the office for one hour and as he wished to report the number of words that could be sent through the cable in that time to the company, he desired him to put his best operators at work. The Doctor complied with the desire, and at the end of the specified time succeeded getting exactly sixty-one words through the cable, or little more than one word per minute. Subsequent experiments, however showed that there was very little reliance

to be put upon even this rate of transmission, for it not unfrequently occurred that the electricians were unable to send a single letter through correctly. It became apparent that Dr. Whitehouse could not do what he [i.e. the director] was led to believe he could do, as he had stated in his report, and the company resolved that the cable should be thrown open to other electricians and that they should be invited to test their systems.

The company, obviously not wanting to fail in this critical area, and perhaps believing that there was some merit in what Thomson had been saying, decided to invite others to test their instruments on the cable. It now became apparent why Field had brought Hughes into the project. Hughes's telegraph was familiar to him, and he had played a key role in launching it in America. He knew it was capable of high speeds and was already in production, whereas Whitehouse's instrument had the performance and appearance of an instrument still in development.[32] Field's reasons for inviting Hughes to try out his instruments on the cable were sound, but would there be time to adjust the instruments and complete the tests? The squadron would soon be departing and if the cable was laid successfully, the full focus would be on getting messages through it. If the company was not prepared (and had not heeded warnings from competent scientists) there would be an outcry. The newspapers continued to keep their American readers up to date:[33]

> The cable ships Agamemnon and Niagara returned to England, and according to agreement went into Plymouth, where the cable was all landed and carefully coiled in a watertight tank. About twenty-one hundred miles of it were placed here near the beginning of November....
>
> Three gentlemen have been invited by the company to make experiments upon the whole length, and are requested to make a full report of the result. These are Mr. Thomson a gentleman who occupies a high position in the English world of science; Mr. Henley an electrician of much merit and Mr. David Edward Hughes the inventor of the instrument which is known by his name.
>
> Dr. Whitehouse told this correspondent that he (your correspondent) should not expect anything as he (Dr. W.) felt confident that Mr. Hughes could not get a current through twenty miles of the wire with his appliances—that is with his instrument, &c; that we knew nothing at all about induction in the United States, and that he (Dr. W.) regretted we should have formed any expectations that it was impossible to have realized.
>
> At last Mr. Hughes did arrive and with him Mr. Hyram Hyde a gentleman who has a large interest in his patent. He was accompanied by two assistant electricians Henry Bishop and Chas. P. Craig.

While it was reported that the cable was coiled in watertight tanks, and this appeared to have been the original intention, this was not in fact the case, as the tanks had been incorrectly constructed and leaked badly. Consequently, the tanks were never filled with water and were left dry: an important point, as retardation was much less of a problem in a dry cable than in a submerged one.[34]

Hughes finally got his turn with the cable and set up his instruments:[35]

> Wednesday 28 April he sent current through whole twenty six hundred miles. This was more than the chief electrician and his staff expected and they were accordingly much disappointed.... Before he left the office he printed not only one letter, but forty continuously, and then wound up by making the currents spell his own name and the names of his assistants.

He further recorded in his own notes:[36]

> Whitehouse made proposal that the instrument should be patented in his name. Mr. Hyde indignantly refused and wrote to the Co. explaining the whole affair.

Was Whitehouse trying to eliminate the competition, save face, or protect his financial interests? Whitehouse reported the incident differently; he believed that a great effort would be made to induce the directors to purchase the patent rights or obtain a license to use Hughes's instrument at an exorbitant price. While he decried Hughes's instrument, at the same time he offered to help make it work on the Atlantic telegraph cable and suggested that the company should not pay for any of the changes he (Whitehouse) made, but that he (Whitehouse) should benefit from these changes if Hughes's instruments were used on other non-competing telegraph lines.[37]

Whitehouse, of course, as chief electrician and an employee of the company, was receiving a salary and was in line to receive a large bonus if he succeeded, so he had reason to protect his interests, whereas David Hughes and William Thomson were working for free.[38]

Thomson was still working quietly in the background, and in a letter to his brother in April, indicated that he had just returned from Devonport, having conducted tests on the cable in which he had verified his mathematical theory. He had also managed to transmit a letter every three seconds (twenty letters per minute) through the 2,700 miles of cable. He reported that he was having instruments made for both Valentia and Newfoundland and was hoping to have them ready by May 14.[39] Thomson had previously asked the directors for £2,000 to cover the cost of making these new instruments but had received a disappointing reply: that due to the financial state of the company it would not be expedient to advance him such a large sum of money. They did however subsequently allow him £500.

The board of the Atlantic Telegraph Co. was becoming frustrated by the lack of progress. As time was rapidly running out, they set new rules to try to give each of the electricians a fair chance to solve the problem by giving each of the hopefuls equal time in the laboratory, with access to the cable. Of course, Whitehouse was somewhat put out by the board's decision to push him aside and their lack of confidence in his ability, and now he had to let these other electricians into his laboratory. He must have abhorred the interference.

Hughes had realized by now that he had been given erroneous data regarding how fast words could be sent through the cable: it was obvious that they were nowhere close to operating the cable at ten, never mind twenty words per minute. Hughes reported in his notes:[40]

> Worked the Instrument through 2500 miles of cable at the rate of two words & half per minute, but that it was necessary to alter the train of wheels before we could work reliably.

Hughes had to rethink the situation and consider further modifications to his instruments so that they could run at this much slower speed. Whitehouse reported that Hughes had to use his hand to slow the instrument down so that it would print correctly, which was probably correct, given that his instrument was set to run too fast.[41]

By now, Hughes had a better understanding of the requirements for operating with the undersea cable and was in a scramble to make the necessary changes to his instruments. This involved making new parts as well as modifying existing components so that the instruments would run significantly slower. To accomplish all this he needed the use of Whitehouse's workshop, electricians and mechanics. Hughes had worked up to two and a half words a minute and was hoping to achieve eight words a minute. However, Whitehouse was creating a roadblock and denying Hughes any help, presumably hoping to stall his effort until the squadron sailed.

The directors back in London, who Thomson reported were now meeting almost daily, were under the misapprehension that their instructions had been followed and that Whitehouse had facilitated and accommodated the other electricians' experiments, and that all the necessary tests had been completed. They had therefore given the go-ahead to start loading the cable. Cyrus Field, as confident as ever, sent a message to David Hughes at the Royal Hotel, Plymouth on May 12 inquiring what the results of his tests were:[42]

> Will you have the kindness to give me direct answers to the following questions?
>
> 1st What is the greatest rate of speed that you have been able to send printed messages through the entire length of the cable (2900 miles) now at Devonport, with your instrument?
>
> 2nd How much do you think you will be able to increase this speed before the Expedition sails on the experimental trip about 2 weeks from this time?
>
> 3rd At what rate do you think you will be able by your improved instrument to work thro' the cable from Ireland to Newfoundland, within one month after the cable shall have successfully laid?"

Of course, Hughes was not making any progress and Whitehouse's tactics of denying him access to the cable prompted his business partner Mr. Hyde to appeal directly

The Atlantic cable being fed in from above and carefully coiled in the hold of the Agamemnon.

to the directors of the Atlantic Telegraph Company in a letter written on May 13.[43] His letter clearly shows how desperate the situation was at that point in time. Hyde politely thanks the board for the opportunity to participate in the project. He goes on to say that on Monday, Cyrus Field had been to Plymouth to witness the results of tests by the three participants, Whitehouse, Thomson and Hughes. Professor Hughes was selected to demonstrate his instruments first and attained a speed of two and a half words per minute on the 2,900-mile-long cable; Thomson had difficulties with his instrument; and Whitehouse did not submit a machine to any experiment, admitting that he could not do better than one word per minute until he got his new instrument down from London. "What this instrument will do nobody knows but it must do a great deal to sustain the Doctor's sinking reputation," Hyde wrote, and went on to say that, "we have carefully abstained from making remarks relative to the induction coils and instruments that he uses but think this is part of your problem."

Cyrus Field was quick to respond, and the board immediately sent orders to Whitehouse directing him to place the cable at Hughes's disposal during a fair portion of the time that remained before the departure of the expedition. However, time was running out, as the cable was already being loaded on board the two cable ships. Hughes chased the cable onto the *Agamemnon*, still trying desperately to complete the tests and get the answers requested by Field. He made a note:[44]

Tried the Inst (after some necessary alterations) through 1500 miles of cable on board the Agamemnon found it worked perfectly and reliably.

The ships were making ready to depart, and with them departed Hughes's hopes of completing all of his tests. Now he had to think what his next step would be, since the two ends of the cable would soon be separated not by a few yards, but by 2,000 miles.

On May 29 the squadron departed to conduct cable laying trials in the Bay of Biscay (Hughes stayed on shore to continue modifying his instruments so that they would work well on the cable). Whitehouse, as chief electrician, was supposed to accompany the expedition to carry out the electrical testing but indicated that he was not well enough to sail, and Thomson had to take his place on board as electrician.[45] Just before they departed a package arrived for Thomson: it was his anxiously awaited marine mirror galvanometer. Field and Bright also came along for the sea trials, which went well, and the ships returned to Plymouth on June 3. While the cable laying operations seemed to be in hand, the situation with Whitehouse's telegraph instruments was not. An unsettling report by George Saward, the secretary of the company, which he delivered upon the ships' return, made it clear that things were not as they should be. It appears that some of the directors were still under the misconception that operations were running smoothly in the electrical department. Apparently, the previous warnings and furious activity by Thomson, Hughes and Hyde had not been understood by all of the board members. Possibly they had only been reading the positive reports made by their own electrician! Saward indicated that Whitehouse had been instructed to use the several months that the cable was in storage to have the operators practice sending and receiving messages with the instruments that were to be used with the cable. However:[46]

> The Directors were, therefore greatly disappointed to find that not only had this not been done, but they found on their assembly at Plymouth that the instruments were not in a state, nor of a nature calculated to work the cable to a commercial profit.

It is interesting to note that Whitehouse, later in September, recalled their visit somewhat differently:[47]

> The Directors came down to examine the working of our instruments, with the accuracy and certainty of which I understood they were well satisfied.

The state of affairs just prior to the departure of the expedition was not encouraging. The squadron stayed in port only long enough to take on coal and supplies and left for the Atlantic on June 10. The expedition consisted of the two main cable-laying ships and a number of support vessels. As Whitehouse was still claiming he was unwell, Thomson again took his place on board to supervise operations in the cable testing room. Here he was in an awkward position, as he was expected to make use

The cable ships Niagara *and* Agamemnon *being loaded with cable while Prof. Hughes was still trying desperately to complete his testing.*

of Whitehouse's instruments, none of which he had used or tested and in which he appeared to have no confidence. He was, however, given permission to take on board and use his own marine galvanometer.

Whitehouse appeared to have every confidence in his own instruments and set about transporting them to the cable terminus at Valentia in Ireland in preparation for the cable's landfall there. It appeared that he had defeated Hughes and Thomson, at least for the time being. But while he was relocating to Valentia, Hughes made use of his absence to finally get access to his workshop and start making the necessary changes to his instruments.

HMS Agamemnon was one of Britain's finest ships of the line, and had seen service during the bombardment of Sebastopol in the Crimean War. It was one of the typical hybrid ships of the period, a three-masted wooden sailing vessel of 3,102 tons (230 ft long, 55.5 ft beam with a 24.5 ft deep hold) with a screw propeller powered by a coal-fired steam engine. The other cable ship, which was the larger of the two, was on loan from the American government. This was the US frigate *Niagara*, a screw frigate of 5,200 tons (345 ft long, 55 ft beam, 31.5 ft deep hold). This also was a three-masted sailing vessel with screw propeller powered by a coal-fired steam engine. The holds of both ships had been modified to each take on half of the cable, which was in the region of 1160 tons.

The objective of the expedition was clear but the outcome was far from certain. The plan this time was to proceed to the mid-Atlantic and splice the two halves of the cable together. The *Niagara* would then head for Trinity Bay, Newfoundland, and the *Agamemnon* would proceed to the island of Valentia off the west coast of Ireland. Unfortunately the squadron lacked long-range weather forecasts and set off unaware that they were sailing into a major depression over the Atlantic that almost spelled doom for all of them. A hair-raising account of the voyage is contained in Charles Bright's *Story of the Atlantic Cable* in which he quotes a narrative by a reporter from the London *Times* who was on the voyage. The following short description is excerpted and condensed from this account.

As they headed west, the barometer kept falling and the weather started to deteriorate, with high winds and angry seas. The *Agamemnon*, with Bright and Thomson on board, was the smaller of the two cable ships and was getting the worst of it. The weight of the cable and also its location severely strained the ship's timbers: not all of the cable would fit below decks, and so some 250 tons of it were stowed on the forward deck. In addition, the lower coal bunkers had been removed to make room for the cable below decks, and as a result not only the 250 tons of cable but also coal was also stowed on the upper deck. All of this made the ship overloaded and top heavy, never a good situation in a storm!

The seas were tumultuous and frightening; the ship was rolling almost on her side. Things were breaking loose and timbers giving way under the tremendous onslaught of the sea and wind. There was great fear that their precious cargo, the cable, would break loose from the deck and go over the side. The barometer kept falling, and when it was believed it could not go any lower, it did. The coal stored on deck broke loose, taking everything on deck with it—crew, hatches and equipment—as it moved with great force from side to side and down companionways. The masts had started to loosen and the stays were flapping and limp. This was not what the electricians and engineers had envisaged; now there was no thought of laying the cable, but only of surviving. The seas increased and the *Agamemnon* rolled to 45 degrees, threatening to turn turtle. The cable below decks had started to work loose and was getting tangled. Water poured over the decks and down through broken hatchways, shutting down one of the boilers. Everyone was getting thrown around and numerous injuries were occurring. In desperation, the captain brought the ship about to run before the storm; the foresails were raised, full steam got up, and full speed ahead called for. Finally, the glass started to rise and the ordeal was over after sixteen days of hell, quite a start to the expedition.

As the seas diminished, the *Agamemnon* headed back to the rendezvous point, not sure what to expect. Had they all survived? Luckily both cable ships and all the support ships reported in, although not in the best of shape; the storm had taken its toll. Nevertheless, on June 26 the cable ends were spliced and the ships set sail in opposite directions. But the cable broke twice and they had to return each time to splice it and then try again. On the third attempt the cable again broke, but now they were beyond the range previously agreed to as the point of no return. With their supply of coal running low, the squadron abandoned the effort and headed back to Queenstown, Ireland.

The failure caused significant despair to the board of the company. Field and his supporters, though, were able to bring them around and the board voted to make another attempt that same summer. The ships were refueled, and on July 17, 1858, the expedition once again set sail for the Atlantic, again rendezvousing mid-ocean, splicing the cable and setting sail in opposite directions. There were a few incidents during this attempt, but the two ends of cable were successfully landed at Bull Arm in Trinity Bay, Newfoundland, and at Valentia, Ireland, and on August 5 a current was transmitted across the cable. An electrical telegraph link was established for the first time between Britain and America. The great event caused jubilation in both countries and Queen Victoria knighted the Chief Engineer Charles Bright for his contribution (at only twenty-six).

During the cable laying process, the insulation and also the continuity of the cable between the two ships had been continually checked. It was noticed that transmission through the cable seemed to improve once the cable was submerged. This was attributed to the cold in the deep waters, as copper conducted electricity better at lower temperatures. The considerable pressure at depth was also believed to have compressed the gutta percha insulation and to have consolidated any gaps.[48]

Field and the electrician Charles de Sauty arrived in Newfoundland to supervise the shore end of the cable and to set up the instruments in the telegraph building. They had taken ashore the equipment from the *Niagara* which included Whitehouse's apparatus as well as one each of Thomson's and H. Moore's galvanometers.[49] Field then departed on the *Niagara* for New York via St. Johns, leaving Charles de Sauty in charge at Trinity Bay to operate the cable.

In Valentia Thomson handed over the cable operation to Whitehouse, also leaving one of his sensitive mirror galvanometers there before returning to Glasgow. Whitehouse had at his disposal a total of 500 battery cells and had installed immense induction coils five feet in length.[50] This arrangement was capable of sending pulses of approximately 2,000 volts into the cable. To receive messages he was ready with his own relay-type receiver. He set about performing tests on the cable and communicating with Charles de Sauty in Newfoundland

The first message from Newfoundland to Valentia was received on August 13. The cable, though, was proving very flighty and tremendous effort and perseverance was required to interpret messages. Messages such as "send again," "send slower," and "do you receive," "your currents very weak" and "repeat" dominated the early traffic. On August 16 there was an interchange of congratulatory messages between Queen Victoria and President James Buchanan. Later, it was learned that sending the Queen's speech, which consisted of only 100 words, had taken sixteen hours. By the middle of August things did not seem to have improved; messages were passed but with great difficulty. There are references in the messages to the use of galvanometers.

Of course, New York was going wild with the news of the successful cable link and Field got caught up in the revelry for a while. However, he kept in touch with de Sauty to monitor progress. Whitehouse had indicated that he needed about six weeks to carry out his tests on the cable before it would be ready for commercial service. To the many who wanted to get the cable into operation, this seemed an inordinate length of time, and there was pressure on the company to open up the line for business. There were also a few skeptics who believed the whole thing was a scam by Field, and that the cable did not exist. Others thought that to send a message it was necessary to tug on the cable.

After the initial jubilation over the successful laying of the cable, disappointment must have set in with the realization that all was not well with the sending and receiving instruments. This had become obvious from the painfully low volume of messages transmitted on the cable, which ranged from one to twelve per day.[51] This was not the volume that had been anticipated, and was far too low for commercial success.

And the company had another problem: the board finally came to realize Whitehouse's ineptitude when some of his skullduggery in Ireland was exposed, and the day of reckoning arrived on August 17. His services were abruptly terminated and William Thomson was appointed to take over operations at Valentia. It came to light that Whitehouse had been rather devious in his reports or lack thereof to the board in London; specifically, that he had been using Thomson's mirror galvanometer from time to time while claiming that he was only using his own equipment. Normally Whitehouse would have received the pulses representing the dots and dashes via his own receiving relay. This, in turn, would have activated a local automatic Morse recorder that would print the dots and dashes on a strip of paper. However, as his relay did not work satisfactorily, he substituted Thomson's mirror galvanometer in its place. He, or a clerk, would watch the moving light spot on the screen and note its movement, interpreting the movements as dots and dashes. They would then manually input these dots and dashes via a telegraph key connected to the Morse recorder. The resultant printed strips of paper with the messages were then sent to the board of directors in London as if they had been received directly off the cable with Whitehouse's own instrument. It was also revealed that he had deduced that there was a problem with the cable close to shore and had attempted to investigate by raising the cable, contrary to the wishes of the company.

When Thomson took over the operation in Valentia, he installed his mirror galvanometer and discontinued the use of the high voltage induction coils, reverting to battery power only, and instructed de Sauty in Newfoundland to do the same. Unfortunately, though, the cable was ailing, and on September 4 the Atlantic Telegraph Company in London issued a statement indicating that there was no longer any communication over the cable.

The situation in America prior to this disturbing news had been one of celebration and jubilation. Cyrus Field was preparing to participate in the official celebration of the joining of the continents by the Atlantic telegraph cable in New York City. On September 1 and 2 the celebration was in full swing, and consisted of a large parade followed by a banquet and fireworks. The fireworks ended with a tumultuous finale, setting fire to the cupola on top of City Hall.

But during the days leading up to this celebration Cyrus Field had been monitoring the situation up in Newfoundland and was becoming perturbed over the lack of progress in increasing the speed and reliability of sending and receiving messages. If the situation persisted it would put the company in an untenable business position. The public and press were already putting great pressure on Field to open the line for business. He thought it imperative that they discontinue their current course of using what he presumably thought were Whitehouse's instruments and substitute Hughes's instruments as soon as possible. At this point there was every confidence in the integrity of the cable and it was believed that the bottleneck lay with Whitehouse's sending and receiving instruments.

In late August Field had written to Hughes and Hyde in England, confirming his support and expressing his hope that they would come to a contractual arrangement for the use of his instruments with the Atlantic Telegraph Company.[52]

To H. Hyde Esq. or Prof D.E. Hughes care R. Stuart Liverpool

Fully believing from the evidence I have witnessed that the Hughes invention possesses great merit and not doubting but that the machines could be made with reasonable time for experiments of great value to the Atlantic Telegraph Company for working the cable. I earnestly hope that you will be disposed to make and that the Atlantic Co. will be disposed to receive and entertain from you a fair proposition whereby you may make such demonstrations with your machines in connection with the cable as will satisfy you and the company as to the value of your invention as compared with the invention of others. Correctness and expedition in the transmission of messages through the cable are the important points to strive for, and I have no doubt but that all the Directors will agree with me that no time should be lost in availing themselves of the very best telegraphic system that science and skill can produce. You are at liberty to show this communication to the Directors of the Atlantic Company and I shall hope to hear soon that you have made satisfactory arrangements with them.

Signed
Cyrus W. Field

Mr. Hyde did make a financial proposal to the Atlantic Telegraph Company for the use of Hughes's telegraph instruments on the cable.[53]

When the celebrations in New York were over, Field's worst fear was realized when Charles de Sauty indicated that the signals had become so weak that he could no longer receive messages from Ireland. Field's heart must have sunk.[54]

Cyrus Field was now isolated from London when he most needed the cable to coordinate with the company. The brief teaser of "instant" transatlantic communications had created great excitement and had confirmed his vision of the value of connecting the continents. By now, however, he had only a sketchy idea of what was transpiring back in England, as they were back to communicating the old way—by steamers crossing the Atlantic.

Field, ever optimistic and believing the latest glitch was only temporary, issued the following statement from New York on September 8:[55]

> Sir: I have received from Newfoundland a dispatch informing me that although the insulation of the ocean cable remains perfect no message has come over it for several days.
>
> The last telegraphic dispatch that I received from England was dated London September 1.
>
> What may be the cause of the cessation we do not know but conjecture that it is the change of the shore end at Valentia, which I was informed was about to be made; but it should also be stated that Professor Thomson was about to succeed Professor Whitehouse in a series of experiments on the cable; and, although his system was regarded by all practical telegraphers in England as perfectly childish, it is quite possible that the present delay in transmitting intelligence is attributable to Thomson's experiments.
>
> It is also known at the sailing of the Africa that the directors despairing of satisfactory results from the systems of Whitehouse and Thomson, had arranged with Professor Hughes to take charge of the electrical department of the company's business, and it was expected that Hughes's printing telegraph instrument would be placed at Trinity Bay and Valentia on or about 20th or 21st inst.; and from the experiments made with the cable at Plymouth, there is no reasonable doubt that Professor Hughes will be able to transmit intelligence through the cable reliably at a rate of about 300 words per hour.
>
> Cyrus W. Field
> NY Sept 8

For Hughes, the whole situation had suddenly been turned upside down; he and Hyde now found themselves as the new hope to make the cable a success. While Thomson's apparatus appeared to be adequate, the directors (or at least Field) must have thought that the Hughes instruments could do even better.[56]

Prompted by the directive from Field, Hughes had dispatched his assistant and equipment to Liverpool on a special steamer about September 10, bound for Trinity Bay, Newfoundland, and the assistant was expected to arrive around September 20 or 21. At this point, nobody knew for sure what the problem was with the cable, but it had happened before that following a problem the cable had miraculously cured itself and returned to operation, so hope had not been abandoned.

Unfortunately, the cable did not recover, and all of those involved soon realized that its brief life had come to an end. Cyrus Field's dream had almost come true. Remarkably, he did not give up and was able to raise enough capital for a new attempt, but his plans were again foiled, this time in America by increasing tension between the Northern and

Southern States which led to the US Civil War. It was not until 1865–6 that the next attempt was made and successful telegraph communications were finally established between Britain and America.

For David Hughes and Hyde, their dreams were dashed; Hughes's position as electrician for the Atlantic Telegraph Company had been short lived, and his equipment was never tested on the 2,000 miles of submerged Atlantic cable. They could ill afford to wait around and Hyde was eager to move on and find other customers. But would Hughes's telegraph have worked on the cable?

It is highly probable that his instrument did work on the full length of cable while it was in dry storage as he states in his notes. Electrical signals sent over the cable under those conditions were less subject to retardation, drifting and earth fluctuations. Further, he had added to his instrument a sensitive detector based on the galvanometer to receive the weak signals; he was certainly familiar with construction and implementation of these devices,[57] and it is known that such galvanometers were sensitive enough to receive signals over the full length of the submerged cable. It is therefore probable that Hughes's galvanometer receiver could have detected signals sent over the full length of the submerged cable. Hughes later showed that he could transmit over these long distances in tests at the East India dock and also on land lines from St. Petersburg to Paris, a distance of 2,200 kilometers.

It is doubtful though that Hughes's instrument would have worked on the submerged Atlantic cable, or if it had, it would have been with extreme difficulty. The main problem would have been maintaining synchronization between the instruments at each end of the cable. Thomson's mirror galvanometer for instance relied on human interpretation of the light spot's movement; human interpretation was necessary as the cable's electrical characteristics were not particularly stable. Similarly for the other galvanometers which were used: they employed a pointer that could swing left or right of a center zero position that required human observation and interpretation. Hughes's instrument, on the other hand, operated automatically and required the transmitting and the receiving telegraph instruments to operate in tightly maintained synchronism. Establishing this synchronism would have been the first task to be performed, and while Hughes had a procedure for it, coordination would have been challenging. It probably would have required the use of one of Thomson's mirror galvanometers in the circuit to coordinate instructions. While Hughes's instrument could deal with the retardation effect and weak signals, it could not tolerate variations in determining at what point in time an electrical pulse arrived, as the instrument operated based on pulse position modulation. The apparently random drifting and fluctuations in the electrical signals on the cable would probably have led to errors in detecting the time of arrival of the electrical pulses and so caused the instrument to suffer a loss of synchronism, and thus to print out incorrect letters and garbled messages.

As cable technology improved, Hughes's instruments were successfully operated on many shorter undersea cables, such as across the English Channel. Eventually synchronized systems were also successfully used on the transatlantic cables.

As for Hughes, he remained in England a while longer, carrying out tests on undersea cables. It had been determined that the cable had failed because of a breakdown in the gutta percha insulation, believed to have been punched through by the high voltages used by Whitehouse. This had allowed the seawater (earth/ground) to penetrate into the cable and short circuit the central copper conductor. However, while this may have been the final nail in the coffin, the situation was more complex than that. There were many other factors that had contributed to the cable's failure. The conductivity of the copper core had not been controlled in manufacturing, resulting in a wide variation which was further exacerbated by the early decision to use a thin copper conductor rather than a thick one. There were many splices in the cable, resulting in many joints which compromised its performance. The cable had been stored in conditions that had left it exposed to the heat of the sun, allowing the gutta percha insulation to soften and thus the copper conductor to move from its central location within the insulation. It was suspected that this had allowed the copper conductor to come dangerously close to the protective steel wires and the conductive sea water. The many loadings and unloadings of the cable from the ships and its having been being dashed about and kinked in the storm had also probably damaged it.

Initially, most of the suspicion fell on the breakdown of the insulation and Hughes reasoned that if an undersea cable could be self-repairing it would prevent similar problems in the future, which would be a great boon, especially as it was so difficult to locate where the fault lay in a cable, find it, raise the cable from great depths, repair the fault, and re-lay the cable. Hughes put his inventive mind to work and came up with a semi-fluid self-sealing insulating substance that could be inserted in the gutta percha tube surrounding the copper conductor. Thus, if the insulation was pierced or was faulty, the fluid would ooze out to fill the fissure and solidify. He patented the invention in January of 1859. His formula for the semi-fluid was kept secret, but his patent gives some hint that it was based on rosin dissolved in turpentine.[58]

> The chief object of the invention is to maintain the insulation of submarine telegraph wire even after the gutta percha covering has become injured and no longer able to protect the wire from contact with water. One mode by which I attain this end is to insert in the gutta percha tube that encloses the conducting wire a semi fluid substance which, when the gutta percha coating is pierced or cut, will ooze out and fill up the fissure, and thus restore and maintain the insulation.

A demonstration section of cable was made and tested and the self-sealing insulation was shown to work. While there was interest in this novel approach, it was not adopted: it was an invention before its time.

After the cable failure, the British government formed a board of inquiry in 1859 which was referred to as "The Lords of the Committee of the Privy Council for Trade" or just The Board of Trade. The board was made up of prominent scientists and engineers. Hughes carried out various tests on undersea cables for Josiah Latimer Clark, the electrical engineer with the Electric Telegraph Company, in support of the inquiry. He was then called upon to give evidence and provide opinions and recommendations. In July of 1863 the board issued its report and concluded that a well designed cable utilizing quality controls during manufacture and paid out from a cable ship with improved machinery stood a good chance of working and of operating for many years.[59] The causes for the failure were put down to design, manufacturing and quality control problems which had been exacerbated by the great haste with which the project had been carried out. While these were all contributory factors, it is probable that the cable could have operated for some years if it had not been subject to the extremely high voltage abuse by Whitehouse which eventually created short circuit faults by puncturing the insulation.[60]

William Thomson continued his association with the Atlantic telegraph cable but first returned to his duties as a professor at Glasgow University. When the enterprise recommenced in 1865, it was his mirror galvanometer that was used. He went on to develop further instruments based on its principle, in particular the "siphon recorder" which was used for receiving signals on undersea cables for many years. He became one of the most distinguished scientists of his day and was knighted in 1866 and given the title of Lord Kelvin in 1892. He and Hughes would meet again in a few years, this time in connection with another new technology, the telephone.

Hughes spent some time promoting his telegraph in Britain, but found it difficult to unseat the systems already in use, and early in the 1860s he went to France to try his luck there.

As for Hyram Hyde, he apparently ran out of patience in waiting for a return on his investment and decided to do a disappearing act! The supposedly moneyed man who had told Hughes he was expecting great financial resources soon to be at his disposal, and whom Hughes had entrusted with two $1,000 bonds as well as lending him additional money, suddenly took off in the direction of Nova Scotia and was never heard from again.[61] Worse, Hyde had not been paying their expenses as he had agreed to do: Hughes soon learned that he had failed to make the necessary payments for the French patents. The applications had lapsed and Hughes had to settle for patenting the improvements he had made to his instrument.

Dr. Whitehouse spent quite a bit of time trying to rescue his reputation and exchanging barbed letters and pamphlets with his critics.[62]

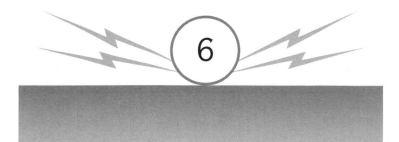

6

FINANCIAL SUCCESS AT LAST

PARIS, FRANCE, 1860

Running short of money, and unable to break into the British market with his telegraph, Professor David Edward Hughes headed across the Channel to try his luck in France. There he faced a very different situation. In France, as in the rest of continental Europe, the telegraph service was operated by the government: there was no need to deal with a myriad of companies as in Britain—just the one relevant government ministry. While this made his job easier, it also carried a much higher risk: if he were successful, the business he would get could be considerable, but if he failed, then it was all over—at least in France. His first task was to arrange a demonstration of his telegraph for the government. Hughes was able to do this, and his friend, the author John Munro, wrote about the demonstration sometime later in *The Telegraphist*. According to this article and other notes Munro made, the demonstration proceeded as follows.[1]

Hughes sat perched on the edge of his chair in front of his telegraph instrument at the Paris telegraph office, his fingers rapidly darting over the now familiar keyboard as he typed a message to the Lyons telegraph office, located 300 miles away. As he finished the last word, another message was handed to him and then another after that, at a hectic pace. While he was typing, the printer was chattering away, pumping out paper tape with messages printed on it; these were copies of the transmitted messages repeated back to him from the telegraph office at Lyons. Every so often, his assistant would tear off the paper strip and compare the two: so far, so good. The tests were going well, which was essential if he were to have any chance of selling his telegraph instruments to the French government. However, he could feel the pressure mounting as he kept typing, checking the printer, and winding up the heavy weight that kept the instrument powered, all the while under the careful scrutiny of his adjudicators. These were some of the most eminent scientific men in France and included the Count du Moncel, a well respected electrical engineer, author, and advisor to the Telegraph Administration; Edouard Blavier, an inspector for the Telegraph Administration; Paul-Gustave Froment, an electrical engineer and inventor; and Monsieur Gaugain, also from the Telegraph Administration. This austere group had been appointed by the French Telegraph Administration to examine Hughes's telegraph system and report on its performance.

As Hughes typed in yet another message for transmission, the printer, which had been chattering away, suddenly stopped mid-word. He looked over at the paper tape, waiting for it to restart, but it did not. He typed in a query message to Lyons, "REPETEZ," repeating it several times, but there was no response. The telegraph system appeared to be as dead as a doornail. The commissioners, who had been checking the accuracy and the speed of the sent messages, looked at their pocket watches, but Hughes did not notice their exchange of glances and almost imperceptible nods.

Paris c. 1860—Hughes's move to France marked the beginning of his financial success, and the city came to be one of his favorites.

He could feel panic welling up inside him and fought to regain control, quickly checking his electrical connections and that the battery was still functioning. He checked that the weight drive was fully wound up, but could find no faults, and became more and more perplexed. This was not a good sign, and just some moments earlier, everything had been going so well. While he racked his brain for the source of the problem, his distinguished audience, who had been quietly watching, unexpectedly broke their silence and crowded noisily around him, congratulating him: "Très bien, Monsieur Hughes, très bien, nous vous félicitons!" smiling all around and bowing. Now he was really confused; their congratulations seemed ironic under the circumstances.

The following morning saw a dejected Hughes making his way to a meeting with the commissioners, unsure of what to make of the previous day's events, and fearing the worst. It was then that they let him in on their secret. The commissioners had arranged a test to ensure that he was actually communicating over the whole length of the telegraph wire between the two cities. They had instructed the telegraph operator at Lyons to "earth" the telegraph line at a prearranged time, which would stop the transmission of electrical signals. They had made this test, they explained, because the government had nearly been duped on a previous occasion by an unscrupulous telegraph speculator who had faked the operation of the telegraph he was trying to promote. Hughes's relief upon learning that the apparent failure of his instrument had been a test was quickly followed by elation when he learned that the commissioners had given a favorable report to the Telegraph Administration, which then arranged to install his instruments on trial for a six month period. Success at last!

It probably had not hurt his case to have had a letter of recommendation from the American Telegraph Company, which he had presented along with his credentials.[2] The letter praised his instruments, which had been in use for two years on the company's East Coast lines across distances of up to 700 miles. The instruments were working accurately and with ease at 2,000 words per hour. The letter finished by saying that the company would not hesitate to recommend Hughes's telegraph instruments in preference to any other.

Hughes had left Britain for France after a stay of about two years at the suggestion of his friend Josiah Latimer Clark after Hughes had become disillusioned at his inability to sell any of his telegraph instruments or license his patents. The failure of the Atlantic cable and his partner Hyde's absconding with his money had only added to his despondency. Hughes's stay in Britain was what might be called an interesting scientific adventure, but the adventure had failed to put bread on the table.

Josiah Latimer Clark was a respected and experienced telegraph engineer who presumably could see that Hughes was wasting his time trying to break into the British market. Knowledgeable about the telegraph business on the Continent, and believing there was more opportunity there for Hughes, he furnished him with a letter of introduction to the French government, which turned out to be key to Hughes's future success.

Hughes's stay in Britain had, however, resulted in some useful relationships which would serve him well later. His association with Cyrus Field and the Atlantic Telegraph Company had helped to publicize his name and telegraph instrument, and to make the scientific men and electricians of Britain aware of his work. As a consequence, Hughes had been invited to give a presentation to the Society of Arts on his inventions.[3] This occurred on April 13, 1859, when he presented a paper titled "On Professor Hughes' System of Type Printing Telegraphs and Methods of Insulating with Special Reference to Submarine Cables."

It is interesting that William Fothergill Cooke chaired the meeting; he was no doubt interested in learning all he could about Hughes and his telegraph instrument, as it was a potential competitor to his own. The paper was actually read by Hyde, while Hughes carried out the demonstrations. The presentation was critical of the needle telegraph of Cooke and Wheatstone, which was widely used in Great Britain at the time, and the Morse instruments were said to use a "primitive method." The presentation was followed by a polite discussion. However, Hyde and Hughes's criticism did not go unanswered. A letter appeared in the journal *Engineer* by writers calling themselves by the nom de plume "Double-Needle, Morse, and Co.," who wrote the following as if it was the instruments themselves complaining:[4]

> Sir, We were very much disappointed that at the Society of Arts, on the 13th inst., when the paper on the Hughes instrument was read, no champion appeared to assert our rights. We consider ourselves parties who have been much traduced. We hold ourselves greatly aggrieved. Our leading partner, in particular, considers himself grossly insulted by the contemptuous tone in which Mr. Hyde designated him as being a *primitive* creature. The second member of our firm is burning with rage at the inaccurate statements that were made of his merits and public performance; and the "Co." are indignant that they should have been overlooked and slighted for a mere Yankee infant, scarcely yet out of the cradle, who has accomplished nothing at present but shrieking and screaming, and promises in their opinion to be a complicated and useless member of society.

Welcome to Britain! The letter did end with kinder words about Hughes's telegraph apparatus, calling it "a most ingenious and beautiful instrument," but it was obvious that Hughes would not have an easy time penetrating the British market. Some years earlier his fellow American, Samuel Morse, had had an even rockier reception, and had not even been able to obtain a patent.[5]

Hughes's spirits were raised briefly when Cyrus Field returned to England in June of 1859, determined to try once again to connect the two continents. However, the business attitude in the country towards undersea telegraph cables had soured. The chances of once again raising large amounts of money were slim without a guarantee of success. One way he considered to satisfy this requirement was to seek the backing of the British government; after all, it could be argued that the transatlantic cable was in the nation's interest. However, the timing could not have been worse, as the government was still smarting from its recent experience with the Red Sea cable, which had also failed. They had provided funding for that project, regardless of whether it worked or not, and had been left holding the bag, so to speak. They were not about to make the same mistake again, and before funding any new cable venture they would seek guarantees of performance, thus putting the onus on the cable promoter. No matter how enthusiastic Field was, industry, government, and investors had become skeptical about undersea telegraph cables. There had been too many failures, and rumblings of a re-examination of the whole situation were in the air. The government convened a board of inquiry into undersea cable failures and how they could be prevented. There was not much Field could do but wait for the board's report, and so he decided to return to New York and his original paper business.

One of those appointed to the board of inquiry was Josiah Latimer Clark, the electrical engineer for the Electric Telegraph Company, and he engaged Hughes to assist in a number of tests on undersea cables as part of the inquiry. In particular, they tested the gutta percha insulation and found that they could punch through it with a high voltage. If this occurred in practice, the sea water would penetrate the insulation and short-circuit the copper core. This test was inspired by suspicions that the transatlantic cable had failed due to the very high voltages transmitted on the cable by Edward Whitehouse, the Atlantic Telegraph Company electrician.

Hughes was later called to give evidence to the committee, and he stated that he believed that three causes had led to the cable failure.[6] First, there was the heat to which the cable had been exposed after its manufacture. It was believed that the storage of the cable outside in the yard in the sun had caused the gutta percha insulation to soften, allowing it to become thin in some areas and making the cable more susceptible to short-circuits. Second, there were the numerous joints due to the many splices required to join the sections of cable, and also the many splices where parts had been cut out during its manufacture due to faults, the splices made at sea to fix breaks, and the joints to connect the ends of the cable on shore. Third, there were the high voltages, in the range of 2,000 volts, that had been used to send signals into the cable. Hughes's tests showed that these were most damaging when the cable at the receiving end was open circuit, that is, when it was not connected to any receiving instrument. Hughes added that the sensitivity of the receiving instrument was one of the important parameters to ensure future success, as sensitive receivers would allow signals to be sent and received through the cable with low voltages. He stated that his test showed this could be done with ten to twenty Daniell Cells (ten to twenty volts).

During this period Hughes carried out a significant number of experiments at the East India Dock in London. This facility, which was close to many of the cable manufacturers, had access to various lengths of undersea cable in storage, as well as space for experimentation. The records of these experiments clearly show that for an experimenter like Hughes, success and discoveries only came with hours and hours of hard work. His notebook indicates that he was experimenting six to seven days a week, and he easily filled 160-odd pages of his notebooks in four months.[7] His experiments concentrated on a few topics, one of which was measuring the time delay a pulse experienced when traversing various lengths of cable (he preferred to have his own experimental data rather than rely on Thomson's Square Law). For this he was able to use his own telegraph instrument. The instrument, by virtue of using a mechanism based on the frequency of oscillation of a spring element (similar to a clock), provided an accurate time base. The speed of rotation of the print wheel and the rotation of the contactor that scanned the keyboard was directly governed by this precision oscillator. By connecting the telegraph transmitter to one end of a cable and the telegraph receiver to the other end, the cable delay (the time it took for an electrical pulse to traverse the cable) could be measured. If there was no delay, then when the letter "A" was sent, the letter "A" would be printed. When Hughes introduced a length of cable of 77 miles, a "B" was printed, for 154 miles a "C," for 231 miles a "D," and so on. From this information and knowledge of the speed of the print wheel and the number of letters spaced around it, the time delay could be deduced.[8] The tests were carried out on undersea cables, but these were not submerged at the time. So, while Hughes was able to work through 2,000 miles of cable, the results he obtained were not entirely representative of those that would be obtained when the cable was submerged, where there would be a much greater retardation as well as potential problems from ground currents.

Hughes also carried out experiments to determine the capacitive charge, or as Hughes called it, the "inductive capacity," of the cables.[9] In addition, he determined how long the cable held the charge and explored methods for neutralizing the cable by grounding it or reversing the polarity. He also investigated the effects of different types of insulation, including his semi-fluid insulation, their relative capacitive charges, and the effects caused by varying the diameter of the copper core and the ratio of insulation thickness to core diameter. Further, he demonstrated that on a cable whose insulation was defective and which was exhibiting a lower resistance path to ground at some point along its length, it was possible to signal faster. This was due to the fact that the lower resistance path allowed the capacitive charge to leak away faster.

After he had carried out tests for the board of inquiry, he continued his experiments to optimize his instrument for use on undersea cables, evaluating various relays to provide the polarity change-over function. (It had been found that alternating the polarity of the electrical pulses on the cable, i.e. changing them from positive to negative, neutralized the charge on the cable more quickly and hence allowed faster transmission.)

He carried out demonstrations for a number of people, including the Red Sea Company's Mr. Laws, Mr. William Siemens, Sir Charles Tilston Bright, and the editor of *The Engineer*. He had been making comparison tests using a Morse instrument that used a sensitive relay built by Cromwell Varley, electrician to the Electric Telegraph Company. In side-by-side tests, Hughes was transmitting seventeen words per minute vs. the Morse at only six words per minute through a 460 mile length of the undersea cable coiled up in dry storage. Varley must have got wind of Hughes's tests, and when Hughes invited him down to witness the demonstration, he was far from cooperative:[10]

Invited Varley who used insulting language! Then I told him that nothing but the utmost cowardice could prevent him from accepting the invitation to try fairly his instrument against mine.

Varley, however, never did go and see the tests. Hughes was trying to promote his telegraph with the Electric Telegraph Company but was not having much success, and making an enemy of Varley would not have helped his cause, as he was the company's chief engineer. Ironically, Hughes later made use of Varley's sensitive relays.

His luck with the undersea cable companies was not improving. He did try his telegraph instrument on the Amsterdam cable of the Electric Telegraph Company on May 18, 1861, but he was unable to get it to work due to problems with earth current interference and insufficient time.[11]

It took about fifteen months for the *Report of the Joint Committee Appointed by the Lords of the Committee of the Privy Council for Trade and the Atlantic Telegraph Company to Inquire into the Construction of Submarine Telegraph Cables* to be completed. It was a voluminous document often referred to as the "blue book." It was one of the first scientific boards of inquiry, and set the standard for such inquiries in the future. It provided an in-depth analysis and explanation of the problems and recommendations for improvements or "principles that should be followed in the future." These recommendations resulted in significant improvements in undersea cable manufacturing, quality, cable laying, and instrumentation, and as a consequence, future undersea telegraph cables functioned reliably.

As 1860 rolled around, storm clouds were gathering in America and Hughes had become more and more concerned about his family's safety at home. The Southern States were threatening to secede from the Union; while there were numerous points of contention between the Southern and Northern States, the most important was the issue of slavery. Events in America continued their downward spiral and the situation turned very bleak as the unrest and dispute escalated, eventually erupting into civil war in April of 1861. The war proved divisive in Britain as well: the mill owners and cotton merchants sympathized with the South, while the working class and radicals supported the North. Britain also faced a difficult diplomatic problem: whether it should recognize the Southern Confederacy. For Hughes, traveling back to the American South was now out of the question, as he assumed that Kentucky was supporting the South, and the Southern ports were being blockaded by the Northern Unionists. There was little he could do but remain in Europe and hope that his family would be safe. By now his finances were running low, and Hyde's defection with his pockets full of Hughes's money, together with his uncertainty whether he would receive any further payment from the American Telegraph Company due to the war, had put him in a tenuous situation.

It was at this point that he took the good advice of Josiah Latimer Clark and proceeded to France to try his fortunes there. However, before entering France he had to obtain an American passport from the American Legation in London, where he declared his age as twenty-nine years (a couple of years younger than he actually was, a legacy of his "child prodigy" days). He landed in Boulogne on May 27, 1860, and went directly to Paris.[12]

Hughes found the situation in France quite different from that in Britain, which had forged ahead of its Continental neighbors during the Industrial Revolution. Britain had attained supremacy in shipbuilding, engineering, and heavy industries. Its parliamentary government was a civilian body rather than a military one, and provided a model that would be followed by other European countries. On the Continent, on the other hand, many countries were still dominated by monarchies which wielded a degree of power unknown today.

In France, Napoleon III had become Emperor following a *coup d'état* in 1851. During the 1850s, which are often referred to as the "authoritarian" period, he ruled with a strong hand by means of a centralized administration. It was, however, a prosperous period which saw a great expansion of the railways, the road network, industry in general, public works, banking, and the telegraph system. The importance of the telegraph cannot be overstated; in addition to its use by citizens and businesses, it was vital to the successful operation of the centralized government.

By the 1860s Napoleon had shifted to a more liberal stance following the improvements in the economy and social life; Paris was being transformed and restructured with wide new boulevards and parks. There was a movement towards a parliamentary system modeled after that in Britain, and a free trade agreement was signed between the two countries. Thus when Hughes entered France in 1860 conditions were very conducive to business.

France's state-controlled telegraph system used the double wire "French State Telegraph" called the Foy and Bréguet. The government telegraph infrastructure had originated in the early 1800s, when the government had controlled and used the extensive network of visual semaphores established by Claude Chappe and his brothers. When the government introduced the electrical telegraph in the 1840s, they had required it to use the same signals as the Chappe semaphore, which resulted in a double-needle receiving instrument. Each needle could rotate to one of eight positions, and the two needles together could indicate sixty-four different signals.[13] The sending device, called the "manipulateur," had two handles, each of which could be rotated to one of eight radial positions. The system required two wires for its operation. The implementation was along the lines of the Cooke and Wheatstone double-needle system. For international messages the Morse system (called the "American System" in Europe) was used. Dispatches were not direct or immediate; they were transmitted between intermediate stations, received, written down, and passed to the next operator, who forwarded them for retransmission. Messages also stopped at the country's borders, going through the same lengthy procedure.

The French telegraph system operated as a separate state department under the supervision of a director general. At times, esteemed scientists were invited to participate in a council for deciding on improvements to the telegraph system. As the dial telegraph system of Foy and Bréguet had been in place since the 1840s, by 1860 it was certainly time to look at a new system which was easier to use, faster, and used only a single telegraph wire.[14] So when Hughes arrived in 1860 with his telegraph instruments, he was in the right place with the right product at the right time.

The French Telegraph Administration liked what Hughes had to offer and proposed a trial period during which he would oversee the installation of the telegraph instruments and the training of operators in their use and maintenance. Once the system was operational, its performance was monitored to ensure it met the standards set by the administration. The system went into use on the Paris-Lyons line, then the Marseilles-Lyons, Paris-Bordeaux, followed by Paris-Le Havre and Paris-Lille.[15] Hughes passed the trial period and a contract was signed for Fr. 200,000.[16]

The administration arranged to have Paul-Gustave Froment and his workshop in Paris manufacture Hughes's telegraph instruments, and this turned out to be an excellent choice.[17] Unlike the uneasy relationship Hughes had with George Phelps in America, this relationship was synergistic. The older Froment had made his own telegraph instrument which had used a piano-type keyboard, as well as a type of mechanical helical scanner.[18] Thus, there was some similarity in the way the two men had gone about their inventions. With Froment's help and skill Hughes was able to continually improve the durability and reliability of his telegraph and put it into production. By 1861–2, instruments were being used on all of the important French trunk lines and were sending fifty messages per hour, with an average of twenty words per message. Transmission speeds of up to forty words per minute could be attained with the instrument running at 120 revolutions per minute.[19] The French were so pleased with the improvement that Hughes's instruments brought to their telegraph operations that he was later decorated by Emperor Napoleon III with the order of Chevalier de la Légion d'Honneur.[20]

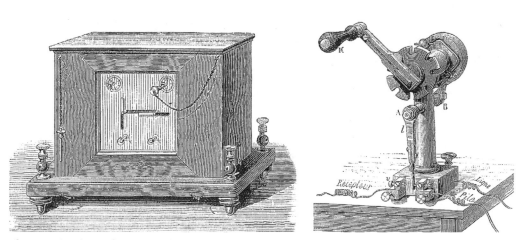

The French telegraph system of Foy and Bréguet, the Récepteur and Manipulateur that were soon replaced by Hughes's system.

It was probably natural that France's close neighbor, Italy, was the next country to become interested in Hughes's telegraph.[21] Count Camillo di Cavour was the driving force in the Northern Italian provinces, and an admirer of France and Britain, particularly of Britain's parliamentary system. He saw that the way to prosperity was to modernize agriculture, industry and finance and to use modern scientific methods. To accomplish this, an efficient telegraph network was essential. Communications had become the lifeblood of commerce, and with the adoption of Hughes's telegraph system, Italy could not only improve its own infrastructure but also enable direct cross-border communications with France. Hughes made a number of trips to Turin to help install his instruments and instruct the telegraph staff in the operation of his system. The contract with Italy netted Hughes Fr. 125,000.[22] Later King Victor Emmanuel II of Italy conferred on Hughes L'Ordine dei Santi Maurizio e Lazzaro (Order of St. Maurice and St. Lazzaro).

By September of 1862 there were new developments in England. The United Kingdom Electric Telegraph Company, which had languished since 1851, had been re-energized in 1861 when it acquired sufficient capital to recommence operations.[23] The company had considered using Thomas Allen's needle telegraph, but started out using Morse inkers on all of its circuits. However, in 1862, persuaded by its dynamic chairman Alexander Angus Croll, the company decided to use the Hughes printing telegraph system. Hughes was requested to attend a meeting in London with the company. According to the contract they signed, the company bought the rights to Hughes's telegraph patent for £12,000, which amount was paid in stock.[24] As Hughes now owned 10 percent of the company, he was also appointed to the board of directors. Hughes found himself in distinguished company when he joined the board, which boasted among its members the chairman A. A. Croll, a major gas entrepreneur; James Pilkington, the glass manufacturer; Lord Alfred Churchill; and a number of bankers. The company was installing its lines along canals between the major population areas and centers of industry: London, Liverpool, Manchester, and Birmingham. Its flat rate tariff of one shilling per message, irrespective of distance, became very popular with business users. In 1863 the company started introducing Hughes instruments on the trunk line between London and Birmingham which sent fifty telegrams per hour.[25]

Hughes's American business apprenticeship under the tutelage of Daniel Craig and Cyrus Field was finally paying off. He felt proud of the contracts he now had with France, Italy, and the United Kingdom. The next piece of business acumen he needed was advice on what to do with all of his new-found wealth. No doubt he received such advice from his new banking associates on the board of directors. He seems to have received sound advice, as he started investing his money in bonds and securities.

Out of his experience with his current customers Hughes formulated a "model" contract that he could use in future. This was based on his observations of how his telegraph was used and integrated into existing systems, and of what was required to make the program a success, such as planning the details of the electrical installation, checking the integrity of the telegraph lines, and securing battery supplies. Also essential was adequate training of the staff in the instruments' use, adjustment, and maintenance. He had decided that just selling telegraph instruments without proper training and support would not work.

Whether Hughes realized it or not, he was creating a system that would lead to significant financial rewards through market domination. There were three conditions that helped bring this about. First, a growing telegraph market; second, customers believed that Hughes's telegraph could improve their efficiency while increasing their revenue; and third, fortuitous timing.

With regard to the second point, most western countries were using the Morse system, often supplemented by a needle or step-by-step system of older vintage. Hughes's instrument offered advantages over these systems. Telegraphy was a growth market, and in fact had been growing at a phenomenal rate. New lines were constantly being installed, reaching into all corners of many countries. While it was important for a country to develop its own internal network, it was also of growing importance to have smooth communications with other countries to facilitate commerce and political discourse.

Up to that time, telegraph communications had suffered from a lack of compatibility between equipment and tariffs in different countries. Messages often stopped at the border and were written down, passed to a telegraph station on the other side, and retransmitted. This was recognized to be cumbersome and inefficient, and in order to effect some standardization, the International Telegraph Union was formed. With respect to timing, Hughes was bringing a superior instrument to market at a moment when many governments were looking to upgrade from their existing equipment or wanted a more efficient instrument that communicated in plain language rather than code.[26]

There were two technical factors that also gave Hughes an advantage. First, his instrument had a unique electrical interface that required identical (Hughes) instruments on both ends of the line. That is, it was not compatible with Morse, needle, or step-by-step instruments. This might have been a disadvantage if countries were looking to introduce a new instrument compatible with their existing instruments, but in fact it worked to Hughes's advantage. He had established his system in France, which was one of the most important European countries at the time. French was the international diplomatic language, and many embassies and legations were located in Paris. Other countries found it advantageous to be able to communicate directly with France using compatible equipment, and to do that it was necessary to use one of Hughes's instruments. This is what Italy did, and soon other countries followed suit, until eventually it became a disadvantage to be incompatible with the Hughes network. Hence, the domino effect led to his supremacy in the market.

The second technical advantage of Hughes's system was that it provided significantly more security than the Morse system. A telegraph line carrying Morse signals could easily be tapped by connecting onto the line with a Morse sounder or register (receiver) and the message could be read. In addition, false messages could be sent using a single key (on/off switch) and battery. Messages could be and were encrypted, but this required additional time and trained operators at both the transmitting and receiving ends. In Hughes's system single pulses were transmitted on the telegraph line in what appeared to be a random sequence, and thus the messages could not be interpreted without a Hughes instrument.

Since Hughes had set foot on French soil, business had been excellent, and he was ever grateful to the French government for giving him his start. With installations proceeding in France, Britain, and Italy he was busier than ever, and Froment's workshop was occupied making instruments to meet the demand.

Hughes found Paris to be a bustling and vital city, and now that he was on a firmer financial footing and was becoming better known in scientific circles, he was able to enjoy what it had to offer. He had become fluent in the French language, glad that he had learned it in his youth, for his ability to communicate in French was a distinct advantage, not only in France but in many of the other countries where he would do business. It was during 1862 that he met Anna Chadbourne, also an American, who had lost her husband tragically some five years earlier. This strikingly beautiful and talented woman must have made an impression on him, as their friendship continued for many years. Anna, however, returned to America at some point in the 1860s, later returning to Paris in the 1870s.[27]

After Froment had produced a number of Hughes's telegraph instruments it became apparent that some changes were necessary for them to stand up to the rigors of constant use.[28] One item which tended to fail was the precision vibrating timing rod, and so Hughes started looking into an alternative timing method. Also, there had been a request by the Telegraph Administration to make it possible to send numerals and punctuation marks. Froment and Hughes took the opportunity to upgrade the instrument, making the gears and other components more robust, changing the method of precision timing, and implementing a fifty-six character set.[29] They removed the vibrating spring rod and escapement timing mechanism and replaced it with what Hughes called a rotating pendulum. This was a form of speed governor that consisted of a rod fixed at one end and connected at the other end to the perimeter of a flywheel. On the rod was mounted a weighted ball. When the flywheel rotated, the rod prescribed a cone and the weight was flung out by centrifugal motion. As the speed increased, this action slowed the rotation by applying a brake so that a constant speed was maintained.[30] These modifications were patented in January of 1863 and started to appear in models manufactured from about 1864 onwards.[31]

Hughes's business success had now put him in a strong position to promote his telegraph system in other Continental countries. He also contacted the American Telegraph Company to see if they would be interested in the new model of his instrument.[32] He probably was unaware that by this time the American Telegraph Company had switched over to the Phelps combination telegraph instrument. As the name suggests, it was a new instrument in which Phelps had combined the best ideas of Hughes and the House telegraph instrument together with some of his own. The company wrote back saying

Front view of the instrument showing the keyboard and printing mechanism.

he should send over two instruments for evaluation. However, it is believed that he never pursued this opportunity any further.

Early in 1864 he carried out an extensive study of electromagnets. Although this study was primarily intended to improve the relay he used in his own instrument, his investigation and experiments ranged much wider. He derived guidelines for optimizing magnetic circuits to maximize the magnetic force. Hughes had a lifelong fascination with magnetism and often returned to it in his researches in his attempt to answer the question "What is magnetism?" The earliest results of his research into electromagnets were published in *Annales Télégraphiques* in 1862, and he also published an article on electromagnets in *The Telegraphic Journal* in 1864.[33]

Hughes's earlier association with Sir Charles Bright and Josiah Latimer Clark in connection with submarine cables appears to have paid off when a renewed effort got underway to connect Britain with India. The failure of the 1859 Red Sea Cable had been a setback to speedier communications with this important part of the British Empire. At the request of Lt. Col. Patrick Stewart, Director General of the Indian Telegraph Services, Hughes had provided a proposal for the use of his instruments. The new route was based on an agreement between Britain, Turkey, and the Persian governments to connect their landlines. To avoid some difficult terrain a submarine cable was to be run through the Persian Gulf from Fao to Bushire to Gwadar and on to Karachi. According to articles that appeared in the technical journals, Hughes's instruments were used on the Persian Gulf cable, but it does not appear that Hughes traveled to the area.[34]

Representatives from Russia had made some inquires with Hughes about the possibility of using his instruments, and they now appeared to be ready for more serious talks: General Guerhardt, Director General of the Russian Telegraph Administration, visited the Froment workshop in April, 1865.[35] One of the technical issues was how to handle the Russian Cyrillic alphabet which consisted of more than twenty-six letters. After some discussion, Hughes and Guerhardt eventually settled on a thirty-character set.[36] Hughes recorded in his notebook how he came up with the mechanism to accommodate the fifty-six character set and its modification for Cyrillic characters:[37]

> Studied several weeks to find a good method of introducing letters in series of figures without having a blank separation: every means tried up to this time was without practical value. This eve after studying several hours could find nothing but on taking off my coat to go to bed saw at once clearly and distinctly the manner to arrive at this end by a simple lever acted upon by the figure changing lever during its movement but not afterwards. This upon trial next morning gave most perfect results never failing since being the most simple at the same time most perfect of any tried. These experiments were for the Instruments being constructed for Russia.

The first print-out in the Russian language on one of the modified instruments took place on May 24, 1865 in the workshop in Paris.[38]

Hughes was intrigued by the possibility of taking his telegraph into Russia and called it his "Russian Campaign." The wanderlust he had inherited from his father continued to pull at him, and the mystique of what lay out there in the vast expanses to the east no doubt contributed to his decision. Certainly, opportunities closer to home

A telegraph message in Russian printed on one of Hughes's instruments modified for the Russian market.

would have made more business sense at the time, but he was keen to go to Russia. This is evident from his notebooks. Usually he restricted his jottings to technical matters, but his notebooks from this period include notes related to his trip and about the Russian officials involved, the intrigue, and the final success as they embraced him and his telegraph.

While Froment was busy in the workshop constructing the new instruments to be shipped to Russia, he no doubt talked to Hughes of how circumstances in that country had changed. It was only some fifty years since Napoleon had invaded Russia with an army of 500,000 men in 1812; Napoleon had been defeated and had returned with less than half of his troops. Unlike Napoleon's army, who had slogged their way on foot and had borne the brunt of the Russian winter, Hughes traveled in relative comfort by train, and in the summer. On the long journey Hughes probably learned about what he might expect from his fellow travelers. Alexander II was the current tsar; he had risen to the throne in 1855 after the death of his father and Russia's demoralizing defeat at the hands of France and Britain in the Crimean War. Russia traditionally had a strong, autocratic regime supported by a strong army and police. However, Alexander II had sought to relax some of the old ways and had emancipated the serfs from bondage, for example: the more liberal and democratic practices of the West had apparently influenced Russia. But the old ways remained just below the surface, as became clear when the Poles, who had suffered greatly under the previous Russian monarch, took advantage of the more liberal atmosphere to push for independence. This rebellion was crushed with great severity by the Russian government, and to ensure against the surfacing of similar ideas in Russia, the state ended its reforms and tightened its control once again. A good communications system was essential to the functioning of the centralized government. The Morse telegraph system was used extensively in Russia, but there was a desire to bring about improvements in the telegraph network.

On August 1, 1865, Hughes arrived in St. Petersburg, which was a center of culture and fashion for the nobles and bourgeoisie. During his visit Hughes did not see the poverty in which the vast majority of the population lived. The telegraph instruments had already arrived and were waiting at the telegraph office, along with General Guerhardt and a Colonel Ispolatoff, who were there to greet him. The first task was to check the instruments to see whether they had been damaged in the journey, and the second was to set about training four employees in their operation. The official test was to last one month, after which the results and recommendations would be presented to a commission. The tests commenced early in October over the St. Petersburg to Moscow line, a distance of 630 km, and also on some loop lines.[39]

The next test was to demonstrate operation over the long distance telegraph lines between St. Petersburg and Paris. Initially Hughes had difficulty in these tests:[40]

Sunday Oct 15 made an experiment with Paris direct without relay, we had 150 elements Paris 200. I could receive his call at intervals but impossible to speak, the current disappearing in fits and starts. A relay was then put at Berlin. The result was little better as I was able to receive 10 words very perfect though the rest illegible—no doubt the distance too great for the relays to act and I believe there should be three.

Due to the great distance (2,200 km) and varying quality of the lines in each of the countries through which the transmission passed, the signal was very weak by the time it reached its destination. There was also a large amount of electrical noise on the line, making it difficult or impossible for the telegraph instrument to discriminate between the signal and noise. In an effort to overcome these problems, Hughes used higher voltages than normal, in the range of 150 to 200 volts DC, and also slowed the instrument down from 120 to 75 revolutions per minute. To boost the signal en route, Hughes decided to make use of sensitive repeater relays made by Siemens and Varley, which he had tested previously. These were spaced out along the route and took the weak signals and boosted their strength using a local battery; this also allowed him to return the speed of the instrument to 120 rpm.[41]

Sunday October 22. Victory!!! We placed the relay Siemens at all stations en route for Paris and first spoke by the Morse which worked tolerably well. Then at ½ past 11 took

my instrument and was able at once to speak and work perfectly for nearly 2 hours when experiment ceased.

This was a cause for celebration, and everyone was congratulating Hughes and probably toasting him with vodka, as Hughes complained he got an awful headache after the celebration. Not everything went this smoothly, as Hughes notes he suffered an equipment failure when a timing spring broke.

The relays had been placed at Königsberg, Berlin, and Cologne. The Russian instrument was unique as it could either communicate in Cyrillic for in country use or Roman characters for diplomatic correspondence. To accomplish this, the keyboard had both alphabets engraved on its keys. The receiver incorporated dual co-axle print wheels, one with Roman characters and the other with Cyrillic characters that could alternately be selected.

On Friday, October 27, Colonel Ispolatoff completed his report to the commissioners and showed it to Hughes, who was delighted at how favorable it was. However, the next day the Colonel hurriedly called on Hughes again, telling him that all was not well, as another member of the commission had submitted a damning report on his instrument.[42]

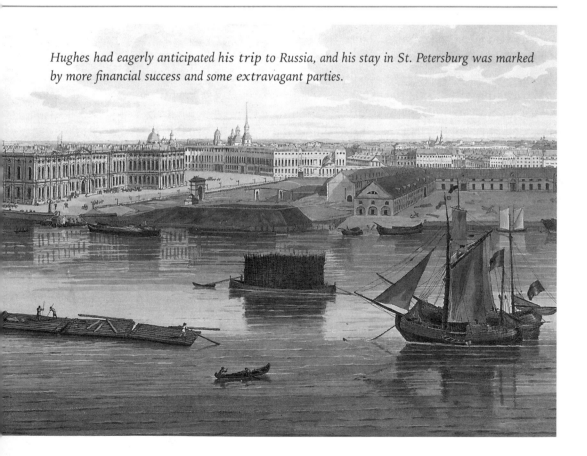

Hughes had eagerly anticipated his trip to Russia, and his stay in St. Petersburg was marked by more financial success and some extravagant parties.

Saturday Oct 28. Inst worked perfectly all day to Moscow. Col. Ispolatoff showed me a report on my Inst by Mr. Parott written in the most "bad will" possible saying that the Inst cost more than the Morse that it requires better clerks & & also trying to show that my Inst was not practical and this notwithstanding the brilliant results obtained with Moscow—Prof. Parott is the Prof. teaching the Morse clerks and has acted in a most jealous and forbidding manner towards me since my arrival—unfortunately he is a member of the commission to decide on my Inst.

This was not good news, and Parott obviously saw Hughes as a threat to his entrenched power. Nonetheless Hughes's instruments had impressed the commissioners enough that he won their approval. The news leaked out that the administration was proceeding to prepare an act to be signed by the minister to pay Hughes to install the equipment on a permanent basis. Hughes wrote in his notebook "Hope it is so!!"

On Monday, November 6, he was invited to breakfast with General Guerhardt, where they talked at length about the telegraph, and he learned that the general had paved the way for him to approach Prussia with his telegraph. He was told he should call at Berlin on his way back to Paris. Hughes wrote "Vive General Guerhardt." On November 10 telegraph service on Hughes instruments was initiated between Moscow and St. Petersburg, with two telegraph lines in service and a number of others planned. Gen. Guerhardt, meanwhile, told Hughes that the report had been accepted and that the minister, named Tolstoy, was impressed with it and had invited him to dinner.

It was while Hughes was in Russia that he learned of the death of his friend M. Froment in Paris. This sad event raised some concern over the future of Froment's workshop and the manufacture of the instruments.[43] Possibly with this concern in mind, Hughes approached the electrical manufacturer Siemens and Halske, who had a division in St. Petersburg.[44] They had probably heard that Hughes was about to be awarded a contract from the Russian government and could see other opportunities opening up in the East, and so were quite eager to sign a contract with Hughes for the manufacture of his telegraph instruments. The agreement allowed them to construct and sell his instruments to the governments he authorized. The highest price they could charge for an instrument was Fr. 1500.[45]

On Monday, November 20, Gen. Guerhardt and Hughes dined with Minister Tolstoy and Madam Tolstoy. As the Tolstoys showed great interest in the new telegraph system and its operation, Hughes offered to bring one of his instruments to show to Madam Tolstoy, and also to give them a lecture with illustrative experiments on electricity. They were enchanted with the idea.

Hughes heard from Gen. Guerhardt that the act had been signed, and Col. Ispolatoff translated it and read it to him. Hughes commented that it was the most favorable report possible, and that a copy of it would be of immense service to him in other countries.

On Saturday, November 25, as Hughes prepared to give his lecture to Minister Tolstoy, he was surprised to see so many aristocrats in attendance. The reason for their

Hughes during his time in St. Petersburg (1865), radiating the confidence of his success.

presence became apparent when the minister created him Commander of the Order of St. Anne to the felicitations of the crowd.

Hughes went on to present his lecture on electricity and its applications, performing some twenty experiments. After the lecture Tolstoy informed Hughes that the emperor wished him to repeat the lecture for him and the court. Hughes, Col. Ispolatoff, and Gen. Guerhardt retired to drink champagne in honor of his knighting.

On Wednesday, November 29, Hughes started preparing for the "grand soirée," and he and Col. Ispolatoff rerouted some telegraph wires to the Czarskoizelo Palace and set up the equipment and experiments for his lecture. At nine p.m. the emperor, followed by the empress, the grand dukes, the princes and rest of the court entered. Tolstoy introduced Hughes, and Hughes gave his lecture, which was received enthusiastically.[46] The emperor then sent and received dispatches over Hughes's instrument. When the event was over, well past midnight, Col. Ispolatoff and Hughes again celebrated with champagne and drank to the health of the emperor, Hughes toasting "Vive la Russie."

Hughes had asked for his payment to be in French francs so that it could be drawn on a bank in Paris, which the Russians agreed to do, and he was given a check for Fr. 200,000. In addition he received 1,900 rubles as a payment for some of his instruments.

Hughes's business was now concluded; he had been in Russia almost six months, and he prepared to return to Paris, but first Gen. Guerhardt asked him to assist in preparing a paper to present on the Russian telegraph system. In addition, the general invited him to a grand dinner on Saturday, December 15. Hughes describes it as magnificent, with meals prepared by fourteen chefs, an orchestra, and wine that cost

Fr. 800 for each guest. In his notebook the next day, though, Hughes exclaims "Sunday ill all day!!!" Then it was back at it on Monday as it was Col. Ispolatoff's birthday and there was another magnificent dinner. Hughes made plans to return to Paris on Sunday, December 30. He was clearly impressed by all of this merriment and by the apparent partiality of his hosts to imbibing, and made a note and some sketches in his notebook in connection with another business opportunity: this section of the notebook is titled "Studies upon an Alcoholmeter"![47]

Gen. Guerhardt and Col. Ispolatoff tried to persuade Hughes to remain, and Gen. Guerhardt even offered Hughes a job in an attempt to entice him to stay. During his visit he had made many friends, and had he stayed, he would have been able to live the good life experienced by the aristocracy, but it was time to return. When Hughes went to the railway station, there was a send-off group consisting of Gen. Guerhardt, Col. Ispolatoff, various officers, and the many friends he had made. This type of support and enthusiasm from his customers is a testament to the wisdom of Hughes's approach to business. In promoting his telegraph system he poured his heart and soul into making the project a success from top to bottom, making sure that his telegraph system was well integrated into the communications infrastructure of the country and that it also communicated smoothly across borders with the systems in other countries, and took pains to make sure that the operators and telegraph electricians were well trained. His advice to employers was that "Employees should be chosen from a lower grade so as to hope for promotion."[48]

Hughes arrived back in Paris on January 4, 1866, after another successful and eventful year.[49] He went to the Froment workshop, which must have seemed empty without his old friend present to greet him, but the workshop continued to operate under the name of Dumoulin-Froment. His next business appointment, arranged by his friend General Guerhardt, was in Prussia, and he set about preparing instruments to take with him.[50] By March he was ready, and headed for Berlin to meet the director general of the telegraph service, Colonel Chauvin. Prussia already had an extensive telegraph network which had been greatly expanded with the help of Werner Siemens, and used instruments based on Morse's provided by the manufacturer Siemens and Halske. Their interest in Hughes's system was for use on the international and main trunk telegraph lines. Hughes installed his equipment and started experimental operation and tests on the Berlin to Paris line of 880 km with a repeater relay in Cologne. Next, tests were conducted on the Berlin to St. Petersburg line, which stretched 1,330 km, with a relay in Königsberg—whence he sent a message to General Guerhardt updating him on recent events and progress. The conditions on the long telegraph lines, however, varied constantly: some days they could not transmit due to all the electrical noise, or they could transmit intermittently, but other days the lines were fine. Col. Chauvin nonetheless told Hughes that he was pleased with the progress and was going to prepare a positive report to the minister, which gave Hughes cause for celebration.

But Hughes was sensing that things were not quite right: it was as if they were expecting something to happen, but he could not quite put his finger on what it was.

When he next met with Col. Chauvin, the colonel announced that Prussia was gearing up for war and that it would be impossible to proceed under the circumstances. Colonel Chauvin assured Hughes, as if by way of consolation, that the instruments had met all of their expectations, and that on the return of peace they would certainly make an agreement with him. While Hughes must have felt dejected at having come so close to a contract without being able to sign one, he must also have concluded that Prussia was not going to be the safest place if hostilities broke out, and made arrangements for a hasty retreat.[51]

> The chiefs and employees regretted most bitterly me taking the Instruments away and certainly the impression left by the experiments is one highly favorable to my instrument. After saying adieus etc. I returned to Paris on Thursday. So ended my first Prussian Campaign.

Hughes found himself caught in Prussia just when it decided to flex its military muscles. The complex political situation involved the confederation of German states within which Prussia considered Austria its chief rival. Previous attempts to unify Germany had failed. Prussia was under the rule of William I and guided by his ambitious minister Otto von Bismarck, who believed that it was his country's mission to unify Germany. Bismarck, who had a distaste for liberalism and parliamentary rule, had issued his famous warning "that the great question of the day will not be decided by speeches and resolutions of the majorities—but by blood and iron." He had embarked on his plan for unification in 1864 when Prussia had declared war on Denmark, which had resulted in a swift Danish defeat and Prussian gain in territory. Now it was Austria's turn.

While Hughes had every intention of leaving Berlin before the conflict started, and had already sent his instruments back to Paris, he reports that:[52]

> The last page was written under the impression of leaving but unforeseen circumstances prevented it.

Hughes had pulled a rabbit out of the hat at the eleventh hour. Instead of leaving with no contract or sale he made a new proposal to Col. Chauvin, telling him that instead of concerning himself with purchasing instruments for the whole of the German Confederation, he should buy an installation for Prussia alone, and that he (Hughes) would later undertake to market his instruments to the rest of the Confederation. This would be much less costly for Prussia, and Hughes gave a revised price to Col. Chauvin. The new offer went over well and Hughes was asked to stay in Berlin while the colonel went to see the minister. The result was that a contract was drawn up for Fr. 100,000, and on Saturday, June 2 it was signed. Hughes telegraphed Paris and ordered the instruments to be sent back and additional new instruments to be manufactured. When they arrived, he started instructing the telegraph employees just as war was declared on June 14, 1866. He records:[53]

War has broken out this day between Austria with the German Confederation against Prussia and Italy. The telegraph wires are cut in all directions and expect a grand battle very shortly. I am afraid that this event will cause great difficulty in carrying out my contract.

While the conflagration raged far to the south, there was little that could be accomplished, and he spent his time carrying out experiments on his instrument and studying the effects of electrical noise on the telegraph lines. Then, on July 6, 1866, the Prussian government called Hughes to a meeting and paid him the sum of Fr. 100,000 one month ahead of schedule. The war had been short and swift, and Austria had been defeated in a matter of weeks. It had been a new type of war, one waged from a central command post based in Berlin and which used the speed and reach of the telegraph system to direct the army and coordinate its movements, and the railways to rapidly move forces into position. The war machine was quickly adapting to make use of modern technology.[54] Hughes finally left Prussia after receiving his payment in gold coin and returned to Paris in July of 1866.[55]

Upon his return he spent some time catching up on events back in America. The Civil War had ended and he learned from his sister Maggie, who was his main correspondent, that all the family were safe, although they had had a tough time. His father had suffered the most and had decided to move out of the South and relocate to Chicago with his brother John and family. It was probably about this time that Hughes set up an arrangement with Maggie to help the family financially by sending her regular payments. In other developments, Hughes was delighted when he heard the news that the Atlantic cable had finally been laid successfully. He made a big entry in his notebook at this time: "Atlantic Cable successfully laid the 27 July 1866." Hughes had received a letter the previous year from George Saward of the Atlantic Telegraph Company, inviting him to participate in the new attempt to establish a transatlantic telegraph system:[56]

The directors of the Atlantic Telegraph Co and myself are very desirous that the Hughes Instrument should if possible be tried on upon the new cable now in the course of manufacture and ready for sea by the first week in June next year. The directors will willingly arrange... to secure for you every possible facility for making arrangements for working through the line when coiled on board the Great Eastern. W Shaw and W Andrews have informed me of the very gratifying results of the working of your instrument—at which I very much rejoice looking at the great amount of labour and talent you have devoted to it.

When Hughes received this letter he was in Russia engaged in telegraph negotiations, and appears to have declined the offer.

In Froment's workshop Hughes saw a large, impressive, two-meter-tall instrument which incorporated a large swinging pendulum. It was a "pantelegraph," the invention of Giovanni Caselli. The instrument could transmit images and drawings over the telegraph lines: it was an early telefacsimile machine, in fact.

Hughes was intrigued by this impressive instrument; its inventor Caselli had had to face many of the same problems that Hughes had solved with his telegraph, such as maintaining synchronism between the transmitting and receiving instruments. Froment himself had also made a version of a writing telegraph some years earlier.[57] Hughes saw how he could improve on these devices and make a much smaller table-top instrument using many of the components from his own instrument. The sketches Hughes made in his notebook show a compact device that he called an "autograph," with a rotating drum onto which the document with the information to be copied was wrapped.[58] The image was usually drawn or stenciled onto thin tinfoil with non-conducting ink. A stylus was arranged so that it could scan back and forth over the image; by incrementally rotating the drum and moving the stylus back and forth across the page, the whole page could be scanned.[59] A series of electrical pulses was generated by the scanning process. The receiver was a similar device except that it used a chemically treated paper that was wrapped on the drum. As the stylus passed back and forth, the electrical pulses passed through the paper, changing its color, thus reproducing the transmitted image. As in his telegraph, it was necessary to have the two instruments operate in synchronism. Hughes made a pair of the instruments, and examples of the images he transmitted are contained in his notebook, one titled "The first specimen worked by the Hughes autographie telegraph sent from one instrument to the other October 26th 1866." Other examples are of a butterfly and a castle. However, by December, he notes that the "Autographie is a real Humbug." And that was the end of his experiments on a device that was ahead of its time.[60]

By now the situation had stabilized in Prussia, and as promised, Hughes returned to promote his telegraph among the other members of the German Confederation, starting with Austria. He arrived in Vienna in January of 1867, met with the Director General Mr. Brunner, and commenced service right away with Berlin. Hughes was now starting to benefit from already having his telegraph instruments established at some key telegraph nodes such as Paris and Berlin: this is demonstrated by how quickly he started up communications from Vienna. After a month, Hughes worked out a contract based on the Prussian contract for Fr. 100,000 and was so confident that it would be awarded to him that he ordered four more instruments from Paris. Mr. Brunner informed him one day that he was going to Constantinople on business, and while he was there, he was willing to talk to the Turkish government about adopting Hughes's instrument. Hughes agreed enthusiastically. Brunner wanted to take a blank contract with him and they discussed what might be a suitable price, settling on Fr. 60,000. On May 13 the Austrian contract was signed and Hughes received the Fr. 100,000 as well as 36,000 guilders for six instruments. This good news was closely followed by a telegraph message from Mr. Brunner saying that the Turkish government and the Sultan had signed his contract![61]

For his contribution to improving the telegraph operation in Austria Hughes was awarded the Order of the Iron Crown.

Hughes's notebook showing his thoughts on modifying his instrument to handle Turkish characters.

Everything had happened so fast with Turkey that he had not had time to consider some of the challenges that the contract posed. After a bit of hasty research done with the help of the Austrian telegraph staff he was able to locate a German book that described the Turkish alphabet.[62] Certainly the script was different, and it also used more than twenty-six characters, but he had already dealt with that type of problem in creating the Russian version of his instrument. However, there was another wrinkle: Turkish writing was read from right to left, and his instrument was set up to print out for reading left to right. He came up with a rather ingenious solution to this problem, which was to engrave the type wheel with the Turkish characters upside down; after the characters were printed and the paper strip was torn off, it had only to be turned around, and the message read correctly right to left. In addition, the print wheel had to be made wider to accommodate the variations in the height of the letters. He also worked on a method for making the paper strip turn around and run backwards so that it could read right to left, but this presented a number of problems and early attempts led to blurred characters. The final configuration, unfortunately, was not documented, although a solution must have been arrived at, as the instruments went into service.

Hughes left Vienna for Paris on July 6 and arranged for the new Turkish instruments to be made at the workshop. While in Paris he attended the International Exhibition, where he received the gold medal, the highest honor awarded, in recognition of his great achievements.[63] Hughes was now able to enjoy Paris, and the whole city was in high spirits, with the exhibition in full swing. He had seen the city slowly transformed each time he returned over the last few years. It was becoming beautiful, with its wide tree-lined boulevards and grand buildings, the big bronze lamps, and splendid shops. Now he could take pleasure in sitting outside at one of the many cafés, savoring his refreshment in the warm summer air.

Not one to let the grass grow under his feet, Hughes set off once again for Vienna en route to Constantinople, where he arrived on August 1, 1867, and met with the Director General Agthon Effendi. Hughes received Fr. 30,000, the first installment specified by his contract. He tried transmitting on a telegraph line from Constantinople to Vienna and Semlin near Belgrade, but Serbia refused to give them a direct line, even though the country had signed an agreement with the Austrian and Turkish governments to permit just this type of access. So Hughes resorted to working on some internal lines, although he complained that they were very poor and noisy. Finally, in October, the Serbian government gave its consent for a direct wire to Semlin.[64] By November the instruments were up and running and the staff trained, and Hughes returned to Paris, stopping on the way in Belgrade and Vienna.

For his services to Turkey the Sultan bestowed on Hughes the Grand Cross of the Medjidie.

Training an operator to be able to touch type on Hughes's instrument by covering the keys.

In December Hughes was off to Holland to negotiate a contract with the Dutch. The Dutch turned out to be tough negotiators and told Hughes that his prices were too high. Gaining a foothold in Holland was vital to Hughes, as Holland was the terminus of a number of cross-channel undersea cables from Britain, and he was keen to operate on them. The Dutch knew this, and also that they were in an excellent bargaining position. They eventually agreed to pay 25,000 florins. Hughes started training the staff and the instruments were installed on the Rotterdam-Amsterdam and Amsterdam-Berlin lines.

Hughes's instruments had now been in service for several years and he felt it was time for an upgrade. He had been gathering feedback from various operators about problems, recommendations, and suggestions for improvements, and he collected them together and reviewed them with Mr. Schiffler of the Austrian telegraph administration in Vienna in July of 1868. They ended up with a list of improvements with sketches indicating how the necessary changes should be made. They then discussed the changes with the Paris workshop and with Siemens and Halske. The opportunity was taken to add a couple of extra features such as a paper tape cutter so that the messages could be neatly sliced off. Also, for those telegraph organizations that pasted the paper strips onto a telegram form, a gum dispenser that automatically applied gum to the back of the tape was incorporated.

It was during 1868 that Hughes received the sad news that his father had died in Chicago; he may have received the news on one of his own telegraph instruments while in Paris. He did not return to America for the funeral, though, as he would have had to travel by boat across the Atlantic and then overland to Chicago, which would have meant a protracted journey, and it probably would have been impractical for the funeral to have been delayed so long.

As the political situation seemed to have stabilized in the German Confederation, Hughes returned there on January 27, 1869, this time to Bavaria and Württemberg. This was the final phase of the expansion of his telegraph system to embrace all of Germany. Installations went smoothly, with the first tests occurring on the Munich-Frankfurt and Munich-Stuttgart telegraph lines, followed by tests on the Munich-Berlin and Munich-Amsterdam lines. By the beginning of April the project was completed, he had received his payment, and he returned to Paris. He had now reduced the time required for a typical installation to about two and a half months, and the largest variable was how quickly operators could be trained. For his contribution and service to the telegraph in Bavaria, Hughes was awarded the noble Order of St. Michael.

Hughes traveled to London in July of 1869 to pursue a long-held goal, which was to transmit on an undersea cable; specifically, he planned to transmit over the London-Amsterdam cable, as he already had instruments in Holland.[65] He had researched the unique problems of operating on submarine cables, and how best to arrange his instruments to deal with their different electrical characteristics. As his standard instruments used only positive pulses, they would tend to charge up the undersea cable, thus making it difficult or impossible to detect the signals at the receiving end. It was, therefore, necessary to neutralize the cable after the transmission of each pulse. This was accomplished by switching relays which enabled first a positive pulse to be transmitted, then a negative pulse (by reversing the battery connections), and then the cable was grounded; he called this device a double relay. The tests were successful on the London-Amsterdam cable, as he sent thirty-five messages with his instrument operating at a slightly slower speed of 110 revolutions per minute vs. the normal landline speed of 120.

Although the tests were successful he had to break them off to attend to business in Switzerland, and by September 12, 1869, he was off to Bern with six instruments. He soon had them communicating on the Bern, Geneva, Zurich and Basel lines. He received a first payment of 8,500 francs from the Swiss and then he moved on to Belgium, and as it was now Christmas time, Hughes noted:[66]

Commenced the instruction of 18 elves. 15 Dec.

The later model of the Hughes instrument with a DC electric motor drive and rotating governor.

By January his instruments were handling communications between Brussels and Antwerp, and soon thereafter between Brussels and Berlin. Belgium later awarded Hughes the title of Officer of the Royal Order of Leopold. By March Hughes was back in Paris. [67]

Although the workshop was as busy as ever producing telegraph instruments, the workers were now discontent and grumbling: the newspapers were running story after story about the political dispute brewing between France, Prussia, and Spain, and the workers were not happy making instruments that would be used in the German countries. Every day the tension seemed to be worsening, and Hughes, who had dealt with these countries, tried to allay their fears by pointing out that with the telegraph these political disputes could be more easily negotiated and settled. But his words had no effect and the war drums started to beat once again. The newspapers helped fan the flames of nationalistic pride in France. Hughes, not wanting to be trapped if war broke out, decided to leave for England. It is from records relating to this flight to safety that we first learn that Hughes had a wife by the name of Maria! There is no record of his marriage or where in his travels he had met her. Was she Parisian? Hughes, who is full of surprises for his biographers, had sprung another one in this case: his notebooks and other documents provide no clues about this marriage or his wife.[68]

Hughes and his wife departed just in time, as France's old fear over the rise of Prussia proved to be justified. Bismarck, through political manipulation, caused France to declare war on Prussia, resulting in the Franco-Prussian war which was declared on July 19, 1870. The Emperor Napoleon III was now ill and the days of the empire and mighty French army were gone, and the French were no match for the Prussian Army with its precision and superior artillery. The Prussian victory was speedy and decisive, and disastrous for France. Napoleon III and his army capitulated following the battle of Sedan in September of 1870. The Prussian army marched on Paris and laid siege to the city from September to January 1871, when an armistice was signed. Napoleon went into exile in Britain and Bismarck forced elections. A new national assembly was formed and France became a republic. France also gave up territory, as Alsace and Lorraine became part of Germany, and Bismarck used the defeat of France to complete his unification of Germany. King William I of Prussia was declared the German emperor in 1871.

While Hughes had escaped just in time from France, when he landed in England he faced more turmoil: the government and the Post Office were creating a major upheaval in the telegraph industry. Hughes, who was a director of the United Kingdom Electric Telegraph Company, was faced with the prospect of a government takeover. The Post Office had decided to nationalize all of the telegraph companies in the country. There were several reasons put forward for this move, such as that there was not sufficient coverage by the private telegraph offices, and many towns or villages had no access; opening hours were short; charges were exorbitant; and messages were slow to be delivered. Further, it had been suggested that telegrams were a form of letter and therefore should naturally come under the control of the Post

Office. The implication was that all of the independent telegraph companies should be acquired by the government, which would result in a situation similar to that in Continental countries. The initial government estimate of the cost of purchasing the companies' property and rights was £2.5 million, and a parliamentary act had been passed in 1868 to allow the Post Office to proceed. The telegraph companies, however, protested and opposed the act—or at least were holding out for a better deal. Consequently, a second act had to be passed in 1869 to increase the amount to £8 million.

The directors of the United Kingdom Electric Telegraph Company then issued a letter indicating that they withdrew their opposition to the Electric Telegraph Bill, and stating their conditions for the purchase by the government.[69] These conditions were that the government (1) purchase twenty years of present net profits; (2) purchase the patent for the Hughes Type Printing Telegraph for £12,000; and (3) purchase the ordinary shares plus the prospective profits. The purchase of the company by the Post Office put all of the rights to Hughes's instruments in government hands. To ensure continuity of service, he was called upon to provide training to government operators, which he did from September 1870 until January 1871, free of charge:[70]

> Having been driven from France by the war, he has taken residence in London, and from no other motivation than a love of science has voluntarily given instruction daily to a certain number of our clerks and candidates for admission in the working of his instrument and general principles. Professor Hughes is so situated as not to stand in need of any remuneration which could be given to him for his services, and the Department has great reason to congratulate itself on having been able to obtain the voluntary co-operation of so eminent a man.

As the British government now owned all of the telegraph systems in the country, it became necessary for the government to consider the recommendations and guidelines of the International Telegraph Union (ITU) which the rest of Europe followed. Britain had previously been precluded from joining the Union, as its telegraph systems had all been privately owned.

The ITU had been formed to standardize telegraph communications across international boundaries. At the Union's 1865 conference, agreements had been reached on the use of French as the official language, a system of uniform tariffs, the adoption of the gold French franc as the monetary unit, and the use of the Morse system for use on international lines. At the second ITU conference in 1868 the Hughes telegraph was recommended for use on all major international lines. This was a major boon for Hughes as it now required all countries to use his instruments for compatibility.

In 1871, Britain was connected with the Continent using the Hughes equipment through the Submarine Telegraph Company, which operated a number of cross-channel cables. By October of 1871 his equipment was sending messages between London and Paris on the Boulogne cable, between London and Amsterdam on the Dutch cable, and between London and Paris direct through the Le Havre cable, running at 110 revolutions per minute. The test was then extended from London to Marseilles with all three stations on line.[71] The tests were successful and Hughes entered into a contract with the Submarine Telegraph Company on February 1, 1872, in which the company made an initial purchase of four instruments.[72] There was a one-month trial period and a payment of £800. Finally, Britain was connected into the Hughes European telegraph network, enabling London to communicate with the major European cities such as Amsterdam, Brussels, Berlin, Paris, Lyons, and Marseilles. The connection was averaging fifty-five messages per hour with his system. By 1878 the company had twenty Hughes instruments, and by 1886, forty.[73] All of the Continental news for the *Times* and *Daily Telegraph* was received on Hughes instruments.[74] By 1891, telegraph operations were centralized at the Post Office facility at St. Martin's-le-Grand, where fifty-two lines were devoted to foreign cable work with the French, Dutch, Germans and Belgians. A through line to Vienna handled the messages for Austria, Hungary and Bulgaria, and traffic for Constantinople passed through Rome.[75]

After the Franco-Prussian War had ended, Hughes returned to France, and in 1875 Spain contracted Hughes to install his telegraph equipment for 50,000 Francs and honored him by making him a Commander of the Royal and Distinguished Order of Carlos III. Portugal, Hungary, and Serbia followed shortly after, giving Hughes virtually total coverage of Europe with his system. His last foreign recognition came in October of 1896, when the Royal Serbian Legation wrote to him, saying it believed that as "it would be an honor for the Knights of the Serbian Royal Orders to number you among them, His Majesty has been pleased to confer on you the Grand Officer's Star and Collar of his Royal Order of Takovo."

Hughes's telegraph went on to reach as far as South America, although it is unlikely that he went there as he was not a good sailor. There are a few references which indicate that his telegraph instrument was used in Peru, Argentina and Brazil.[76] By the end of the 1800s there were some 2,500 Hughes telegraph instruments in operation in Europe.[77] The instruments continued in service well into the 1900s, with the last one going out of service in France in the 1940s, Belgium in 1947, and the Netherlands in 1950.[78] It is a powerful testimonial to the quality of Hughes's work that instruments of his design continued in service for almost a hundred years. The total number of his instruments manufactured over the years was probably about 3,000. During the long life of Hughes's instruments a number of upgrades were made, many of them by Siemens and Halske: for example, they were changed to operate by electric motor power with a centrifugal governor.[79] There was also a version in the UK that used a compressed air motor.

As for Hughes himself, by the mid 1870s he was ready for a change of pace. Up to that time all of his energies had been directed towards the telegraph, both to promote it and then to obtain contracts for which he personally trained the operators and installed his equipment. He had been traveling continually, and what time there was between trips he spent in experimenting to improve the operation and reliability of the instruments. He also experimented with telegraph lines to enable his instruments to function on lines with a high degree of electrical noise, to develop sensitive polarized relays, and to enable his equipment to work over submarine cables. The French government also had him work with Prof. Guillemin to investigate various telegraph problems and lightning protection methods, for which he was made a member of the Commission de Perfectionnments.

Hughes's experimentation to improve the understanding and operation of electromagnets and relays helped many other inventors, and in Europe his sensitive relay was widely known as the "Hughes Relay or "Hughes electromagnet." One important use was in railway block safety and signaling systems. His relay was incorporated into Henry Lartigue's first automatic block system on the French railroad and by Sykes in Britain.

By the mid 1870s Hughes's situation was significantly different from what it had been ten years earlier. The European telegraph market, originally wide open, was now well developed thanks to his success, and therefore he saw his future role changing. The countries using his equipment would continue to do so as there was no major

Hughes telegraph operators at the busy Berlin telegraph office.

competitor or reason for them to change.[80] They would also buy new machines as their economies grew, as well as spare parts to maintain existing machines. Siemens and Halske, as well as Dumoulin-Froment, were in a better position to make upgrades, in which Hughes would still be involved. He had attained financial independence, and with more free time, there was no need for him to continue to work with so much vigor. He was, at heart, an experimenter and inventor, as is evident in his notebooks, where every so often he jotted down ideas and experiments unrelated to the telegraph. These covered a wide spectrum of topics such as steam and hot air engines, improved magnetic compasses, needle guns, an autograph telegraph, gas and water meters, electric intrusion alarms for banks, techniques for decomposing water into hydrogen and oxygen, and better methods of converting iron into steel. Now that he had become successful he was in a position to pursue his dreams and get back into the laboratory to tinker with some of these ideas.

In the summer of 1876, David Hughes decided to return to America to visit his family. He left few notes about the trip other than to remark that he went to Kentucky to see his sister Maggie and brother-in-law and their two daughters and two sons, as well as his brother John and his wife and their two daughters. According to a later passport application, he returned from America on October 14, 1876.[81]

Hughes had become well known not only as a businessman, but also as a skilled and respected engineer. The many honors that had been bestowed on him had made his name familiar throughout Europe. While France had its share of scientific men, London was the real scientific hub, with its many scientists, scientific societies, technical publications, and forums. It is also possible that Paris had lost its luster for him or for his wife; in any case, it was time for a change. So in the fall of 1877 he and his wife moved to London to enable him to pursue his desire for independent research.

7

IF ONLY WE HAD A TELEPHONE WE COULD SORT THIS OUT!

Self-appointed prophets had predicted that once the continents were connected by the Atlantic telegraph cable, peace would reign, conflicts could be avoided, and misunderstandings smoothed away. Unfortunately, not everyone got this message.

New Jersey, June 1878. The daily sack of mail had just arrived at Thomas Edison's laboratory in Menlo Park, and Stockton Griffin, Edison's secretary, dumped it onto the table for sorting.[1] Among the items was the latest issue of the British technical journal *Engineering*. He opened it and flipped through the pages, and something caught his eye. There was no mistake; Edison had to see this right away. When Edison saw the article he raced through it, becoming more and more infuriated, and when he finished he exploded into action, going over to his telegraph key and pounding out two searing messages.[2] The first was to William Preece, the Assistant Engineer-in-Chief and Electrician of the British Post Office in London, accusing him and Professor David Edward Hughes of "piracy," "plagiarism," and "abuse of confidence." The second, which he sent just to make sure it was understood that he meant business, was to Sir William Thomson, one of the most respected British scientists of the day, complaining about Preece's underhanded behavior.[3]

Thomas A. Edison, whom the American press called "The Wizard of Menlo Park."

Edison's impetuous action was to start a scientific fracas that raged across the two continents for several months—so much for the Atlantic telegraph's smoothing influence.

When William Preece received the telegraph message at the Post Office headquarters in London, he was taken aback. It was like a slap in the face, and such accusations were not taken lightly in Victorian Britain, especially when made against such a prominent government official: some years earlier such an accusation would have led to pistols at dawn. Moreover, this was not an accusation from some unknown person, but from someone he thought was a friend, none other than the "Wizard of Menlo Park" himself.[4] Preece, upset by the attack on his honor, sent a copy of the telegraph message to his friend Hughes, adding the question:[5]

What do you think of the enclosed message from Edison? Is he mad?

Edison, without waiting for a reply to his telegraph messages, made his accusations public in the newspapers.[6] He accused Hughes of stealing his invention, and Preece of aiding and abetting him by passing on his trade secrets. The *New York Herald* took up the cause under the headline "Brain Stealing."[7] Previously Hughes had had some respect for Edison, referring to him as a "talented humbug," but he, like many others in Europe, soon changed his mind and switched to calling him a "snake" and "charlatan."[8] As the war of words escalated, Hughes came out of his corner swinging, and wrote to Preece, encouraging him to write a rebuttal to Edison's accusations:[9]

William Preece, Electrician to the Post Office, who became an ally and friend of Hughes in his dispute with Edison over the credit for inventing the microphone.

I mean you to give a stunning crushing reply—every sentence a hammer blow—He has tried to ruin you… but now you must knock him down…. My Welsh blood is up and now there will be no quarter not the slightest mercy as the villain does not deserve it.

Edison's associates, Charles Batchelor and James Adams, not wanting to be left out of the fray, rallied in Edison's support:[10]

…damnedest steal in the country and Preece knew it all the time…. We intend to go for them bad… we will make Preece so damned sick he will wish he had never been born. We will spend $5000 if necessary to expose it.

These were fighting words indeed. The European scientific community and press rallied behind their champions, Hughes and Preece, while the American press rallied behind Edison, but none of this was the behavior expected from scientific men. So, what was the hullabaloo about?

It was about the creation of a new industry, the telephone industry, which would not only put a phone in every house, but also, eventually, in everyone's pocket. It was about a technology that would encompass the world and surpass everyone's wildest dreams, and about a business opportunity that would make some people and companies very rich.

By 1876, people had become accustomed to the seemingly instantaneous distribution of news and exchange of information over the network of telegraph wires that connected towns, cities and continents.[11] Now it was time for the next leap forward in communications, a shift from dots and dashes and the awkward phrases of "telegraphese" to the transmission of the spoken word over great distances. Professor Alexander Graham Bell began it all with his invention of the telephone in 1876.[12]

People had different reactions to the possibility of talking to other people over wires: some believed that it was nothing more than a toy, while others saw it as a revolutionary discovery. Telegraph companies gave the technology a mixed reception, unsure how the "talking telegraph" would affect their business. Some of them started their own research to produce a competing device. Scientists and inventors enamored of the new talking telegraph set about improving on what Bell had invented—and also looking for ways around his patents. Hovering on the sidelines were the capitalists, attentively watching the action and ready to invest in promising opportunities. As the stakes became higher, the competition became keener and sometimes downright underhanded. Even the scientists and inventors were not immune from the plotting and maneuvering. Who would control this new technology, and who would profit from it?

While Bell's telephone worked, it was far from perfect, and needed substantial improvements before it could reach its full potential. Contributions from several people would be needed before it could evolve into the dynamic instrument that became the cornerstone of the communications industry. William Preece, of the British Post Office, made a prophetic observation about the telephone around the time of its invention:[13]

> The accounts of the telephone were received in this country with great scepticism. Many even now doubt its truth until they actually test its reality. When once however, a new thing is shown to be true, a host of detractors delight in proving that it is not new. The inventor has to pass through the ordeal of abuse. He is shown to be a plagiarist or a purloiner or something worse. Others are instanced to have done the same thing years ago, though perhaps their own existence, apart from their ideas, have never before been heard of. Professor Bell will have to go through all of this; nevertheless the telephone will always be associated with his name and it will remain one of the marvels of this marvelous age, while its chief marvel will be its beautiful and exquisite simplicity.

Professor Alexander Graham Bell had sprung the telephone on the world in June of 1876 at the Centennial Exhibition in Philadelphia. Bell demonstrated his invention to the judging committee on a Sunday, when the exhibition was closed to the public; the committee was headed by Sir William Thomson, a pre-eminent scientist of the day who was visiting from Great Britain. They were amazed at the new device which actually allowed them to speak and hear each other over a greater distance than they could shout! Bell's invention suddenly moved from obscurity to center stage. Bell won an award, and Thomson was so impressed with the "speaking telegraph," as the telephone was often called, that he arranged to have a second demonstration in Boston, where Bell was based. Thomson probably noticed that this dynamic young professor of twenty-nine years, who had a rather pale complexion with jet-black whiskers and flashing eyes, was a fellow Scotsman. Bell presented him with a set of telephones to take back to Britain. When Thomson arrived home in Scotland, he attended a meeting of the British Association in Glasgow. It was here that he presented this new technology for the first time in Britain and he attempted to demonstrate the telephone's operation, but unfortunately the instruments had been damaged during the journey and failed to work.[14]

At the same Philadelphia exhibition Thomson also met Thomas Edison, who had been awarded a prize for his "electric pen" and "automatic telegraph." Before returning home, Thomson paid a visit to Edison at his Menlo Park laboratory. Edison at age thirty-one was often criticized for his dress and mannerisms, and had been described in one popular newspaper as having:[15]

> the characteristic features of an American, the nasal accent of a down-easter and the slovenliness to be expected of a genius. Mr. Edison is certainly not graceful or elegant. He shuffled about the platform in an ungainly way, and his stooping, swinging figure was lacking in dignity. But his eyes were wonderfully expressive, his face frank and cordial, and his frequent smile hearty and irresistible. If his sentences were not rounded, they went to the point.

The fifty-four year old Thomson, a professor at Glasgow University, was a slender and lively man who sported the popular Victorian whiskers and walked with a slight limp, a legacy of a broken leg suffered some years previously. He was probably making profuse notes in his ever-handy notebook. However, Edison had this to say about Thomson:[16]

> I remember Sir William Thomson when he came to see me had on a suit of clothes— I tell you. His trousers were too short for him; his coat was old and greasy, the collar came up above his ears and his hat looked as if he had boiled soup in it. And that was his bang up suit too.

Edison was not formally trained, but that had not impeded his success as an inventor. He had created a large, well-equipped laboratory in Menlo Park, New Jersey, several miles outside New York City. It was staffed by a dozen skilled associates, and was probably the best laboratory in the country, and had been founded for the sole purpose of creating inventions; it became known as the invention factory. Edison was a workaholic; he ate and slept at his laboratory, and was as often found working at night as by day. He probably spent more time there with his associates than at home with his wife.

He was hailed as the "Wizard of Menlo Park" by the press. His laboratory had become a pilgrimage site for visitors and journalists and was flooded with mail. Edison proposed "to invent some minor thing every ten days and some big thing every six months."[17]

Constant invention of products with patent protection was the order of the day.[18] Having gained recognition in America, Edison desired to become well known in Europe, and to be accepted by the European scientific community.

Edison considered patent protection essential: it was what guaranteed the inventor a return on his investment of hard work, experimentation, and innovation. Patents turned innovation into property that had value, and this was never truer than in the emerging telephone industry. This factor was probably more important in America, which supported free enterprise, than in Europe, where communications were under government control (this had been one of the first industries to be nationalized). Nevertheless, patents were closely guarded and fiercely defended, and Bell, as well as Edison, would undergo many challenges to their patents over the years.

Following Bell's surprise introduction of his telephone at the Philadelphia Exhibition, the Western Union Company, with whom Edison had signed an agreement in March of 1877, began to take a serious interest in the instrument. Edison had recognized that the weak link in Bell's telephone was his transmitter, and in early 1877, he started serious research into better telephone transmitters. By the summer he had developed a device that showed promising results. Later in 1877 Hughes also recognized that the transmitter was the weak link in Bell's telephone and embarked on experiments to find a solution—which resulted in his discovery of the microphone.

The unfortunate conflict that would soon erupt between Edison and Hughes was between two men with very different goals, each of whose perception of the other was totally askew. Hughes was an individual inventor starting a new phase in his life as an independent researcher, who only sought recognition for his work and had no interest in seeking patents or remuneration. Edison, on the other hand, was the leader of an invention factory on a mission to solve a problem with the commercial telephone and make money from that solution.

Hughes's discovery of the carbon microphone, an amplifier of sound, had a wide range of uses and he gave the technology away freely to all who wished to use it. As a researcher, he spent time studying the loose contact phenomenon so that he could explain its operation to the satisfaction of the scientific community. His discovery was a huge stimulus to the design of microphones and telephone transmitters based on his carbon pencil and carbon particle experiments. Both of the technologies were to be exploited widely by other researchers and manufactures.

Edison, on the other hand, had invented a specific device for a specific application: a transmitter for the telephone. His device was also based on a carbon compound. He patented his telephone transmitter as part of his obligation to Western Union, and was in the business of making money and protecting his patents. The two inventors did however have one thing in common, and that was the desire for respect and recognition for their work. While Edison had gained this status in America he was less known in Europe, a situation he very much wanted to change. He had been making some progress in this direction, but Hughes's claim to have invented the microphone and the publicity surrounding it looked like they could dash his hopes.

Edison's accusations would have caused great damage to Hughes's reputation (and of course to Preece's also) if they were left unchallenged and if Edison were to prevail. Hughes, only newly established in the British scientific community, dreaded the thought of being maligned and marginalized for something he knew he had not done; it was the last thing he wanted.

Was Edison correct in his accusations? Had Hughes stolen his invention and had Preece leaked the details to Hughes so that he could claim the glory? And where was Alexander Graham Bell in all this? After all, had he not invented the telephone? There are two sides to all such stories, and in this case, the story will be told in two parts.

The first part of the story revolves around Professor Hughes and William Preece. Hughes's story is one of a scientist on the path to the discovery of the microphone. William Preece was a prominent member of the technical staff of the Post Office, an organization which was responsible for the telegraph system in Britain, and which was now considering what policy to adopt with regard to the "speaking telegraph." Preece was to play a prominent role in this decision, attempting to balance the interests of the Post Office in this new device with those of various inventors and companies. Hughes and Preece began as colleagues, but their relationship developed into a friendship and finally into a close bond, as they were compelled to defend their honor.

The second part of the story, which follows later in the chapter, relates to the Wizard of Menlo Park, his accusations, his telephone receiver, and his relationship with Preece.

>━━<

In the autumn of 1877, Professor David Edward Hughes and his wife Maria decided to move from Paris to London, where they took up residence at 94 Great Portland Street. Paris had proved a convenient base from which to conduct his highly successful telegraph business, and due to the success of that business Hughes now found himself with more free time and money in the bank. London had become the center of the scientific world. Here there were many experimenters and scientists; there were technical societies and respected technical journals, all of which provided an environment conducive to new discoveries and inventions—just what he was looking for as he shifted from telegraph engineer to independent researcher. As he was already well known and respected both on the Continent and in Britain, when he moved to London, he was warmly accepted into the scientific community.[19]

When he arrived in London, this community was abuzz over Alexander Graham Bell's new invention, the telephone, and Bell happened to be in Britain at the time promoting it. Hughes was probably one of the many who crowded in to see one of Bell's demonstrations at the Society of Arts that November. He too became caught up in the excitement, as he made an entry in his notebook for November 5, 1877, "Studies upon a Telephone": he had chosen his research project.[20] Like many others who had attended Bell's telephone demonstration, he had realized the instrument's limitations as well as its potential, and he started to think about ways to improve it.

Alexander Graham Bell had been in Britain since July on his honeymoon, and was showing his new bride, Mabel Hubbard, his homeland. He was also there to promote his telephone, in which he was helped by William Preece, electrician to the Post Office. Preece had recently returned from a tour of telegraph facilities in North America during which he had met Bell and been impressed by his invention. Preece had also visited Thomas Edison and seen the competing telephone receiver which he was developing.

Once back in Britain, Preece had wasted no time in publicizing what he had learned on his trip, and took the opportunity to present a technical paper "On the Telephone" at the British Association meeting at Plymouth in August, inviting Bell to attend.[21] Preece, known as a good public speaker and lively presenter, had pulled off a coup: he was not only about to conduct the first successful demonstration of the telephone in England, but also had the inventor in the audience. The meeting created tremendous excitement.[22]

Preece began his presentation with a history of early telephone experiments, describing the work of Philipp Reis of Germany in 1861, of Elisha Gray in Chicago in 1873, and of a number of other contributors. He next described Bell's telephone and researches in glowing terms, saying "He has rendered it possible to reproduce the human voice with all its modulations at distant points. I have spoken with a person at various distances up to 32 miles." He described the instrument's principles of operation and how it was made, indicating that the transmitter and receiver were identical and connected together by telegraph wires.[23] Bell's telephone consisted of a polarized electromagnet (a magnet with a coil of many turns of wire wound around it) and a very thin iron diaphragm (disc) that was mounted very close to the end of the electromagnet (but not touching it).[24] Sound waves created by the voice caused the diaphragm to vibrate in sympathy with it. As the diaphragm vibrated in the magnetic field, it caused fluctuations to occur in this field, which in turn caused small electrical currents to be induced in the coil. When this electrical signal was sent over a pair of wires to an identical device, the fluctuating currents had the opposite effect. That is, the small electric currents fluctuating in the coil caused fluctuations in the magnetic field, which in turn caused the diaphragm to vibrate and recreate the sound waves of the original voice. While the device was simple in principle, the arrangement of the various components and the interconnecting wire had a significant influence on the quality and intelligibility of the speech. The advantage of Bell's telephone was that no batteries were necessary for its operation. This was considered a benefit at that time, as batteries were considered a nuisance to the user. Preece's published paper included a diagram of Philipp Reis's and Bell's instruments that aided in the description.

Preece concluded his remarks with the caveats that Bell's telephone was limited in range and that the currents were weak and were susceptible to electrical interference from other lines. This led him to describe how Thomas Edison had sought to rectify these problems, modifying Reis's transmitter by using a small cylinder of plumbago in conjunction with the diaphragm. This acted as a resistor which varied its value in relation to the pressure exerted by a diaphragm. He also described Edison's novel and

Alexander Graham Bell's telephone in use; its weakness was that the transmitter was only good for short distances.

peculiar telephone receiver and showed a diagram of it. The lecture concluded with the remark that Edison's telephone was not yet in practical use, whereas Bell had hundreds of telephones in use in Boston, Providence, and New York.[25] Preece then introduced Bell, probably to thunderous applause, who also was a good orator and who went on to give an address and demonstration. He had located one telephone in the hall and another about a mile away. Sir William Thomson attended and participated in the demonstration.

Use of Bell's telephone often led to amusement or frustration as it required an interesting combination of movements that had to be synchronized with those of the party at the other end of the wire. Early models combined the transmitter and receiver in one unit, so after speaking into it one had to move it quickly up to the ear to hear the other party's response. Variety show comedians had a field day with the telephone, imitating two people either trying to talk at once or listen at the same time and then shouting into it "Hello," "Hello?" "Are you there?" "Where did you go?" "Nowhere, where did you go?" and so on. Later, separate instruments were used for speaking and listening.

Hughes was not in England when Preece gave this lecture. However, he came to the same conclusion that Edison had reached, namely that Bell's transmitter was the weak link.[26] In the early part of November, Hughes mulled over the problem and decided that in order to proceed with experiments he needed to obtain a pair of Bell's telephones.

Hughes's notebooks for this period read like a scientific detective story: he analyses the problem, reviews various lines of inquiry, selects a promising approach, performs extensive experiments to determine whether it is fruitful, makes a breakthrough, pursues it with vigor, brings it to practicality, and presents it to the scientific community.

His starting point was to revisit the work of the German experimenter Philipp Reis.[27] He was quite familiar with Reis's "Telephon," as he had used one in his demonstration to the Czar in Russia over ten years earlier in 1865.[28] He had this to say about his experiments with Reis's apparatus:[29]

> Prof. Philipp Reis, of Friedericksdorf, Frankfort-on-Main, sent to Russia his new telephone, with which I was enabled to transmit and receive perfectly all musical sounds and also a few spoken words, though these were rather uncertain, for at moments a word could be clearly heard and then from some unexplained cause no words were possible.

Reis had used a diaphragm that could operate a set of make-and-break electrical contacts. A sketch in Hughes's notebook depicts a similar set-up of a diaphragm with an adjustable contact resting against it.

However, he was aware that this arrangement was far from satisfactory because of the make-and-break nature of the electrical contacts, and decided that some form of continuous contact or material was necessary, and sketched in his notebook the waveform of a typical speech pattern converted into varying current (today such a waveform would be displayed on an oscilloscope).[30]

> Studies upon a Telephone—requisites 1st a variable strength of current in proportion to force of vibrations thus. This could be done by a varying resistance such as a contact in Glycerin or oil, but a metallic one composed of several small thin discs of tin or gold foil laid on one another to the required thickness, this would give a great resistance when not tightly pressed but when pressure was exerted by a diaphragm it would be greatly reduced as per experiments we have made 4 years since upon condensers.

Hughes was looking for a material that would directly convert sound waves (sonorous vibrations) into a corresponding varying electrical current. He reasoned that such a material or substance could exist, as other substances were known which translated one physical parameter into another; for example:

- Willoughby Smith had shown that the metal selenium varied its electrical resistance in response to light.
- Wire changes its electrical resistance when heated.
- Iron wire elongated microscopically when an electric current was passed through it.
- Switching on and off an electrical current to an electromagnet could be heard as a series of clicks (the magnetostriction effect).
- Two dissimilar metals in contact with each other produced an electrical current when heated.
- Sir William Thomson had shown that wire, when strained (for example when it was pulled) changed its resistance.

Hughes decided to pursue this last example as a starting point. He reasoned that a wire plucked and set in vibration would experience rapid variations in strain, and that these strains would cause changes in its electrical resistance.[31] To test this theory he made use of his musical background and came up with an experimental arrangement that looked similar to a bass violin or double bass. It consisted of a sounding box with a bridge in the center, over which he stretched a tight iron wire.

This apparatus did present a problem, though, which was how to measure the rapid changes in resistance. Up to that time electrical technology had revolved around DC voltages, which were static, slowly varying, or switched on or off. With the introduction of the telephone, however, the situation had changed, as it pushed technology into the realm of alternating voltages and into the spectrum of audio frequencies. Measuring instruments for these new signals did not exist, as galvanometers and relay recorders were far too slow in their responses. Hughes, however, recognized that the human ear was exceedingly sensitive to both amplitude and frequency, and that in combination with the telephone receiver, could be a very useful piece of test equipment. In fact, it enabled these parameters to be determined over a wide dynamic range for the first time. It was here that Hughes's background in music and his ability to determine a frequency and amplitude to a high degree of accuracy and repeatability were to be put to good use.

He called the telephone receiver in this apparatus a "phonoscope," and summed his thoughts on the device as follows:[32]

The introduction of the telephone has tended to develop our knowledge of acoustics with great rapidity. It offers to us an instrument of great delicacy for further research into the mysteries of acoustic phenomena. It detects the presence of currents of electricity that have hitherto only been suspected and it shows variations in the strengths of currents which no other instrument has ever indicated. It has led me to investigate the effect of sonorous vibrations upon the electrical behavior of matter.

Hughes experimented with a stretched wire with an electrical current running through it; when the wire broke it made a sound in the telephone receiver, and this gave him the idea to pursue the loose contact microphone.

To carry out his experiments with the stretched wire, he needed one of Bell's telephones to use as a detector; if there were any electrical perturbations, he should be able to hear them in the telephone. By November 24 he had managed to obtain a telephone on loan, and was then able to proceed with his experiment.[33] He set up the apparatus, which consisted of a battery, a telephone receiver, and the stretched wire, all connected in series. He then tried plucking the wire as well as speaking to it (to see if he could set it to vibrate), but was unable to detect any effect. He kept increasing the tension on the wire but was still unable to detect any sound in the telephone receiver until the wire broke. He described this important moment as follows:[34]

> The effect was but momentary, but invariably at the moment of breaking a peculiar "rush" or sound was heard. I then sought to imitate the condition of the wire at the moment of rupture by replacing the broken ends and pressing them together with constant and varying force by the application of weights. It was found that if the broken ends rested upon one another with a slight pressure of not more than one ounce to the square inch on the joints, sounds were distinctly reproduced although the effects were very imperfect.

It is fortunate that the experiment failed, because it was this failure that set him on the path of discovery. Hughes tried to reproduce the sound he had heard when the wire ruptured by pressing the broken ends back together, but heard only crackling noises in the telephone receiver. He then laid the wires on top of each other under slight pressure. This time he heard something different; the sounds were not distinct, but he was certain that sounds that were traveling through the air as acoustic vibrations were being converted into electrical signals that he could hear in the telephone receiver. This must have been an exciting moment for him, as this was exactly what he had been looking for: an acoustic to electrical converter.[35]

Hughes was a great experimentalist and had a gift for determining the best way to proceed. The broken wire would have been an annoyance to most experimenters, but he had heard the small noise when the wire broke, realized the potential, and experimented until he found a way to exploit that potential. Following up on the broken wire turned out to be crucial to discovering what he called the "loose contact" effect as a means of converting sound into an electrical signal.

Hughes next experimented with some parts that he had at hand, namely a few nails. These he arranged in a horizontal "H" and mounted them on a sounding board. Two were laid parallel to each other, with the third resting loosely on top of them, so that it did not make perfect electrical contact. He connected one battery terminal to one of the parallel nails, and the other battery terminal to the other parallel nail via the telephone receiver. When Hughes tapped on the sounding board, the loose contact with the upper nail varied its contact resistance, causing fluctuations in the current flowing through the receiver, which he could hear. He stated that he was able to hear the sound of large vibrations but not the finer inflections. He was able to improve the

Working with materials at hand, Hughes made one of the first loose contact microphones in what he called the "French nail experiment."

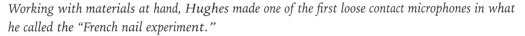

effect by adding fine metallic filings, a mixture of tin and zinc (white bronze), at the points of contact and declared that at this stage he was able to hear articulated speech. He called this his "French nail experiment." He observed that many conducting materials, mounted so as to be in slight contact, produced the same effect.

Hughes knew that at some point he would have to return the loaned Bell telephone receiver, so he spent some time making his own and seeing if he could improve on the performance of the original. Assembling this device would have been straightforward for him, as he had spent years experimenting with various configurations and arrangements of electromagnets in connection with his telegraph work. In fact he was able to take one of the polarized electromagnets he had used in his telegraph and mount an iron diaphragm in front of it. It is highly likely that he was able to improve on the sensitivity of Bell's receiver.[36]

Unlike Edison with his well-equipped and well-staffed invention laboratory, Hughes carried out his experiments by himself on a table spread with newspapers in his sitting room, constructing his apparatus from the most basic items and using copious amounts of sealing wax (the Victorian super glue) to hold the parts together.[37]

Having determined the basic principle by which his device would operate, he now focused on searching out and evaluating different materials, configurations, and contact arrangements to determine which produced a louder sound and better fidelity. To do so,

Hughes experimented with a variety of glass and quill tubes filled with metallic filings, carbon pieces, granules, and powder for his microphone, and would later use them in wireless detectors.

he made experiments with a closed loop circuit using three Daniell cells in series with the telephone receiver (phonoscope), and the material/loose contact he was evaluating.[38] He used a variety of sounds to test the device, such as scratching or tapping on the sounding board, and brushing it with a feather. To test its reproduction of speech he presumably had an assistant speak to the device.

He continued his research with the loose contact concept and experimented with a glass tube containing metallic filings which was sealed at both ends while under strain to keep the pressure constant.[39] He tried tin, zinc, and then bronze powder. Any metal appeared to produce results, provided the particles were small enough and that the material did not oxidize. For instance, he tried platinum and mercury and found that they gave excellent results, while lead soon exhibited high resistance due to its surface oxidization. This led him to investigate carbon, as its surface was free from oxidization. It was also a convenient material to work with as it could be easily made into small blocks, granules or powder, and it was cheap. He experimented with a glass tube two inches long by a quarter inch wide, packed with six pieces of charcoal.[40] He also experimented with packing carbon filings into quill sections, and with metalizing the charcoal by heating pieces made from willow and pine until they were white hot and plunging them into mercury so that it penetrated into the pores, which seemed to work well, as did charcoal impregnated with platinum-perchloride.[41]

Hughes, who had been described as "one who thinks with his hands," was making progress. He had settled on carbon as his preferred base material, and after experimenting with many mounting configurations, settled on two small blocks of carbon with indentations, with a third piece of carbon in the form of a rod or pencil supported between them, its ends having been shaped to fit loosely into the indentations of the blocks. The whole was then mounted on a sounding board. He showed this configuration in his notebook on January 4, 1878. Later he refined this into a vertical configuration, with a more lozenge-shaped vertical carbon pencil about one inch long by a quarter inch thick. By this time the device was ultra-sensitive, and he was able to hear a fingernail or feather brushing along the sounding board. He reported that speech was being clearly and distinctively reproduced, including its timbre.[42]

Next came his party trick: he took a jar with a fly in it and held the jar's mouth against the board, and when the fly alighted on the board its footsteps could be heard! The sound may not have been high fidelity but nevertheless there were clicks, clumps or scratches that were caused by the fly moving on the board. What Hughes had created was a sensitive sound magnifier—a microphone, although he did not use this term until later.

Hughes started to describe how the phenomenon was occurring:[43]

> It is quite evident that these effects are due to a difference of pressure at the different points of contact and they are dependent for the perfection of action upon the number of these points of contact. Thus an undulatory current would appear to be produced by infinite change in the number of fresh contacts.

In explaining the loose contact effect he took as his starting point the idea that when someone spoke in a room, it set the whole atmosphere into vibration. This atmosphere was composed of an infinite number of infinitely small molecules, all of which were in a state of vibration. When these sound waves, or molecules moving with the sound waves, impinged on the eardrum, they created the sensation of sound. However,

The material Hughes settled on for the microphone was carbon, as it was cheap, easy to work with, and did not corrode.

it was not only the eardrums that were affected, but also the walls, woodwork, windows, and so on—all would be trembling as they were acted on by the vibration of the molecules. This included the components that made up his loose contact device. He then asked himself how a sonorous wave could affect the body of a conductor so as to influence its electrical resistance, for it was this fluctuation in resistance that was causing the change in electrical current which could be heard in the telephone receiver. He gave the following explanation: if two separate conductors were joined by contact, the contact offered a certain electrical resistance. This resistance could be varied by increasing or decreasing the pressure, thus bringing more or fewer points into contact. If a constant pressure was applied to the contact, then when it was subject to sonorous vibrations, more or fewer points would come in contact in accordance with the movement due to sound waves.

He explained the effect diagrammatically using an illustration of a row of rubber balls all touching each other. If the pressure was increased on them, they squeezed together, and when the pressure was decreased, they expanded or elongated. In the former case the resistance would decrease as more of the surfaces came into contact, decreasing the resistance, while in the latter case the resistance would increase.[44]

While little was known about molecules at that period, they were invoked to explain various phenomena. Hughes was on the right track in suggesting that it was the multiple contact points that created the effect.

Hughes continued his experiments through February in an attempt to obtain consistent pieces of charcoal, as some conducted too well while others did not conduct at all: he was after a semiconductor. He constructed a small cantilever test apparatus so that he could evaluate samples under controlled conditions. In this apparatus he had two pieces of the test material, such as two pieces of charcoal, resting on each other, and with the cantilever he could adjust the pressure between them. It was this arrangement that he housed in a box and named his "speaking box." His notebooks indicate that he took two such boxes to the Submarine Telegraph Company in March for a demonstration for his friend Mr. Despointes and others.[45]

By April, Hughes felt confident enough to show his discovery to a wider audience, and specifically to William Preece of the Post Office. At the time Hughes knew Preece only through his association with the Society of Telegraph Engineers, and used a presentation of Preece's that he had attended as a pretext for contacting him, and sent Preece a letter congratulating him on the presentation.[46] He then told Preece that like many others he had been making experiments with the telephone, and that he had found some compounds that were sensitive to sound. He had enclosed the compound in a box and said it was louder than Bell's telephone.[47]

I am not yet prepared to tell the secret of this compound, because it is in too defective a state and as I have not much time for experiments I want to try and work it out quietly. In the meantime however it will perhaps be found out by many others—and if they do so from their own investigations it is perfectly fair—So at present the compound like

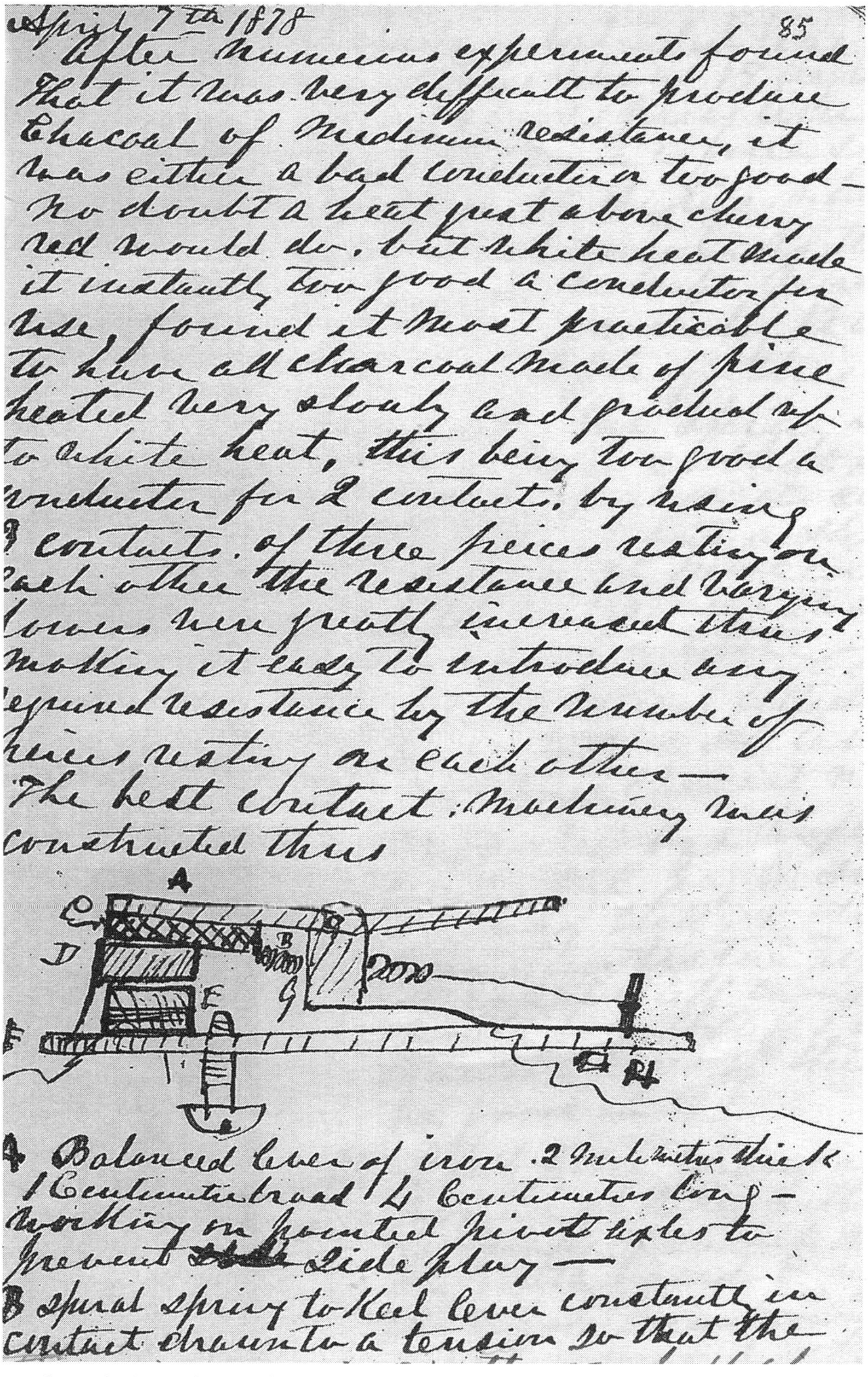

April 7th 1878

85

After numerous experiments found that it was very difficult to produce charcoal of medium resistance, it was either a bad conductor or too good — no doubt a heat just above cherry red would do, but white heat made it instantly too good a conductor for use, found it most practicable to have all charcoal made of pine heated very slowly and produced up to white heat, this being too good a conductor for 2 contacts. by using 3 contacts. of three pieces resting on each other the resistance and varying lowers were greatly increased thus making it easy to introduce any required resistance by the number of pieces resting on each other —
The best contact Machinery was constructed thus

A Balanced lever of iron .2 millimetre thick 1 centimetre broad 4 centimeter long — working on pointed pivot axles to prevent side side play —
B spiral spring to keep lever constantly in contact drawn to a tension so that the

Hughes's design in his notebook for the cantilever microphone; the realization of this design can be seen in the following illustration.

<u>Halloways pills</u> is a secret—but if you would like to see or hear the result I will bring a couple of speaking boxes to your office and you can try them.

Preece invited Hughes to show him what he had, and saw the "speaking boxes" for the first time on April 10, with Hughes keeping him guessing as to what he had created:[48]

Still they seemed very much astonished and tried by every means to find out the secret. Mr. Preece said he was never more impressed in his life....

Hughes wrote to Preece, thanking him for his kind attention and saying he had also shown the speaking boxes to a number of other scientific friends (Prof. Huxley, Prof. Locker, Mr. C.W. Cook, and Mr. P.F. Nursey), who visited his rooms in Great Portland Street—so that "the cat is now out of the bag."[49] Hughes suggested demonstrating the speaking boxes to the Society of Telegraph Engineers before the discovery was claimed by someone else, as he did want to ensure that he was recognized for it.[50]

...so that there is a wide field now open to inventors of Telephones, everyone can invent one for himself using a different material as transmitter and a different magnet as recepteur—"No home complete without its own invented Telephone."

Hughes did finally let them all in on the secret of the speaking boxes, and they must have been surprised when they saw how simple the device was.

Preece observed that the sounds produced were loud and did not interfere with each other, and that two people could talk at the same time without confusion, giving a duplex action. By this time Preece had experimented with Bell's telephone and knew some of the words that were a good test of performance; these were the sibilant sounds such as "s," "c," and "sh." It seems that Hughes's transmitter passed the test, as Preece

Hughes's most sensitive microphone was the cantilever arrangement; the audience at a demonstration at the Royal Society was amazed that the device enabled them to hear a fly walking.

said that the articulation was absolutely perfect, and that one of its peculiarities was the fact that all the sounds were faithfully reproduced.[51] Preece's use of the word "peculiarities" clearly indicates that other early telephones struggled to reproduce speech correctly: Hughes's was unusual in that it did this well.

Hughes and Preece were of similar age, in their 40s, and shared a Welsh kinship, both having roots in North Wales. Thus it was natural that a friendship should arise between them. Initially their correspondence had been quite formal, with Hughes addressing Preece as "Dear Sir." As the relationship warmed up, Hughes started to refer to him as "Dear Preece," and Preece responding with "My Dear Professor" and inviting him to his house "Gothic Lodge" in Wimbledon to dine and to discuss the paper he would present to the Society of Telegraph Engineers. Hughes decided to give a name to his speaking boxes and called them "microphones," first using the name in a letter to Preece. The name was appropriate, as people were already familiar with the microscope which magnified light, and Hughes's device magnified sound.[52]

The first public announcement of Hughes's discovery appeared in the *Times* of London on Tuesday April 30, 1878, under the title "Transmission of Sound."[53] An excited Preece dashed off a note which he sent to Hughes's residence:[54]

> My dear Hughes, Pray look at the Times this morning and you will see my paragraph in a very prominent position indeed immediately after the leading articles.

Hughes must have been delighted, and the article provided an extra incentive for him to complete his technical paper. It had been assumed that this would be read before the Society of Telegraph Engineers, and in a letter from Hughes to Preece written in early May there was some discussion of the issue, Hughes remarking:[55]

> Of course it is understood that you will read the paper—as you are a splendid speaker—and I anything but that.

It is interesting that Preece was to deliver the paper, and not Hughes: this was yet another coup for Preece. Hughes, though possibly not as charismatic a speaker as Preece, would not have been bashful, as he had performed as a musician before heads of state. Earlier in their correspondence, though, Hughes had indicated there was not so much to talk about, but many experiments to demonstrate.

Hughes's paper had been put on the agenda to be read before the Royal Society by his friend Prof. T.H. Huxley, secretary of the Society, who had seen an earlier demonstration of the microphone. It appears that the Royal Society was quicker off the mark than the Society of Telegraph Engineers, as his paper was read there first on May 9, by Huxley. As the Royal Society was one of the most prestigious scientific societies in Europe, this was certainly an honor for Hughes, particularly as he desired to become a member of the Society some day. His paper was titled "On the Action of Sonorous Vibrations in Varying the Force of an Electric Current."[56]

The paper described how he had carried out his experiments, his discovery of the loose contact, the French nail experiment, and the testing of various materials and combinations, through which he had arrived at his present carbon pencil arrangement. He suggested that the effect was taking place through molecular action and expounded his points-of-contact theory. Hughes referred to the various configurations of his microphone as "transmitters." He paid tribute to Reis and Bell as well as Edison, of which he had this to say:

> Edison and others have produced variations in the strengths of a constant current by causing the diaphragm to press directly upon some elastic conductor, such as carbon, spongy platinum &c., the varying pressure upon these materials varying the resistance of the circuit and consequently the strength of current flowing. Graham Bell and others have produced the same effect, by causing the vibrations of the diaphragm to vary the electromotive force in the circuit. It will be seen, however, in experiments made by myself, the diaphragm has been altogether discarded, resting as it does upon changes produced by molecular action, and that the variation in the strengths of currents flowing are produced simply and solely by the direct effect of the sonorous vibrations.

The point Hughes makes, that his microphone does not require a diaphragm, is an important part of his argument that his discovery is distinct from others', especially Edison's. He explains the mechanism at work:[57]

> I resolved this by the discovery that when an electric conducting matter in a divided state, either in the form of powder, filings, or surfaces, is put under slight pressure, far less than that which would produce cohesion and more than would allow it to be separated by sonorous vibrations, the following state of things occurs. The molecules at these surfaces being in a comparatively free state, although electrically joined, do themselves so arrange their form, their number in contact, or their pressure (by increase size of or orbit of revolution) that the increase and decrease of electrical resistance of the circuit is altered in a very remarkable manner, so much so as to be almost fabulous.

In his concluding remarks to the Royal Society, Hughes added:

> I do not desire to assert that there is anything in what I have brought forward that is superior to or equal to other transmitters used for telephony. It is as loud and far more sensitive than any I have yet heard.... I only wished to show that it is possible to transmit clear and intelligent articulated speech, and to render audible sounds which have hitherto been inaudible by the mere operation of sonorous vibrations upon the conducting power of matter. My warmest thanks are due to Mr. W.H. Preece, electrician to the Post Office, for his appreciation of importance of the facts I have stated, and for his kind counsel and aid in the preparation of this paper. I do not intend to take out a patent, as the facts I have mentioned belong more to the domain of discovery than invention.

No doubt inventors will ere long improve on the form and materials employed. I have already my reward in being allowed to submit my researches to the Royal Society.

This was the first demonstration in Britain of a working "microphone," a device that had a far wider application than just as a telephone transmitter. Not seeking a patent was a magnanimous gesture on Hughes's part, as it would probably have earned him handsome profits. However, he believed, as did his hero Michael Faraday, that discoveries should be available for the benefit of all.

His discovery of the microphone, and its superiority over Bell's telephone transmitter, had obviously caught Preece's attention, and Preece was no doubt considering it as a way to improve Bell's telephone. Alexander Graham Bell, who was not at the Royal Society presentation, soon learned of the sensation that Hughes's microphone had created, and wrote to him from his London residence:[58]

If it is not trespassing too much upon you I should like very much to have the opportunity of meeting you and learning something about your researches.

Hughes replied enthusiastically, considering it an honor to meet Bell. Bell confirmed the invitation in a letter and requested permission to bring along Sir William Thomson and Mr. Ellis.[59] Upon hearing that Hughes had had to make his own telephone receivers, Bell offered to lend him a couple of his good telephones. Bell also requested that he be allowed to refer to Hughes's research as well as exhibit his apparatus at a lecture he was to give at the Royal Institution in conjunction with one of their Friday lectures on "Speech."

At about this time Preece contacted Hughes indicating that he was convening a special general meeting of the Society of Telegraph Engineers for May 23 in order to bring Hughes's microphone discoveries before the members. Preece said that it would be a discourse on the connection between sound and electricity illustrated by Hughes's recent discoveries, and asked whether Hughes would be prepared to assist him by exhibiting his apparatus and making the experiments. There appears to have been some discussion between Hughes and Preece, with Hughes expressing some concern about his reputation with the telegraph engineers as well as over Bell and Edison. Preece reassured Hughes, saying:[60]

I am quite shocked at your expression about the TE [Telegraph Engineers] "I dont know much about them and they dont about me" [Oh!]
There is no man in the Telegraphic World who is more liked than DEH.
Your wishes shall be strictly attended to—Edison and Bell may go to H---
I would only use my old friend Hughes and d -- his eyes whoever wants to rob a poor man of his [illegible word].
Have nothing to do with Bell. He is a skunk.

These are rather strong words by Preece about Bell and Edison. The situation must have sorted itself out, as on May 23 Preece presented the paper on the microphone to the Society with Hughes's assistance.

By now, reports of Hughes's discovery had made it into the technical journals and started to appear in America; they came to the attention of Thomas Edison, who wrote to Preece concerning an article that he had seen in the journal *Nature*:[61]

> In Nature I see Hughes has discovered that some substances are sensitive to sound like selenium is to light—Evidently Mr. H don't read the papers that is nothing but my carbon telephone—he varies the resistance by disturbing the pressure that's all....

Edison, who had successfully experimented at improving Bell's telephone transmitter, had also pursued carbon materials, specifically plumbago, and had patented a transmitter that used this substance. When more articles appeared in the technical journals and in the press about Hughes and his microphone discovery, Edison was unable to contain himself any longer, and sent his infamous telegraph messages to William Preece and Sir William Thomson. He believed not only that he was the inventor of the device, but also that Preece, with whom he had been corresponding, had tipped off Hughes—thus allowing him to claim the invention. No doubt he felt confirmed in this belief when he read about Hughes's methodology and his exhaustive evaluation of many materials, especially semi-conducting materials: he must have seen the parallelism to his own research and thought that Hughes's efforts were derivative.

A review of Hughes's notebooks, his line of research, and his conclusions on how his microphone worked makes it difficult to believe that he stole or had knowledge of Edison's work during the period when he discovered the microphone. If he had, he surely would have investigated the properties of plumbago, but he did not, and in fact there is no record of him even considering plumbago. Instead he started by reviewing Reis's work and then progressed to his tensioned wire experiments, searching for a material that would translate one form of physical energy, sound, into another, an electrical current. It was this research that led him to the loose contact phenomenon and carbon. It is also worth noting that Hughes was never trying to fit his microphone components into a telephone mouthpiece as Edison was.

Hughes was not in England when Preece gave his lecture in Plymouth, in which he discussed Edison's work, and Hughes did not become friends with Preece until April of the following year—after he had discovered the microphone. Hughes was certainly aware of Edison's researches by May, as he mentions him in the paper he gave to the Royal Society. It is possible that Hughes read an account of Preece's Plymouth paper which was published in the journal *Nature*, which was widely read at the time, but there is no copy in his collected papers or any reference to it.

The goals and motives of these two experimentalists were very different. Edison was under contract to Western Union and his work was narrowly focused on the telephone and the replacement of Bell's transmitter so that it could transmit signals further and be less susceptible to interference. He was less concerned with science and more concerned with the practicalities of carbon and its variable resistance when inserted into an electrical circuit. When he applied his findings to the telephone or other devices he could protect those applications via patents. Hughes on the other hand was neither seeking nor required any financial rewards and did not contemplate patenting any of his discoveries. He was interested in the science and in understanding the principles involved so that he could explain them to the technical societies and publish them in the technical journals; he considered recognition to be his reward.

Hughes believed that his microphone worked on a principle totally different from Edison's, who said that his transmitter operated through the pressure applied to the plumbago button by a diaphragm. Hughes described his device as not requiring a diaphragm and working on the principle of the loose contact, in which the number of points of surface contact increased or decreased as a result of the sonorous vibrations. Hughes also pointed out that while carbon was the preferred material, his microphone could operate using a range of materials.

It should also be emphasized that Hughes was researching a device that had a broad range of applications: an amplifier of sound. It happened that one of these applications was as a telephone transmitter, although in its basic configuration it did not even look like one.

During his experiments Hughes discovered an interesting phenomenon whose importance was not recognized at the time: this was the feedback effect. What he experienced is recognized today as the penetrating screech from a public address system when a microphone and loudspeaker are placed too close together and the sounds from the speakers can couple back into the microphone.[62]

> I have recently made the following curious observation: A microphone on a resonant board is placed in a battery-circuit together with two telephones. When one of these is placed on a resonant board, a continuous sound will emanate from the other. The sound is started by the vibration which is imparted to the board when the telephone is placed on it; this impulse passing through the microphone, sets both telephone-discs in motion; and the instrument on the board, reacting through the microphone, causes a continues sound to be produced, which is permanent so long as the independent current of electricity is maintained through the microphone. It follows that the question of providing a *relay* for the human voice in telephony is thus solved.

What Hughes had discovered was positive feedback, which could have been adapted to create a rudimentary audio oscillator for testing telephone and telephone circuits, had its potential utility been recognized. As it was, discovery and understanding of the feedback effect would not come until 1926, when Harvey Fletcher of the Bell Laboratory analyzed positive feedback, and 1927, when Harold Steven Black, also of the Bell Laboratory, discovered negative feedback. Both effects are used extensively in electronic control circuits today.

The point Hughes made with regard to a relay for the human voice, however, was explored by Edwin Houston and Elihu Thomson in America. They had been attempting, without success, to make a telephone relay, that is, a device that could take the weak telephone voice signals of Bell's telephone and boost them so that they could either be more easily heard or passed to another telephone line. When they read about Hughes's carbon microphone they applied it to their problem and were immediately successful. This device consisted of a Bell receiver joined with a Hughes microphone: three small carbon pencils mounted in carbon blocks were attached directly to the receiver diaphragm. The device, an "amplifier," proved to be exceedingly sensitive.[63]

The second part of the story examines what prompted the Wizard of Menlo Park to make his accusations, his relationship with William Preece, and whether his accusations had any foundation. To follow this part of the story it is necessary to step back to April of 1877. This was when William Preece, Engineer to the Post Office, and H. C. Fischer were sent to the United States and Canada for two months to inspect the telegraph equipment, technology, practices, and operations of the various telegraph companies.[64]

Preece was five feet nine inches tall, squarely built with a large head, brown hair, a full beard and moustache, and luxuriant side-whiskers that merged into his beard. He looked the part of the English gentleman, complete with monocle. Preece had lost his wife a few years earlier and had been left with seven young children to bring up. With the help of one of his sisters, he was able to cope, but the loss of his wife had taken its toll, and he had lost some of his usual zest both for work and for participation in the various technical societies to which he belonged. However, a tour of Europe followed by the North American tour appeared to rekindle his interest in his work.[65]

In New York he attended a lecture on the telephone by Alexander Graham Bell. Impressed, and seeing the importance that the new device might have for the Post Office, he visited Bell a number of times during his stay in order to get a better understanding of the invention.

Preece also met Edison, seeing him for the first time when he sat in on a trial in New York City involving the "quadruplex telegraph," where Edison was on the witness stand.[66] Preece wrote in his diary with reference to Edison:[67]

> Orton told me in England of him "that young man has a vacuum where his conscience ought to be" and is known here as the professor of Duplicity.

Preece and Fischer visited Edison at Menlo Park on May 18, but Preece, in his diary, had little to say about what he saw. He wrote the comment, "an ingenious electrician—experimenting and examining apparatus."[68] At the time Edison was attempting to develop a telephone transmitter that would cure the problems that Bell's electromagneto transmitter exhibited, and also to circumvent his patents. Edison, who was under contract to the Western Union Telegraph Company, showed Preece the telephone tranmitter he was working on as well as his novel receiver, the electromotograph, and various other telegraph instruments.[69] Western Union by this time had become an industry giant and had a monopoly over the telegraph in the United States. The rest of Preece's diary entry was taken up with a description of the train journey to Menlo Park and the strange lunch Edison served them of raw ham.

Preece probably noted that it would be worth monitoring Edison's progress on his transmitter, since, if it were successful, it might make for a better telephone. Edison claimed that during Preece's visit he had made Preece his agent to represent his interests in England.[70]

Because Preece recognized the telephone as an important new technology, he paid a further visit to Bell at Boston in June, where Bell gave him a pair of telephones to take back to Britain. Preece and Fischer returned to New York City and on July 3 they visited the Western Union headquarters, where Edison was demonstrating one of his telegraph instruments called a recorder-repeater. The demonstration did not go well as the device had a number of problems.

Preece and Fischer departed New York on July 4 to return to Britain, and were shortly followed by Bell, who was going on his honeymoon, and also planned to promote his telephone while in Britain and on the Continent—a visit that ended up being an eighteen-month tour.

Once back in Britain, Preece presented his technical paper "On the Telephone" at the British Association meeting at Plymouth in August, with Bell in attendance.[71] In addition to describing Bell's telephone he also described Edison's work, but in less detail, saying that Edison had sought to rectify the weak signals of Bell's telephone by introducing a transmitter based on the variation of the resistance of plumbago. Plumbago was a form of carbon derived from lampblack, the residue left on the glass chimney of a kerosene lamp misadjusted to give a smoky yellow flame. Edison's transmitter consisted of a small cylinder of plumbago whose resistance varied with the pressure of the vibration of a diaphragm. The paper did not contain any diagram of this device. Edison had also invented a telephone receiver so as to stay clear of Bell's patent; this was called an electromotograph, but it was rather an impractical device. Preece only supplied a diagram of this device in the published version of his paper. The lecture was concluded with a remark that Edison's telephone was not yet in practical use.[72]

Preece was impressed with what Bell had to offer, as he was already producing telephones while Edison was still in the development phase, and recommended to Mr. R.S. Culley, Engineer-in-Chief of the Post Office, that the Post Office enter into an agreement with Bell for the use of his telephone, together with the rights to manufacture it. Culley did not appear to share Preece's enthusiasm for the telephone; he did give him the go-ahead to evaluate and conduct trials, but not for any procurement.

Edison started corresponding with Preece (his agent) on a regular basis, providing him with updates on his telephone progress. He had an additional motive for courting Preece, which was that up to that time, Edison was not widely known in Europe, and he wished to change this and be accepted by the European scientific community. Preece was well positioned to help him in this: he was a respected telegraph engineer, was well connected in the technical societies, and held an important title at the Post Office.

On September 3, in a letter to Preece, Edison apologized for not having sent him some telephones, but promised to send a pair in a week or two and said that they would cost about $3. He also provided Preece with an updated comparison between his and Bell's telephone (this comparison really relates to his transmitter, as he was using a Bell receiver):[73]

1. That the articulation of mine was far better.
2. That it was four times louder.
3. That there was no noise.
4. That it worked in every wire tried and but a few wires were found that Bell's could be worked on owing to the cross leakage sounds overpowered the talking.

This was good news for Preece, as it appeared that Edison was making progress on his transmitter which would hopefully solve the problem with Bell's telephone. Edison followed up with another letter on September 6 which contained more negative statements about Bell's telephone. On September 19 another letter from Edison arrived in which he indicated that he would send some telephones soon.

But by September 28, as no telephones had arrived, Preece wrote back to Edison saying that he was disappointed not to have received any of his telephones and urging him to send him at least the transmitter portion.[74] Preece appeared already to have one of Edison's receivers called an electromotograph (also called a musical telegraph instrument). In addition, Preece provided Edison with an update on Bell's progress in Britain. The instrument had problems with crossfire (he was referring to interference, as Bell was testing on subterranean telegraph wires coated with gutta percha, buried in dry pipe, certainly more of a challenge than overhead wires). Preece went on to say he did not want to do anything with Edison's instruments while Bell was there.

Preece followed up with a further letter on October 3 saying that he was glad that Edison had sent one of the speaking telephones, and if it did all that he said it did, then it would be a useful thing, and there should be no difficulty in working out satisfactory terms.[75]

Preece was unaware, however, that back in America Edison was making several significant alterations to his transmitter. As Edison had a number of assistants he was able to delegate some of this work and testing, which allowed him to work on several inventions simultaneously. His laboratory was a pretty impressive operation, and there was some merit to its nickname of the "invention factory." Even while he was working on the telephone transmitter, he was also working on other telegraph instruments, as well as a significant new invention, "the phonograph." This was a device that would record speech and then replay it.

It was at about this time that Hughes moved from Paris to London and started his researches into the microphone.

In November, Edison sent Preece yet another letter, promising to send the telephones, and mentioning that he had learned that Bell was now using two separate wires for his telephone, which had brought about an improvement (that is, two wires instead of one wire and an earth return).

As it seemed that Edison's telephone would soon be ready for commercial operation, the Western Union Telegraph Company decided to become more serious about the telephone and established the American Speaking Telephone Company to compete with the Bell Telephone Company, which had been established on July 9.

On November 25, Edison wrote to Preece saying that he was having difficulty making the telephones but still promised to send some.[76] In fact Edison had been struggling for some time to improve the quality of the signal from his telephone transmitter, particularly the reproduction of sibilant or hissing sounds, despite experimenting with several different mouth pieces. He had also tried different compounds in the transmitter, testing plumbago rubbed into wool, and then replacing the wool with a type of silk called fluff or floss silk. However, he found that the plumbago would shake out after use, and therefore tried silk with a thicker plumbago paste mixed with other compounds such as rubber, making them into discs. Finally he settled on pure lampblack compressed into a button with a heavy diaphragm pressing on it. It was also about this time that he introduced a further innovation by adding an induction coil (transformer) into his transmitter circuit to amplify the signal and provide a better match between the lower resistance of the plumbago and the telephone line. Thus his telephone transmitter consisted of the plumbago button connected in series with a battery and the primary winding of the induction coil. The secondary winding was connected to the telephone line and ground. It was this configuration that gave Edison's telephone transmitter superior performance over Bell's transmitter: it was able to transmit over longer distances, and because of its stronger signal, was less susceptible to line interference.

By December 24 Preece was desperate, having waited nearly six months without any sight of Edison's telephones. He had arranged to give a lecture at the Royal Institution and was depending on having Edison's telephone available. Preece was now pleading that he send them by the New Year.[77] It was at this time that Preece learned a possible reason for the delay, and understood that perhaps the telephone was not as high on Edison's priority list as he had assumed. An account of a new Edison invention appeared in the *English Mechanic* in December 1877 and later in the *Times* of London in January: this was the "phonograph."[78]

The New Year of 1878 came, and Edison sent a letter to Preece on February 11:[79]

> I suppose you think by this time I promise many things and send none—However, I have this day sent you by Austin Baldwin's Express an experimental phonograph suitable for lecture purposes.

He continued:

> About my speaking telephone, I shall send you a complete set soon and I think they will be satisfactory on your wires. The reason of my delay lies in the fact that I _must_ get something to work on wires that Bell's _will not_ and you know how difficult that is.

So, while Preece was waiting patiently for the telephones to show up, he found that Edison was instead sending him a different invention, the phonograph, for him to present to the various societies.[80] Edison evidently had no problem treating Preece as his agent, and it seemed that he interpreted this term in the broadest sense. He had already had Preece present his alternate telephone receiver, the electromotograph (musical telephone), and now he was expecting him to present his phonograph to the scientific community, thought it had nothing to do with the telegraph or telephone.

It was during February that a management change came about at the Post Office. R.S. Culley, the Engineer-in-Chief, retired, and William Preece was promoted to the position of Assistant Engineer-in-Chief, which gave him more authority to promote the telephone. Preece now took over the responsibility for engineering, testing, experimenting, and standardization. Preece and the Post Office had been working with Bell during this time, testing his telephones on the Post Office lines.[81] However, Bell was still struggling with both interference from other lines and the weakness of the signal, due to the inadequacy of its transmitter. It did not matter how loud one shouted into the transmitter, the signal was still weak, and Preece needed a solution to that problem: eventually, people would want to talk over longer distances than thirty miles. Given his new management position and his role as the promoter of the telephone for the Post Office, he was eager to have success with the device, and concerned about criticism if there were problems. This probably led him to keep more than one iron in the fire by working with Bell while monitoring Edison's progress.

Edison next sent Preece detailed instructions on how to operate the phonograph and how to install the metal foil on the rotating drum for recording. With regard to his telephone, he said that that he had no other agent in England except Preece. Then on March 15 Preece received a telegram from Edison which said:[82]

> Telephones great success Adams leaves for England Tuesday.

This was followed by a letter dated March 18 which declared:[83]

> At last Telephones I send you one of my assistants Jas Adams who you will perhaps remember, with apparatus and he has instructions to conduct whatever experiments you desire on BPO Telegraphs.... I think after full investigation that you will conclude that the Carbon Telephone is a great advance in the art.

While Edison appeared upbeat, he had actually just endured a three-month struggle against others within Western Union, such as George Phelps, to have his telephone adopted by the company.[84] It was during this same time that with the encouragement and support of William Orton as well as the assistance of Henry Bentley of the Philadelphia Local Telegraph Company, a Western Union affiliate, that Edison had been able to refine his instrument to make it ready for commercial use.[85] Western Union was now ready to go into business as they had Edison's superior telephone transmitter and the magneto receiver of Phelps. Edison was probably happy with the way things were now going and had an article published on his telephone transmitter in the *Washington Star* on April 19. He sent a copy to Preece, who received it in the mail towards the end of April.

In Britain, though, Preece was struggling with the slow progress Bell was making and the annoying situation with Edison, which only worsened when his man Adams failed to appear. It was at this low point for Preece that a sudden ray of light appeared. Hughes contacted him, telling him that he had a promising new device that was better than Bell's, and that he would like to show to him his "speaking box." Preece must have breathed a sigh of relief when on April 10 he saw Hughes's microphone, and confirmed that it did in fact work significantly better than Bell's.

In early May, Preece received another letter from Edison.[86] This letter implied that the first set of telephones which he had sent had problems, and that he was sending new ones. There was some mention of the salt air from the sea (possibly relating to some corrosion problems, as he was sending some new carbons in a sealed tin case). He asked Preece to tell Adams to write to him with details of the problem. Edison also asked Preece for help with his patent claims in England,[87] urging Preece to tell him what had to be disclosed in the patent claims. The letter continues:[88]

> I have been backward in asking you to spend your time looking after my interests because I could not see where you was to receive any consideration therefrom. If you will point out where I can reciprocate financially (outside of telegraph matters which you could have no interest). I will brush up sufficient "cheek" to ask you to assist me. Have you a private laboratory if not you ought to have one. Why not make jack the public pay for one when we do so much for him.

Edison was almost addressing Preece as his employee and seemed to be suggesting some sort of financial arrangement with him, even though Preece was a government official. Edison did not appear to have a problem with conflicts of interest, exhibiting a somewhat cavalier attitude towards the interests of his associates.[89]

Preece of course had neither seen Edison's elusive man, Adams, nor received any telephones. Light was shed on the mystery when a letter was sent to Edison from London by an associate, Mr. Gouraud, telling him that Adams was confined to bed with a severe attack of pleurisy, and that he would deliver the telephones to Preece himself.[90]

By this time, though, Preece had turned his attention to other matters, and had transferred his hopes for improving the telephone to the new discoveries of David Hughes, whom he was now advising and assisting in preparing a technical paper. On May 9 Hughes's microphone discovery was shared with the scientific community at the Royal Society meeting, and within weeks, his paper and related articles were published in the technical journals and in the popular press.

The Post Office finally received Edison's telephones in early May; however, the demonstration did not go well. David Hughes, in the company of many others, was present at the demonstration and described the apparatus and the results:[91]

> It consisted of an Edison transmitter, and an exact copy of Professor Bell's receiver, which he called an Edison receiver. The transmitter consisted of a diaphragm (of the same form and materials of Professor Bell's) pressing upon a button of carbon, the varying pressure of the diaphragm upon the carbon producing a varying current of electricity. It was complicated, required not only the use of batteries, but induction coils, and the results were inferior to those of Professor Bell's against which it was tried in my presence. The Edison receiver was identically the same as Professor Bell's the only difference being that the natural magnet was brought round so as to touch the diaphragm, in fact it was so transparent a device to infringe Bell's patent, that the Bell Company at once said they would not permit its use.

The test was conducted by Edison's man Mr. Adams, and if we can believe Hughes's account it was not a particularly successful test. Edison's transmitter could be easily disarranged, as is pointed out in the circular that accompanied Edison's transmitting boxes:[92]

> The carbon button of the Edison transmitter is delicate and liable to disarrangement from a slight jar. The instrument should therefore be transported with great care, and the box fastened to the wall before the transmitter is put in place.

Edison's copying Bell's receiver and claiming it as part of his telephone arrangement would never have been acceptable to the Post Office,[93] and when the transmitter did not perform as anticipated, it must have been the last straw for Preece. He had kept his end of the bargain, stepping up every time Edison had asked for help, even demonstrating his phonograph and working on his patents. But in the end, he must have been frustrated and disappointed at having put so much faith in him, only to end up almost a year later without a solution for improving the telephone.

Luckily for Preece, Hughes had appeared with his microphone which did work well. Hughes seemed to have a knack for being in the right place at the right time. As Hughes had stated, he did not intend to patent his microphone, but would provide the technology free to whoever wished to use it, including the Post Office. How could Preece lose? He immediately embraced Hughes.

By mid-May, reports of Hughes's discovery had started to appear in America and came to Edison's attention. He asked Preece to tell Adams to write and provide him with details as to what was wrong with his telephones, not bothering to inquire about poor Adams's health.[94] Then he commented on an article he had read in the journal *Nature* on Hughes's discovery of a substance sensitive to sound, saying that it was the same as his carbon telephone.

Preece replied to Edison's letter, beginning by speaking of Adams and his illness and then telling him:[95]

> It is unfortunate that he has been so unsuccessful with your telephone for the recent discoveries of Professor Hughes have thrown your telephone completely in the shade. Hughes' doings borders so closely upon yours that it difficult to distinguish between what you have done and what he has done. You were on the very threshold of a great discovery, in fact had it not been for the phonograph distracting your attention you must have anticipated what Hughes has done. You must have seen the papers and know exactly what he has done and therefore it is useless my going into the matter. Have not tried it practically and only seen his results which are certainly startling. I am going to bring them before the Society of Telegraph Engineers tomorrow night (May 23) and will send you a report as soon as it is printed. I am glad you have closed terms with [illegible, probably referring to Western Union] for Hughes having thrown his invention open to the world makes it rather awkward for patentees like yourself.

A few days later, Preece wrote a follow-up letter to Edison, telling him how Adams had been ill and about the lack of success with his telephones. He stated:[96]

> The fact is his heart is much diseased and the doctor says that any sudden shock or disappointment might be fatal to him. I have not liked to tell him much about the failure of the experiment for fear it might hurt him.

These letters took a couple of weeks to reach America, and when they arrived they caused an explosive reaction in Edison.

They suggest that Preece's patience with Edison had run out: he presumably saw that the way forward was to supplement Bell's telephone with Hughes's microphone. This seemed to be an ideal solution, especially as Hughes was providing the microphone for free. It can only be speculated that this was the purpose of a meeting that Preece arranged at his club between Hughes and the manager of the "Telephone Company Ltd."—Bell's newly formed company in England.[97]

The company had been formed after Bell's representative in Britain, Colonel Reynolds, had become disillusioned waiting for the government to procure the Bell telephone. Wanting to stay ahead of any competition, Reynolds had decided to promote the telephone to a group of capitalists, with the aim of setting up a private company. In March, he had Bell write a prospectus; this document was visionary, the promotion was successful, and the new company was formed.[98]

For some reason the company did not reach an agreement with Hughes, possibly due to the company's rocky start and management problems. There was also a movement in parliament to include the telephone under the Telegraph Act. Of course nationalizing the telephone service was the last thing the Bell Company wanted, and they were spending time lobbying against this proposal.[99]

Hughes's paper on the microphone was presented to the Society of Telegraph Engineers on May 23. Preece was the presenter and was assisted by Hughes. The fact that Preece presented Hughes's paper only further enraged Edison, as he had considered Preece to be his man. The paper was similar to the one previously given to the Royal Society; the apparatus was simply made and focused on the properties of the microphone. Preece, however, introduced Hughes in fairly glowing terms:[100]

> It is therefore to me, as I am sure it is to you a great gratification to have brought before us an invention which is the offspring of British soil. During the last few months the science of acoustics has made marvelous and rapid strides. First of all we had the telephone, which enabled us to transmit human speech to distances far beyond the reach of the ear and the eye. Then we had the phonograph, which enabled us to reproduce sounds uttered at any place at any time; and now we have that still more wonderful instrument, which not only enables us to hear sounds that would otherwise be inaudible, but also enables us to magnify sounds that are audible; in other words, the instrument which I shall have the pleasure of bringing before you to-night, is one that acts towards the ear in the same capacity as the microscope acts towards the eye.
>
> I may point out in the first instance, that the telephone and the phonograph depends essentially upon the fact—and a great fact it is—that the mere vibrations of a diaphragm can reproduce all the tones of the human voice.... But in this new instrument diaphragms are cast aside and we have direct conversion of sonorous vibrations or sound waves, into forms of electrical action.
>
> Now, if it had been the habit or the custom of this society to give papers and discussions delivered here sensational titles, I should have been inclined to call the few remarks I am going to make to-night, "A Philosopher Unearthed," Prof. Hughes is well known to us; he has been more or less associated with the society since its inception. Whenever he is in London he is amongst us. His instrument is well known to us as one of the most exquisite pieces of mechanism ever invented; and his works, though few, are known because they are sound. The chief characteristic of this philosopher whom I have succeeded in unearthing is his extreme modesty.

The following day Hughes wrote to Preece, congratulating him on his magnificent lecture on his (Hughes's) discovery.[101] "Bravo! Bravo it was *splendid*." While Preece talked, Hughes had carried out the demonstrations, including one that involved listening to a fly walking, "the flies putting on their best footing." Hughes must also have sung into his microphone as he received some applause for it.

The Duke of Argyle, who had been present, praised the presentation and made an interesting prediction, one that was to come true and would lead to one of the darker uses of the microphone—that of spying. He had this to say:[102]

> It was quite obvious they were in the presence of one of the most remarkable discoveries of the age which was full of discoveries, discoveries which were sure to be utilized in a thousand ways which at present they could not foresee. They were close to Downing-Street. If Professor Hughes were to place one of his little boxes in the chamber where the Cabinet sat, why, they should have the whole of the secrets of that assembly heard quite distinctly in the hall of the engineers (Laughter.) And if by any of those tricks which conjurors were aware of one of the boxes were only inserted into the pocket of his distinguished friend Count Schouvaloff, or Lord Salisbury, he had no doubt they should be in a possession of all those secrets which the whole of this country and of Europe desired to know.

The letter Preece had written to Edison a few weeks earlier finally arrived in America, and Edison, who was already agitated over articles appearing in the press about Hughes, became even more agitated when he read those tormenting comments:[103]

> — Hughes has thrown your telephone completely in the shade.
> — You were on the very threshold of a great discovery, in fact had it not been for the phonograph distracting your attention you must have anticipated what Hughes has done.

It must have been like waving a red flag in front of a bull! To make matters worse, Preece's letters were followed by the arrival of a couple of English technical journals with in-depth coverage of Hughes's discoveries.[104] First came the journal *Engineering* which contained the article "The Hughes Telephone" with its glowing review:[105]

> This marvelous apparatus, rough as it is…. is the most delicate instrument we have ever seen in the whole realm of physics. Not only is articulated speech taken up by it and transmitted by it to a distant station with great power and distinctness, but it detects and converts into loud noises the minutest possible vibrations.

The next issue of the same journal contained a reprint of Hughes's presentation to the Royal Society, complete with Hughes's concluding remark:[106]

My warmest thanks are due to Mr. W.H. Preece electrician to the Post Office, for his appreciation of the importance of the facts I have stated, and for his kind counsel and aid in the preparation of this paper.

Edison could not hold back his anger any longer. He saw what had transpired as a theft of his invention by Hughes with the complicity of Preece. His reaction was immediate: he fired off the two telegraph messages:[107]

To Preece London
I regard Hughes heat measurer and direct impact telephone as abuse of confidence I send you and others papers describing it also in letter about trouble in expansion telephones if you do not set things right I shall with details.
    Edison

To Sir Wm Thomson London
Direct impact carbon telephones sent Preece two months ago also publication and letters describing its use as heat measurer great abuse of confidence his part in Hughes matter I send you publications of proofs.
    From Edison

These messages were not particularly clear, and strangely Edison sent no message to Hughes, the person who he believed was taking credit for his invention. Part of the problem at this point was miscommunication. Edison's reference to the heat measurer came about through a reporter's misunderstanding, which resulted in a misleading article on what Hughes's device could do: in fact Hughes had no device like that described in the article. However, this article convinced Edison that Hughes had stolen his heat measurer as well as his microphone.[108]

Edison misunderstood the situation in Britain and reacted hastily; his subsequent actions only made matters worse. He could not understand how Preece had given up on him after waiting so long for the telephones, or how incapacitated and consequently ineffective Adams had been with his telephone in Britain. He seemed to think that everything had gone well and that the staff of the Post Office was as excited as people in America over the great improvement his telephones represented over Bell's. He believed that Preece had been his agent and had been looking out for his interests. So, when he started to read the reports in the press, he could only think there was some sort of conspiracy against him. His attitude is summed up in a letter to an associate, Henry Edmunds, in London:[109]

I am very much grieved at the Hughes article in the Engineering. That Mr. Preece should announce before the B.A. [i.e. the British Association's meeting in Plymouth] my discovery of the variation of resistance of carbon and other semi conductors by pressure and the same fact published and broadcast for over two years and within the past 6 months of the great success of my carbon telephone & Adams in England with the apparatus it is incomprehensible that the article should appear giving the credit to Hughes it is not <u>co invention</u> because after a thing is known all over the world for two years its sudden invention is clear stealing.... It is a notorious fact in this country that G.M. Phelps Supt. of the W U [Western Union] Tel shops was the inventor of the Hughes apparatus [referring to the Hughes printing telegraph] so it is only his second attempt... and then to have it stolen without comment especially in England where I want to stand well.

While Preece understood that Edison's and Hughes's discoveries were based on similar technology, Hughes had shown his to work and Edison had not. Preece's view can be seen in remarks he made when he delivered Hughes's paper to the Society of Telegraph Engineers:[110]

No one has ever been nearer a great discovery than Mr. Edison. His telephone is based on the variation of resistance due to pressure. He used carbon and finely divided matter, but he worked on the idea that the difference in pressure was produced by the vibrations of a diaphragm. Had he thrown away his diaphragm he would have forestalled Prof. Hughes in this respect, and found that the sonorous vibrations themselves produced the differences of pressure. The great secret of Prof. Hughes is that sonorous vibrations and electrical waves are to a certain extent synonymous.

When Preece received Edison's telegraph message he was puzzled, and it certainly generated some excitement when he sent a copy to Hughes with the comment:[111]

What do you think of the enclosed message from Edison? Is he mad?

Edison was in an impetuous mood and decided not to wait for a reply from London, but took his case directly to the American newspapers.[112] He claimed he, and not Hughes, was the inventor of the microphone and the heat measurer (tasimeter), and accused Preece of aiding and abetting Hughes and of divulging his (Edison's) secrets to Hughes. It was at this point that Edison decided to terminate Preece as his agent and to switch to Gouraud. He cabled Gouraud in London on June 1, urging him to "Take charge of my telephone in England."

Preece did not reply immediately to Edison's telegraph message, probably because he was taken aback by his attack and his decision to make the whole affair public. The matter quickly mushroomed into an international scientific scandal. Newspapers and journals were soon full of claims and counterclaims, opinions and letters.

Hughes wrote many letters to Preece over the next couple of weeks, repeatedly expressing his confidence in him:[113]

There is one splendid thing about you and that is you're a real warrior and can sniff the battle from afar—Edison will get more than his match if he speaks about you in the first and last place. You have truth and justice on your side and you are not the man to be frightened by a pop gun.

On June 24 Hughes again wrote to Preece, urging him to pen a rebuttal to the allegations Edison was heaping on him.[114] Hughes had received a package of American newspaper cuttings from his brother in Cincinnati, who was the editor of the journal *American Inventor*. His brother had written to the technical journals in America asking them to reserve judgment until Mr. Preece could be heard from, and suggested that Preece get in touch with the Associated Press agent in London to state his views. They also learned that Edison had sent copies of all his accusations and supporting publications to leading scientific men in Europe such as William Thomson, the Count du Moncel, Hermann von Helmholtz, and Werner Siemens.

Up to this time Preece had not divulged to Hughes the contents of the letter he had sent to Edison earlier in May, but now he came clean and showed him a copy. Hughes was far from pleased with the contents, as he wrote:[115]

> That was a most unfortunate letter you wrote Edison in which you say you saw so little difference between his and microphone that you can hardly tell which or where it is. If this was so and your opinion at that time, why did you not say so, for I could have most easily demonstrated at any time the vital and all important differences.

Hughes also seemed puzzled over the way Edison had portrayed Preece in the press as his "agent"—if Preece and Edison did have any arrangement, which is not entirely clear, certainly Hughes at any rate was not aware of it:

> He seems to speak as if you were simply his agent ignoring the high official position you so worthily occupy and which you have so long held long before he was heard of.

At the end of June, Hughes wrote an eight-page letter to Preece, stating that he had responded to Edison's charges and encouraging Preece to do the same, saying that his honor was at stake. He laid out several weak points in Edison's accusations, and offered affidavits confirming that Preece had not seen his (Hughes's) microphone until April, at a public meeting. Hughes also claimed that since his microphone had been made public:[116]

> From statistics I have made there are some 50,000 microphones already sold—one firm has sold 2000— (Halifax) —another from Paris writes several thousand. Say only 10,000 in all or 1000 or 100. How many has Edison Humbug in use or really sold in Europe. Echo answers None.

This was quite a claim and probably a wild guess; his point was that a number of manufacturers were already making microphones based on his technology. The reference to Halifax was no doubt to the microphones being produced by Louis John Crossley of Halifax, Yorkshire, England, which used four carbon pencils in a diamond pattern, and the reference to Paris was to those produced by Clément Ader, which used ten carbon pencils. There were advertisements in the press from several companies offering Hughes microphones for sale; an advertisement in *The English Mechanic* offered Hughes microphones for a price of 21 shillings. The journal *Engineering* carried articles with diagrams on how to construct a Hughes microphone in its May 10 issue. Hughes said he had already received many letters asking where his microphone could be purchased. A pamphlet by Hughes titled *The Microphone or Sound Magnifier* was published by the London Stereoscopic Company, and it described how one could use the microphone to "hear a fly walk and sometimes hear its cry, also the minutest sounds in nature never heard before."

Preece congratulated Hughes on his response to Edison, which had been published in the *Telegraph Journal*, July 1, 1878, pp. 266–268, as did representatives of the Telegraph and Civil Engineering Societies: he was told that his "letter reads beautifully in print." Preece said:[117]

> The fact is you and I have played such trump cards that Edison will find some bother to follow. Let Engineering [i.e. the journal *Engineering*] have its whack and then we can rest on our oars.

Preece did finally send out a rebuttal letter to the press, and on July 13 Hughes received a letter from Preece referring to a note he had received from Sir William Thomson. Preece commented:[118]

> Sir W. Thomson's note puzzles me very much. I cannot believe in it.... I have written him about it but he is on the sea somewhere. I certainly never showed how sound could be magnified at Plymouth. I merely explained the carbon telephone and what I said is in print. But in any case I think your letter and the Engineering article are conclusive.

It is assumed that the note he referred to is the one Sir William Thomson wrote to Preece back in June. The long delay between when Thomson wrote it and when Preece responded was probably due to the fact that Thomson was at sea, sailing on his yacht, during this period. The note was certainly not to the liking of Preece or Hughes, as it sided with Edison. In the note Thomson suggested that Preece write to Edison telling him that he had no idea of doing him an injustice, and went on to say:[119]

> He does I think deserve the first place in respect for the credit for the microphone on account of what you told me at Plymouth of what he had done which involved the essentials and some of the details of the affair very clearly I think. I should think Hughes has worked out what he had done so well quite independently.

It was at this point that Preece had a visit from Mr. Gouraud (now Edison's agent) whom he had met previously when they had demonstrated the phonograph. Preece told Hughes in a letter:[120]

I had a visit from a friend of Edison and have sent him away an altered being.

Some light is thrown on Gourard's perspective on this meeting by Gouraud's description of it in a letter to Edison. It was a meeting that Gouraud indicated Preece had requested, although it is not clear that he went away an "altered being" as Preece had declared:[121]

> I saw Preece at his request and he was anxious to convince me of your entire and as he expressed it "unaccountable error." He feels greatly grieved and confident that you will in the end see your mistake. He was anxious to convince me of his entire right in the question—I emphatically declared that I should take no sides in the question personally—I told him that you evidently felt that you had indisputable grounds for your suspicion and your charges and that you had taken measures to substantiate these and to document evidence which would be forwarded to your council here.—Upon this you would stand or fall. That it would be finally no question of opinion.
>
> I told Preece that there seemed some doubt as to Adams having received fair play— He repudiated the insinuation and declared that he had no interest whatsoever in any bodies telephone—nor would have—that no telephone yet seen Bells, Grays, or any bodies was practical or satisfactory—that he had publicly stated his opinion that yours was most likely to be practical. He is anxious to see yours and let me believe that every facility will be at your command in the Post Office.
>
> He read to me two letters from Hughes and one from Thomson which I thought you might like to see.

Gouraud made hand copies of Hughes's letters of April 8 and 30 as well as of Thomson's. These were Preece's evidence regarding when he first learned of and first saw Hughes's microphone. It is unclear why he gave him a copy of Thomson's letter, since he was dissatisfied with it, as he had stated to Hughes. Perhaps he was trying to appease Edison, as this letter was favorable to him. Gouraud sent the copies of the letters to Edison.

In mid-July, Sir William Thomson wrote to Hughes on his family crested notepaper with the heading "Yacht *Lalla Rookh*." The letter was written in Thomson's characteristic fluid hand, which led the reader to believe that his missives had been written at sea in a storm. He wrote about visiting Hughes in Portland Street to see his experiments on the microphone, and the various meetings at which Hughes had presented papers when he had been present:[122]

> I fully understood it then as a development of the principle of which I had heard of at the Brit. Ass. Meeting at Plymouth from W. Preece as having been discovered by Edison.

That variation of pressure produced in suitable materials variation enough of electrical resistance to magnify it, as it were by relay, telegraphic effects. From both Mr. Edison and your work having been brought forward by Mr. Preece I believe that there must be a complete understanding across all concerned as to the relations of priority and independent invention between you and Mr. Edison. I am exceedingly sorry to find that it is not so and I only wish I could do something to reconcile conflicting claims.

It is varying pressure and <u>nothing but varying pressure</u> that produces the results in your microphone and everything that I have seen of printed communications on the subject in "Nature" and several other journals which have been sent to me for which I am indebted to you and for some, I suppose to Mr. Edison confirms the opinion I entertained when I first heard of it in the latter part of your communication to the Royal Society of the microphone that it was a carrying out of the principles and practical method which Mr. Preece had told me of at Plymouth.

I was as was everyone who saw your experiments greatly charmed with what you shewed us and I have never for a moment doubted but that you worked out your results in a thoroughly genuine manner from what you heard of Edison's invention. I wrote to Sir H. Thompson and Mr. Preece and to Mr. Edison. I sent a copy of my letter to Sir H. Thompson to the same effect.

I hope and trust that two such thoroughly original and genuine men as you and Mr. Edison will come to a perfect understanding on a subject of such great scientific and general interest in which you have both worked so well.

Hughes replied to Thomson's letter, and Preece wrote to Hughes, congratulating him on it. Preece still believed that Thomson had misunderstood the situation:[123]

I think he must have confused what he said about Edison's "electro-motograph" with the "carbon telephone" at the Plymouth meeting he said he thought Edison deserves the first place based on what he heard at Plymouth but he never intended to magnify sound. It was also what I thought and you probably thought the same thing. I do not think so much of what Sir W. T. has said as you seem to. Cook puts it right in Engineering. I think we ought to let the matter rest for now until we see the support in America of what we have said.

Thomson, still yachting, wrote to Preece from Le Havre, France, at the end of July:[124]

I trust everyone will see there has been no intentional misappreciation of Edison on the part of you and Hughes or anyone else concerned; though as you will see from my letter to Hughes I do not think you have quite seen how [illegible word] is the principle on which Hughes worked with that described on Edison in your own Plymouth lecture. Hughes is clearly entitled to very high credit in the beautiful way in which he brought out the interesting results by the very principle appliances which he used.

Sir William Thomson was still aboard his yacht at Cowes on the Isle of Wight on July 30, where he was waiting for a replacement jib boom. Perhaps this delay gave him the opportunity to read about the situation more carefully and to contemplate the whole affair, as he seems to have reconsidered his position. He became less sympathetic towards Edison, who had kept up his barrage of allegations in the press. He wrote up his final judgment on the affair and sent a copy to Preece, Hughes, and Edison.[125] As Edison had elected to make his allegations public in the newspapers, Thomson must have felt obliged to respond in kind. He therefore sent his reply to the journal *Nature* as well as to the New York *Herald* and *Tribune*.

After the first few sentences, Thomson dispensed with the niceties and set about dressing down Edison, as a teacher might do to discipline one of his students. This was probably not what Edison had been expecting, and it must have been humiliating for him that this was happening in the public eye and at the hands of one of the pre-eminent scientists of the day. He chastised him for his attack on Preece and Hughes and for his charges of "piracy," "plagiarism," and "abuse of confidence," and said that these accusations were completely unfounded. He insisted that Preece had given a clear and thorough appreciation and description of Edison's carbon telephone at Plymouth. He continued:[126]

> The beautiful results shown since the beginning of the present year by Mr. Hughes with his microphone were described by himself in such a manner as to leave no doubt but that he had worked them out quite independently, and that he had not the slightest intention of appropriating any credit due to Mr. Edison. It does seem to me that the physical principle used by Edison in his carbon telephone and by Hughes in the microphone is one and the same and that it is the same as that used by M. Clerac of the French "Administration des Lignes Telegraphiques" in the "variable resistance carbon tubes" which he had given to Mr. Hughes and others for important practical applications as early as 1866, and that it depends entirely on the fact long time pointed out by Du Moncel that increase of pressure between two conductors in contact produce diminution of electrical resistance between them.
>
> I cannot but think that Mr. Edison will see that he has let himself be hurried into an injustice and that he will, therefore not rest until he retracts his accusations of bad faith publicly and amply as he made them. I remain sir, your obedient servant,
> William Thomson

Edison never did apologize to Hughes and Preece. The closest he came to explaining himself was in a letter to William Barrett in October, when Edison clarified what he meant by "abusing confidence":[127]

> I did not imply that he gave to Hughes any ideas, but that he had abused the confidence I placed in his promise that he would bring my carbon telephone before the authorities and societies there a result which I had hoped for and which I sent him one of my assis-

tants with telephones. I gave him every chance to explain the matters because in my first telegram which was widely published I said, "If you do not set the matter straight I shall with details." After waiting some time and receiving no reply I then wrote the letters. The hard words spoken came mainly from newspaper reporters.

Later in November Thomson wrote to Preece:[128]

I am sorry Edison has not written to you. I had some hope that he would do so in a handsome manly way. There is no doubt he is an exceedingly ingenious inventor and I should have thought that he had it in him to rise above the deleterious influence of the kind of puffing of which there has been so much.

By the end of the summer it seemed that Hughes, Preece, and Edison had had enough of the matter, although others continued with their letters, comments, and debate about the affair into 1879.

Edison took a break from his hectic laboratory schedule and escaped New Jersey for an expedition to Wyoming to view an eclipse. Unfortunately, his hasty accusations had stirred up so much ill will towards him in Britain and on the Continent that his reputation in Europe was damaged for some time, and thus the effect of his accusations was the opposite of what he had hoped for. It is unfortunate that he jumped to conclusions without considering the possibility that another scientist could simultaneously and independently be working on a technology similar to his own. When he did return to Menlo Park, he focused his attention on the incandescent electric light bulb.

William Preece emerged unscathed from the attack, one of the many that he would fend off during his lifetime. The telephone became a reality in Britain and helped to advance Preece's career. When the British telephone industry was nationalized, this significantly increased the role and size of the Post Office, and along with it, Preece's importance.

Hughes picked up his hat and dusted it off, feeling that he and Preece had been vindicated. In Europe, there was no doubt about who was the true inventor of the microphone. Hughes enjoyed traveling in the summer, usually looking up old friends on the Continent, and it seems that this summer was no exception, judging by the lack of entries in his notebook for this period. When he came back to London, he turned his attention to another technical problem that was holding back the telephone — research which led to yet more inventions and discoveries.

Hughes's discovery of the microphone is commemorated by an English Heritage Blue Plaque Historical Marker on the building at 94 Great Portland Street, London.

In conclusion, it is clear that Edison had patented his carbon transmitter prior to Hughes's discovery, but as Thomson and du Moncel pointed out, M. Clerac of France had shown that carbon exhibited a variable resistance under pressure before either Edison or Hughes, although neither was aware of his discovery. It appears that Hughes made his discovery independent of Edison, and that Preece did not divulge Edison's secrets to Hughes.

The work of Alexander Graham Bell, Thomas Edison, David Hughes, and many others helped to make the telephone industry a commercial success, although in the short term there were many more battles to be fought. Initially the technological path taken in Britain and on the Continent was different to some extent from that taken in America. Eventually, though, the various nations settled on a telephone receiver based on the electromagneto, and a transmitter based on carbon granules.[129]

SUBSEQUENT TELEPHONE DEVELOPMENTS IN EUROPE AND AMERICA

Bell had to return to America in November of 1878, just as Edison's associate was heading to England with Edison's carbon transmitter and their version of Bell's receiver. The Bell Company learned of this violation of its patent, threatened litigation, and put a stop to Edison's efforts. An urgent request was sent to Edison to find a way round Bell's patented receiver. This he did by trotting out his electromotograph receiver again and the "Edison Telephone Company of London" was formed the following year, in August of 1879. The electromotograph consisted of a chalk cylinder that had to be kept moist with the chemical potassium iodide. A stylus connected to a diaphragm rode on the cylinder as it was rotated by hand. As the fluctuating currents were received and passed through the stylus and cylinder, they caused more or less friction on the stylus, which transferred these mechanical modulations to the diaphragm of an earpiece. If the operator stopped turning or let the chalk dry out he or she would lose the conversation: the receiver was novel but not practical for the long term. It was, however, enough for the Edison Company to start up their telephone business with George Bernard Shaw as their front man.

The competition between the Bell and Edison companies heated up, with Bell installing its first British telephone exchange in August.

While these companies were growing, a large threat loomed over them in the form of the Post Office. The Post Office executives viewed the telephone as a form of the telegraph, and if this view was shown to be valid, then the telephone, like the telegraph before it, would be nationalized under the Telegraph Act of 1869. The Edison and Bell companies, anticipating the Post Office's appetite for all things connected by wires, decided to amalgamate in 1880 to better defend themselves (the companies had by this time already consolidated in America). The new company was called the United Telephone Company. They also bought the rights to the Crossley carbon transmitter, which was based on Hughes's microphone. Despite the British telephone companies' efforts to defend themselves, in December of 1880 they were swallowed

The interior of one of Clément Ader's telephones which used a Hughes microphone comprising of ten carbon rods (two are missing) from about 1880.

up by the Telegraph Act. Companies now had to obtain licenses to operate from the Post Office. It is widely believed that this nationalization held back the development and expansion of the telephone business in Britain for many years.

Hughes's carbon microphone technology was selected by a number of telephone companies. Louis John Crossley in Halifax, Yorkshire, constructed a telephone using a Hughes microphone which was used by the United Telephone Company and the Post Office, as well as by many overseas countries.[130]

Another new telephone company was the Gower-Bell Company (Gower had originally worked for Bell; however, this company was not associated with Bell). They had seized on the opportunity previously offered to Bell to use the Hughes microphone. Their design used a radial pattern of eight carbon pencils mounted on a sounding board together with a slightly modified Bell receiver. The company published a circular to help inform the public of the advantages of its system:[131]

There are broadly speaking four classes of telephones: 1. *The Original Telephone* of Mr. Bell; 2. *The Electro-Chemical Telephone* of Mr. Edison; 3. The *Gower-Bell Telephone* formed on the principle of the Bell telephone, but much more effective; 4. The *Gower-Bell Loud Speaking Telephone*, the latest and best form of instrument, being the combination of the microphone transmitter of Professor Hughes, F.R.S. with the Gower-Bell telephone as a receiver.

Other designs that incorporated Hughes's technology were those of Johnson, Swinton, and S. Thompson. Several manufactures on the Continent used Hughes's carbon microphone in their telephones: these included Clement Ader, d'Arsonval, de Jongh, and Mix and Genest. Hughes's carbon pencil based microphone continued in use until the end of the nineteenth century.

Hughes must have been especially proud when the first cross Channel telephone link went into service in 1892, connecting Paris and London by undersea telephone cable. At the London end, a Gower-Bell telephone was used, and at the Paris end one of Ader's telephones, both of which used Hughes carbon pencils in their microphones.

There were many modifications and refinements to the telephone over the years, and one of the more important of these refinements was based on Hughes's work on carbon in a finely divided state: this was the microphone devised by Henry Hunnings in September, 1878. He carried Hughes's experiments with carbon pieces and powder encapsulated in a glass tube one stage further by using carbon granules sandwiched between two metal discs. A microphone transmitter based on this technology eventually became the dominant telephone transmitter throughout the telephone industry. In the UK it was known as Post Office insert #13 microphone, and in America it was known as the "solid back" transmitter, and had been developed by Anthony White of the Bell Company. The carbon granule transmitter was in use for most of the twentieth century.

In America a much larger battle had occurred. After Bell had left for England in 1877, the promotion of his telephone in America was left to Thomas Watson, Thomas Sanders, and Theodore Vail. As the fledgling Bell Company struggled to secure financing, it offered to sell the Bell patents to Western Union for $100,000, an offer which William Orton, the president of Western Union, turned down. This decision would later cost him dearly.

Western Union, of course, dwarfed Bell in terms of assets, infrastructure, and rights of way for wires. Its superior position was solidified once Edison perfected his carbon transmitter, which operated in conjunction with an induction coil and a Phelps magneto receiver. To further bolster its position, the company hired Elisha Gray and Amos Dolbear. However, in September of 1878 the Bell Company brought suit in federal court in Boston against Western Union and its American Speaking Telephone Company for manufacturing and selling telephones covered by Bell's patents. David had decided to take on Goliath. It was the filing of this suit that drew Alexander Graham Bell back from London to America in November of 1878 to help in the prosecution.

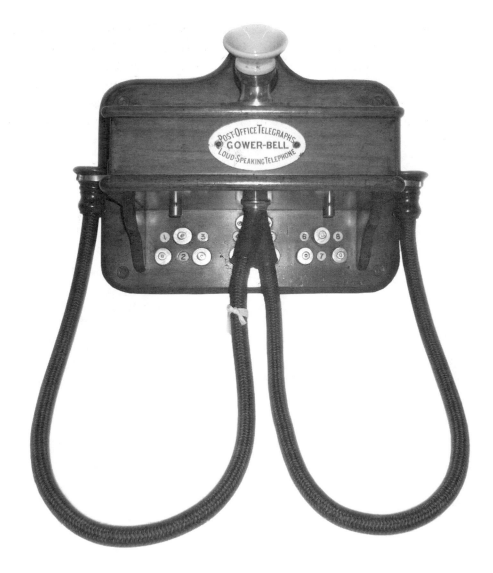

A telephone by Gower Bell, which became one of the major UK companies using Hughes's microphone.

The Bell Company had been persevering with Bell's original transmitter, although they knew that it was inferior to Edison's. To strengthen its position the company hired Emile Berliner, who had filed a telephone transmitter caveat several days before Edison had filed for his patent. Berliner's was not a carbon transmitter, but it was more ammunition in their arsenal to fight Western Union. Next they hired Francis Blake, who had studied Reis's and Hughes's transmitters and had put together a carbon transmitter of his own which was comparable to Edison's, but more robust. The proceedings generated a significant amount of testimony—the transcript ran to more than 600 pages by the time it all ended in November, 1879. The outcome was a negotiated settlement that pooled the patent rights of both groups, with one-fifth going to Western Union and four-fifths to the Bell Company. Western Union promised to stay out of the telephone business and Bell promised to stay out of the telegraph business. With this major victory, the Bell Company stock price shot up. Alexander Graham Bell continued to remain active in the telephone business, but also went on to pursue other interests.

8

A MATTER OF LIFE OR DEATH

WASHINGTON DC, JULY 2, 1881

President Garfield, in conversation with James Blain, his Secretary of State, strides into the waiting room of the Baltimore and Ohio Railroad station in Washington DC. From across the room, Charles Guiteau, a deranged lawyer, watches them enter and moves closer, pulling out a .44 Bulldog revolver which he levels and fires. The explosion of the gunshot shatters the calm in the room, and the President, grazed in the arm, jerks around to see where the shot came from. Bang! Another shot rings out, and the President crumples to the floor in agony. Charles Guiteau stands watching with his smoking revolver; he had avenged himself for being turned down for a government job.

The President was rushed back to the Executive Mansion (later known as the White House) by horse and carriage, conscious throughout the whole ordeal. One bullet had merely grazed him, but the other had lodged in his lower back, its precise location unknown. In the ensuing panic numerous doctors were summoned to the Executive Mansion to attend to the President. Each of them inspected the wound and attempted to locate the bullet using a variety of probes. Unsuccessful, they then probed with their fingers, but to no avail: the bullet could not be found, and they had no other techniques for locating it, as X-rays had not yet been discovered. As the days dragged on, the nation was eager for every scrap of news about their President. Garfield's condition was critical. Medical techniques at the time were rudimentary at best, and doctors did not know whether it was better to leave the bullet in place and let it become encysted, as had been done for many wounded soldiers during the Civil War, or to extract it. The doctors feared that if they could not locate the lead slug they would lose the President.

Many people offered their advice and suggestions. Professor Simon Newcomb in Washington suggested using a magnetic needle to determine the bullet's position by the retardation of its rotation when it was near the bullet. The *New York Tribune* was publishing letters under the heading "Letters from the People—The Bullet Fired by Guiteau." One of these letters was by Mr. George Hopkins of the journal *Scientific American*, who wrote "A suggestion that the Induction Balance be used to discover its position in the President's body." The induction balance he was referring to was an early form of metal detector that had been invented by Professor David Edward Hughes a few years earlier. Hopkins stated in his letter that he owned one of these devices and had already carried out feasibility experiments. He referred to the induction balance as a most sensitive instrument for detecting the presence of metal, and suggested that a modified form of the device could easily be applied with reasonable expectations of success as a painless and harmless means of locating the bullet.

The tragic shooting of President Garfield on July 2, 1881, just some months after his inauguration.

Hopkins contacted the President's Private Secretary, Mr. J. Stanley Brown, offering to send him the Hughes device, which he subsequently did. Hopkins, however, was not the only person who had thought of this idea: it also occurred to Alexander Graham Bell, who was already familiar with Hughes's metal detector. Bell, of course, had met Hughes when he had been in Britain promoting his telephone. Since returning to America he had learned of Hughes's device, which had been widely written about in the technical journals.

Bell had been intrigued by what he read about the instrument, especially as Hughes had once again made use of one of his (Bell's) telephone receivers as part of the apparatus. He wrote to Hughes, saying that he intended to perform tests with the device and that he would send him further details. Bell constructed one of the devices and experimented with it, telling Hughes:[1]

Your Induction Balance seems to be a very valuable contribution to Science.

When Bell learned of President Garfield's precarious state Hughes's metal detector immediately came to mind, and he recommenced his earlier experiments with a view to determining whether he could be of some assistance. Bell was in Boston at the time, and decided to return to his laboratory in Washington with Mr. Charles Sumner Tainter, his assistant. Upon his arrival he learned that George Hopkins had already sent his Hughes induction balance to the Executive Mansion. Bell contacted J. Stanley Brown to offer his assistance; Brown encouraged him to pursue this approach with all haste and gave him the induction balance so that he could conduct experiments with it. Bell immediately got to work, thinking about what would be required to modify the instrument from its laboratory version to a tool for searching for a bullet in a human body. It was at this point that he decided to seek advice from the inventor himself. He sent a telegraph message to Hughes in England, and to ensure that the message was delivered quickly, he sent it via William Preece, chief electrician of the Post Office.[2]

THE ANGLO-AMERICAN TELEGRAPH COMPANY LIMITED
ATLANTIC CABLE MESSAGE

July 16 1881

To Preece Lon

Can Hughes suggest form of induction balance to locate leaden bullet in President if so cable at my expense.

Graham Bell

Upon receiving the telegram, Hughes, recognizing the urgency of the situation, immediately carried out several experiments to determine the configurations and modifications necessary to adapt his induction balance to this new task. He put the information and sketches into a letter to Bell, and Preece telegraphed back a reply:[3]

GENERAL POST OFFICE, LONDON, ENGLAND. 19 July 1881

My Dear Bell: The enclosed very interesting letter from Hughes will enable you to make some experiments, which I trust will result in success.

Yours sincerely
W.H. PREECE

Hughes's induction balance/metal detector was now involved in a life or death struggle. It was several days before Bell received Hughes's letter with the recommendations and sketches.[4]

Hughes's induction balance was a highly sensitive device used to detect very small quantities of metal, or differences between metals or their alloys. The sample was normally examined by being placed in the center of a small coil of wire which formed part of the sensing element of the induction balance; usually the device sat atop a laboratory bench. Neither this method of sensing nor this method of support was suitable for locating a piece of metal external to the device and buried deep within a human body. Hughes nonetheless provided suggestions as to how this might be accomplished and how the sensing coils could be connected for remote sensing, although he warned that lead was more difficult to detect than say copper. If Hughes's device could be modified to perform this new task, then it would offer an alternative to the probe and knife and a way to spare the patient painful and dangerous procedures. This would be the first safe and non-intrusive procedure for locating a metal object within a patient, as the magnetic induction field had no detrimental effect.

The onus now fell on Bell to quickly modify Hughes's apparatus so that it could detect the bullet. He started with Hughes's basic configuration which consisted of two sets of identical coils connected so as to cancel out each other's magnetic fields. Introducing a small piece of metal into one of the coils unbalanced this equilibrium, resulting in a signal that could be heard in a telephone receiver. One set of coils was energized by a battery which was pulsed by an interrupter (rheotome). The other set of coils was coupled to the first set electromagnetically and was also connected to the telephone receiver.

Bell, together with his assistant Sumner Tainter, worked furiously, as there was no way to know how much longer the President could hold out. They constructed the necessary new components and wound the coils of wire to form the sensing probe. They connected an electrical buzzer interrupter to provide the test signal, and assembled these with a battery and a telephone receiver. They tested the metal detector by putting bullets in their mouths and fists and under their armpits; and by firing bullets into wooden boards to flatten them and then inserting them into bags of wet bran and joints of meat, to simulate the characteristics of the human body. The sensing coil was waved over the area where the bullet was buried and the invisible pulsing electromagnetic waves penetrated the surrounding material. If they encountered the metal bullet, the waves were disturbed, the sensing coil detected it, and Bell heard a signal in his

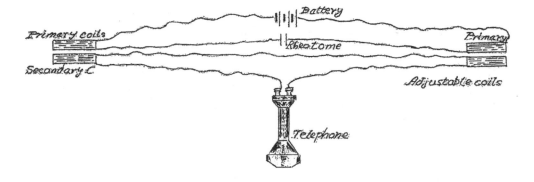

Now, suppose we take coil A and move it over a body with a bullet, thus:

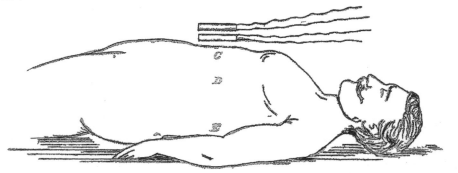

Hughes's instructions to Bell on how to best to adapt his induction balance to locate the bullet.

telephone receiver. The first experiments showed some promise, and by experimenting with coils in a coaxial configuration and varying the number of battery cells, they were able to work up to detecting a bullet four centimeters away.

Encouraged by this result, and cognizant of the urgency of the situation, Bell decided not to waste any more time but to make an attempt to locate the bullet in the President right away. He was ushered into the Executive Mansion and into the President's bedroom. Bell saw a President who only three months earlier had been hale and hearty as he took the oath of office now lying on his bed in a most distressing state. Bell was saddened by his paleness and somewhat taken aback by the wound when the President turned on his side for Bell to access his back. The wound had by now been enlarged to a length of several inches by the many physicians' probing fingers and incisions made in order to drain the wound.

Bell set up his apparatus, the connecting wires trailing over the President's body while the President watched apprehensively. Bell waved the sensing coil back and forth over the area of the wound, listening intently to the telephone receiver for the tell-tale signal that would indicate that he had located the lead bullet. The physicians looked on, skeptical of this non-invasive contraption. In the end the test was unsuccessful.

Bell, dejected and discouraged, returned to the Volta Laboratory on Connecticut Avenue, the sweltering heat of that July only adding to his misery.[5]

It was the horse drawn era and the city, in Bell's own phrase, swarmed with flies and smelled like a stable. A warm malarial wind blew from the undrained Potomac swamps below the White House, and the President was moved from his southern sickroom to a northwest exposure. Cold air was pumped up from the basement through the hot air registers.

While connecting his equipment in the laboratory, Bell realized he had made an error in connecting the wires at the Executive Mansion, and that this was the probable cause of the failure. Time was ticking by for the ailing President, and his condition remained grave. So, with renewed energy, Bell worked ceaselessly to improve the sensitivity of the equipment.

Bell, surrounded by anxious and skeptical doctors, uses the induction balance to try to locate

They were now using a motor driven interrupter whose speed could be increased up to 600 interruptions per second. They settled on 100 as the optimum. Bell had also found that a condenser (capacitor) added across the contactor seemed to give better results. In addition, he had found that the sensing coils were more effective when they were overlapping or eccentrically arranged. With this configuration they were able to detect metal at a distance of up to thirteen centimeters (five inches).

At the end of July, Bell wrote to Dr. Bliss, the attending physician. He said that experiments in a simulated body had given "brilliant promise of success" in detecting a flattened bullet at a depth of three inches, with the possibility of detecting it at a depth of up to five inches. Bell returned to the White House with the country watching and waiting, hoping for him to succeed. Another attempt was made to locate the bullet. The White House posted an official bulletin: "The test is successful." "The wonderful bullet seeker" was effusively praised in the newspapers. However, the experiment had not been successful, and the results were inconclusive.

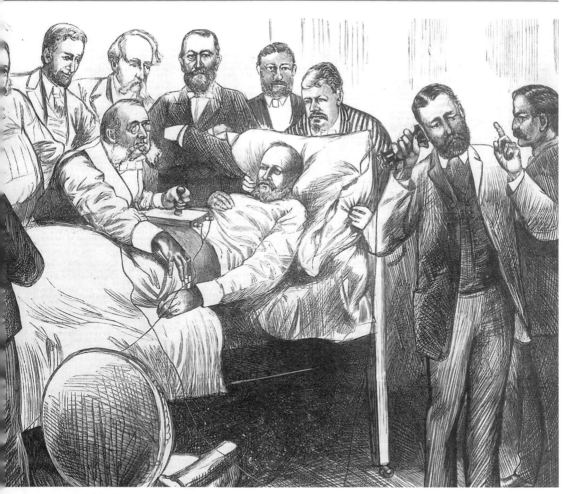

the lead bullet in President Garfield.

Bell once more returned to the laboratory, believing the device was a failure. Or was it? He had been puzzled by a faint buzzing sound he had heard while searching for the bullet over a wide area.[6] On a hunch, he returned to the White House to ask whether all of the metal had been removed from the President's bed. Upon inspection, it was found that underneath the horsehair mattress was another mattress composed of steel wires and springs (a relatively new invention). The presence of such a large amount of metal in relatively close proximity could have interfered with the sensitive induction balance—or perhaps the bullet was just too deeply buried.[7] The inability of the apparatus to find the bullet provided the skeptical White House physicians with ammunition to criticize Bell's involvement and ridicule him. This reaction was unfortunate and misguided, as Bell had worked ceaselessly with the best of intentions. Bell was unable to make any further tests before the President died on September 19. The nation mourned.

The sad irony of the situation was that the President's death was probably due not to the bullet itself, but rather to an infection caused by the probing of the wound by the unsanitary fingers of the many physicians. It is difficult to believe that the physicians were so ignorant or cavalier about the use of antiseptics and the importance of cleanliness, particularly in the case of such a high-profile patient. Over ten years earlier Joseph Lister had published articles on the need for physicians to use carbolic acid as an antiseptic for hands, instruments, incisions and dressings.

Charles Guiteau, the assassin, was put on trial, and in his defense suggested that the doctors should be on trial rather than him. He was sentenced to death and hanged on June 30, 1882.

As for Hughes's induction balance/ metal detector, Bell and Tainter went on to demonstrate its effectiveness by locating bullets embedded in Civil War veterans, thus vindicating both their devoted effort and the equipment. Hughes also demonstrated it and showed that it could locate a needle in William Preece's daughter's finger, as well as a metal fragment in a doubting Elisha Gray's finger.

Hughes's device was a contribution to non-invasive medical diagnostic techniques that was eventually superseded by X-rays at the end of the 1800s. Today, metal detectors are in widespread use in applications ranging from the casual, such as scanning beaches for buried treasure, to the more serious, such as land mine detection and security at airports and other high-risk facilities.

<hr>

Despite their best efforts, Bell and Hughes were unable to prevent the tragic death of President Garfield, and both men, saddened, returned to their experiments. This was an age in which scientists enjoyed an advantage that few have today. They had time to think, to share their discoveries, to experiment, and to pursue whatever intrigued them. They had a broad range of knowledge and interests and were free from the modern shackles of funding which is limited to specific projects.

In the case of Hughes, when one looks at his life and considers all of his inventions and discoveries in order, it is tempting to think that he had a plan as to where all his countless hours of research and experimentation would lead him, for his inventions and discoveries seem to fit together like the pieces of a jigsaw puzzle. This chapter deals with his induction balance, while previous chapters have dealt with Hughes's telegraph, microphone, and his innovative use of the telephone receiver. Considered separately, these devices do not seem closely related, but in fact they contained the elements that together would lead Hughes to his greatest discovery, that of wireless waves.

At this time of course Hughes had no idea where the sum of his inventions would lead him—he was focused on the individual pieces of this jigsaw puzzle. There were many paths he could have taken in his experimentation, but he had a gift for taking the one that led to important new discoveries.

In this chapter we will see how Hughes added one more piece to the puzzle. In 1878 upon returning to London after his summer vacation, and with the microphone affair behind him, Hughes undertook research on a growing problem that had been created by the very success of the telegraph system, and which now threatened the growth of the telephone system. This was the unglamorous problem of electrical interference, which occurred when a telegraph message on one telegraph line showed up on an adjacent line, or could be plainly heard on a telephone. Hughes's investigation of this problem led him to discover ways to suppress it, which led him to the induction balance or metal detector described above, and later to another invention adopted by the medical profession, the audiometer, or as Hughes called it, the sonometer.

The interference problem had been getting worse as more and more telegraph lines came into operation and the volume of signals had increased: the hundreds of wires crowded together on the many cross arms of telegraph poles were a prime source of interference. Interference was bad for business as it led to errors in messages and entailed "send again" requests. Too many of these, of course, cut down on the number of paying messages that could be sent, and thus ate into profits.

Telephone conversations suffered from clicks, pops, and rushing noises that were not only an annoyance to the user but threatened to limit the adoption of the instrument. These noises were mostly caused by electrical interference from telegraph systems. When the telephone was introduced, it was treated as an offshoot of the telegraph, as its name "the talking telegraph" implied. Thus many practices of the telegraph industry were adopted by the telephone industry. Telephone systems used a single iron wire with an earth return, just like telegraph systems, to carry the signal. Economically, this made sense, but this practice, along with that of running phone lines in close proximity to telegraph lines, or in some cases of switching an existing telegraph wire for use by the telephone, caused many problems. Telegraph systems such as the Morse systems relied on robust electrical pulses for successful transmission and reception, whereas the telephone relied on more delicate analog signals whose amplitude and frequency had to be preserved while they traversed the telephone lines. Of course at the time, the science of speech transmission was in its infancy. In 1879 the problems with telephone systems were described as follows:[8]

No wonder there was electrical interference! A typical cityscape during the heyday of the telegraph and growth of the telephone.

It is found next to impossible to work the instrument (*the telephone*) for business purposes in many places during business hours by reason of induced currents produced in its conductors by the interference of neighboring lines conveying telegraphic messages.

Or, in the eloquent Victorian prose of the era:[9]

The effect of these induced currents on a very sensitive receiving instrument, such as the speaking telephone, is to perturb its signal causing a confused clamor of sounds which quite smothers up the small voice of the instrument.

Hughes had started to investigate the telegraph interference problem several years earlier in 1868, at the request of the French Telegraph Administration. Now he took up the problem again.

In the fall of 1878 Hughes may be pictured sitting at his table near the window in his house on Great Portland Street, with newspapers spread about to catch the inevitable dribbles of the sealing wax that he used so profusely, probably smoking a French cigarette, with the smoke slowly curling up towards the ceiling.

Hughes started his investigation into the interference problem (or as he liked to call it, the lateral voltaic induction problem) by setting up a replica of a typical section of telegraph line. He did this by stretching out two twenty-foot lengths of wire parallel to each other. However, he soon found that these were not long enough to reproduce typical real-world interference, where telegraph lines were many miles in length. So he decided to simulate long telegraph wires using two parallel coils, each consisting of 100 yards of wire. These not only provided additional length but also served to concentrate the interference effect, whose strength he could vary by moving the coils closer or further away from each other or by changing the angle that they made with each other. To simulate the interfering signal (there were no oscillators or signal generators at that time) he used a wind-up mechanical clock that had a loud tick and mounted one of his microphones next to it, powered by a battery consisting of three Daniell cells. This provided a steady stream of repetitive electrical pulses for test purposes. He connected this signal up to one of the coils and a telephone receiver to the other.

He had previously expounded on the fact that the telephone receiver, when used in conjunction with the human ear, proved to be a formidable detection device. Up until that time, there had not been a need or a satisfactory method of detecting and quantifying the amplitude or frequency of repetitive signals.[10] He experimented by moving the coils closer or farther away from each other to increase or decrease the magnetic coupling or interference effect. He also experimented by reversing the connections to one of the coils, which eliminated the interference altogether. This was because the signal in one coil and the induced signal in the second coil were equal and opposite, and canceled each other out. He thus had a method that could be applied on one telegraph line to suppress the interference from an adjacent line, but his goal was to provide protection for multiple lines, not just one.

He expanded his experiments to simulate additional telegraph lines by making use of four coils which he could connect in various combinations. He also experimented by introducing magnets and metal into the core of the coils. On the basis of these experiments he was able to provide a solution for eliminating the interference between multiple telegraph lines, as well as between telegraph lines and telephone lines. His experimental apparatus had now taken on the form of two interconnected coils which together represented a long telegraph line. Parallel to these was another identical set, representing a second telegraph line. He used his combination of clock, microphone, and battery, which provided a series of electrical pulses, to simulate a telegraph signal on one of the lines, while on the other line he used his telephone receiver to monitor the level of interference. To suppress this interference it was necessary to send equal and opposite electrical signals on the two lines. To accomplish this he inserted into each of the lines (at the transmitter end) a small copper wire coil. These coils were mounted on a common wooden dowel and so were all coupled together through their electromagnetic fields so as to form a transformer. Each coil in the lines that were to be suppressed was connected in reverse polarity.

The number of turns of copper wire on each of these coils was in proportion to the length of the telegraph wires to which they would be attached, for example, 20 yards of wire on the coil for each 100 miles of telegraph wire. This made the level of interference similar to that expected on the telegraph line. Since they were mounted on a common

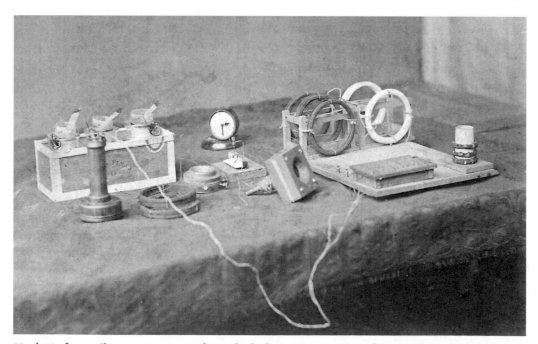

Hughes's four-coil apparatus to study methods for suppressing interference. Shown are the battery, clock/microphone signal generator, telephone receivers, coils for simulating the telegraph or telephone lines, and the suppression coils.

spool the coils could be slid closer or further away from each other to change their electromagnetic coupling and hence fine tune the interference suppression.[11]

Hughes's method of suppressing interference was as follows. Consider two telegraph lines, one identified as the primary line and the other as the secondary. A telegraph message (consisting of a series of electrical pulses) passing down the primary line would induce interfering pulses in the secondary line. Each of these lines had an interference suppression coil in series with it, inserted at the transmitting end. These two coils were coupled together on a common spool. As previously mentioned, the characteristics of these coils were arranged to be in proportion to the telegraph line length and their separation from each other. The polarity of the coil attached to the secondary line was reversed, so that it would send into the line pulses of equal voltage and opposite polarity to the interfering pulses, thus canceling them out. This scheme could be expanded to accommodate several lines, and could also be applied to telephone lines, by the addition of more suppression coils. In practice, as any of the lines could be acting as the primary it was necessary to initially have all of the coils connected with the same polarity, but with the ability to reverse the connections on the coil associated with the transmitting line.[12]

Hughes presented his results to the Society of Telegraph Engineers in London on March 12, 1879.[13] The technical paper also provided other solutions to combat interference on the telephone lines. He stated that using a separate pair of wires which were twisted together for each telephone circuit (versus the then-current practice of using one wire and earth return) would eliminate interference. At the time, however, using two wires was considered an extra and unnecessary expense. He indicated that the same protection could be obtained for a pole-mounted pair of wires by installing them so that they were twisted about each other at one turn per mile. This solution was eventually adopted, along with the switch to twisted copper wire for telephone circuits, and it became standard practice for telephone landlines. Another method Hughes devised to reduce interference was to use shielded wire, that is, a central wire surrounded by insulation which was surrounded by a second conductor which was used as the return: this was the forerunner of coaxial cable. Coaxial cable, however, had to wait many years before its potential was realized in more demanding applications.

It took a while for old habits to change, but eventually Hughes's methods were adopted and reports on their success started to appear in the technical journals. The Great Northern Telegraph Company wrote about the use of "Hughes Induction Compensators" on their telegraph lines and how successful they were.[14] The adoption of twin copper wires for telephone use, however, was slow; a report on their use by the Post Office and the New Telephone Company did not appear in the papers until 1892.[15]

The results of Hughes's research were presented to technical societies and recorded in technical journals. As he pointed out, his objective was not to present any new instruments or patent any of the technology, but to discuss the problem of interference generally. He was not claiming any invention, and gave credit to those who had done similar work in the field. It was not long, though, before Thomas Edison protested. After reading of Hughes's research into combating interference on telegraph and telephone wires, he claimed that he had been there first. This time, presumably having learned his lesson from the microphone affair, he took a much lower-key approach in his challenge. He contacted the journal *Engineering*, claiming that he had anticipated Hughes in the invention of a system to eliminate the effect of interference and referring to his patents in both the UK and in America.[16] The journal responded by stating that it wished to give equal time to all parties, and therefore reviewed Edison's claim and patent along with Hughes's and the work of Charles Wilson of Chicago. Their conclusion was that their approaches were similar. However, Edison had only addressed suppressing interference on one wire, whereas Hughes had addressed suppression on multiple wires. In a letter that he wrote to the journal, Hughes pointed out that in his publications he had given credit to others who had looked into ways of curbing interference, such as Alexander Graham Bell, Charles Wilson, and David Brooks of Philadelphia. He stated if he had known of Edison's work he would have given him credit also. Edison's challenge seems to have fizzled there.[17]

While Hughes was carrying out his experiments he had noticed that when he adjusted all of the coils to suppress the interference and the system was in balance, it could be affected by the presence of metal near the suppression coils. While this had been an inconvenience at the time, it intrigued him, and he went back to investigate. He was thinking that it might lead to a method to investigate various metals, and he made the following comment:[18]

> Continuing this line of inquiry, I thought I might again attempt to investigate the molecular construction of metals and alloys.

He had been interested in the structure of minerals and metals since his gold mining days in Virginia. More recently he had tried to understand the mechanism by which the microphone translated sonorous vibrations into electrical signals. He was now wondering whether he could use electromagnetic induction to peer into the molecular make-up of materials.

Starting with the four coil arrangement he had used to investigate interference and his methods for balancing the various electromagnetic fields, he rearranged his apparatus, this time using four identical but smaller diameter coils. He mounted two of these on one spool, and the other two on another spool. One coil from each spool was connected in series with his clock, microphone, and battery system which supplied a repetitive test signal. Through electromagnetic induction the test signal was induced into the other two coils, which were connected in series with the telephone receiver. These coils were connected so that the signal produced in the two coils canceled each other out, and with careful adjustment, he was able to reduce the signal he heard in the receiver to zero, indicating that the circuit was in perfect balance. When he inserted a small piece of metal into the center of one of the coils, the balance was upset, and he could detect this by an increased signal (louder clock ticks) in the telephone. He found

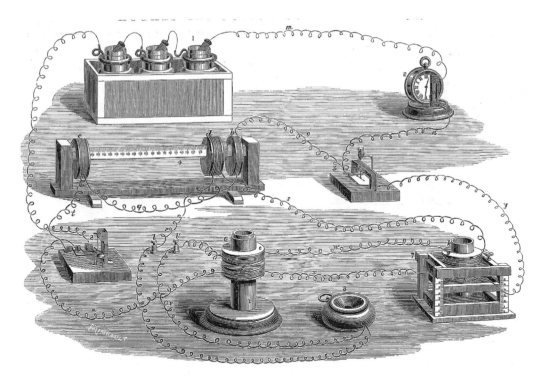

Hughes's induction balance (foreground) and sonometer (background) with the switch for toggling between the two. Metal samples to be tested were introduced into the center of the coil.

that he could detect very small quantities of metal, in the range of a milligram of copper, and with further refinement of the apparatus, an iron wire finer than a human hair. He could also detect differences between metal types and between metal alloys, and variations in coins of the same denominations but produced from different metal batches. Hughes called this apparatus an induction balance.[19]

While his ear was a good gauge of relative amplitude, he needed a better measuring device for accurate comparison of samples, so he constructed another apparatus. This was also based on the induction balance principle, but only used three coils, which were mounted on a rod forty centimeters long. One coil was fixed at one end and another at the opposite end; the third coil was free to slide along the rod between the other two. The rod had a scale inscribed in millimeters (though he often referred to this scale as degrees). The two end coils were connected in series with the clock and microphone apparatus which provided the test signal. These coils were connected in such a way that the magnetic fields they produced canceled each other out mid-way between them. The third, movable coil was connected to the telephone receiver. The movable coil could be slid along the rod until no signal was heard in the telephone receiver, which occurred midway between the end coils. This was the zero position. If the movable coil was slid towards one of the end coils, the signal in the telephone gradually increased in volume. So now he had a device for measuring the loudness of the signal (this was not an absolute measurement but a relative measurement). This new apparatus he called an electrical sonometer.

To make a measurement he would adjust his induction balance so that it was in perfect balance, that is, so that he could hear no signal in the telephone receiver. Next, a sample of metal was introduced into one of the coils of the induction balance. This would unbalance it, producing a signal of a certain loudness in the telephone. By quickly switching the telephone over from the induction balance to the sonometer, he could slide the movable coil along the rod until the loudness from the two sources was equal. Then the value could be read off the scale. By this means, he took readings for different metals (using uniform sample sizes in this case), as shown in this table:[20]

METAL	READING
Silver	125
Gold	117
Aluminum	112
Copper	100
Zinc	80
Bronze	76
Tin	74
Iron	52
Lead	38

Hughes presented this invention to the Royal Society on May 15, 1879, again giving away the technology to anyone who wished to use it, just as he had done with the microphone and methods of interference suppression. [21] The induction balance became a popular device and was sold by his instrument maker friend W. Grove, who resided close by in Portland Place.

Mr. Chandler Roberts, FRS, the chemist at the Royal Mint, used an induction balance to monitor the quality of the mint's coins, metals and alloys.[22] It was claimed that a difference of one part in 10,000 of a metal alloy could be detected. Also, in this application, an exact comparison between a standard coin and one to be tested could easily be made. One coin was placed into the center of one set of coils of the induction balance and the second one was put into the second set of coils. If they were identical then no tone was heard in the telephone.

Dr. Benjamin Ward Richardson, FRS, a friend of Hughes's, explored the medical uses of the apparatus. Working with Hughes, he took the sonometer component of the induction balance and demonstrated its use for testing a person's hearing and presented the results to the Royal Society, publicizing the device's merits.[23] It was renamed the audiometer and was widely adopted by physicians;[24] the firm of Thomas Hawksley manufactured and sold it into the early 1900s.

Hughes came up with another medical application for one of his inventions, and had even suggested its use to Bell as another method to locate the bullet in President Garfield:[25]

> The microphone is invaluable as a probe for bullets. I made the first for Sir Henry Thomson to find out stones in bladder. But it is even more applicable to bullets. It consists of a simple hammer and anvil microphone adjusted upon the handle of the ordinary probe. The instant this probe touches any hard substance a sharp click is heard in the telephone. The smallest shot can be heard.... This instrument is well known to surgeons, so I need not say more about it.

This would probably have been a much more successful approach, and was a method familiar in Britain, like Lister's antiseptic procedures. However, it did not appear to be in widespread use in America at the time. It was later found that for locating metal objects such as lead musket balls, all that was necessary was a telephone receiver—the microphone component could be dispensed with. One wire was placed in the patient's mouth and the other connected to a needle probe. When the needle touched the lead, a click could be heard in the receiver, the body and the metal acting as a battery.

Some evidence, albeit politically incorrect, of the entry of Hughes's audiometer into popular culture is provided by the following quotation:[26]

> The Audiometer—It appears from the audiometric researches of Dr. Richardson that contrary to all expectations, the ears of women are much inferior to those of men both

Hughes's own experimental model of his induction balance. A commercial version could be purchased complete for £3/10/0 from W. Groves of Portland Place, London.

in acuteness and range of hearing. This apparent anomaly is thought by some philosophers from the feminine habit of never listening to reason. Be this as it may, however, the deficiency in question is unfortunately more than compensated for by the greater perfection of the female articulating organ. Would our ears be blunter!

Hughes used the induction balance and its variants in many other experiments over the following years. His interest in the molecular make-up of metals impelled him to investigate iron and steel and their magnetic properties. This research led to the invention of two more instruments; one was the "magnetic balance," an instrument for measuring and comparing the magnetic force exhibited by different metallic samples; the second, a simpler one, permitted the study the magnetic effects of torsion on a wire. The device consisted of a coil of wire with a wide opening through which an iron wire could be passed; the wire was held tight at one end but could be twisted from the other end. The interesting effect he noted was that the wire produced "molecular sounds" due to the previously known phenomenon of magnetostriction. He also probably heard a tone in the receiver when the wire was plucked while using a magnet and coil close to the wire—but the world would have to wait some decades for the invention of the electric guitar.

With the completion of the induction balance, Hughes had collected most of the pieces of a jigsaw puzzle, but he had no idea that they would fit together, or that together they would help him to achieve a great new invention. There was no picture or blueprint; in fact, he had not even decided what to do next. But when he did, it was to be a revelation.

9

THE ETHERIC FORCE

"An Etheric Force discharged itself into the Luminiferous Ether." This statement represents one of mankind's first legitimate recognitions of invisible energy waves. Professor Hughes had come to the realization that the energy waves he was creating in his Great Portland Street laboratory were radiating outwards and traveling through the air and through walls, doors, and the floors. Further, he had developed a detector that let him pluck these invisible energy waves right out of the air. What a discovery! This was the birth of a technology that would enable communication without the encumbrance of wires. Excited to test how far these "wire-less" waves traveled, he set his transmitter to automatically send out signals from his laboratory. Then he exited his house with his portable wireless receiver and was amazed to find that he could still pick up the signals as he walked up and down Great Portland Street.

The wireless era was about to dawn, and wireless technology would soon allow communications from any place in the world to any other, and even out to the furthest reaches of our solar system.[1] Professor David Edward Hughes was there at the start. This chapter recalls the excitement he experienced during a frantic four-month period when he filled some 200 pages in his notebooks with experiment after experiment, remarking in the margins "Good," "Important," "Meaningful," and "Most Wonderful." The modern researcher who consults his notebooks is left dizzy trying to decipher his handwriting, interpret his diagrams, follow his reasoning, and understand the language of the period. Hughes had cracked open the door to a technology whose potential would take futurists another twenty years to realize, a technology which the twentieth century would embrace, and without which the world of the twenty-first century could not function. The empty silence of space was about to be shaken up with electromagnetic activity, and previously vacant frequency spectrums would soon be filled with signals.

Here the reader must attempt to cleanse his or her mind of all knowledge of modern electronics, radio, TV, cell phones, WiFi and computers, so as to travel back to the time of Hughes. This is a tall order, but it is also the only way to appreciate the problem that Hughes faced and the limited knowledge base and set of tools he had to work with in 1879 in order to solve it. Scientists were still at a loss as to what electricity and magnetism were: the two forces seemed to keep themselves cloaked in invisibility, only making their presence known through their effects. When it was found that these two different forces were inextricably linked, the mystery only deepened. Now these twins, not content with being held captive in a Leyden jar, Daniell cell, a piece of iron, or a coil of wire, were about to demonstrate a great new feat: they would take flight. At that time, wireless and electromagnetic waves were unknown, and Hughes and other scientists had to come to terms with the fact that such things were possible.

During this period two parallel research paths—closely related, but at the same time very different—were being independently pursued. The brilliant experimenter David Edward Hughes, considered one of the "practical men" and by no means a theoretician, was following one path. He started a new line of research that would take him into the realm of communicating wirelessly via electromagnetic waves. He would discover how to generate and detect them, but struggled to understand what they were, and also to convince others of the validity of his discovery.

The other path was wholly theoretical and revolved around the work of the physicist James Clerk Maxwell, who devised a brilliant theory which predicted the existence of electromagnetic waves, the basis of wireless, and generated some of the mathematical equations governing their behavior. But his highly theoretical work contained no information about how to generate such waves or detect them.

⋙⋘

In 1879 Hughes took his usual Continental summer tour to visit some of his telegraph customers and manufacturers. On these trips he never missed an opportunity to stop in his beloved Paris, this time to demonstrate to his colleagues his recently-developed microphone and induction balance. By September he was back in his laboratory in Great Portland Street carrying out further experiments with the induction balance. He was experimenting with different batteries and testing various metals, including

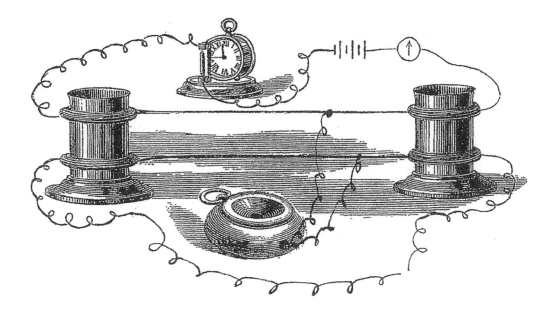

This experiment with the induction balance started Hughes on a four-month flurry of activity which led to the discovery of wireless waves.

---

metals in a finely divided state (particles).[2] He also tinkered with different wiring arrangements of his apparatus.

Hughes's standard configuration of his induction balance consists of two sets of identical coils mounted in close proximity to each other. One set of coils was being pulsed by current from a "clock-microphone" (as Hughes called it)[3] and battery; the other set of coils formed a secondary circuit and was normally connected to a telephone receiver as a detector. If the circuit was balanced then no signal would be heard in the telephone receiver; if the circuit was unbalanced by the presence of a small piece of metal in one set of coils, then the clock ticks could be heard in the telephone receiver. The more the circuit was unbalanced, the louder the signal would be. To make measurements that would permit comparisons between different samples, Hughes would switch the telephone receiver over to his sonometer, adjust it until the loudness was the same, and then note the measurement on the sonometer's scale. The diagram above depicts an arrangement which was different from his usual one: Hughes had connected the telephone across his primary and secondary circuit and had left the secondary circuit open.

This configuration gave him strange results: although the circuit was incomplete, he could still hear the signal on his telephone receiver.[4]

This is so distinct and so evident that this must be studied clearly to know why.

He first thought that this effect was the result of a problem with the insulation of the coils, but on further investigation found that there was a loose or bad connection, or what he liked to call a "microphonic joint," that excited some portion of the circuit.[5] The effects of the loose connection set him to explore further; after all, it was a loose connection which had led to his discovery of the microphone. He connected components in different arrangements, disconnected wires, touched various points in the circuit with his finger, changed to different batteries,[6] and connected one of the wires to a gas pipe (as an earth). Making this earth connection was natural for a telegraph engineer who was used to employing an earth return for proper telegraph operation. But still he was puzzled:[7]

This is not due to bad insulation but either induction or some new effect.

He struggled to understand how, if the circuit was incomplete, that is, with wires disconnected, he could hear the signal so well in the telephone receiver:[8]

The resistance of the air circuit must be enormous.

He was wondering whether the signal was actually returning through his body and the floor, or else through the air by conduction. It was always considered necessary to have a closed loop or a complete circuit, so that there was a path for the current to flow from one terminal of the battery through a circuit and back to the other terminal. Everyone knew that electrical current could not flow round a circuit that was open or incomplete. He wondered if he was observing what Thomas Edison had noticed:[9]

It seems to be the identical etheric force of Americans which is simply due to high intensity of Extra current.

The "extra current" referred to had been observed by many experimenters. It occurred when the current passing through a coil of wire was quickly switched off and the energy stored in the coil collapsed and tried to continue to flow. This manifested itself as sparking or arcing across the switch contacts as they were opened up. A modern example is the ignition coil used in a gasoline engine to create a spark across the points of the spark plug.

Much of what Hughes was observing was not making sense to him, and we can imagine him hunched over his apparatus listening to the telephone receiver, connecting and disconnecting components, and wearing a puzzled expression on his face as he hastily scrawled in his notebook, the air full of the smoke given off by a spirit lamp and by the melting sealing wax. The table was no doubt cluttered with coils of wire, horseshoe and bar magnets, condensers, batteries, and jars and bottles for making Daniell or Grove cells; mechanical clocks, pieces of carbon, an assortment of microphones and telephone receivers, resistance tubes, empty pill boxes, and plenty of red sealing wax and bootmaker's wax, his universal sticking and gluing compounds. He had never fallen out of the habit of making his own apparatus.

While this might seem to be a lot of clutter to some, to Hughes it was an experimental stimulus. Having parts readily available meant that he could easily insert them into a circuit to see what effect they had. He could build something out of a collection of components where others only saw a mess. He was about to make history with an important discovery because he was a great experimenter, because he tried different combinations—and because he had an instinct that led him to try the right combinations. Also important was the fact that through his prior inventions of the microphone and induction balance he had unknowingly equipped himself with precisely the tools necessary for his next great discovery. These factors would prove to be the discriminators between him and others who had dabbled with the "extra current" but had drawn a blank.[10]

By early October he had begun an intensive series of experiments relating to this "extra current" using the induction balance. His aim was to determine why the clock ticking could still be heard when certain wires were disconnected. Holding one of the wires in loose contact, or, as he referred to it, in "microphonic contact," he was still able to hear the loud ticking of the clock in the telephone receiver. In most experiments a bad connection in a circuit was something to be avoided like the plague, but in this case for Hughes it was something to be exploited, and was similar to his loose contact carbon microphone. It was therefore only natural for him to insert one of his carbon pencil microphones into the circuit, considering it a "more robust bad connection," but he was dissatisfied with the results and commented:[11]

> It seems as if one side becomes charged and passed to other by a spark…. Seems as if a metallic microphone contact would be better.

The introduction of a "microphonic contact" turned out to be a crucial and brilliant idea, as we shall see. He had evaluated many types of microphonic contacts prior to his discovery of the carbon microphone, including several metallic contacts, coke, carbon, and various metal particles packed into a glass tube. He decided to try using what he referred to as the "old thermo-microphone loop,"[12] which consisted of two copper wires with intertwined loops that had been oxidized in the flame of his spirit lamp. Confusingly, he also termed this device a "joint." Although they seemed simple, these joints were tricky to prepare and there were many variants.

During the weeks of these experiments he had been using his original clock microphone as a source to excite the induction balance coils, but also tried a clockwork-driven interrupter.[13] It was over the course of these experiments that he permanently switched to using the clockwork interrupter to pulse the primary coils. This gave him improved excitation and consequently higher voltage swings from the coils, providing a more intense "extra current" and spark across the contacts of the interrupter. He also experimented with different coils and settled on using two flat ones, one for the primary and the other for the secondary, instead of the induction balance configuration. After further experiments he again makes reference in his notebook to the "Etheric force of the Americans." He was aware of Thomas Edison's earlier experiments,[14] following which he declared that he had discovered a "new force," but Edison was unfortunately ridiculed in the press over it:[15]

> ...the "Etheric experiment". This was noticed by friend Edison in 1875 published in Scientific American Dec 1875.

Of course it would be interesting to know what emphasis he put on the word "friend" after the microphone affair.

Elihu Thomson and Edwin Houston in America had repeated Edison's experiment and they concluded that the effect he had observed was not a "new force" but produced by "induction currents." In England the young Silvanus P. Thompson had also repeated Edison's experiment, concluded that the effects Edison had observed were due to "electrostatic induction," and published his results in the *Philosophical Magazine* in September 1876.[16] Unfortunately these authors were wrong, and the publication of their incorrect conclusions probably only served to cloud the issue for other scientists. Thompson did observe though that the effect was of an oscillatory nature, an important point that seemed to go unobserved. Of course later in their lives when the etheric force's true nature was uncovered they realized what an opportunity they all had missed.

Hughes was not one for accepting others' results without investigating himself, and he carried on with his experiments. It is just as well, as otherwise he might have given up at this point. Hughes was using different components in his investigation of the extra current and the etheric force than Edison and the others had used, and it was these that were to prove the difference. At this point in his research Hughes renames and reconfigures his microphonic joint and now calls it a "key." One form of this device was an iron wire that was heated red-hot, then cooled gradually to preserve the oxide, and placed in contact with an unoxidized iron wire. By now he had filled one notebook and started the next on October 15, 1879.

His apparatus was now taking on a new form, separated into two parts.[17] One part consisted of a battery, a clockwork-driven interrupter, and a coil, all connected in series. The other part consisted of a telephone receiver across which was connected the microphonic joint or key. (To judge from his sketches, he now appears to have removed the coil from this circuit, but perhaps he just omitted it from the drawing). He decided to see what the effect would be if these two parts were separated by moving the telephone receiver and microphonic joint to the next room. They were still connected by a single wire which he called an "air line" or "extra current line." He found that he could still hear the signal on the telephone receiver even though only a single wire, i.e. an incomplete circuit, connected the interrupter and the receiver. He found that the extra current was creating a full spark and was so forceful that it influenced the wires at great distances. He struggled to understand how all this worked. Surely a return path was necessary for the current in order for the circuit to operate, and his only explanation was that this must be through the earth, via the telephone's wooden case, his ear, head, and body, through the floor and back through the wooden case of the battery.

His experiments on the "extra current" included inserting a condenser[18] into the circuit at various points as well as connecting the circuit to an earth, which was usually the water pipe or gas pipe.

After further tests he deduced that the effects were due not to an induction reaction but possibly to an electromagnetic effect induced in the coil.[19] It was perhaps

Like a cell splitting for the first time Hughes starts on a path to divide his circuit into two parts that would eventually become the wireless transmitter and receiver.

inevitable that he would take his next step as he worked his way through different configurations of his apparatus. This was a major step, a "Eureka!" moment, though he likely did not grasp its full import at the time: he disconnected the wire (his "air line") between the two separate parts of his circuit, and was very surprised that he could still distinctly hear in the telephone receiver the "make and break" of the clockwork-driven contactor.

He recorded his deductions in his notebook:[20]

> Thus it is evident that it is not by induction of the coil in line but simply by pure conduction through large mass or surface of battery through table to line and also earth. It is however wonderful that 1st it should work through such an enormous resistance, 2nd and as there must be enormous relative escape to earth by walls etc. it is wonderful that there is still enough to work the telephone sound quite loudly. From this we should suppose that we might even get the sounds louder in next room provided we had a large surface on wall to catch the direction.

He comments that the extra spark is bright and strong, and is amazed that the current in the circuit can be flowing through the house structure by "conduction," since to do so it must be overcoming an enormous electrical resistance. He disconnected the ground wire and found that the signal disappeared. His use of the word "conduction"

The transmitter and receiver are now separated, with no wire connecting them. The transmitter consists of a battery, interrupter/spark gap, and coil with an earth connection, while the receiver consists of an aerial wire, detector, and telephone receiver plus an earth connection.

---

to explain the effect, while an obvious choice to him, was unfortunate, and would come back to haunt him. His conclusion that it was conduction was based on the idea that an electrical circuit must have a complete path in order for the electrical current to flow. It was still incomprehensible to him that a current could travel in or excite an open circuit, that is, a circuit without a return path.

He was unaware that he was actually creating electromagnetic waves in the coil and spark gap at the circuit interrupter which were radiating out through the air. Just as importantly, he was capturing them with his air line and detecting them with his microphonic joint in a continuous[21] manner which he could hear in the telephone receiver.

After separating the two parts of his apparatus he began to realize how important the microphonic joint was,[22] so he devoted considerable time to its improvement, a task that was to be repeated many times. From October 24 to November 11 he filled twenty-two pages with scrawled notes about the different metals, combinations of metals and wire loops, and processes to oxidize and carbonize them that he tried. He wanted to determine the type of wire, configuration, and process that would yield the most consistent results. There is also a hint in his notes that he tried heating the microphonic joint with a small lamp while it was in the circuit to determine whether that helped.

He made one of his more important discoveries when he tried an iron and mercury device:[23]

Oct 24 Good Important
Found that a mercury bottle with iron wires gives out tones equal to best and that it was

wonderfully improved by using a battery over shunt circuit, that battery makes such a difference that is probable that a battery alone would do it if we manage it so that it gives the continuous sound of polarization—sounds which resemble Strohs magnet.

It was during this period (November 4) that his friend Mr. Jean François Despointes[24] paid him a visit and Hughes eagerly showed off his experiments, commenting in his notebook that Despointes was surprised by what he saw. On November 12 he decided to go mobile: he left the clock interrupter running in his laboratory and took what he had now started to call his receiver out into Great Portland Street and walked over to the Public Baths in Tottenham Court Road.[25]

Took the extra current arrangement the necessary part to the Public Baths in Tottenham Court Road about ½ mile—could not hear at all the noise in the baths was very great so as to drown any faint tones if there were any. I thought several times that I heard traces of the clock in Portland Street but it was not by any means sure, should say that there were none or so feeble as to be overpowered by the noise of the baths, thus evidently this kind of electricity diminishes rapidly with distance having no conductor to confine its operation in one direction. Tried at house again by taking the receiver down to the W. Closet could then hear perfectly well quite equal to upstairs if not better. Found that if one end of Telephone is shunt with thermopile was connected to gas and the other to water that we could hear much more powerful…. The water pipe gave a current as a battery now is it the influence of a battery to earth in the second wire or is the mass of metal which causing it.

While Hughes was experimenting with microphonic components he was actually discovering the properties of semi-conductors: it was this mechanism that provided the detection of the electromagnetic waves. This mobile experiment over a distance of half a mile was premature, as he had not yet hit on the best microphonic joint or configuration of the receiver. It will be noticed that he called the latest configuration of the microphonic joint a "thermopile" or "thermo joint," probably because the joint consisted of dissimilar metals.[26] He had noted that the signal was louder when he took the receiver down to the cellar WC (water closet, i.e. the toilet) and connected an earth wire up to the water pipe (not a gas pipe as had been used for an earth in the extra current circuit upstairs), and reasoned that the dissimilar metals used for these connections[27] were creating a small voltage potential at the receiver. As this was an improvement he decided to add a small battery to the receiver circuit, and made tests to determine the right type of battery. Experimenters at this time usually made their own batteries and Hughes was no exception; while there were some standards such as a Daniell or Grove cell, Hughes had some of his own design. He realized that he needed a battery that was not too powerful or it would destroy the microphonic joint; it also had to be small and not spill any acid as he wanted it to be portable.[28]

1ˢᵗ Found after innumerable experiments that the best battery for the Thermojoint is a small cell Carbon Zinc Sal Ammoniac must be small else quantity too great burning wire destroying it and producing a hissing boiling sound. 2ⁿᵈ Found that the thermo joint could be placed in closed bottle acting even more perfectly from non liability to being touched as once adjusted it goes always.

The receiver was now taking shape with the addition of a small bias battery and a detector enclosed inside a small bottle for protection. For the detector or "thermo joint" he had settled on a steel wire that had been placed in the smoke from the spirit lamp which was then put in contact with a copper loop that had been heated and oxidized.

He was still wrestling with how the signals were getting from one room to the other and was having second thoughts about his previous conclusion that it was by "conduction." He reasoned that the tremendous electrical resistance of the house structure precluded an electrical current traveling through it, but was at a loss as to how he could hear the signal so clearly with the receiver. One thing he was sure of was that the signals were not traveling by "induction," as had been concluded by previous researchers. Induction would imply that the coil being pulsed by the circuit interrupter was magnetically affecting the receiver. However, it was known that the inductive effect dropped off rapidly between two coils as they were moved further apart, and the parts of his apparatus were certainly far apart. Then there was also the overriding fact there was no coil in the receiver to couple to anyway.

He was probably one of the few living scientists who understood induction from a practical point of view. He had spent a significant amount of time investigating induction effects as they pertained to the problem of interference on telegraph and telephone lines and had found solutions for their suppression. Of course he had also done extensive experiments with the induction balance.

He had now demonstrated that he could transmit some sixty feet within his own residence, and at some point he decided to try the experiment over at his friend Mr. Stroh's instrument manufactory:[29]

> Mr. Stroh and myself could hear perfectly the currents transmitted from the third story to the basement, but I could not detect clear signals at my residence about a mile distant. The innumerable gas and water pipes intervening seemed to absorb or weaken too much the feeble transmitted extra current from a small coil.

He took up his experimentation again with renewed vigor and set out to see if he could shed some light on what was happening. First he took the earth wire from the circuit interrupter and coil that had been connected to the gas pipe (earth), disconnected it, and reconnected it to a metal fender[30] by the stove. Then the earth wire from the receiver was disconnected from the earth.

He found that he was still receiving a "good tone" and noted:[31]

thus the current evidently travels from fender through wood stone etc. to the roof in next room. The resistance must be very great.

He was still unable to let go of the idea that there might be some type of signal path between the two circuits other than a physical, material path. This assumption was natural, as in all of his previous experience electrical signals had needed to flow through wires or some other conductor. The other possibility, that the signal was being transmitted by induction, he had already rejected. Believing that the floor of the room was acting as a conductor which he called a "false earth," he carried out a number of experiments using his Clerac Tube variable resistor.[32] He substituted this in the earth circuit to try to determine what the value of this mysterious high resistance was; but the tests were inconclusive.

As we turn to the next page of his notebook we are surprised to read about a new and lofty objective: not content with being able to send a signal in one direction, he experiments to see whether he can send in both directions simultaneously and obtain duplex operation. The setup he used to perform these tests was complex

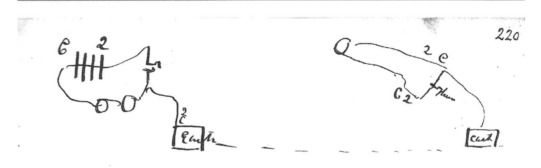

Hughes's sketch of his transmitter and receiver.

and probably produced mixed results. However, by now he has started to call his extra current generator a transmitter. Putting this digression aside, he returned to his main line of inquiry and made some adjustments to increase the effectiveness of the transmitter coil.

He was now (around the end of November) coming to the realization that the signal was traveling from his transmitter to his receiver by some means that he did not understand:[33]

> 1 Good The current decidedly decreases as the distance perhaps as the square... thus no doubt the circuit is completed through the carpet tables etc.—but there are many preceding experiments which goes to show that it is rather in the nature of a static charge not requiring a circuit but rather the electric inertia or absorption.

It is an interesting deduction that the strength of the signal drops as the square of the distance. Now we come to the experimental *pièce de résistance*. Hughes isolated the receiver by hanging it on strings from the ceiling and connected it to a tin-foil-covered board which acted as an antenna, which he also isolated. Only a single line earth was connected to the

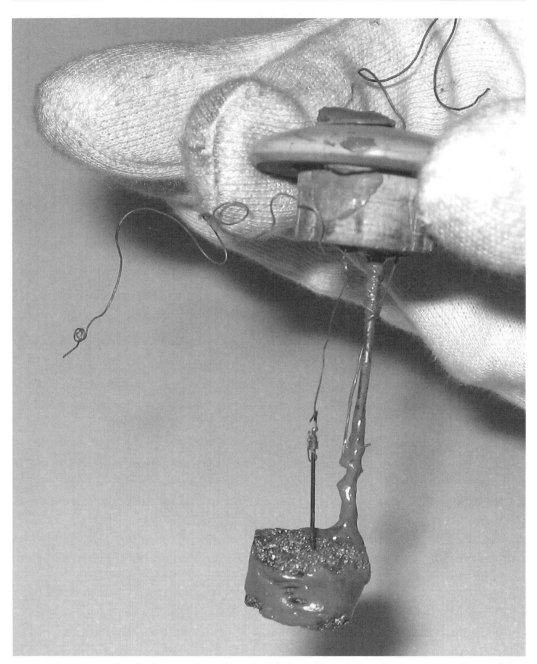

One of the many coke (carbon) and steel needle wireless detectors Hughes constructed. Note his basic construction methods and the extensive use of sealing wax to hold everything in place.

receiver. This test proved to him finally that there was no return path through the floor or structure of the house, and that he was receiving his signal directly through the air, or as the scientists of the day liked to call it, the "ether." Here are his own words:[34]

2 Good To see if the tin foil covered board increased sound because it made a better return circuit through table, we slung by a string this board and the receiver to the gas pipe from which it received its sound thus if any loss of insulation would be to its own earth through the string as the receiver and board could not touch either the table nor any return current except through air—found that sound was decidedly increased by use of board with 1 element.... but the currents must travel through the air as static induction or the absorption by inertia takes place in either case there was no possibility of return by a separate route from the board except through its own gas pipe thus the air itself must be charged.

3 Good In order to determine fully if current traveled through carpet table etc. was necessary—we insulated the receiver as above connected with its own receiving earth and in order that no current should travel through the feet of body to telephone we placed the tin foil on a chair and connected this direct to same receiver earth. Now when we stood on this board we were in direct communication through feet to same receiving earth, as any current coming up through chair must have been cut off—in these conditions we still hear plainly and much stronger when we touched receiver as usual. Now we could only act either as a shunt or an absorber and as we have seen no shunt improves it. It must be either been as an absorber or as a direct static charge from air. If we touched gas pipe with the other hand it made no difference although we increased our direct communication with earth. We believe thus far that large surfaces can act both as a surface charge to air and also in so doing it absorbs force thus if it makes a charge against walls or other bodies it must also do work and the amount absorbed will be in direct proportion to the work done.

What a revelation! Now he understood that the signals were actually traveling through the air, and just as important, that work was being done. This implies that energy was being transferred through the air from the transmitter to the receiver. If energy were not being transferred the signal could not be received, so this deduction perhaps seems obvious in retrospect, but it was nonetheless an important step forward in understanding what was happening. Of course, the question now became how the signal was traveling through the air, or rather through the more complex medium the theoretical scientists had dreamed up called "the luminiferous ether."[35] His first guess was that it was traveling by a static charge.

Hughes next experimented to see whether he could increase this unknown force by using a larger surface area for the transmitter aerials, and the stove fender was again pressed into service. The results were promising, and he was now certain that he was on to something new: we detect a note of confidence in his notebook:[36]

...thus showing the enormous superiority of my receiver.

He finished another notebook and began a new one on December 5. The remainder of the month was consumed by experiments with different configurations of his aerials (antenna) and new attempts to improve the thermo joint detector.

The aerial tests were carried out with the transmitter and receiver in separate rooms and the air lines (aerials) stretched out to candles on separate small tables, well insulated from earth. Noticing that the sound increased as he moved away and decreased as he approached the table, he added a condenser to the receiver and claimed a significant improvement, stating:[37]

> This proves that the whole atmosphere is influenced even to the great distance of 15 meters with the door closed—closing the door makes not the slightest difference.

Hughes deduced that the force was acting on the wires of his receiver and was being converted into a thermo current by the thermo joint, and that this in turn caused the sound in the telephone receiver. He was right that the thermo joint was responsible for detecting the transmitted signals but it was not through a thermo-electric current. The joint was acting as a detector similar to a nonlinear device such as a semiconductor diode.[38] He reasoned that adding a battery improved the receiver much as heating the thermo joint with a lamp would have, that is, it would have generated a small voltage.

Further tests were conducted with the air lines (aerials) for the transmitter and receiver; if they were straight and parallel to each other the reception was good, but if they were at right angles the reception was poor. When the air lines were tried straight up to the ceiling and supported by sticks or laths the reception was good, and Hughes made the following note:[39]

> 1 good.... It might seem to point out the direction of force nothing more.
> 2 If held vertical it increases sound double at least and this at either pole of receiver thus this does not bring receiver nearer but simply cuts more lines of force—showing that the whole atmosphere is impregnated and the more lines we can cut naturally the greater the force.

The revelations were coming fast and furious and he was making remarkable progress in improving his understanding of what was happening. He had now realized that

Hughes isolated the aerial wires from ground by stringing them to wax candles mounted on tables.

the waves were everywhere, and believed that they manifested themselves as lines of force[40] emanating from the transmitter aerial, and that the receiver aerial was being cut by them, so the larger the aerial the better. The fact that he noted changes in signal strength when he changed the receiving aerial from being parallel to the transmitting aerial to being at right angles to it was due to the effects of polarization. His use of a grounded transmitter with the antenna positioned vertically is typical of the configuration of today's dipole antenna. Although he was discovering all of these important attributes of transmitters and receivers he was still struggling to understand what exactly it was that he had discovered.

He tried the mobile receiver experiment again, transmitting from Great Portland Street and taking his receiver to his friend Mr. Grove's house 500 yards away, but could not hear anything. He says:[41]

> Thus the current does not travel any great distance and most likely the effect is altogether due to air circuit anyway the effect is only local and no hopes of its usefulness.

Despite these negative results he was not discouraged, and plowed ahead, inserting a "microphone/telephone receiver amplifier"[42] to see if he could boost the received signal, but this did not seem to have a significant effect. He carried out some tests to determine whether the signals were directional by using two round tin discs (milk tin lids), but concluded that they were radiating in all directions. He also concluded that a large surface area air line worked just as well as a copper wire, as long as they were well insulated from earth. He also refers to his air line at this point as an "Eariel" (spelled thus).[43]

During this part of December[44] he invited several friends to see his invention. These were William Preece,[45] Sir William Crookes FRS, Sir William Roberts-Austen FRS, Prof. W. Grylls Adams FRS and Mr. Grove. The experiments must have made an impression on these visitors, as Sir William Crookes was later to write about the future possibilities of these wireless waves.

It was getting close to Christmas and Hughes once more returned to his efforts to improve the microphonic joint or thermo joint. He recorded his tests of the following materials on several notebook pages:

> Comparative values of different microphonic materials for extra (current).
> Zinc filings—clear and good
> Charcoal filings—no sound
> Brass filings—good but not as good as zinc
> Lead—ditto
> Sheet lead, sheet resting on its oxide not quite as good as thermo joint
> Black steel—not good
> Plus many other combinations that were calibrated against one of the existing thermo joints.

On January 15, 1880, Hughes remarked in his notebook:[46]

> Have passed many days trying to remake thermo joints. Have not as yet succeeded in repeating barely any one.

However, the situation did improve and finally he was able to encapsulate nine thermo joints in small bottles. Some of these were his carbon steel detector configurations, one of which consisted of a carbon pencil touching a steel needle with an adjustable spring to regulate the contact pressure. Another was a small piece of carbon in the form of coke with a steel needle placed vertically whose position could be adjusted, all mounted inside a small bottle.

At times he must have wondered if his experiments would ever result in anything useful, but by February he was feeling more confident and finally attained success by receiving a signal with his portable receiver at a distance of almost 500 yards from the transmitter:[47]

> After trying successfully all distances allowed in my residence in Portland Street, my usual method was to put the transmitter in operation and walk up and down Great Portland Street with my receiver in my hand, with the telephone to the ear. The sounds seemed to slightly increase for a distance of 60 yards, then gradually diminish, until at 500 yards I could no longer with certainty hear the transmitted signals. What struck me as remarkable was that, opposite certain houses, I could hear better, whilst at others the signals could hardly be perceived.

He was now ready to share his discovery.[48] After all, in four months he had made significant progress. He had created a transmitter that filled the atmosphere with some sort of energy in the form of lines of force. These could penetrate walls and doors and travel outside and down the street. He had also found a way to receive this energy by intercepting these lines of force as they traveled through the air anywhere within a radius of close to 500 yards. It was this receiver with its microphonic detector and its ability to detect a continuous stream of transmitted signals that separated him from others who had investigated the etheric force. The fact that the signal faded opposite certain buildings and then reappeared opposite others may have been due to shielding from iron railings, or as some have suggested, to interference between the incident and reflected transmitted wireless waves that caused peaks and valleys in the signal strength in different spots. But this theory was well beyond Hughes's knowledge, and he was still wrestling with a much more basic question: What was the nature of the force being transmitted? He had started out thinking that the energy was transmitted via "conduction" through the structure of the building and earth. As his experiments progressed he imagined it to be via "conduction" through the surrounding air, then possibly by static charge, and finally by radiating lines of force that could be cut or intercepted by the receiver air line (aerial). This was a very reasonable

An artist's recreation made in 1922 of Hughes walking on Great Portland Street receiving wireless signals.

hypothesis, particularly considering that it was a newly discovered phenomenon, and even though electricity and magnetism had been studied for quite a while, no one knew what they were, let alone what they might become when they started acting in concert and flying through the air.

Hughes contacted Mr. William Spottiswoode, the president of the Royal Society, to set up a demonstration. Spottiswoode replied on February 14, 1880:[49]

> Dear Sir, Let me sincerely congratulate you on the remarkable results at which you have arrived; and at the same time to thank you for the kindness you have shewn in communicating them to me. I have spoken to Professor Stokes, who could come on Friday next at 3.30. P.M.; and I have written to Professor Huxley proposing that day and hour. If therefore you do not hear from me again, please expect us at that time. I need hardly add with what interest I look forward to the meeting. It will give me great pleasure to arrange for the reading of a communication from you to the Royal Society, whenever you think that the time has arrived.
>
> Believe me yours very truly, W. Spottiswoode

This was a complimentary letter, as was to be expected, for Hughes had now established a remarkable track record with the technical community. Within the past three years he had presented the microphone, discoveries on how to deal with interference

The components used by Hughes in his wireless experiments: from left to right, a clockwork drive circuit interrupter and spark gap, three detectors, a portable spill-proof battery, and Hughes's telephone receiver.

on telegraph and telephone lines, the induction balance, and the sonometer—and now he had yet another new discovery.

Hughes was not one for putting personal details in his laboratory notebooks; they were not a diary, and the historian generally has to seek this type of information about Hughes from other sources. But in this instance he did record the meeting with and demonstration to the high-level Royal Society personnel. On the afternoon of February 20, Mr. Spottiswoode, the president of the Royal Society, and Prof. Stokes and Prof. Huxley, the secretaries, arrived at Hughes's laboratory and Hughes described the meeting in his notebook:[50]

> They visited me today at ½ past 3pm and remained until ¼ to six pm in order to witness my experiments with the extra current thermopile etc.—The experiments were quite successful—and at first they were astonished at results, but at 5 pm Prof. Stokes commenced maintaining the results were then not due to Conduction but to Induction and that the results were not so remarkable as he would imagine rapid changes of electric tension by Induction. Although I showed several experiments which pointed conclusively to its being conduction he would not listen—but rather pooh poohed all the results from that moment this unpleasant discussion was then kept up <u>by</u> him: the others following his suit until they hardly paid any attention to the experiment even to the one working through the gas pipe in Portland Street to Langham Place on roof—They did not sincerely compliment me at the end in results, seemed all to be very much displeased because I would not give at once my Thermo pile to Royal Society so <u>others</u>; could make their results—I told them that when Prof. Hughes made an Instrument of research it was for Prof. Hughes researches and no one else. They left very coldly! And with none of the enthusiasm with which they commenced the experiments—I am sorry at these results of so much labor, but cannot help it—
>
> D. E. Hughes

Hughes's notebook entry for February 21:[51]

I wrote to Mr. Spottiswoode, that my opinion firmly fixed based on true experiments that it was conduction nothing else! So I have made matters worse: and expect nothing more from them, except that they will probably copy my apparatus and make their own experiments.

Spottiswoode replied on February 22:[52]

Dear Mr. Hughes, You have very little to regret in the course of the experiment which you were good enough to show us the other day; for I am sure we could have not spent our time better, or more agreeably than we did. Nor indeed did it make the slightest difference to us that they were performed in your rooms. The results are marvelous; and I shall only be too glad to arrange for a meeting all to yourself at the Royal Society whenever you are prepared to make them public.

The question of conduction v induction is certainly one of importance in the explanation of facts—so much so that I should much like to arrange another séance with you on this special point, if you are kind enough to give it to us and we can get Prof. Stokes again.

Believe me yours very sincerely,
W. Spottiswoode.

What a let down! It is easy to imagine Hughes's anger and frustration at this point. He had made a significant discovery, but try as he might he could not get these three adjudicators to see it for what it was. He had demonstrated the effect over a distance of between 200 and 500 yards from his laboratory to Langham Place, and induction almost certainly could not act at such a distance. But we can only speculate. Stokes certainly misunderstood what he was witnessing.

Spottiswoode, probably trapped in the middle, had offered an olive branch, but even if there was another demonstration Hughes still would have to deal with the main roadblock, Prof. Stokes, and it appears that he declined this offer. It was bad luck that Prof. George Gabriel Stokes, Lucasian Professor of Mathematics at Cambridge, was the senior scientist to review his work together with William Spottiswoode, also a mathematician. Stokes had made his mark at Cambridge and now was mainly engaged with his secretarial duties at the Royal Society. As such he was the gatekeeper to publishing papers and presentations at the Society. His theoretical background and possible recollections of previous experiments by other scientists who had concluded that the "extra current" was due to induction may have biased his opinion. Stokes[53] was held in high esteem by other scientists, and as a result Hughes, though angry and disappointed, was unlikely to cross him. Hughes's insistence that the effect he demonstrated was caused by "conduction" is puzzling and most unfortunate as it only seems to have confused the issue. There are many instances where scientists[54] coined or used inaccurate terms, and Hughes was not immune to this problem. The results of his demonstration could well have been very different if he had been able to communicate his belief that lines of force that were emanating and traveling outward from his transmitter and filling the surrounding space, and that it was this force that he was capturing with his receiver.

Hughes never published his work, perhaps bowing to someone with superior theoretical knowledge, or he may have had doubts about his theory and failed to come up with a better explanation. As a practical scientist and experimenter his work was devoid of any theoretical or mathematical foundation, something Stokes would have been more comfortable with. Spottiswoode's insistence that it had not made the slightest difference that the experiments had been carried out in Hughes's rooms must have been a reply to some comment made by Stokes. Certainly Hughes's laboratory, which was part of his sitting room, together with his homemade apparatus, may have projected an amateurish atmosphere and turned Stokes off. Stokes was probably more familiar with university research facilities such as the Cavendish Laboratory at Cambridge, a place where one might more naturally expect ground-breaking research to be done.

Hughes's reluctance to give up his thermo pile for others to investigate was certainly to have been expected. He had had his ideas stolen once before. If only he had had the opportunity to present his discovery and be given credit for it, there is no doubt that he would have given away the technology freely as he had done on other occasions.

It is also possible that Hughes had heard that he was being proposed for membership in the Royal Society and so did not wish to upset these executives. It was a life-long desire of most scientists to be honored with this distinction, and Hughes was no exception. The proposers[55] had started the "The Certificate of a Candidate for Election" in January of 1880, and so by February it had probably gathered the necessary signatures. It was also in February[56] that the council met and decided on recommendations for "new fellows." Thus it was just at about the time of Hughes's demonstration that these same officials of the Royal Society were acting on his membership. Hughes was elected a fellow, and ironically it was Prof. Stokes who notified him by formal letter on June 4, 1880. Hughes went back and made a note in the margin of the page of his notebook relating to the unsuccessful demonstration that he had been elected to the Royal Society on June 3.

Some of his friends who had seen his experiments tried to persuade him to publish his results, and one these was the author John Munro:[57]

One Day, after lunching with him at the restaurant Frascati, he showed me his experiment. The transmitter, sparking coil, battery and clockwork interrupter, with a stiff wire from it sticking up in the air was on the working table, spread with newspapers by the north window in the corner of the sitting room. The receiver, a telephone connected with short wires to a small bottle coated on the outside with strips of blue paper, stood on another table in the adjoining room. Bidding me listen to the telephone he went into the front room, shutting the door behind him and left me alone. Holding the telephone to my ear I distinctly heard, through the walls, the rhythm of the "make and break" thirty

Prof. George Gabriel Stokes, Lucasian Professor of Mathematics at Cambridge University. Stokes's skepticism about Hughes's wireless experiments discouraged Hughes from pursuing them further.

feet away. He told me the bottle was a little "pile" or "thermopile" which he had found sensitive to electricity. I understood it was not an ordinary thermopile, but a new and somewhat mysterious instrument.... I suggested the publication of his experiment but he would not hear of it, and I gathered that he wanted to sift the matter out.

Perhaps the ridicule that Edison had suffered over the etheric force, and the statements by the press which implied that it was the same as the "Odic" force or "psychic force" responsible for spiritual and occult phenomena, had given Hughes pause. Or maybe he believed that he could figure out what this mysterious force was by himself. Unfortunately he was at a theoretical disadvantage, and it would take the combined theoretical knowledge and work of three scientists who were followers of James Clerk Maxwell, namely George Francis FitzGerald, Oliver J. Lodge, and Oliver Heaviside, as well as Heinrich Hertz, several years to understand and explain the phenomenon.

It is difficult to believe that the Hughes who abandoned this discovery was the same Hughes who only the previous year had taken on Thomas Edison and defended William Preece with so much gusto. We might have wished that in this case Hughes had defended and pursued his discovery further. But that was not to be, and that part of Hughes's story was over. There are a few more pages of notes on experiments and then the notebook ends. He does not start his next notebook until September of 1880, and his interests appear to have shifted to another subject.

BEFORE WE WENT WIRELESS

The public did not have knowledge of Hughes's discovery, or an appreciation of how close he had come to launching the wireless era, until twenty years later. Before we close this chapter it is worth seeing how knowledge of wireless waves was finally achieved.

⊁⌢⌁

On November 5, while Hughes was in the middle of his experiments, the one person who knew what the mysterious waves were unfortunately died at an early age. He was James Clerk Maxwell, a professor of experimental physics who was responsible for the Cavendish Laboratory at Cambridge. Maxwell had determined through some amazing foresight that when electrical and magnetic changes took place they would generate an electromagnetic disturbance that would manifest itself as a wave motion which could travel through the ether (air). He then realized that the wave motion of electromagnetic disturbances and those of light were of the same nature, he calculated that they traveled at the same speed, and deduced that light was a very high frequency electromagnetic disturbance.

Maxwell built his theory on the earlier work of Michael Faraday, who had published the results of his many electrical, magnetic, and electromagnetic experiments in his *Experimental Researches in Electricity* (1839). Faraday later showed that magnetism had an effect on light, which really set scientists pondering. He was a self-taught experimental genius but lacked knowledge of mathematics. His explanation of magnetism was that there were lines of force surrounding a magnet, and similarly his explanation of electrostatics was that there were lines of force between electrically charged bodies.

William Thomson read Faraday's work and was amazed that it did not contain any mathematical equations. After further study he was able to contribute the necessary mathematical treatment which he published in his multi-part article "On the Mathematical Theory of Electricity in Equilibrium." Maxwell while at King's College, London, made use of Thomson's work and published "On Faraday's Lines of Force" in 1855, and "On Physical Lines of Force" in 1861.[58]

Maxwell's major work however was his *Treatise on Electricity and Magnetism*, which he published in 1873. This two-volume set was difficult to follow and not for the faint of heart.[59] Within the book was the germ of a theory that would eventually disclose the mystery of wireless waves, although Maxwell left no clue in his work as to how electromagnetic waves could be produced or detected. Maxwell and Stokes were both at Cambridge University and Stokes was familiar with Maxwell's work.

However it would take many years and the diligent work of three other researchers to unlock the secrets of these waves, to interpret them, to expand Maxwell's work into a theory that was more understandable, and to systematize it in what are known today as Maxwell's electromagnetic equations. These researchers, who became known as the Maxwellians, were the Irish mathematical physicist George Francis FitzGerald, resident in Dublin; the physicist and experimenter Oliver J. Lodge, resident in London; and the reclusive mathematician Oliver Heaviside, who

{ 214 }

The great theoretical physicist James Clerk Maxwell (1831–1879), who was developing an understanding of electromagnetic waves at the same time that Hughes was transmitting and receiving them.

also resided in London. They corresponded about their research and thus left a historical record of their work.

It was FitzGerald and Lodge who were the first to be intrigued by Maxwell's *Treatise*. These two met in their late twenties at a British Association (BA) meeting in Dublin in 1878 and became firm friends in their common pursuit of Maxwell's theory. Lodge went on to give a paper "On a Hypothesis Concerning the Ether in Connection with Maxwell's Theory of Electricity" at a BA meeting in August of 1879.

Lodge was particularly interested in the electromagnetic waves associated with light. He reasoned that if he could generate these waves he would be able to use his eye, rather than some as yet uninvented apparatus, as a detector. Lodge's paper stimulated FitzGerald to start looking into electromagnetic waves, and he initially concluded that it would be impossible to generate them. He gave a paper in November 1879 to the Royal Dublin Society "On the Impossibility of Originating Wave Disturbances in the Ether by the Means of Electric Forces."[60]

> However these [displacement currents] may be produced, by any system of fixed or movable conductors charged in any way, and discharged themselves amongst one another, they will never be so distributed as to originate wave-disturbances propagating through space outside the system.

It may or not have had any bearing on Hughes, but FitzGerald was in communication with Stokes[61] on the subject of light and the effect of magnetism in November of 1879 and mentioned to Stokes that he had just given a paper on the impossibility of generating waves electrically. This was only three months before Stokes witnessed Hughes's experiments. In 1883 after further consideration FitzGerald reversed this opinion about the impossibility of generating the waves.

All of this theoretical speculation was taking place while Hughes was actually generating the mysterious waves and detecting them! Thus there were two brilliant theorists wondering whether it were possible, and if so, how, to produce and detect electromagnetic waves, at the same time that Hughes was walking up and down Great Portland Street generating the waves and wondering what on earth they could be. But these practical and theoretical lines of investigation did not meet, at least not yet. Hughes, discouraged by Stokes, never published his paper, and so Lodge and FitzGerald remained unaware of his work; and Hughes had not read Maxwell's *Treatise*, whose mathematical approach was largely beyond his grasp, and he had no knowledge of the theoretical works of Lodge and FitzGerald, which might have helped him understand what was happening in his experiments.

In February of 1880 Lodge wrote to FitzGerald with his ideas for generating electromagnetic waves of frequency high enough to be in the visible spectrum by a method of multiple cascading coils that would double the waves' frequency at each stage, or alternatively using the discharge of a condenser (capacitor). However Fitzgerald's negative reaction put Lodge off any further exploration of how to produce ether waves. In 1881 Lodge moved from London to take up a position as professor of physics at Liverpool University and became preoccupied with establishing a program and a department. He would go on to play an important role in wireless discovery and technology, but not until later in the 1880s.

By 1882 FitzGerald realized his error regarding the impossibility of generating electromagnetic waves and issued corrections and additions to his earlier paper, stating that it was possible, and he tried to calculate how much energy would be radiated by an oscillating electrical current. In 1883 he suggested that they could be generated using a circuit consisting of inductance, capacitance, and resistance, but he was at a loss as to how to detect the waves. At the time neither he nor Lodge assumed there would be enough power in the electromagnetic wave to generate sparks. FitzGerald went on to make important contributions to the development of Maxwell's equations.

It was thus left to Heinrich Hertz in Germany in 1888 to generate electromagnetic waves in the ether, to detect them, and to prove that Maxwell had it right all along. He was followed by Guglielmo Marconi who saw the great potential of wireless and set about developing it.

Hughes's work did not come to light until many years later, when Sir William Crookes wrote an article "On Some Possibilities of Electricity" in the *Fortnightly Review*[62] in February of 1892. Crookes's article was wide-ranging and farsighted in predicting the future of wireless at a time when Guglielmo Marconi was just starting his experiments. In one paragraph in the article he alluded to wireless experiments that he had witnessed some years earlier:

> This is no mere dream of a visionary philosopher. All the requisites needed to bring it within the grasp of daily life are well within the possibilities of discovery, and are so reasonable and so clear in the path of researches which are now being actively prosecuted in every capital of Europe that we may any day expect to hear that they have emerged from the realm of speculation into those of sober fact. Even now, indeed, telegraphing without wires is possible within a restricted radius of a few hundred yards and some years ago I assisted at experiments where messages were transmitted from one part of a house to another without intervening wire by almost identical means here described.

In 1899, The author John Joseph Fahie was completing a book titled *A History of Wireless Telegraphy* and asked Sir William Crookes about the experiments he was alluding to. Crookes wrote back[63] saying that the experimenter had been Prof. Hughes, and added:

> I have not ceased since then urging on him to publish an account of his experiments. I do not feel justified in saying more about them, but if you were to write to him, telling him what I say, it might induce him to publish. It is a pity that a man who was so far ahead all other workers in the field of wireless telegraphy should lose all other credit due to his great ingenuity and prevision.

Fahie then wrote to Hughes:

> Dear Prof. Hughes; I have now in the press a History of Wireless Telegraph from 1838 to 1899, and in writing to Sir William Crookes for information he tells me that many years ago he saw some experiments of yours with the microphone in which you signaled from one part of a house to another without connecting wires, and he desires me to refer to you for particulars. I think with Sir William, that it is a pity you have not hitherto published your results, and I sincerely hope you will now do so. If you would kindly favor me with a short account, I could find room for it in my book, which now is in the printer's hands.—Sincerely yours,
>
> J.J. Fahie

Hughes replied:[64]

> Your letter of 26th instant has brought on me a flood of old souvenirs in relation to my past experiments on aerial telegraphy. They were completely unknown to the general public, and I feared that a few distinguished men who saw them had forgotten them, or at least had forgotten how the results showed them were produced.... At this late date I do not wish to set up any claim to priority, as I have never published a word on the subject; and it

would be unfair to later workers in the same field to spring an unforeseen claimant to the experiments which they have certainly made without any knowledge of my work.

But in the end Hughes seems to have been persuaded, and he sent another letter to Fahie (April 29, 1899) outlining the experiments he carried out and who had witnessed them. It is a softer version than the one in his notebook and there is no mention of the difference of opinion with Prof. Stokes over induction vs. conduction. Hughes also gives credit to Hertz, Lodge, Marconi, and Branly, who had all made great progress in the field since his 1879 experiments. In addition to the account in Fahie's book, descriptions of Hughes's experiments appeared in *The Electrician* of May 5, 1899, pp. 40–41, and in *The Electrical Review* 44.1123 (June 2, 1899), in the latter case with sketches of Hughes's apparatus.

Years later Sir Oliver Lodge[65] reflected on Hughes's discovery and referred to him as a singular genius and brilliant experimenter and as a man who thought with his fingers:

All this was in the early 'eighties and before either Hertz or me. Hughes was a telegraphist, and though he would have never worked out the subject mathematically as Hertz did, and would have not been interested in matters of theory, he might well have stumbled, even at that early date, on something like a rudimentary system of wireless signaling had he been encouraged. But he was not encouraged. He showed his results to the great and splendid mathematical physicist Sir George Stokes; and Stokes, alas, turned them down, considering that they were explicable either by leakage or some other known kind of fact. That is the danger of too great knowledge; it looks askance at anything lying beyond or beneath its extensive scope; whereas an experimenter operating at first hand on Nature may quite well occasionally stumble on a fact which lies outside the purview of contemporary science, and which accordingly neither he nor anyone else at the time understands. Crookes himself had a similar experience.

If Hughes had been encouraged or if different referees had reviewed his experiment, perhaps wireless communications would have been launched twenty years earlier than they were, and maybe we would be measuring frequencies in units called hughes, kilohughes and megahughes instead of hertz, kilohertz and megahertz.

While Heinrich Hertz is credited with discovering wireless waves in 1888, Hughes had actually built a transmitter and receiver and operated them simultaneously in a demonstration in 1879, nine years earlier. Hughes's first public disclosure of his discovery was to a rather large group of his peers starting in November of 1879 and continued into early 1880, facts that are well documented.

Although he is best known for having walked up and down Great Portland Street with his mobile receiver, his demonstration of transmission from his Great Portland Street laboratory and reception at Langham Place, a distance of 200 to 300 yards, which was witnessed by members of the Royal Society, is a more significant milestone. It is of course ironic that Langham Place was where the British Broadcasting Corporation later established its headquarters.

While Hughes used a range of descriptive words for what he believed he had discovered, many have blamed his choice of the word "conduction" for the referees' confusion. However, it was an age when new terms were frequently being invented and existing ones misused, especially by the practical men like Hughes. The following note in a letter to Latimer Clark about his experiment shows how Hughes could certainly be confusing in his descriptions:[66]

> When you find time I will show you (in confidence) some experiments on aerial transmission which forces me to believe that induction is simply the result of polarization or rather a previous conduction—my time would be between 3 and 5 pm—but as I might be absent or engaged in some other experiment you had better name a day in advance so I would be free—we can talk over this when we meet.

Regardless of any confusion about terminology, the fact that Hughes could get a signal to travel such a long distance without connecting wires should not have been so readily dismissed, and should have elicited some further investigation by the referees. Stokes's conclusion that it was due to induction over such a long distance was clearly incorrect.

Hughes in his notes says that he had deduced that the signals were actually traveling through the air and visualized them as lines of force that radiated everywhere, with the receiving aerial being cut by these lines. He postulated that work was being done, which implied energy transfer, a necessary condition for reception and detection of the signal. The larger the aerial, the better the reception was, although he noted that the signal strength appeared to decrease in proportion to the square of the distance from his transmitting aerial. He found that by using a vertical aerial and ground transmitter he increased his transmitting signal strength. This was one of Hughes's breakthroughs, which Marconi rediscovered in 1885 and which enabled him to extend his transmission beyond 500 yards.

Stokes is consistently named as the one who derailed Hughes's wireless research, and in 1922 Sir Joseph Larmor, Stokes's successor at Cambridge, came out in his defense.[67] While he makes a number of points relating to ambiguity in Hughes's experiments, he admits that he only spent one day perusing Hughes's notebooks. He implies that there was some embellishment of the facts regarding Hughes's experiments when they came to light some twenty years later. This is true to some extent. For instance the word "coherer" was introduced to refer to Hughes's detectors, but this word did not come into use until well after Hughes's experiments. Also, the distances over which Hughes had successfully transmitted a signal were extended somewhat: according to the original account, "sounds seem to slightly increase for a distance of 60 yards, then gradually diminish, until at 500 yards I could no longer with certainty hear the transmitted signals," but in the later retelling, it was claimed that the sounds "could be heard at a distance of 500 yards up and down the street."

But it cannot be denied that one of Hughes's historically significant discoveries was his development of methods to receive and detect wireless waves. The key element of the receiver was his signal detector. Hughes can actually be credited with three types of detector: the carbon and steel, the metal oxide, and the mercury iron.[68] These were all detectors that would later be called self-restoring coherers. That is, they could detect signals continuously, remaining sensitive after repeated exposure to electromagnetic waves, such as receiving a continuous series of blips from his transmitter. This name distinguished this type of detector from non-restoring coherers which could only detect a single event or blip, after which they had to be manually reset. Hughes had actually experimented with these types of coherers with his metal-particle-filled glass tubes, which Edouard Branly was credited with discovering later in 1890, and which wireless developers unfortunately became enamored with for the next several years.[69] Hughes abandoned these devices due to their inability to detect continuous signals such as those generated by his clockwork driven repetitive pulse transmitter.

It is interesting to note that while Hughes's experiments were witnessed (but not published) in 1879–80, in the twenty years up to when the experiments were published in 1899, no other detector (rectifier) had appeared on the wireless scene.

Hughes's carbon steel detector consisted of a carbon pencil contact resting on a bright steel needle, which Hughes often referred to as a microphonic joint. This device was in effect a contact rectifier using a point contact to form a semiconductor junction. Another configuration used coke rather than a carbon pencil. There were a number of configurations which were often mounted in glass bottles for protection. It was not until 1908 that Louis Austin of the US Bureau of Standards characterized the carbon steel junction as a contact rectifier and published data on its voltage vs. current characteristics which showed its non-linearity.[70]

In 1902 H. Shoemaker and Greenleaf Pickard filed a patent assigned to the American Wireless and Telegraph Co. for a detector consisting of five steel needles sandwiched between two carbon blocks.[71] The device could be tilted to alter the pressure of the needles on the carbon. Writing later in 1919 on "How I Invented the Crystal Detector," Pickard explicitly tied his work to that of Hughes, essentially starting his experimental work from where Hughes had left off twenty or so years earlier with the carbon steel detector. In the article he notes:[72]

> A simple carbon steel microphone consisting of a sewing needle resting lightly against a carbon block in series with a cell or two of dry battery and a telephone receiver formed a most effective detector exceeding the coherer in sensitiveness, speed of working and reliability.

In addition to Pickard's work there was much activity in the early 1900s as a new batch of experimenters started searching for a better detection apparatus than the

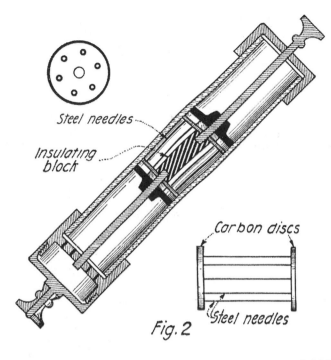

Steel needles

Insulating block

Carbon discs

Steel needles

Fig. 2

Dissatisfied with the then current coherer detectors and their inherent need to be constantly mechanically reset, Greenleaf Whittier Pickard successfully resumed Hughes line of research by experimenting with the point contact detector of carbon and steel needle.

coherer.[73] Pickard continued his research, moving from carbon to mineral crystal such as galena. These mineral crystals had various impurities both inside them and on their surface, and when the right point was located with a steel needle, they acted as a diode rectifier. This needle probe became known as a cat's whisker.[74]

As crystal detectors developed, more robust devices were made using a fixed spring contact or compression connections to the crystal, precluding the need to probe for a hot spot and making the devices significantly more shock-proof. Modern developments led to the semiconductor P-N diode.

There was a common belief among experimenters of the time that these devices detected by thermo-couple action, something Hughes had also believed.[75] It was not until George Pierce published a paper on "Crystal Rectifiers for Electric Currents and Electric Oscillations" in July of 1907 that scientists came to understand that it was actually rectification that was taking place in these solid-state devices.[76]

Hughes's carbon steel detector continued to see service into World War II, when it was used in prisoner-of-war camps to receive AM wireless broadcasts and was known as the fox-hole crystal set. It was made from scavenged parts that included the broken end of a lead pencil resting on the edge of a razor blade as the detector.

Hughes's second type of detector—the copper oxide detector—was a copper wire loop which Hughes states that he prepared by heating it in the flame of a lamp; this would have caused two thin layers of oxide to form. First, next to the base copper would have been cuprous oxide (Cu_2O), which takes on a deep salmon color. This active layer has the characteristics of a semiconductor. On top of this was a layer of

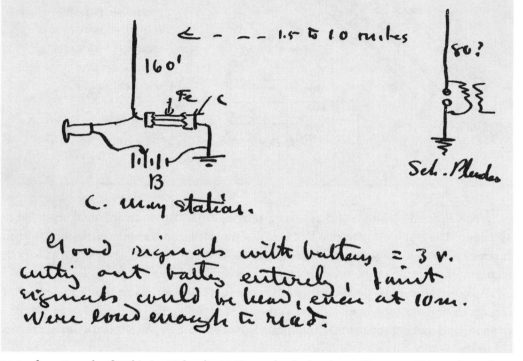

Notes from Greenleaf Whittier Pickard's 1902 notebook showing a diagram of his receiver of the same configuration as Hughes using a carbon and steel needle detector and telephone receiver where he was able to receive signals over considerable distances.

cupric oxide (CuO), which takes on a black color and is a non-conductor. In his hundreds of experiments Hughes must have hit on the fact that the black oxide layer first needed to be cleaned off, exposing the cuprous oxide layer underneath. His detector thus consisted of a copper wire with one end formed into a small loop that had the cuprous oxide layer on it. Into this loop was inserted a steel needle that was in contact with the oxide layer. The copper wire and the steel needle formed the two detector contacts.

A copper oxide junction acts as a diode rectifier, and it is assumed that this is what Hughes had created. Copper oxide rectifiers came into widespread use in the 1900s, and were known as metal rectifiers. They were eventually eclipsed by selenium rectifiers which in turn were replaced by the solid-state semiconductor diode.

Hughes's third type of detector was the iron wire mercury detector. This consisted of iron wires dipping into mercury. While Hughes appeared to prefer the other detectors, this was a significant discovery and worked well (it was also self-restoring). Iron mercury detectors were further used and developed in Italy by Prof. Thomas Tommasina, Luigi Solari, and Paolo Castelli, who used a tube with a drop of mercury placed between two iron electrodes. This device was also known as the Italian Navy Coherer and was used by Marconi in his 1901 transatlantic wireless experiment.[77]

It is unfortunate that Hughes died before seeing these detectors put into use with the many wireless applications of the early 1900s. But at least the authors J. J. Fahie and J. Munro were able to document Hughes's wireless experiments, which otherwise might easily have gone unnoticed.

In 1897 Hughes went back and inserted a note into the front of his December 5, 1879 notebook. This had the heading "Nov 30 1897—Persons who saw* my Aerial Transmission Experiments."[78] It turned out that 1897 was an important year as it was when Marconi obtained his first wireless patent; it was also when Crookes's article of 1892 which mentioned Hughes's earlier wireless experiments was reprinted in the *Electrician*.[79] Oliver Lodge also brought up Crookes's article the following month in his own article on "The History of the Coherer Principle" in the November issue of the *Electrician*, which may have triggered Hughes's memory. There was quite a bit of resentment at the time by British scientists, including Lodge, over the broad claims made by Marconi in his patent. Consequently there was much discussion and several articles about earlier work in this same area as part of an attempt to weaken Marconi's patent. By making this note Hughes was probably preparing in case he should be called on for support or in case someone followed up on Crookes's article.

Hughes had been knocking at the gate of radiotelegraphy with his experiments. He was using an automatic transmitter (his clock interrupter) which was putting out a series of single pulses—we could stretch a bit and say that he was transmitting the Morse letter "E." As telegraphy was never far from his mind, it was probably only a matter of time before he would have tried to connect a Morse key to the interrupter and transmit a message in Morse code. This might then have led to him trying his own telegraph instrument with his wireless link.

It would have surprised Hughes to learn that in 1923 not only was his printing telegraph still in use, but it was part of a duplex wireless link between London and Berlin. The route was from the GPO in London by land wire to Stonehaven, and thence by wireless link to Zellendorf. The other route was from Königswusterhausen to an aerial on the roof of the GPO in London. Twenty-five messages per hour were being handled in each direction:[80]

In January this year some hundreds of public telegrams were exchanged over the Anglo-German Government owned wireless systems between Berlin and London by means of the Hughes direct printing telegraph apparatus, an invention of the late professor of that name. Curiously enough, one of the oldest forms of printing telegraph (it was invented over 50 years ago) has become associated with and proved itself adaptable to the most modern system of telegraphic communication.

10

THE JOYOUS YEARS

LONDON, JUNE 1880.

"**P**rofessor David Edward Hughes, Fellow of the Royal Society"—the sight of that title appended to his name must have thrilled him. Being elected to that illustrious body had long been one of his ambitions, and now it had happened. In fact, Hughes was one of only two candidates elected out of a pool of fifty-two that year. The letter of notification was signed by the President of the Society, Sir Gabriel Stokes.[1]

Hughes had not been on the best of terms with Stokes since Stokes had dismissed his "ether waves" experiments as nothing more than electrical induction. It has always puzzled historians that Hughes, having discovered and demonstrated wireless waves and knowing that he was onto something totally new, never pursued the issue further, and did not even publish his results. His demeanor during this period was certainly uncharacteristic, and he did not appear to be the same person who, only a short time earlier, had clearly had fire in his belly, battling it out with Edison and defending Preece's honor. Some possible causes for his failure to pursue this line of research were mentioned in the previous chapter—his desire not to cross Stokes, concern about being disparaged in the press for describing a new force which he did not understand, his changing interests—but there may have been a personal cause as well.

This period was not a happy one for Hughes and it is certainly understandable that he may have been despondent. His wife Maria, who was not a well person and was described as being an invalid in 1878, died, although little is known about her or the circumstances.[2] The grim reaper however was not done with Hughes. He received a telegram from his brother John in America in November of 1879 telling him that his wife Fanny had unexpectedly passed away. Hughes knew his brother was ill and before opening the telegram may have thought that it was about him. No sooner had Christmas passed than he received another telegram, this one from John's daughter Lilly, with the sad news that his brother had passed away on January 15, 1880.

Hughes's friend, William Preece, had also lost his wife some years earlier and could certainly empathize with Hughes.[3] He had eventually overcome his despondency by traveling abroad. Possibly feeling that the same remedy might work for Hughes, he selected him as a commissioner for the forthcoming Paris Electrical Exhibition. Preece was at that time President of the Society of Telegraph-Engineers, and as such, was able to arrange the position for Hughes. In his capacity as an advisor to the Post Office, Preece also kept Hughes busy testing iron wires.

The Paris Electrical Exhibition was to be a significant event as it was the first exclusively electrical exhibition. It represented the coming of age of electricity and was also a celebration of the fiftieth anniversary of Michael Faraday's discovery that moving a magnet in and out of a coil of wire resulted in the generation of electricity. Electricity, once just a novelty, was now growing in importance and becoming a separate branch of science. The broad diffusion of electricity had been assured by its first serious application, the telegraph, for the function of the telegraph was communications, which meant that any area that was connected to the telegraph network would quickly learn about other electrical inventions. News and discoveries from many nations were now easily and rapidly disseminated. New applications for electricity seemed limitless as dynamos, motors, electric lights, electric tramcars, telephones and many more products were being rolled out.

France announced it would hold the exhibition at the Palais de l'Industrie on the Champs-Élysées in Paris from August to November of 1881, and the British government was invited to participate. The exhibition was to coincide with the International Electrical Congress where discussions would take place on "Electrical Units," "International Telegraphy" and "The Diverse Applications of Electricity."

The British government, however, appeared to be strapped for cash to support the event, as the author J. Munro reported:[4]

> ...the British Government unlike the Governments of other countries, contributed nothing, except a few yards of national bunting. Fortunately the Society of Telegraph Engineers and Electricians came to the rescue.

The Society of Telegraph-Engineers and Electricians recognized the importance of the exhibition and congress to the industry, and named Hughes, as well as Sir Charles Bright, as commissioners.[5] Hughes, of course, was an ideal choice, as he was well known on the Continent and fluent in French and German. As August approached, Hughes was busier than ever, raising money from private subscribers and industry to fund Britain's participation in the exhibition and making the final preparations.

It was at this point that he had received the urgent telegraph message from Alexander Graham Bell in America seeking Hughes's advice on how to use his metal detector to locate the assassin's bullet in President Garfield. Hughes dropped what he was doing to address the problem and must have felt the sudden weight of the responsibility for this man's life on his shoulders. After Hughes sent his recommendations all he could do was to wait and hope that Bell would be successful. The weeks of waiting dragged into months and Hughes had to attend to his duties at the exhibition, but was saddened to learn in September that the battle for Garfield's life had been lost.

The Paris exhibition was an opportunity for each country to showcase its electrical technology and inventions. The British section of the exhibition had on show the Wheatstone automatic telegraph, historical instruments of Cooke and Wheatstone, and the Hughes induction balance. There was a large display associated with submarine telegraph cables, an area in which Great Britain excelled. It included one of Sir William Thomson's sensitive siphon recorders which was used for receiving the weak signals on undersea cables. There was no Hughes printing telegraph equipment on display in the British section, but it was adequately represented as it was displayed by many of the Continental countries.[6]

An amusing incident occurred one day when Hughes was introduced to M. Cochery, the French Minister of Posts and Telegraphs, who was visiting the British section. During the introductions he did not hear Hughes's name. Hughes conducted the minister around the various exhibits, showing him the Wheatstone automatic telegraph machine. Cochery, not in a mood to be outdone by his cross-Channel rivals, commented that the machine was worth nothing, and he could get better results from the Hughes printing telegraph that they used in France. Upon hearing this, Hughes thanked the minister for his compliment. Cochery stared at him in disbelief. Turning to an associate he marveled that someone would thank him for insulting their equipment. Of course, Cochery had not realized that he had been talking to the inventor of the Hughes instrument.

Hughes did have an induction balance on display, and when Elisha Gray, the American inventor, came by, he sought out Hughes, intending to see if his device could actually do what he had read it could do. He told Hughes that fifteen years earlier an iron filing had become embedded in his finger, and while it was no longer painful, he asked Hughes to see if he could find it. Hughes tested each finger in turn and correctly located it. After this demonstration Gray's finger was in constant demand.

In the French section, visitors could see Hughes's sensitive relays which were used on the French railways in their signaling and safety systems, installed by M. Latigue.[7] One of the more popular nightly events which must have amused Hughes was the "theatrophone," which made use of his carbon microphone.[8] M. Clément Ader had set up a demonstration of the first stereophonic sound system that people could experience, and word soon got around about this new wonder. Visitors were amazed to be able not only to hear a live opera performance from the opera house some miles away, but also to be able to visualize the singer's position on stage and to follow his or her movements from left to right, or vice versa. The phenomenon was described as giving an "auditive perspective" and as being based on the "theory of binauricular audition." The microphones used at the opera house were of Hughes's carbon pencil design. Ten microphones were spread across the front of the stage, covering the full span in order to capture the stereophonic sound effect.[9]

The demonstration was given in the exhibition hall between eight and eleven o'clock in the evening. An enormous number of people crowded around the entrance to the building before the doors opened, and visitors queued up in the gallery adjacent to the three telephone rooms.[10]

> The visitor was ushered into a mystical saloon that was hung with tapestry and thickly carpeted, to silence the footfalls. Sets of telephones were placed at intervals round the walls, and each person holding a pair to his ears stood waiting for a signal. An alarm bell tinkled and lo! The strains of Gounod or of Verdi burst upon the ear as if by magic....

There was an American section in the exhibition that featured many of Edison's Menlo Park creations. It is not known whether Hughes made his way there to see his "friend" Edison.

When the Electrical Congress convened on September 30, Hughes was serving with some of the most respected scientists of the day such as Prof. Helmholtz, Sir William Thomson, and M. Cochery, and was selected to chair some of the working meetings.[11]

Parisians don their headphones for a live stereo performance from the opera house, a system which was a descendant of the "Theatrophone."

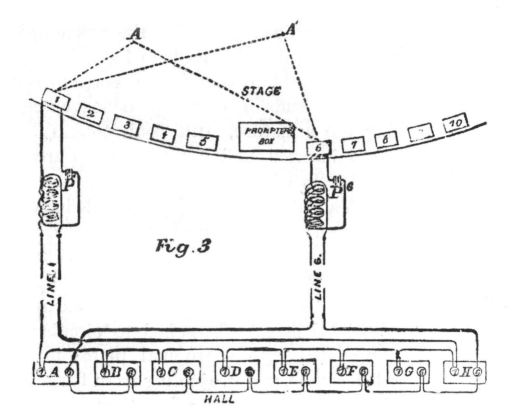

Diagram showing how Clément Ader had arranged the microphones, each of them based on Hughes's carbon microphone design, along the front of the stage to obtain the stereoscopic effect.

Hughes, of course, relished the extended stay in Paris; he enjoyed the city and the French way of life, and it gave him an opportunity to visit with the friends he had made when he had resided there. This time was to be different, though, as he sought out one very special person, and that was Anna Chadbourne (then residing at 83, Rue des Petits Champs), whom he described in a letter to his sister Maggie in America:[12]

When I first knew Anna in Paris she was quite a young girl but that was more than twenty years since. Her relations were friends with Mrs. Lett—perhaps whom you remember—it was she who introduced me at a dinner party—we became friends—I had again to visit the family to report the death of Mrs. Lett the visits were constantly more and more repeated—we became more and more friends then I had to run off in Italy for my Telegraph—on my return saw them all again—I had again to run off to Russia and this kept up—getting more and more friends—but constantly running off to some country with my Telegraph time slipped by—we have both become much older and now neither of us can be considered young.

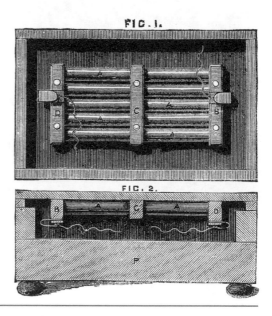

Each microphone had ten carbon pencils mounted on a thin pine board to receive the sound vibrations. The board was mounted to a large lead slab on rubber feet to isolate it from the stage.

Hughes was not sure of Anna's exact age but believed she was some years younger than him. He describes his and her ages and appearances as the letter continues:[13]

> Now why wont Ladies tell the truth about their age? I always do about mine saying I am some five or ten years younger than I am—!!—of course I cannot be very exact as I don't remember the event and I am not so foolish to believe other peoples talk.... Any way I look much the oldest. My moustache has all gone white. Not a blessed brown or black hair left. My hair is all grey—half and half—but fast turning completely white— (oh dear) but Anna has not a grey hair—it is a beautiful brown—and she is very proud of it—There is no doubt she has beautiful hair and the most perfect teeth possible—not a single faulty or plugged tooth—whilst many of mine are gone.

Historians had assumed that it was during the fall of 1881 or spring of 1882 that David Hughes finally proposed marriage to Anna Chadbourne, and that she accepted, setting the marriage for August of 1882 in Paris.[14] But this is not correct: the April 1881 London census tells a different tale and gives up a secret. It lists two residents at 108 Great Portland Street, London, by the names of David E. Hughes and Anna Hughes, and lists them as married![15] So it appears they were cohabiting some eighteen months before their official marriage, certainly not the norm for Victorian times in Britain. Perhaps a bit of the Parisian Bohemian lifestyle had slipped across the Channel. It is impossible to know when Anna joined him in London, as Hughes left no trace in his notes.

Anna Chadbourne was a charismatic woman of striking beauty, an American by birth and a long-time resident of Paris. She was an accomplished artist and pianist, highly resourceful, with an adventurous spirit. Her marriage to David Hughes came at an appropriate time for both of them. In addition to providing companionship, she played an important part in his life as he more and more took on the role of a leading scientific figure. It was still very much a man's world, but she was able to subtly influence Hughes over the coming years. It was also due to her that some of Hughes's history was recorded, as she took the time to jot down notes about his life. This marriage was an important milestone in Hughes's life, and obviously one taken after much thought. As the rest of his life was to involve Anna Chadbourne, it is worth looking at who she really was—and it turns out that her life was filled with just as much drama as her husband's. To do this it is necessary to step back nearly thirty years.

＞━～━＜

The American artist George P.A. Healy's studio, Paris, 1856.[16]

Healy was busy arranging his studio when a knock came on the door.
"Why! Mr. Goodyear! How wonderful to see you!"

Healy had previously met Charles Goodyear back in America where they had been introduced by Daniel Webster. Goodyear was the inventor of vulcanized rubber and was over in Europe promoting his products.

"Mr. Healy, I told you I would come and bring the gutta-percha panels you thought impossible. Here they are—and here I am. Will you paint my portrait?"

Healy positioned his subject and started to paint, commenting on the smoothness of the panels and the joy to paint on them. After some time Healy ended the session and suggested continuing the following day.

"Where can I reach you Mr. Goodyear?"

"At my shop—40 rue Vivienne...."

"Oh, of course!"

"If I am not in, give the message to my partner, Mr. Morey; he's almost as interested in this as we are...."

Healy recognized the name as he had painted Morey's wife Mrs. Anna Chadburne Morey's portrait the previous year.[17]

After Goodyear had left, the newspaper was delivered to Healy's studio. Casually reading through the day's news, he was startled to see Goodyear's name in reference to his partner Mr. Morey. He re-read the paragraph and couldn't believe it: Morey was dead! He was sure that Goodyear had no knowledge of the tragic news of his partner when he was there.

In a matter of hours, Anna Chadbourne's life was drained of all the gaiety that Paris had to offer and was filled with misery and despair as the circumstances surrounding her husband's tragic death unfolded. She was widowed at only thirty years of age.

Her and her husband's life in Paris had been idyllic, almost fairytale-like. They had arrived in Paris as a young married couple, and through Charles Morey's

Anna Chadbourne shown engaged in her great passion, painting, in a portrait by George P. A. Healy. Healy painted many eminent Americans, from Charles Goodyear to President Ulysses S. Grant. Photograph © 2011 Museum of Fine Arts, Boston.

entrepreneurial skills, had risen financially to enjoy plush accommodation in the heart of Paris, where they experienced a fast-paced life and extensive travel. They seemed to have flourished.

Anna Chadbourne was born on February 22, 1826, the daughter of Dr. Thomas Chadbourne and Clarissa Dwight Green, an established New England family in Concord, New Hampshire. Anna married Charles Morey in 1849 and they moved to a residence just off Broadway in New York City. In a letter to her brother Anna described herself as a "wild country girl" arriving in the city.[18] Her father described her as "the same laughing, giggling girl as ever" as she enjoyed the outdoors and horseback riding and was also becoming an accomplished musician and artist. It appears that the Chadbournes were an entrepreneurial family, for Anna's uncle, Robert Eastman, had invented a machine for dressing, shaping, and ornamenting stone for architectural use. It is believed that it was through her uncle that Anna met her husband, as Charles Morey was an agent and promoter for this machine.

Anna and Charles Morey's residence in New York was short lived, as they soon headed off for Europe to pursue Charles's business opportunities.[19] From 1849 to 1851 they seem to have alternated between London, Le Havre and Paris, as well as traveling extensively on the Continent, often joined by Anna's father, Dr. Thomas Chadbourne. To further promote the business Morey exhibited the architectural stone dressing machinery in the Crystal Palace at London's Great Exhibition of 1851. It was here that he met a fellow Yankee exhibitor from New Haven, Connecticut, by the name of Charles Goodyear, the inventor of vulcanized rubber, a process that revolutionized the rubber industry, who was exhibiting rubber pontoons and lifeboats.[20]

Morey was taken with Goodyear's process of making rubber into a usable form and was no doubt captivated by Goodyear's enthusiastic promotion of its many possibilities. Morey's entrepreneurial spirit kicked in, and he and Goodyear struck an agreement. To Goodyear it seemed a good match as Morey was a young dynamic French-speaking American with goals similar to his—which were to succeed and become rich. Morey devoted himself to the new business venture, traveling to Paris to start promoting vulcanized rubber, sensing that the market was ready for the introduction of this new material. During 1852–53 the manufacture of India rubber boots and shoes was in full swing and business was reported to be good.[21]

> For about two years the prospect of large returns from this quarter were very flattering; so much so, that Mr. Goodyear was led to make extraordinary preparations for the opening of the "Exposition Universelle" in Paris, in 1855. He fitted up, at an expense of 50,000 dollars, two elegant courts in the most central part of the exhibition palace....

Charles Morey and Anna started to reap the rewards of her husband's hard work:[22]

> Although quiet in his personal habits, he was elegant, perhaps too expensive in his tastes. He used to occupy a splendid apartment on the first story of the Rue de la Paix,

and drive a pair of horses not easily matched by the finest turn-outs on the Champs Elysees or in the Bois de Bologne.

The Rue de la Paix was and still is a very elegant and fashionable area of Paris. Of course, they had a staff to support their lifestyle, and Anna mentioned engaging a new cook and valet de chambre. There was no doubt a liveried staff to take care of and drive the coach. Anna busied herself with her painting, having permission to go to the Louvre and do studies in the Galerie du Luxembourg, making copies of famous paintings. Paris was, of course, an artists' haven, and it was a time when Monet, Renoir and Manet were developing their styles. Anna may even have benefited from the advice of Monet's early artistic supervisor, Eugène Boudin, when she was in Le Havre.

Charles Goodyear began marketing his rubber process in Belgium and Austria while Morey forged ahead in France:[23]

> Mr. Morey, his agent, speaking French fluently, endowed with remarkable tact for business, had awakened an extraordinary interest in the rubber trade and developed it in a few months into proportions that could only have been reached by a healthy growth in five or six years. Three large companies were formed, and commenced the manufacture of various articles under Mr. Goodyear's licenses.

Morey bought the French rights to Goodyear's vulcanizing process for hard rubber in March 1853 and went on to patent several products of his own, which he manufactured.[24]

As mentioned above, Goodyear saw the exposition which was to take place in Paris in 1855 as a grand opportunity to publicize this new rubber material and display the goods and products that could be produced from it. He spared no expense and put on a display of inlaid India rubber furniture, ornamental objects, finely carved caskets and rich jewelry, while the walls were hung with valuable portraits painted on panels of rubber.[25]

The business was growing, and Goodyear and Morey were excited at the prospects for still further growth. However, events soon took a tragic turn. Goodyear's patents were constantly being challenged in the French courts, and although up to that time, the rulings had been in his favor, there was a new challenge, and the court reversed its earlier decisions. This left Goodyear in a very exposed position financially as his business was based on licensing his patents. The large sums of money he had spent on the exhibition, along with other expenses for machinery, were leading to a cash flow problem. The court's ruling made creditors and licensees feel vulnerable and they started knocking on Goodyear's door, tightening their financial grip. The troubles went on to engulf Morey and he was arrested for non-payment of debt and taken to the "Clichy debtor's prison":[26] French law allowed any foreigner to be arrested for debt on the simple declaration of a Frenchman. Upon hearing the news Anna Morey rushed out to the court to secure his release. The judge granted his release for the following day, December 30.

Morey's stay in prison and the events that surrounded it were recorded later in the *Boston Journal*, from which this account is taken:[27]

An earlier riser than most of the prisoners, he was in the habit of taking a morning walk in a corridor at the end of which, on the third story, was a window looking out towards the barrier of Clichy. At nine o'clock on the 30th December, he was standing before this window with his hands in his pockets, when he was ordered away by the sentinel below, who, upon his remaining, either because he misunderstood or did not hear the order, stupidly and cruelly shot him dead. The explosion of fire-arms brought all the prisoners rushing together, and as soon as the facts of the case were known, there was a general revolt. None of the officers were allowed to approach the corpse or even enter the corridor until the proper civil authorities and the Hon. Mr. Mason, the American Minister, had been sent for and had arrived.

Charles Morey, thirty-one years of age, was laid to rest on January 4, 1857.

The American minister in Paris demanded justice and reparation to Morey's widow. The guard was tried by court-martial and acquitted on the grounds that he had followed the orders given to him. The guard, a soldier from the 88th Regiment, had acted under a misconception of his duty. He remembered that when on guard in the criminal prison he had been ordered to fire on any prisoner who put his head out of the window and refused to retire when warned to do so, and he believed these orders were in force at the Clichy prison. To the American minister, this was far from just and he demanded from the French government liberal reparation to the widow. Negotiations lasted until July, and the government finally settled on a compensation of 76,000 francs (or $15,000).[28]

After the tragedy Anna stayed in Paris; her family took up residence there, and she had the support of her father, mother and brother William. Sadness, however, was not done with Anna as within two years her mother passed away. Anna was fairly secure after the settlement, and continued with her painting. It is here that Professor David Hughes made her acquaintance sometime in the early 1860s when he moved to Paris to promote his telegraph system. Although Hughes traveled extensively for his telegraph work and Anna returned to America for a period they remained in touch.

When Hughes returned from the Paris Electrical Exhibition to London in the fall of 1881 (presumably with Anna), he fell very ill with a throat ailment and remained so through February. He was susceptible to bronchitis, possibly a result of having damaged his health with the fumes of sulfur and mercury when carrying out experiments as a boy, and his cigarette smoking probably aggravated his chest condition, especially as he had the habit of soaking the cigarettes in petroleum spirits, believing that this was good for his throat! Another cause that has been suggested was the ozone present from the electrical machines at the exhibition. When he was finally well again, he started a new line of research on the subject of magnetism.

As summer approached he and Anna took a vacation in Switzerland, touring around the lakes as well as doing some mountain walking, and ending up in Paris in preparation for their marriage.[29] Their plan was to be married by the American ambassador at the American embassy, as both he and Anna were American citizens. However, recent changes in French law had taken this power away from ambassadors. They would now have to be married according to French law, with the ambassador in attendance so that he could verify it and issue the US stamp of approval.

One of the French requirements was for six months' residency in the parish where the marriage was to take place, which Hughes deemed impractical. The ambassador recommended that he "do that which all Americans have been obliged to do... go to England" and get married where requirements were easier to meet, and they took his advice. Hughes commented in a letter to his sister Maggie that he longed for the good old days in Kentucky, when a person only had to run off with the girl and go before a justice of the peace, declare their intentions, and it was all finished. Hughes did expose his softer side in an expression of joy in the same letter to his sister Maggie:[30]

> Oh dear! Oh dear! What an emotional time we shall have to go through in England crying, sobbing—smiles and kisses—all at the same time—I shall not tell anyone about it much more write about it....

Anna appears to have been prudent with her investments, such that they yielded an annual income of $2000 per year; she had invested in railroad bonds and gas shares as well as some property in Boston. Hughes indicated that their combined income would be about $5000, commenting that this was after deducting what he was sending quarterly to Maggie.[31]

David Hughes and Anna Chadbourne were married on September 11, 1882 in the parish church of St. Andrew, Holborn, London, the same church at which David Hughes had been baptized in 1829. Hughes told his sister that they did not intend to buy a house as they did not want to be tied down, but wished to be free to run about, traveling all over Europe or the seaside, as the fancy took them. He implied that they might take an apartment in Richmond while maintaining his laboratory and office in Great Portland Street. There was sufficient room there to enable them to stay if they wished to remain in town.[32]

Over the next few years, David Hughes's standing in the scientific community only increased, and he was constantly presenting papers and giving lectures on his experiments and discoveries regarding magnetism and its effects on various metals.

11

THE RISE OF THE THEORETICIANS

The gavel came down with a resounding bang, and the 150th Ordinary General Meeting of the Society of Telegraph-Engineers and Electricians was called to order. Mr. C. E. Spagnoletti, M. Inst. C.E., the former President, occupied the chair.[1]

Mr. Spagnoletti, after taking care of routine business, quickly moved on to the night's important event. "I now have the great pleasure of introducing to you my successor, Professor Hughes." The new President, Professor D. E. Hughes, F.R.S., then took the chair.

After a vote of thanks to the past president, Hughes stepped up to the podium to deliver his inaugural address. This was probably the most important speech he would ever give. If he followed in the tradition of his predecessors he would talk about the Society's accomplishments, making some mention of his own contributions. Hughes, however, had something completely different in mind: he had decided instead to give a paper on recent experiments he had carried out which were highly germane to their industry.

The meeting hall was full. The opening session, normally a draw, was more so on this occasion as Hughes was giving the speech. He had become one of the most respected scientists of his generation; when he spoke, people listened; when his name was mentioned, one of his inventions or discoveries came to mind. Honors continued to be bestowed on him, the latest the previous year when he was awarded the prestigious Royal Medal by the Royal Society.[2]

His audience sat ready and they sensed from his bearing and from the apparatus behind him that he was about to spring something new on them. He began:[3]

Before commencing the subject of my address this evening, I desire to express my sincere thanks to the Members of the Society of Telegraph-Engineers and Electricians for the great honour they have conferred on me by electing me as their President, and to assure them that I will do all in my power to aid and promote the interests of our Society, which are those of Applied Science in one of its highest branches.

It is the custom in our Society, that the elected president should open the Session by an address containing a general review of the present state of Electrical Science, or researches in some special branch which may be of interest. I have chosen the latter, as it enables me to present to you some researches which I have not yet published, and I propose to present these in the form of a paper rather than an address, in order to allow our members the opportunity of a full discussion on the subject, which I hope may bring forth many new facts in their possession.

The subject I have chosen is "The Self-Induction of an Electric Current in Relation to the Nature and Form of its Conductor."

The title of his presentation would not have raised many eyebrows, and in fact at first it might have seemed a bit anticlimactic. In his opening remarks there was a subtle reminder that the interests of the Society were really those of "applied science." There was also the question of who he was hoping would "bring forth new facts in their possession."

If people knew anything about Hughes, it was that he was never far from controversy, and this time was to be no different. What might have been a speech full of platitudes, a mere formality, was to become a catalyst and turning point not only for the Society, but also for electrical technology in general. The practical men of science (or at least some of them) would come to realize that the small group of theoreticians in their midst might actually be able to help them, and in fact, might hold the answers to many of their problems. This change would not come easily, and would be many years in the making.

The topic of Hughes's paper, self-induction, was not a well-understood electrical phenomenon at the time.[4] It was real, but was treated, through ignorance, as if it were something cloaked in darkness, lingering in the shadows, which only made its presence felt on its own terms. It was considered an evil force by some, while others tried to pretend it did not exist. William Preece, the senior electrician for the Post Office, referred to it as a "bête noire" and something to be eliminated. Self-induction was not a particularly easy phenomenon to comprehend, and had rather crept up on the practical men, becoming a nuisance as more telegraph lines were crowded onto poles and transmission speeds increased. This caused electrical interference between telegraph lines, resulting in incorrect message transmission. The problem had become even more prevalent with the introduction of the telephone, as telegraph lines caused interference on telephone lines, to the extent that in some areas telegraph messages could be heard on the telephone—so much for privacy.[5]

Hughes was primed for his address; perhaps he was not as charismatic a speaker as William Preece, but what he lacked in oratory skills he made up for with his enthusiastic presentation. He had experimented extensively with self-induction and its effects; in fact, he considered himself one of the top experts on the subject and had told William Preece that he thought as much. His latest experiments were first-of-a-kind and the results were not at all what he had expected. This made it all the more important to present them to his peers and see what they could make of them.

In the years prior to 1886, Hughes had tried his hand at theoretical scientific investigation.[6] He had delved into magnetism and presented many papers on the subject.[7] During these investigations he had increased his theoretical understanding of magnetism; perhaps he had not realized it, but in his earlier work his lack of theory had limited him as a research scientist. Other practical men were finding themselves in a similar situation: they were reaching the limit of their electrical knowledge, whether or not they knew it. Their industry had evolved and electrical science was increasing in its complexity, moving into uncharted territory that was severely testing their methods. The danger was that as the practical men clung on to their older ideas and empirical rules of thumb, they themselves would hinder progress. The problem was compounded by the fact that these practical men were often in positions of power, which made it harder for the theoreticians with their new ideas to make themselves heard.

When Hughes learned that he had been nominated for the presidency he probably decided to change course and get back to the practical matters that were of concern to the Society's members. This would have led him to look at the Society's accomplishments, possibly with a view to giving a traditional address based on the state of the art of the telegraph and telephone. The electricians after all had a lot to be proud of, as they had created a telegraph system that encompassed the civilized world. It had been constructed by trial and error, sheer will power, and exhaustive experimentation, one foot in front of the other, with some flashes of brilliance. It was electricians like Hughes, with smart hands guided by ingenious minds, who had invented its instruments and assisted its growth and development, and quite remarkably it had all come about with the benefit of little or no theoretical knowledge!

Their technology had evolved from simple beginnings, when it was just a matter of wiring components together and experimenting with them until they worked. For example, batteries were added at the sending end until there was sufficient signal strength at the receiving end to operate a Morse register or sounder. There was no theory involved, it was simply experimentation. Telegraph signals were sent on iron wires strung along the tops of poles up in the air that had low electrical capacitance. Signals consisted of relatively long pulses generated by manually switching a battery current on and off. Signaling speeds were low and operation was down at the bottom of the frequency spectrum, below ten cycles per second.[8] Test measurements on telegraph equipment and lines were made under static DC conditions using batteries, galvanometers, and Wheatstone bridges.

As the telegraph network grew, more telegraph wires were installed and were crowded onto the same telegraph poles in close proximity to each other. In addition, signals were being sent at a faster rate (more words per minute), and in Britain, some telegraph wires were being buried underground in iron pipes, increasing their electrical capacitance. When the challenge of the 2,000-mile transatlantic telegraph cable came along (which had significantly higher electrical capacitance), it caused a lot of head scratching as it defied the knowledge of the electricians. The simple rules that they had been using did not work anymore; there were obviously new and poorly understood factors in play. Not only was the signal attenuated, as was to be expected on such a long cable, but the cable seemed to swallow up any pulses sent into it, delaying and smearing them, eventually regurgitating them at the far end sometime later in a vastly different form.

The practical electricians, however, continued to apply the same rules that they had followed for landlines, increasing the voltage at the transmitting end until it was large enough to force something out at the receiving end. They found out the hard way that using very high voltages damaged the cable by destroying the insulation that protected the conducting wire from the seawater, thus causing a short circuit and rendering the whole cable useless. So while cut-and-try methods could get them so far, when applied to a major project such as the Atlantic cable, they had major drawbacks.

William Thomson was one of the first scientists to apply himself to understanding electrical phenomena on a theoretical level and to describing them using mathematical equations.[9] He produced an equation, his Square Law, that modeled the electrical parameters of a cable and their relationships, and which could be used to determine the best way to set up a submarine cable. However, this young theoretician had a hard time convincing his peers of the usefulness of his formula, and the practical men went out of their way to show that his equation was not only wrong, but totally contrary to their measurements.[10]

The adoption of faster telegraph speeds entailed the use of more rapid pulses with faster switching times, so that the frequencies of the signals were higher, although the electricians did not know what effect this would have. When the telephone was introduced, there was a move still higher in the frequency spectrum, and the need to deal with frequencies of up to 1,000 cycles per second and beyond. The fact that telephone signals were significantly lower in amplitude than telegraph signals did not help. The technology was shifting from the simpler laws that governed quasi direct current circuits to the more complex laws (many as yet unknown) that governed alternating current circuits and rapid pulse switching. As self-inductance was a byproduct of these conditions, it was becoming a more and more important factor in electrical circuits, and had crept up on the electricians over time.

Thomson's attempt can be considered one of the first to determine the laws that governed electrical technology. After his efforts, though, there was a long drought. The practical men, believing that experience and experiments were the keys to gaining new knowledge, continued to distrust the theoreticians. However, many years later, when the practical men decided to apply equations to transmission lines, they drew on Thomson's equation as the only one available, and applied it to all situations, even where it was not applicable. When Thomson produced his equation he considered four parameters: resistance, capacitance, inductance and leakage.[11] In the transatlantic telegraph cable the inductance was very low and capacitance was a dominating factor, while the signaling speed was low, so he decided to leave self-inductance out of the equation, and this decision was justified. Yet the practical men later applied it to cables where self-inductance was a significant factor, and this led to incorrect results.

The telegraph and telephone were becoming victims of their own success, and several problems were developing that needed solution. Electrical interference, limits on transmission speed, interference between telegraph lines and telephone lines, limits on distance for telephone communication, signal distortion—the situation would only get worse. These problems really needed to be addressed, and the sooner the better.

Perhaps it was meditation on these issues that prompted Hughes to refocus his speech on his industry's problems, and what better way to start than with what he perceived to be a major contributor to those problems—self-inductance. He had made some inroads into the subject several years earlier by solving some of the interference problems associated with telegraph lines.[12] Since then, hc had had gained significant experience with induction effects in his experiments with his induction balance.[13] Hughes hypothesized that many of the industry's problems were the result of self-induction occurring under dynamic conditions when pulse switching took place on telegraph lines. Previous to Hughes's experiments, little attention had been paid to the telegraph lines themselves, many believing that they could not have much effect—"after all it was just a piece of wire!" This myth was shortly to be dispelled by Hughes's experimental results and the discussion of them by the theoreticians.

Hughes was aware through the technical journals that some theorists had shown interest in the topic.[14] In fact, he later stated that he had seen articles by the theoretician Oliver Heaviside in *The Electrician* and was in the habit of cutting them out to save them.[15] However, the theoretician's papers and articles were full of mathematical formulae that went over the heads of the practical men, and consequently, little attention had been paid to them.

Hughes commenced his presentation by recapping some basic discoveries made by Michael Faraday and Joseph Henry and giving his reasons for making his experiments:[16]

> ...Faraday, who proved that on sending a current through a wire a momentary induced
> current in the opposite direction is evoked in its own wire; also that, on the cessation

of the primary current, a second induced or "extra-current" is excited in the direction of the primary. The effect is greatly augmented when the wire forms a coil, as we then have in addition the reaction of superposed currents; but the effect exists to a great extent even when the wire forms but a single loop, or a straight wire with the earth forming the return portion of the loop, as in all telegraph lines.

It has been generally supposed that the nature of the molecular condition of the metal through which the primary current passes exerted no influence upon the extra-currents except that due to resistance. I have previously pointed out that for induced currents "the rapidity of discharge has no direct relation with the electrical conductivity of the metal, for copper is much slower than zinc, and they are both superior to iron." This led me to make a study of these extra-currents, for which I constructed a special Induction Bridge, in order to measure both the primary and its extra-current separately at the instant of action.

He continued:[17]

A curious fact in relation to telegraphy is that all measurements are made during periods of a constant flow of current, whilst all instruments—particularly those working rapid changes in the current—work only during the rise and fall of the current, as in the variable period. Telegraph engineers, however, have not made the mistake of assuming that there is no difference in the resistance of a wire in these two periods, as it is well known that electro-magnets and coils have a far higher resistance during the rise and fall of a current, and coils simply augment the effect of a straight wire of a given length. The speed of telegraph instruments is greatly influenced by the resistance of the wire. I said in 1883 that a great difference would be found in the resistance of an electrical conductor if measured during the variable instead of the stable period, and I have made numerous experiments with the view of ascertaining to what extent the difference would probably be felt on telegraph lines.

Hughes was using the word "resistance" in its broadest sense: today it would be referred to as impedance, the term for the combined effect of resistance, inductance, and capacitance. This loose use of terminology was one of the problems in the communication between the practical men and the theoreticians, and Hughes was one of the main abusers, tending to be fairly flexible in his use of terminology, and certainly not as precise as the theoreticians required. It was necessary to listen carefully to follow his line of reasoning, as can be seen from this example, where he uses his own unique descriptive vocabulary:[18]

I am fully convinced from the results of my experiments that an enormous retardation or resistance is evident in all conductors at the first portion of the variable period, and that this is due to self-induction, the current thus arousing an antagonist in its own path sufficiently powerful, when the primary current has a high electro-motive force, to deflagrate or separate the wire into its constituent separate molecules, as shown by Dr. Warren de la Rue.

Hughes continued his presentation by describing his apparatus and the results he obtained measuring the "inductive capacity," his term for self-induction, of various metal wires, both with steady state current flow and with a rapidly interrupted current like that which would occur on a telegraph line. Many of the practical men in the audience (who were in the majority) would probably have been quite satisfied to nod as Hughes made his various points, then thank him for another interesting presentation, and be done. However, the theoreticians present became somewhat energized as the presentation progressed, for his experimental results were quite contrary to what theory predicted.

Hughes had arranged his experiment to measure the self-inductance of different metallic wires using what he termed his "induction bridge instrument," a combination of his induction balance and a Wheatstone bridge.[19] This was his attempt to shed light on the mysteries of self-induction under dynamic operating conditions. He designed and conducted what were probably the first experiments that explored this area. Hughes had gathered many wires of different cross sections and materials (iron, steel, nickel, copper, brass, silver, etc.) to conduct his tests. These consisted of:

1. A batch of 1 mm diameter wire, 30 cm long.
2. A batch of wire of the same length, but of varying diameters from 0.1 to 10 mm.
3. A batch of different cross sections, round, rectangular, and stranded.

He arranged his apparatus to operate in two modes, a stable mode and a variable mode, which he could easily switch between. He first measured the wire resistance using a Wheatstone bridge configuration in the stable mode, and then switched to the variable mode to measure the self-inductance. As the lengths of wire were short, their resistance and inductance would be quite small, necessitating quite delicate measurements.

His apparatus consisted of an interrupter known as a rheotome which interrupted the battery supply to generate on/off pulses. He could vary the rate from 10 pulses per second to 100 per second. A telephone receiver was used as a detector to listen for silence, which indicated that he had adjusted the apparatus correctly to make a measurement (i.e. that the bridge was balanced). He used an adaptation of his sonometer for balancing out the inductive capacity introduced by the wire being tested. This device he called an "induction sonometer." It consisted of an outer coil with a slightly smaller secondary coil which could be rotated within this outer coil.[20] Thus, the inductive coupling between them could be adjusted from maximum to minimum by the rotation of the secondary coil. The idea was to reduce the induced or extra current to zero by balancing it with an equal and opposite induced current from the induction balance. Fastened to the rotational axis of the secondary coil was a pointer that swept over a dial face. The readings from this dial were recorded as the experimental results. These were

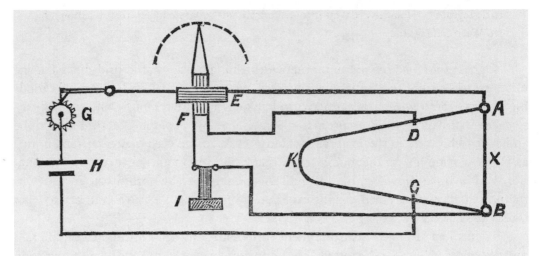

The induction bridge instrument on which Hughes obtained his controversial experimental results. It consists of G (rotonome), H (battery), E (fixed coil), F (rotational coil with pointer), I (telephone receiver), and ABCDXK (bridge components).

not absolute measurements in pure units of resistance or inductance but rather comparative measurements between samples.

In his tests of several types of metal wires which were all of the same diameter and length his results showed that the force and duration of the extra current depended on the type of metal employed as a conductor, its molecular condition, and the form given to the conductor. He presented his results in tables and a graph, as well as in illustrations on a blackboard, of which the following are a summary:

1. The electromotive force from the extra current was highest for iron and lowest for copper by a factor of five.
2. The electromotive force from the extra current increased with an increase in the diameter of the wire to a peak and then decreased. Hughes commented that he was not expecting this result—it was this peak in the results that later fascinated the theoreticians.
3. The charge and discharge of a wire was seven times slower in iron than in copper.
4. He observed big differences in the "resistance" of wire between the stable and variable measurements. For iron wire the resistance was 225% higher in the variable test than in stable test, for solid copper it was 10% higher, and for stranded iron wire it was 8% higher.[21]
5. A ribbon conductor had less self-inductance than round wire.

His testing and comparison of non-magnetic wires with magnetic wires was important, as it brought out the fact that the self-inductance of iron wires was significantly

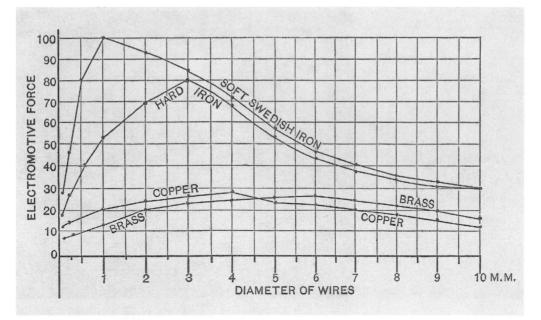

A graph of electromotive force vs. wire diameter for various metals. It was the peak in this graph that aroused the curiosity of the theoreticians.

greater than that of copper wires.[22] The tests on iron wire were also significant for another reason: they were to reveal the operation of an effect that was undiscovered and unknown to all but one person at that time.

As a way of explaining some of the results, Hughes referred to Maxwell's *Treatise on Electricity and Magnetism*, vol. 2, page 291, article 689, "On the Electromotive Force Required to Produce a Current of Varying Intensity along a Cylindrical Conductor." He stated that Maxwell had partially foreseen his results and quoted from his book:[23]

> The electromotive force arising from the induction of the current on itself is different in different parts of the section of wire, being in general a function of the distance from the axis of the wire as well as of the time.

Hughes did not cite the whole of the introductory paragraph of Maxwell's article #689, which sheds additional light on the problem, and which reads as follows (the part that Hughes did quote is placed in italics):

> When a current in a wire is of varying intensity, *the electromotive force arising from the induction of the current on itself is different in different parts of the section of wire, being in general a function of the distance from the axis of the wire as well as of the time.* If we suppose the cylindrical conductor to consist of a bundle of wires all forming part of the same circuit, so that the current is compelled to be of uniform strength in every section of the bundle, the method

Lord Rayleigh became a mentor for Hughes, helping him interpret his experimental results and recommending an improved apparatus with which Hughes was able to more clearly demonstrate the skin effect.

of calculation that we have hitherto used would be strictly applicable. If however, we consider the cylindrical conductor as a solid mass in which electric currents are free to flow in obedience to electromotive force, the intensity of the current will not be the same at different distances from the axis of the cylinder, and electromotive forces themselves will depend on the distribution of the current in the different cylindrical strata of the wire.

Nonetheless it is interesting that Hughes, a practical man, had studied this particular article (and probably its companion #690) in Maxwell's highly mathematical and voluminous treatise; it was to play an important part in the interpretation of his experimental results.

Hughes's talk and demonstration went late into the evening and left no time for the usual discussion period, so his questioners were deprived of their say, and had to wait until the next meeting two weeks later. This, however, gave them additional time to digest his paper and prepare their questions and criticisms. Their ranks were swelled after his paper was published in the technical journals, and theoreticians in Britain and Europe inked their pens for their assault in the press.

What happened next was one of those quirks of scientific discovery. Hughes's unexpected experimental results galvanized the theoretical men into action, led by Lord Rayleigh.[24] Here was Hughes describing phenomena that flew in the face of theory, and worse, he was inventing some terms and misusing others! That could not be allowed to

The brilliant, sharp-tongued, and reclusive theoretician Oliver Heaviside.

go unchallenged. Several prominent scientists waded into the fray, some quite gentlemanly in their comments, while others spared Hughes no mercy with their caustic criticism. The discussion was to last many months, during which time Hughes defended his experiments as he once more became embroiled in controversy. Part of the problem was that Hughes viewed his experiment from a different perspective than that of the theoreticians, and that led to inaccuracies in the way he described and portrayed his work and results. He was an applied scientist, as he stated in the introduction to the inaugural address, and was interested in the total effect manifesting itself on the telegraph lines. Thus, he often lumped many effects together, and gave them ambiguous names such as "inductive capacity"; he therefore tended to use terminology imprecisely. The theoreticians came at the problem from the other end of the spectrum. They built up their equations based on defined individual parameters linked through mathematical and physical relationships. For them to be able to link their theory and equations with experimental results, they had to use consistent terminology and parameters, so that they would be comparing apples to apples and not apples to oranges.

The theoreticians concluded that the results Hughes had obtained were due to the fact that his apparatus was not behaving in the manner he thought. The apparatus was in fact unable to separate out and measure individually the various electrical parameters such as resistance, self-inductance, and the voltage generated by the self-inductance. But while the theoreticians were highly suspicious of Hughes's results, their suspicion did not deter them from trying to interpret those results. It was as if they suspected that there was some mysterious element hidden among his results. And in fact their suspicions were right; there was something else that was contributing to the resistance of the wire when it was subjected to alternating currents. Hughes had again uncovered something new in his experiments. All of this was a lot for the practical men to absorb, for while they were still trying to come to grips with self-inductance, they were now expected to believe that there was also a new hidden effect to understand.

Hughes's inaugural address turned out to be a catalyst that altered the status quo for the theoreticians and resulted in two important accomplishments for them. First, it drew them out of the shadows and into the mainstream, at least for several months, as the arguments went back and forth. When it was all over, they had left their mark by showing that there was a link between theory and practice. The discussion of Hughes's results was also important because it brought out all current knowledge of self-induction, and hence the subject became better understood. While the theoreticians gained some ground, it was a battle they would have to fight repeatedly, at least for a few more years, before the staunchest practical men would admit they were necessary, and before theory made an important contribution to technology.

Second, it engaged the brilliant but reclusive mathematician Oliver Heaviside,[25] whose important work had languished, little read and poorly understood, up to that time. Heaviside was so struck by Hughes's experiments that he interrupted what he was working on to address them. As was his style, Heaviside first admonished Hughes with caustic comments, berating him in the technical journals and pointing out that his experiments, apparatus, and results were flawed. However, buried in Hughes's results Heaviside saw the experimental verification of a phenomenon that he had mathematically shown to exist which he called the "thick wire effect," and which later was to be referred to as the "skin effect."[26] This phenomenon occurred when an alternating electrical current was flowing in a wire. As the frequency of the alternating current increased, the current flow moved to the outer parts of the wire, and at high frequency became confined to a thin outer layer, or the "skin" of the wire. As the current was then using only a fraction of the cross section of the wire, the electrical resistance increased significantly. Heaviside's attitude towards Hughes softened slightly with time, and when his papers were published in book form, he acknowledged Hughes:[27]

> This reprint of my Electrical Papers comes about by the union of a variety of reasons and circumstances.... Thirdly, the experimental work of Hughes in 1886, furnishing the first evidence (in the sense ordinarily understood, though other evidence was convincing to a logical mind) of the truth of the theory of surface conduction along wires under certain circumstances, first advanced by me the year previously....

After it became apparent that his experimental apparatus had in fact given misleading results, Hughes repeated his experiments following the recommendations made by

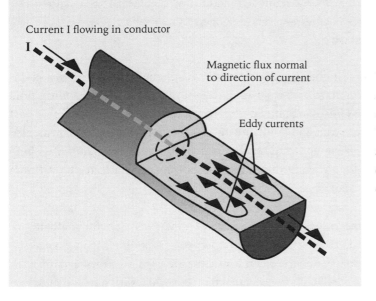

Current I flowing in conductor

I

Magnetic flux normal to direction of current

Eddy currents

The skin effect is produced by eddy currents created by an alternating current. The eddy currents circulate so as to oppose the main current and push it to the outer skin.

the theoreticians. The new results he obtained negated many of his previous results and seem to have been accepted without any further discussion.[28] Hughes reran his frequency tests, which previously had not shown that frequency had any effect. This time he used a wider range of frequencies and found that frequency did have an effect, and the skin effect was more pronounced when he experimented with iron wire. Hughes himself did not subscribe to the skin effect and he continued to argue with Heaviside over it for a number of years.

When the next meeting of the Society was convened two weeks later there was a waiting list of members who wished to comment on Hughes's paper. There were so many, in fact, that the discussion again carried over to the following meetings. Those who had not attended the first meeting but had read Hughes's paper in the technical journals weighed in with their comments in letters to the editor. The theoreticians focused their criticism on Hughes's experimental apparatus, believing that it was responsible for the interesting but probably erroneous results. This, however, did not stop them from trying to explain them. There were some ungentlemanly comments, but there appeared to be a genuine desire to guide this experimentalist through the fog and determine what exactly he had or had not discovered.

Lord Rayleigh was the first to deliver his comments; he had been professor of experimental physics and head of the Cavendish Laboratory at Cambridge after James Clerk Maxwell, and was a well-versed theoretician familiar with Maxwell's work:[29]

I have given attention to some of the points touched upon by Professor Hughes in his very interesting paper; but that paper contains a good many other points which are quite new to me, as also I suspect to most others. I observe that on the first page of the paper

Professor Hughes does not employ the term "self-induction" in quite the same sense—or, at least, with the same definiteness—as has been used by mathematicians, especially by Professor James Clerk Maxwell....

Rayleigh did not dismiss Hughes's experiments, even though he was highly suspicious of them, but instead sought to gain a better understanding of them, spending time with Hughes at his rooms on Great Portland Street. He went on to devote the better part of the year to conducting research and contributing papers on the topic. He was also able to describe Hughes's experiments and results in more precise terms and thus help others understand them. Hughes made the following comment in a letter to William Preece regarding Rayleigh's visit:[30]

Since Rayleigh was with me for two hours on Friday—He went very carefully into all experiments. Critiquing and in some cases I had to repeat some experiments by a change of method—He seemed certainly convinced of the results presented in paper—and if he does not get in another "Maxwell fog"—when left alone. I should regard him as a most valuable ally—to the truth of the results.

Rayleigh doubted that Hughes's experimental apparatus could separately measure resistance and self-inductance and believed that the results he had obtained were a peculiarity of his apparatus. In a subsequent Society meeting Rayleigh followed up his argument with a formula he had worked out to describe what was happening in Hughes's induction bridge apparatus when it was excited by a sinusoidal signal.[31] This formula proved that it was impossible to get a true balance and therefore impossible to separately measure the resistance and self-inductance as Hughes had thought. Also, he showed that the measurements would be frequency dependent, contrary to Hughes's conclusion. Rayleigh was starting to make a strong case in a very gentlemanly fashion that cast doubts on the validity of Hughes's results.

He did praise Hughes, though, for breaking new ground and pursuing such tests, and for his in-depth investigation into both magnetic (iron) and non-magnetic wire (copper). It was at this point that Rayleigh made the comment that he thought that there was more to Hughes's experiments, and that other causes were producing a real and important change in the resistance when intermittent currents were used, though it was not clear what he was alluding to. He went on to advise Hughes on an improved version of his apparatus that would correctly measure the separate parameters.

The next to be given the floor was the well-known visiting American electrician Mr. Frank L. Pope. He related that he and his colleagues had noticed that they could attain a higher transmission speed on a telegraph line that used stranded iron wire than on one that used a solid wire. He surmised that the current was conducted on the surface of the metal rather than through the body and stated that he never heard any good explanation until that of Prof. Hughes. He also said that they had used a copper-clad steel wire that had shown great speed.

The next to speak was Professor Forbes, who had quite a bit of first-hand knowledge of Hughes's experiments, having spent time with him in his laboratory. Forbes had also made his own induction balance based on Hughes's design. However, like Rayleigh, Forbes had difficulty with Hughes's use of terminology. Forbes wanted to see the basic parameters measured, such as the "coefficient of self-induction," rather than the implied parameters that Hughes had used. Again there was not enough time for all of those who wished to speak and so further comments were postponed until the next meeting.

Two weeks later William Preece, who was rarely a brief speaker, did not disappoint and spoke for a considerable time. He was, of course, a friend and admirer of Hughes, and had kind words for him in his opening statement:[32]

> I do not suppose we have ever had a paper brought before us that has formed such food for thought, and possessed such elements for discussion. The paper has the peculiar merit in it that it has brought to the knowledge of the many that which necessarily was possessed previously by but a few. In the telegraph world for many years past, self-induction in various forms has proven a bête noire which required all our knowledge and all our skill, not only to master, but to comprehend; for the effects of self-induction are invariably ill effects, and have various detrimental influences that require to be surmounted.

Preece was in a powerful position as senior electrician at the Post Office, the government organization that essentially controlled all communications in Britain. He had a commanding say in the technical direction the Post Office took and he was a practical man through and through. In his remarks he once again let the "theory men" know where their place was:[33]

> These effects, and his paper, show how our science of electricity has been enriched by practice. Theories always come after the event. I do not know any theory, not even Clerk-Maxwell's theory, that would have predicted what we have seen brought before our Society. There is nobody who has placed in the hands of us practical men such splendid apparatus, such useful tools with which to peer into the internals of matter, as Professor Hughes has done, not only in this paper, but other papers that we have listened to with so much pleasure and delight.

This shows just how much bias the theoreticians had to overcome. Preece probably believed, as the head of the industry, that there were few if any others who had any more knowledge than he did: he was the decider.

There were several others who had comments on Hughes's experiment. Professor Silvanus P. Thompson wanted to know what frequencies Hughes had used in his experiment and whether he had considered using a tone of 100 or 400 cycles per second.[34] He considered a tone (with a sinusoidal wave form) to be more useful in tests as its shape could be easily described mathematically. Hughes responded that his experimental results were frequency independent. Thompson was followed by Dr. J. Hopkinson, Dr. J. A. Fleming, and Professor W. E. Ayrton.

Some of the other comments Hughes had to contend with were printed in the technical journals and were not quite as friendly as those aired at the Society meetings. Professor Heinrich F. Weber of Germany carefully examined Hughes's experiments and sharply criticized him for not providing his results in standard units.[35] He deduced that Hughes's results were dependent on his instrumentation and hence not reliable.

Oliver Heaviside, the reclusive mathematical genius, was an ex-telegraph engineer who had retired early at age twenty-four and communicated with the outside world via personal letters and particularly via articles and letters to the editor of *The Electrician*. For years he had been publishing his work in that journal; his papers were often accompanied by a heavy dose of mathematics and consequently did not attract much attention. Later, when W. H. Snell took over as editor of the journal, he informed Heaviside that he was unable to discover any of his readers who appreciated his articles, and that he was therefore terminating them.[36]

Heaviside's work and brilliance should not be underestimated. He, together with George Francis FitzGerald, Oliver Lodge, and John Henry Poynting, formed the core of the important group that became known as the Maxwellians. They were responsible for taking Maxwell's *Treatise* and deriving from it the now famous equations known as Maxwell's electromagnetic equations, thus shedding light on electromagnetic wave propagation.

Heaviside was not shy about putting the practical men in their place; his attitude is clearly revealed in a comment he published in *The Electrician* in connection with antagonism between the theoreticians and practitioners:[37]

> There is however, one point which does not, I think receive the attention it deserves, which is, that it is the duty of the theorist to try and keep the engineer who has to make the practical application straight, if the engineer should show that he is behind the age, and has got shunted onto a siding. The engineer should be amenable to criticism.

Heaviside had decided he was going to set Hughes straight and his comments were far from flattering:[38]

> NOTE 1. We read in the pages of history of a monarch who was "*supra grammaticam.*" All truly great men are like that monarch. They have their own grammars, syntaxes, and dictionaries. They cannot be judged by ordinary standards, but require interpretation. Fortunately the liberty of private interpretation is conserved.
>
> No man has a more peculiar grammar than Prof. Hughes. Hence, he is liable, in a most unusual degree, to be misunderstood, as I venture to think he has been by many, including Mr. W. Smith, whose interesting letter appears in *The Electrician*, April 16, 1886, p. 455, and Prof. H. Weber, p. 451.

The very first step to understanding a writer is to find out what he means. Before this is done there cannot possibly be a clear comprehension of his utterances. One may, by taking his language in its ordinary significance, hastily conclude that he has either revolutionized the science of induction, or that he is talking nonsense. But to do this would not be fair. We must not judge by what a man says if we have good reason to know that what he means is quite different. To be quite fair, we must conscientiously endeavor to translate his language and ideas into those we are ourselves accustomed to use. Then, and then only, shall we see what is to be seen.

When Prof. Hughes speaks of the resistance of a wire, he does not *always* mean what common men, men of ohms, volts, and farads, mean by the resistance of a wire—only sometimes. He does not exactly define what it is to be when the accepted meaning is departed from. But by a study of the context we may arrive at some notion of its new meaning. It is not a definite quantity, and must be varied to suit circumstances. Again there is his "inductive capacity" of a wire. We can only find roughly what that means by putting together this, that, and the other....

I took great pains of translating Prof. Hughes's language into my own, trying to imagine that I had made the same experiments *in the same manner* (which could not have happened) and then asking what are their interpretations? The discoveries I looked for vanished for the most part into thin air. They became well known facts when put into common language. I have failed to find any departure from the known laws of electromagnetism. In saying this, however, I should make a reservational remark. There may be lying latent in Prof. Hughes's results dozens of discoveries, but it is impossible to get to them.

Besides the criticism, Heaviside did leave open the possibility that the results contained evidence of some latent effect. With respect to Hughes's induction bridge, Heaviside made the following comments, indicating that Hughes could not have obtained a true balance with it, and that it would therefore give mixed results, neither the true resistance nor the true inductance. He had arrived at this conclusion through his own evaluation of several different bridge configurations.[39]

Prof. Hughes's balance is sometimes fairly approximate, sometimes quite false.... It is certainly a rather remarkable thing that the one method out of these seven faulty ways which gave the very loudest sound was the 5 and 6 combination, which is Professor Hughes's method. I do not say it is always the worst, although it was markedly so in my experiments to test for trustworthiness of the method.

Heaviside continued his criticism of Hughes for mixing up the effects of resistance and induction, saying sarcastically that Hughes might actually be inventing a new science of induction. He added that it was remarkable that one with such great experimental skill should have used a method so objectionable. In the end Heaviside did get around to giving Hughes some credit and named the latent result he had been alluding to:[40]

Finally, it was remarkable as containing so far as could be safely guessed at, many verifications of the approximation towards mere surface-conduction in wires. This is, after all, the really important matter, against which all the rest is insignificant.

Heaviside aptly summed it all up: most of Hughes's results were in fact meaningless due to his experimental method and the apparatus he was using—except for one set of results. Heaviside explained:[41]

The most interesting of the experiments are those relating to the effect of increasing diameter on what Prof. Hughes terms the inductive capacity of wires. My own interpretation is roughly this. That the time constant of the wire first increases with the diameter (this is of course what the linear theory shows), and then later decreases rapidly; and the decrease sets in the sooner the higher the conductivity and the higher the inductivity (or magnetic permeability) of the wires. If this be correct it is exactly what I should have expected and predicted. In fact I have already described the phenomenon in this Journal; or rather, the phenomenon I described contains the above interpretation. In *The Electrician* for January 10, 1885, I describe how the current starts in a wire. It begins on its boundary, and is propagated inwards. Thus during the rise of the current it is less strong at the center than at the boundary.

So Heaviside showed that there was another effect in operation here, one previously known only to him, which caused an additional resistive effect that he called the "surface effect" or "thick wire effect." Just when Hughes and the practical men thought that they were getting their arms around self-induction, Heaviside was springing something totally new on them.

After patiently listening to all of the criticism, Hughes responded in the Society's *Journal*, where he continued to argue for the validity of his previous results, and in a letter to the editor of *The Electrician* stated:[42]

Sir: I have noticed several criticisms in your valuable journal upon my paper on "self-induction" which I believe require a few remarks in reply.

The criticisms may be divided into three classes.

First—Prof. H. F. Weber shows that the method which I employed admits of numerous errors, and consequently infers that the results that I have announced are due to an "incorrect interpretation."

Second—Mr. Oliver Heaviside points out that upon a close examination it will be found that all the effects which I have described are well known to mathematicians, and consequently old.

Third—Mr. Willoughby Smith points out that the results which I have announced are contrary to theory and practice, and demonstrates that he is unable to obtain any difference even between iron and copper.

I must say that I am unable to agree with these opposing views, for if we assume with Mr. Heaviside that all my results are contained in some mathematical formula of which I am unaware, then the mathematicians ought to feel extremely grateful for the experimental proof which I have furnished them; if on the other hand we agree with Mr. Willoughby Smith then the formula and my results should at once be abandoned as experimentally untrue.

Prof. Weber's objection is more serious, and I fully admit that it is possible to make very serious errors if the sonometer is not calibrated, or if we do not appreciate the errors that can be easily introduced. I feel sure that Prof. Weber could have seen how such errors could have been avoided, and this even by several means that I have indicated, such as making comparative tests between wires of the same length and resistance, so that no change took place in the bridge adjustment except that due to the differential results.

The only question which I consider important is, Are the effects which I announced true physical effects due to nature or form of the conductor, or are they simply due to some peculiarity of the method I employed? To answer this I have constructed an instrument based on an entirely different method, one of extreme simplicity, and one which does not allow any possible error.

I propose to publish a description of this instrument (together with results obtained) during the coming month when I hope that its demonstration will prove clearly all that I have said as to the influence of the form as well as the nature of the conductor upon its self-induction. — Yours, &c,

D.E. Hughes.

Heaviside was not happy with Hughes's response, especially since he made no mention of the thick wire effect. In the end, the fact that Heaviside had theoretically predicted the skin effect benefited both men: the existence of a possible theoretical explanation for Hughes's results attracted more scientific interest in them, and the existence of a practical proof of Heaviside's theory rescued his work from obscurity.

Heaviside had this to say on the matter:[43]

In Prof. Hughes's researches, which led him to such remarkable conclusions, the method of balancing was not such to ensure, save exceptionally, either a true resistance or a true induction balance. Hence, the complete mixing up of resistance and induction effects due to false balances. And hidden away in the mixture was what I termed the "thick wire effect," causing a true change in resistance and inductance [vol. II., p. 30]. In fact if I had not, in my experiments on cores and similar things, been already familiar with real changes in resistance and inductance, and had not already worked out the theory of the phenomenon of approximation to surface conduction [first general description in vol. I., Art. 30, p. 440; vol. II., p. 30], on which these effects in a wire with current longitudinal depend, it is quite likely that I should have put down all anomalous results to false balances.

Revised configuration of Hughes's experimental apparatus to measure the effects of self-inductance and more clearly demonstrate the increase in resistance of a wire with increased frequency, the so-called "skin effect."

Heaviside's praise of Hughes was something of a coup as he rarely had good words to say about the practical men. However, Heaviside's motives in praising Hughes were mixed, as it was a way of emphasizing the importance of his theoretical work and the priority of his prediction of the skin effect the previous year (1885).

Hughes did take notice of all of this advice and re-ran his tests with a new apparatus that avoided false balances and which yielded the true values of the resistance and inductance of his test wires. . He read a paper describing his experiments at the Royal Society on May 27, 1886.[44] He was unable to repeat his previous results which had shown a peak in the electromotive force at a certain wire diameter, nor could he obtain the same results for many of the other tests—just as the theorists had predicted. This negated many of the controversial results in his earlier paper. Interestingly, he did not dwell on providing explanations, nor did there appear to have been much follow-up discussion. However, some of the tests that he re-ran did produce significant results. He again tested many samples of copper and iron wire and demonstrated that self-inductance was significantly higher in iron wire. Also, when iron wire was subjected to a switched or alternating current he found an increase in what he called "relative resistance," although he did not define what he meant by this. The results showed that the resistance increased with frequency, which others attributed to the skin effect, but Hughes had his own ideas about the cause. He also re-tested insulated stranded iron wires and found that their "relative resistance" was significantly lower than that of a solid conductor.[45]

Hughes's previous experiments had not shown any change in resistance in the variable period with changes in frequency. However, this was not the case when he repeated the experiments. This time he performed the experiments over a much wider range of frequencies, using both a tuning fork contactor as well as his rheotome, to produce pulses at 192, 282, 384, 676, and 768 cycles per second. He found that he could improve his ability to detect the various frequency signals, especially to listen for silence, if he tuned the diaphragm of his telephone receiver to each of these frequencies. These experiments showed that there was an increase in resistance with frequency, providing experimental verification of Heaviside's theoretical prediction of the skin effect.

Hughes never did quite subscribe to Heaviside's theory, but proposed one of his own which traces back to Maxwell's *Treatise* article #689, which Hughes had quoted in his inaugural address.[46] Hughes explained the phenomenon by postulating a constant decrease in the electromotive force of self-induction with increasing cross-sectional area:[47]

> ...we should not consider a current in a wire as a single element reacting solely on exterior wires, but that the current acts precisely as would an infinite number of independent streamlets of current reacting upon each other in the interior of its own wire similarly to their known effect upon exterior wires. My experiments demonstrate this to a degree that leaves no doubt on my mind as to its truth, for according to this view we should be able to reduce the self induction to a very great extent by employing thin flat sheets where the outlying portions are at a comparatively greater distance from the central portions. If the reduction is due to the greater separation of the streamlets, then we should be able to reduce this induction in a still greater degree by employing a conductor composed of numerous small copper wires through which the current is equally divided and which could be separated or brought close together as desired.

Like Hughes, William Preece did not subscribe to the skin effect. This was unfortunate, as it continued to distort his view of the transmission of signals over iron and copper transmission lines. What Heaviside had shown was that while iron wires, like copper wires, did exhibit self-inductance (although to a much smaller extent), this was not the overriding effect creating attenuation and distortion with the use of more rapidly switching currents on telegraph lines and the higher frequencies in use on telephone lines. It was actually the skin effect (which was much more pronounced in iron wires) that was forcing the current into the outer skin of the conductor and hence increasing the impedance of the line.

Hughes continued what appeared to be an amiable correspondence with Heaviside through 1889 regarding their differences on a range of topics.[48] Hughes's reputation was only enhanced by the whole affair and he received praise in the end from the majority of his critics, even Heaviside in a roundabout way. When Sir William Thomson became president of the Society three years later in 1889 he had praise for Hughes as well as for Heaviside:[49]

> In the memorable Presidential Address of Professor Hughes... electro-magnetic induction was very admirably illustrated by experiments that are now more or less familiar to us all, but which have been of immensely suggestive and stimulating character, both

to mathematicians and to experimental workers. The very criticism by mathematicians [e.g. Heaviside!] upon some of the experiments and modes of statements by Professor Hughes have... given a very large body of electrical knowledge and electro-magnetic knowledge which, without such stimulus and such mathematical and experimental scrutiny as it has led to, might have been wanting for many a year.

It is interesting to contrast this controversial discovery, its reception, and its consequences with Hughes's earlier discovery of "wireless waves" and its unsatisfactory reception. In this case, even though the experimental results were not what he had expected, he went ahead with a risky presentation at a high profile event. His experiment and results had not been reviewed by his colleagues before the event, so he really had no idea how they would be received, although he probably believed that he was on solid ground. A lively debate with the theoreticians immediately arose, and though one of the theoreticians' motives may have been to demonstrate that theory could precede experiments, the problem that Hughes had raised was fully investigated, and the effect that was lurking in his results was discovered. Lord Rayleigh's non-combative approach set the tone for the discussions, and his advice and the time he took to frame Hughes's results in more accepted terms helped bring about a satisfactory conclusion.

In contrast, when Professor Stokes reviewed Hughes's wireless experiments he failed to see their merit, dismissed them, and advised Hughes to do the same. As a consequence, the experiments and their results were never presented or published. Just imagine if Hughes had simply gone ahead and presented his wireless experiments to the scientific community. Pandemonium probably would have broken out, and the experiments would have had a large impact: not only would the age of wireless communication have begun years earlier, but the scientific community would have had a much earlier demonstration that theory (Maxwell's) could precede experimental verification.

Hughes's popularity had increased if anything during his term as president of the Society, and the debate that surrounded his inaugural address only served to keep his name and work continually on the pages of the technical journals. He had survived another controversy, furthered the understanding of self-inductance, and whether he liked it or not, was to be credited with being the first to experimentally demonstrate the skin effect. He had also lured Oliver Heaviside out of the shadows, and although it would be a continual struggle for him, Heaviside would finally get recognition for his work.

⚓

Throughout the 1880s the practical men continued to do battle with the men of the "New School." But the theoreticians were gaining ground, and by the end of the 1880s there was no doubt that they could make major contributions to solving the industry's technical problems, and that theory could actually precede experimental evidence of an effect, in spite of Preece's declaration to the contrary.

Depiction of the battle between the practical men and theoreticians—William Preece trium-phantly places his boot on the throat of the theoretician Oliver Lodge.

Interest in self-induction continued, and Heaviside, through theoretical analysis, determined that distortion on telephone lines could be substantially reduced by loading the line with extra inductance. This became known as his "distortionless line";[50] his use of inductance was totally contrary to the views of Preece, who had declared it banned, and who considered resistance and capacitance to be the only important parameters. Oliver Heaviside, together with his brother Arthur, prepared a paper that included Oliver's description of the conditions necessary for distortionless transmission. As Arthur Heaviside was an employee of the Post Office, the paper required Preece's approval before it could be published; since the paper emphasized the importance of inductance and was contrary to his views, he refused permission. This was the start of two years during which Heaviside was troubled by Preece's actions and had difficulty getting his message out and his papers published. He viewed Preece as technically unqualified for such a high-ranking position, and was convinced that Preece was suppressing his work. Heaviside commented:[51]

> But in the year 1887 I came, for a time to a dead stop, exactly when I came to making practical applications in detail of my theory, with novel conclusions of considerable practical significance relating to long-distance telephony... in opposition to the views at that time officially advocated.

In 1888 the situation improved for him through his acquaintance with Oliver Lodge.[52]. Lodge had been requested by the secretary of the Society of Arts to deliver a couple of lectures in memory of the late Dr. Mann who had been an advocate of lightning rods.[53] The lectures, however, brought Lodge into conflict with Preece. The two men held opposing views on the protection of buildings from lightning, a subject on which Preece considered himself an expert. When Lodge carried out experiments in preparation for the lectures he saw evidence of the skin effect and as a consequence read Heaviside's papers on the subject. Through their common theoretical interests and common adversary, Heaviside gained a new ally in Lodge.

Lodge decided that the discharge from a Leyden jar would be the ideal method to produce artificial lightning.[54] It was known that this type of discharge produced a damped oscillatory wave having a frequency dependent on the values of inductance, resistance and capacitance of the circuit. At the time, Lodge believed that lightning was oscillatory, the same as the discharge from a Leyden jar. While experimenting, Lodge and his assistant, Arthur Chattock, investigated what he called the "alternative path,"[55] which consisted of giving the discharge from the Leyden jar a choice of conduction paths that included copper and iron wires or rods or an air gap. What he found was that the discharge did not always follow what appeared to be the obvious path. Lodge's explanation was that this effect was caused by the increased resistance of the conductor due to the skin effect, which was experienced at the high frequencies he was using and which would make some paths less desirable than others. He gave credit to Hughes for experimentally discovering this, and Heaviside for its theory.

Hughes was later to correspond with Lodge, discussing his lightning experiments and comparing them with experiments that he and Prof. Guillemin had carried out as early as 1864. He had made these experiments for the Administration des Lignes Télégraphiques of France to investigate the merits of different lightning protectors and the best methods for investigating them.[56]

Lodge continued experimenting using of a pair of Leyden jars connected to a pair of parallel wires ninety-five feet long wrapped around the walls of the room and insulated from ground. He found that when he discharged the jars into the wires:[57]

> The electricity in the long wires is surging to and fro, like water in a bath tub when it has been tilted; and the long spark at the far end of the wires is due to the recoil impulse or kick at the reflection of the wave.

Lodge was creating waves that ran along the wires and he could create standing waves through their reflection from the far end of the wires. He compared the effect to that of a resonating tube or a vibrating string. He was able to measure the wavelength by observing where the nodes occurred, which was where the spark discharge was largest and smallest. The values of inductance, resistance, and capacitance in the apparatus were very small, resulting in oscillating frequencies in the megacycle range. He stated that he got the largest sparks when the length of each wire was half a wavelength.

He was familiar with John Henry Poynting's paper "On the Transfer of Energy in the Electromagnetic Field" which corroborated his conclusions.[58] Poynting's conclusion was that electromagnetic energy did not flow in the wire but entered it sideways from the field surrounding the wire. The flow of energy was not carried along the conductor but in the surrounding medium. Lodge was sure that his experiments were creating electromagnetic waves that were disturbing the surrounding ether as they radiated.

It was at this point that Lodge read with interest Oliver Heaviside's paper on "Electromagnetic Waves."[59] Lodge and Heaviside then started corresponding, and Heaviside saw how Lodge's experiments confirmed his own theory of propagation of waves along wires. Through Lodge, Heaviside was finally given the credit due to him and was elevated to a much higher standing in the scientific community.

Unfortunately for Lodge, Heinrich Hertz in Germany was also experimenting with electromagnetic waves and went a step further than Lodge by detecting them in free space. The announcement of Hertz's work was made by George Francis FitzGerald in his address to the British Association at its meeting in Bath in September of 1888.[60] Maxwell's theoretical predictions had finally been demonstrated experimentally. Lodge must have felt considerable disappointment, as he had been so close to making the same discovery. Hughes also must have been somewhat frustrated to see the excitement over experiments that he had made ten years earlier. At that time he had been radiating electromagnetic waves from his laboratory and walking up and down Great Portland Street detecting them, but had no idea what they were; now the mystery was solved.

After 1888 the technology balance shifted in favor of the theoreticians; there was now overwhelming evidence that theory could precede experimental verification. Theory could explain many of the mysteries of electricity and magnetism and provide laws and formulae to guide the successful design of practical applications. Preece and his practical men would see their role as deciders slip away as the members of the "New School" took their places.

12

LAST YEARS AND LEGACY

In 1888, Professor David Edward Hughes, together with his wife Anna Chadbourne, boarded a train in London and headed for Wales, in search of his roots. It was a visit that was long overdue, and one that his father had hoped to make before he passed on. Anna's interest in her husband's early years had become obvious from her habit of jotting down on scraps of paper the bits of information about his past that she was occasionally able to glean from him. It may well have been at her urging that he finally decided to make the trip.

They would not have been disappointed with the train journey, especially when they crossed over the border into Wales, as the railway line ran through the picturesque Dee Valley. One of Thomas Telford's marvels of engineering, the Pontcysyllte aqueduct, was like an entrance archway that the train passed under as it followed the river towards the town of Llangollen with its scenic waterfalls. From there it was on to Carrog, the home of Owain Glyndŵr, the Welsh Prince who had fought so gallantly to protect his homeland many centuries ago. The next stop would have been the town of Corwen, and they were now entering the region where Hughes had his roots. They continued a few more miles to their destination, the town of Bala, which is situated by Llyn Tegid (Bala Lake).

Hughes probably remembered some of the stories his father had told about his early life in Bala, and about his grandfather, who had been a bootmaker there. He and Anna no doubt looked for the house where the family had lived and also for their graves, and may also have tried to learn what had become of his father's several brothers and their families. However, determining which of the many Hugheses in the town were his relatives was a challenge. Another challenge was that Welsh was the predominant language, and they would quickly have become familiar with the phrase "Dim Saesneg" (no English). David Hughes mentioned this holiday in a letter, in his usual style when referring to non-scientific events—that is, the account is very brief:[1]

> About 8 years since, we took a Summer holiday and visited Bala in Wales, in the hopes of enjoying our trip, and finding out some of the many relations we must have in Wales, but I found there was so many of the name of Hughes, that it was almost an hopeless task, but we did find out three who seemed to remember my father and all about our family—but as the weather turned out very bad—constant rain, we did not very much enjoy the trip, and it is not likely that I shall go again, particularly as I have been a long sufferer from Bronchitis which prevents me doing anything useful.

They may also have visited the nearby town of Corwen, as some of the Hughes relatives resided there, and he later corresponded with one of those relatives, a cousin by the name of Hugh Hughes. He may have investigated whether there was any truth in the suggestion that he had been born at the cottage Green-y-Ddwyryd just outside Corwen.

David Hughes and his wife returned to London, where they had a wide circle of friends, and they seemed more comfortable in that city than in the countryside of Wales. One of those friends was the author John Munro, who after Hughes's death started writing Hughes's biography, although he never progressed beyond a short summary of his life which was never published.[2] His notes survive, however, and provide insight into Hughes's character and way of life. The following short narrative is excerpted and condensed from them:

> Professor Hughes was a direct and outspoken person who delivered his mind without fear or favor and if some disliked it, thanks to his good sense or tact, he rarely, if ever, caused offence. There was a manly spirit of independence in him. He stood on his own legs, and helped himself, as long as he was able. He would have no coddling or any fuss made about him, even in sickness. He was very determined, wanting to have his own way, and very persevering in his course of action. He had given me the advice once "If you are quiet you will be neglected: if you are modest you will be taken advantage of."
>
> He was a good man of business. Wise and clever enough to secure the privilege of independence early in his life through the invention of his type-printing telegraph instrument, he saved his wealth by economical habits and enlarged it by prudent invest-

ments. He dressed so plainly he gave the appearance of a rather poor man than a rich one. Most men of science have a secondary objective usually wealth, rank or fame. With some it is the main or sole objective and their science is only a means to an end. Hughes was a lover of science pure and simple for its own sake. After providing for his wants by the revenue from the type printing telegraph he devoted with a single heart the rest of his days to the advancement of science.

Besides being an enthusiastic worker in science and a great inventor, Professor Hughes was also one of the best and most genial of companions. He had another side to his character which was always ready with some quick wit and his good-natured laughter was a little roguish that enlivened his companions. He had an inexhaustible supply of information and stories and those who belonged to the little group that used to meet for luncheon three times a week, first at the Horseshoe, Tottenham Court Road, afterwards at the society Nationale Francaise, and ultimately at Frascati's Restaurant were privileged.[3] At Frascati's he was always the life and soul of the party. His arrival was the signal for mirth and his unexpected absence caused a feeling of disappointment.

Hughes amazingly had no formal laboratory, preferring to work in his sitting room mostly with apparatus made by himself out of the simplest material. He would not buy a thing if he could make it and without assistance except from his wife now and again. During his microphonic researches, red sealing wax was a mainstay and he consumed so much that when the young lady in the shop where he bought his materials from saw him enter, she came to greet him with "Sealing wax, Sir!" I am afraid that a dealer in antiques would hardly give the entire collection a second thought.

Although he was drawn to the more serious work of science his music was a recreation as well as a pleasure. He still played his own compositions on the harp, concertina, violin or piano, and often went to hear Paderewski or other famous performers at the public recitals and concerts especially in Queen's Hall.

David Hughes and his wife ate most of their meals out at the restaurants, as was common on the Continent. He was a small eater; his meals were always frugal and wholesome. At eight o'clock in the morning in general he took a light breakfast of bacon, eggs and coffee. Then smoking a "Caporal" cigarette as he did in France, he would begin to work.[4] At one o'clock he lunched with his wife, choosing say a cut of boiled chicken, or veal or ham with vegetables and ale. At 2 or 3 o'clock he was home again, and after a short rest on the sofa, back to work. In the evening he often dined generally at Pagani's but required little more than a steak or a cut off the joint.[5] After that he went to meetings or studied far into the night, sometimes till one in the morning, but very seldom so late that he found it hurtful. As a rule he read about electricity and other physics, but was taken with anatomy and physiology and the mechanisms of the body.

For a while before going to bed he relaxed his mind from the strain of thought by some light reading such as *Tit-bits*.[6] Now and then he enjoyed a novel, which as I recollect he said to me once can show us other ways of life than ours: but latterly he was more interested in biography, and used to think that people should not write their own, because they put in matters better left unwritten.

In the summer as a rule he and his wife took a long holiday on the Continent. He always visited a suburb of Baden in Germany to put flowers on the grave of his old friend Mr. Hirschbuhl the German watchmaker of Louisville Kentucky who constructed his first telegraph instrument. Even in the last year of his life when he could not walk without resting he made this grateful pilgrimage. France was his favorite land though and he liked the French who appreciated him and he was always grateful to them for giving him his start with his telegraph.

The 1880s were a transition period for Hughes, as he continued his research but also became more involved in the various technical societies. In 1885 he became vice president of the Society of Telegraph Engineers and Electricians, and the following year he reached one of the highest positions in the electrical world when he became the Society's president.

Throughout the early 1880s Hughes carried out various experiments and tests on iron wires for William Preece, engineer to the Post Office. These experiments led to Hughes's papers on "Some Effects Produced by the Immersion of Steel and Iron Wires in Acidulated Water," "The Molecular Rigidity of Tempered Steel" followed by "On the Physical Condition of Iron and Steel."[7] Iron wires—and their problems with corrosion—were much on telegraph engineers' minds due to their extensive use in telegraph lines. Some of the investigations that Hughes performed would help Preece build his case for changing over to copper wire for telephone lines.

Hughes also continued to pursue his long held interest in electromagnetic induction and magnetism, a phenomenon which was poorly understood. He noticed that iron and steel changed their electrical characteristics when mechanically altered, such as by hammering or being put under strain, or coming under magnetic influence. Hughes gave a number of papers on what he believed magnetism was, covering such topics as "Molecular Magnetism," the "Theory of Magnetism," and "On Magnetic Polarity and Neutrality."[8] Hughes was a supporter of Weber's theory of molecular magnetism and believed he had made progress in proving that magnetism was due to the alignment of molecules. In the end Hughes's beliefs were not far off the mark, as later research resulted in the "domain theory of magnetism," which is similar to Weber's theory.[9]

His research on the skin effect and interaction with Oliver Heaviside during this period appeared to be Hughes's final burst of experimentation, as following those experiments his entries in his laboratory notebooks come to an end.[10] "When you get old you lose your originality" he said to John Munro one day at the beginning of 1893. "You know too much, when you are young you try all sorts of things."

Hughes began to spend less time on experimenting, and more on other interests. He was acutely aware that as technology progressed, there would be a need for trained engineers and technicians, and was keen to give students a good start and a well-grounded education. To further this goal, he became involved in the mid-1880s with the London Polytechnic Institute in Regent Street (now known as the University of Westminster), and eventually became its president in 1897. He liked to see the young men learning, and would sit up at night writing letters of encouragement and advice, giving them hints and opinions on their inventions or experiments.

He also became involved with another important institution in London, namely the Royal Institution, which for years had been responsible for introducing new technologies and teaching science to the general public. It was where his hero Michael Faraday had carried out his momentous work on electricity and magnetism. Hughes became a member of the Royal Institution in 1882, a manager in 1892, and later a vice president. One of his duties was to administer the popular lecture series for the Institution.[11]

Hughes was also a member of an informal group of leading electrical engineers and scientists called the "Dynamicables," which had first been proposed by W.D. Gooch in March, 1883.[12] Members discussed matters of common interest while dining in comfortable surroundings. Other members of the group included Prof. Forbes, William Crookes, Mr. Charles Biggs (editor of *The Electrician*), Henry Adams, William Preece, Latimer Clark, Fleming Jenkin, Ambrose Fleming, and Sir William Thomson, who was their first president.

By this time in his life, Hughes could look back on his inventions and discoveries and see them in everyday use, making a major contribution to communications and to the medical field all over the world. This must have been extremely satisfying for him.

He was still involved with his telegraph instruments, although his role was now more that of a consultant. Each summer he and Anna took an extended holiday on the Continent, during which he visited friends, government telegraph administrators, and the manufacturers and suppliers of his instruments. The Hughes printing telegraph was eventually superseded by the Baudot telegraph and other high speed teletypes, but it remained in service in some countries until the 1950s, providing almost a century of service.[13]

Hughes's carbon microphone, which he invented in 1878 and whose technology he made available freely to all, was widely adopted by telephone manufacturers both in Britain (Crossley and Gower) and on the Continent (Clement-Agnes Ader). Their telephones used a combination of Hughes's carbon pencil transmitter and a version of Bell's receiver. Telephone usage grew in Britain and Europe, as well as in America, and a major milestone was reached in 1891, when the telephone was first used on a long underwater cable to establish a telephone connection between London and Paris. *The Times* of London reported:[14]

> Fifteen years ago, had anyone predicted that in 1891 a person in London would be able to speak with another in Paris, he would have been regarded as a dreamer, if not a madman. Nevertheless in a few days the magical feat will be accomplished by means of the new telephone line connecting the two cities.

At a quarter to twelve in the morning on March 18, 1891, the Postmaster-General, Mr. Raikes, in London, spoke to Paris:[15]

Monsieur le Ministre, Permettez que je vous offre mes salutations et félicitations.
Le triomphe de la téléphonie internationale est un fait accompli.

A Gower-Bell telephone was used at the London end, and an Ader telephone at the Paris end—and both had Hughes microphones. Besides Hughes's microphones, the new communications link utilized two other features that Hughes had proposed in 1879. First, it used copper wire for both the sending and the return lines. This eliminated the earth circuit and the electrical noise caused by earth currents. Second, these wires were configured on the telegraph poles to rotate about each other as they passed from pole to pole, to preclude disturbances produced by induction from other wires.[16] Hughes must have been pleased with his contributions to the achievement of this milestone.

When Hughes developed the induction balance, he again provided the technology free for all to use. Models could be purchased from Groves of London. Induction balance technology went on to be used in a wide range of products, notably in the metal detector and in non-destructive test instrumentation. The sonometer found its main commercial application in hearing testing. The instrument was used until the early 1900s, when it was superseded by tube (valve) instruments.

An exciting occasion and telephone milestone as the first undersea telephone connection between England and France is made in 1891. Hughes's carbon microphones were used at both ends.

Towards the end of the 1880s, Hughes's wireless experiments were repeated by new experimenters. It started at the British Association meeting in Bath in 1888, when George Francis FitzGerald, the Irish physicist, made the sensational announcement that Heinrich Hertz in Germany had discovered electromagnetic waves. By the early 1890s, many scientists were repeating Hertz's experiments and developing methods of generating and detecting wireless waves. Now there was an explanation for the mysterious waves that Hughes had generated and detected: they had been electromagnetic waves propagated through the ether. Hughes must have felt at least a little smug when he saw the instruments these experimenters were using, especially the crude method of detection used by Hertz (a minute spark gap that had to be viewed with a magnifying lens) as compared with his more sophisticated detector and earphone. Hertz's transmission range of several feet must also have seemed very short compared with the distances he had attained. When Hertz traveled to London to receive the Rumford Medal from the Royal Society in 1890, Hughes met him at the ceremony. Also present was Prof. George G. Stokes. When Stokes saw these two standing together shaking hands he must have connected what Hughes had demonstrated early in 1880 with what Hertz had just accomplished.

When the news about Hughes's wireless experiments finally came out in J.J. Fahie's *A History of Wireless Telegraphy 1838–1899*,[17] there was quite a bit of sentiment for him and criticism of Stokes, although much of it was uttered quietly, as Stokes was now Sir Gabriel Stokes, Member of Parliament, and still a high ranking member of the Royal Society. The author J. Munro, Hughes's friend, summed up the general attitude as follows:[18]

> His golden silence was a fine example to the age of modesty in merit. Nevertheless it is regrettable that he carried his respect for authority so far as to deprive men of his light. On the other hand the criticism of Stokes was honest and weighty. For that reason however it proves the more fatal in this case, and it would be well if theorists, who are prone to criticize practicians, as their inferiors, and with a light heart dismiss in a word the labor of months, perhaps years, remember their fallibility. The tendency of professors to regard themselves as a kind of scientific sauhedrim [*sic*], the appointed judges of natural truth, is perilous, for all theories and rules, all knowledge even, is only an approximation, and it often happens that an outsider, such as Newton, Lavoisier or Darwin, Edison Bell and Hughes reveals the error of their accepted systems or accomplishes what they pronounce impossible.

Hughes, like many other scientists, planted many "technology seeds" that at some time in the future would grow or be rediscovered. His microphone was used to create an amplifier by mounting a carbon microphone next to the diaphragm of a Bell telephone transmitter: the microphone picked up the tiny vibrations of the transmitter diaphragm and amplified them. While experimenting with his microphone he had inadvertently discovered the effects of positive feedback when he placed his microphone too close to a telephone receiver and it began to squeal. This was not only a demonstration of positive feedback, but he had also created an oscillator. Oscillators were not put into use until the 1900s, with the development of tube (valve) circuits.

Hughes was often asked for help in solving particular problems, and he received the following question from a struggling American musician who played the guitar, and who foresaw how Hughes's technology could alter the instrument's role, and hopefully his own destiny:[19]

Dear Sir, - pardon me for writing to you, i write to ask You if you would be Kind enough to tell me how a Microphone is made.... i am a poor Young Married man, Struggling hard to get along, and i play the Guitar, and i thought if i could make the Guitar sound louder, it would be one of the main Instruments in a band.... I ask you either to make the improvement yourself so that I can procure a loud sounding Guitar and introduce it in a Band, and make a living by it or else you tell me how a microphone is made, so that i can experiment on it, and you will receive your reward. Please answer, i will enclose a postage stamp for an answer.

This was a great idea, and it is interesting that Hughes kept the reference. It would be many years before acoustic guitars were fitted with microphones. In fact, a better solution for this musician would have been another phenomenon that Hughes had observed. He had noticed, during his experiments with magnetism, specifically when he was using wire coils, magnets, batteries, a telephone receiver, and a stretched iron wire, that when he plucked the iron wire, he could hear the vibration as a tone in the earphone. These were the rudiments of an electric guitar. Perhaps Hughes was closer than he knew to launching a Victorian rock and roll era!

For his many accomplishments and contributions to science, Hughes was awarded the Albert Medal, which was presented to him in February of 1897 by the Prince of Wales.[20] The staff and students of the London Polytechnic Institute, proud of their popular president, gave him a rousing reception and presented him with an illuminated plaque to celebrate the occasion.

Towards the end of Hughes's life it was said that he had discovered Hertzian waves before Hertz, the Branly "coherer" before Branly, and the "wireless telegraph" before Lodge, Marconi, and others.[21]

By the late 1890s Hughes's health had started to deteriorate, and John Munro captured Hughes's last years in his notes:[22]

A year or two before through an influenza, which affected his mouth, he nearly lost the power of his upper lip. In the spring of 1898 while standing in the sitting-room of his residence in Langham Street, he suddenly grew dizzy and fell striking his head against the fireplace. It was the first of many seizures and falls at home. Soon after it, going out against the will of Mrs. Hughes, he dropped in the roadway and lay helplessly and might have been run over by a cart, had somebody not placed him against a lamp post, and left him to come round. He recovered from these first attacks, but the ailment if not serious, was troublesome to a man so active and made him cautious in his movements.

The following summer, 1899, after the publication of his "wireless experiments," he went abroad for his usual holiday. An invitation from the authorities of the electrical exhibition in memory of the famous Volta who discovered the chemical battery a hundred years before, drew him to Como in August but he was rather unwell and could not mingle in the celebrations. On the way back he stayed some time in Paris and felt the better for it.

As honorary-President of the Engineering Department in the Polytechnic Institution he desired to attend the distribution of prizes before Christmas but was too ill, and for a change went to Brighton. After the New Year on January 3rd. 1900 he lunched at Frascati's for the last time.... In the morning, Friday 12th he rose with assistance at the usual time, but was unable to walk though he did not feel unwell.

His devoted wife prevailed on him to see a doctor, who seemed to think he would recover in a few days, but prescribed a medicine and ordered him to stay in bed. He was troubled with chilliness, and other symptoms of influenza, then very bad at the town, and the warmth of blankets helped the circulation.

Lord Rayleigh was lecturing on flight at the Royal Institution the evening of Friday the 19th and he was most anxious to go, but the doctor would not allow him. Again and again during the small hours of the night, thinking it was day, he asked his wife to get the *Times* newspaper for the report of the lecture. At eight o'clock she read it to him.

The pulse of the invalid was rather feeble.... but neither he nor his wife thought seriously of the illness. He told correspondents in France and Germany that he expected to be up and out in a few days. There was no trace of sadness or discouragement in his manner. He was cheery, pleasant, and happy and would greet the doctor with a smile, or a joke: "Well you've come to see my 'dummy hand'."

About one o'clock Monday the 22nd he asked for his clothes in order that he might go out with his wife and get his luncheon. In the evening about 6 o'clock he spoke with difficulty and his wife could scarcely understand him. His tongue had grown hard. Deeming his throat to be at fault, he wanted some "fleur d'orange" to help it, but wrote the letters one above the other.

About seven o'clock after sipping a little warm milk with a few drops of brandy in it to ease his throat, he sank asleep, and sleeping calmly as a child, at nine he passed away.

On Saturday the 27th January after a touching memorial service in the church of All Souls', Langham Place, his remains were borne to Highgate Cemetery and laid to rest in the eighth vault of the Lebanon Catacombs, amidst evergreens and palms, lilies of the valley, arums and other choice flowers.

It is a fair and sequestered spot with a grassy lawn in front and a fine cedar of Lebanon shedding incense over the tombs.

Hughes's funeral was attended by a large number of mourners which included many of the scientists and dignitaries of the day, and a few words from the Institute of Electrical Engineers summed up their great loss:[23]

> On the 22nd of January in the present year death deprived the world of Science and this Institution of one of the most brilliant experimental discoverers and inventors of the century; and at the same time a large circle of friends lost one of their number whom they loved and greatly admired. His memory will be revered by the world at large, but by the inner circle of his intimate friends that memory will be cherished with loving tenderness.

As he was in life, Hughes was generous after death. His estate was valued at £472,704 ($2,268,979); today this would be worth many millions.[24] A portion of his estate was paid to Anna (who also had her own independent income) and to other members of his family. The majority of the funds, however, went to benefit four London hospitals in the form of the "David Edward Hughes Hospital Trust Fund." These hospitals were The Middlesex Hospital, King's College Hospital, Charing Cross Hospital, and The London Hospital. Under the terms of Hughes's will, the capital was to be held in perpetuity, and the income applied for the general purposes of the hospital. This arrangement continued for some time, but in the hundred years since the Trust was established, there have been a number of organizational changes, one of which was to divide the capital among the hospitals into four independently managed funds, effected through a Charity Commission Scheme on October 22, 1968. Over the years these funds have contributed millions of pounds to benefit the hospitals and their patients and are still making valuable contributions today.

The Middlesex Hospital was merged with University College Hospital in 1994 and closed in 2005, and its fund now comes under the umbrella of the University College London Hospitals Charities. Still held separately and valued at £1,353,000 in 2008, the fund now supports the University College Hospital, Euston Road, London. Each year the capital generates approximately £70,000, which is applied to research and development projects, the purchase of leading-edge medical equipment, and grants for education and skills upgrades for consultants and staff. Over the years the fund has contributed approximately £7 million (in 2010 pounds) to support the hospital.[25]

At King's College Hospital, the Hughes fund was valued at £1,725,000 in December of 2009. Up to 2002 the income generated was used to fund general medical research, but since that time it has been paid over to the general fund for disbursement as grants to the hospital.[26]

The Charing Cross Hospital initially used the Hughes fund for the general purposes of hospital, and then to fund the hospital's medical research committee. Finally in 2000–01 when the hospital wanted to build a primary care and social medicine facility at a cost of £2.5 million, the trustees decided to spend out the fund, which was then valued at £861,000, as a major contribution to the construction of this facility.[27]

David Hughes and Anna's final resting place in the Circle of Lebanon, Highgate Cemetery, London.

In the case of the London Hospital, the fund no longer has a separate existence.[28] However, the present Royal London Hospital still has a building at its Whitechapel facility named in Hughes's honor, and until 1998 had a David Hughes Ward, from which a large marble plaque survives, bearing the following inscription:

> THIS WARD IS DEDICATED TO THE MEMORY OF
> PROFESSOR DAVID EDWARD HUGHES, F.R.S.
> BY WHOSE WILL £90,000 WAS LEFT TO THIS HOSPITAL
> THIS BEING THE LARGEST GIFT EVER MADE TO THE
> LONDON HOSPITAL UP TO 1901 BY ONE PERSON
>
> ———
>
> IT IS WORTHY OF RECORD
> THAT THIS LARGE LEGACY TOGETHER WITH THE LIKE
> AMOUNT LEFT BY HIM TO THREE OTHER HOSPITALS
> WAS THE OUTCOME OF A SUGGESTION MADE TO HIM
> BY HIS DEVOTED WIFE
> ANNA CHADBOURNE HUGHES

Professor David Hughes also bequeathed £4,000 to the Royal Society, £2000 to the Institute of Electrical Engineers (for the David Hughes Scholarship fund), £1000 to

Hughes bequeathed funds to the Royal Society to establish the Hughes Medal, which has been awarded to notable scientists for over 100 years.

the Royal Institution for prizes and gold medals, £4000 to the Academy of Sciences in France (Académie des Sciences de l'Institut), and £2000 to the International Society of Electricians in Paris (Société Internationale des Electriciens).

The money bequeathed to the Royal Society was for establishing a Hughes Medal and award. The awards commenced in 1902 and the Royal Society's Hughes Medal has been awarded annually in recognition of an original discovery in the physical sciences. The recipients have included:

1902 Joseph John Thomson
1905 Augusto Righi
1910 John Ambrose Fleming
1913 Alexander Graham Bell
1916 Elihu Thomson
1921 Niels Henrik David Bohr
1929 Hans Geiger
1933 Edward Victor Appleton
1936 Walder Schottky
1942 Enrico Fermi
1948 Robert Watson-Watt
1950 Max Born
1976 Stephen William Hawking

After Prof. Hughes's death, his wife Anna Chadbourne remained in London and channeled her energies into art, which was the other love of her life. She became captivated by the new technology of photography, abandoned her oils and brushes, and bought a camera and related equipment to practice this new art. This might have been a sufficient outlet for most people, but she had much bigger plans in mind, and photography was only a part of them.

D. E. Hughes and Anna took frequent trips down to Brighton to take in the sea air, and it was there that this undated photograph was taken of Anna.

On December 5, 1902, she embarked with her steamer trunk and camera equipment on a journey that would last six months.[29] She set off by steamer across the Mediterranean, down through the Suez Canal and across the Arabian Sea to India. On her return she stopped in Egypt and visited the Holy Land. Anna was seventy-one years old at the time and had begun a very adventurous journey that few single, unaccompanied women would have attempted at that period.

In India she landed in Bombay, and from there she set out on a tour of the country.[30] This led her to Jaipur, Agra, Delhi, Kapur, Lucknow, and ended in Calcutta; on the way, she detoured into the Himalayan region, specifically to Darjeeling. From Calcutta she returned to Bombay. From there, she sailed on the steamboat *Persia* through the Red Sea to Suez and on to Cairo. She visited the museums to see the Egyptian mummies and pharaohs, and took trips to see the pyramids. Then she sailed up the Nile to see the ancient tombs and went as far as the newly completed Aswan Dam. Anna was obviously serious about her photography, as she made the following comment:[31]

> ...the new interest I take in photography is a joyful study for me and my years of study and experience in drawing and painting are all necessary for the good results in taking "snap shots." So far, the results of my work have been highly spoken of in Calcutta, Bombay and Cairo and I am trying to make progress continually.

Next she went to Palestine and Syria. She sailed for Palestine and the port of Jaffa and then went by train to Jerusalem. Her original plan was to remain in the area for several days and then return home. However, she was so overcome by being, as she put it, on "Holy Ground," that she extended her stay and decided to make an ambitious tour of the region. She hired a "dragoman" or guide who organized her caravan, which consisted of himself and five other persons: the leader of her horse, a tender who took care of the animals, a cook, and two muleteers. There were eight horses and two tents. At times, when they camped near a city, she would also employ a couple of guards. She made this report:[32]

> I left Jerusalem last Monday morning, in a very wide brimmed straw hat, tinted glasses for the eyes, a good steady horse, umbrella and in a thick black cloth skirt I bought in Boston.... I go from 14 to 16 to 24 miles a day as there are here and there places of interest, which lead to side ruins. There is sometimes a path or what they call the places for

Anna took many photographs on her visit to India, including this one of some Indian dignitaries.

a road and often I think neither one or the other, but it is a wonder to me.... I have a good Dragoman as my guide who has been over this ground with many a clergyman as well as myself the "rookie-rider—Anna C. Hughes," each day I am quite fearless in going down steep paths turning around mountains, through fields of fig trees or lemon trees in blossoms, thousands of olive trees—or by miles of cactus as high as a large building, covered with yellow blossoms.

Her trip took her from Jerusalem to Bethlehem, to the Dead Sea and Jericho, to the River Jordan, then north to Nazareth and the Sea of Galilee, to the top of Mount Tabor, and then west to Haifa on the Mediterranean. In all this was a trip of a couple of hundred miles covered by walking and riding, and along the way she took many photographs:[33]

As I expect to be the only one in our family who ever makes this journey, as I have done, I am making it as complete as possible and in the only way to see the various places in the interior, and I have taken so many photographs, you will be able to see some of the interesting places.

From Haifa she went to Beirut and then sailed back to Cairo, returning to London on the *SS Himalaya*, and arriving in port on June 13, 1903. After this adventure, Anna decided to return to her family in America, where she owned a house in Cambridge just outside Boston. It was here that she spent the remaining years of her life until she passed away on July 22, 1919. Her request was to be laid to rest in the mausoleum at Highgate Cemetery, London, alongside her husband. In her will she bequeathed David Hughes's notebooks to the British Museum, an induction balance to The Royal Institution, London, and his medals, harp, and watch to the Smithsonian Institution in Washington DC.

David Hughes's notebooks were sent to the British Museum, and much of Hughes's legacy could have easily been lost were it not for the diligence of the staff of that institution, particularly Alan Campbell-Swinton, FRS. He was requested by the museum to review the notebooks and to make recommendations about their conservation. Luckily, Swinton had known Hughes, recognized the value of the notebooks, and recommended that they be preserved. They were rebound, and are now in the manuscript collection of the British Library, London. After Swinton had dealt with the notebooks, it occurred to him that Hughes must have also possessed a great quantity of experimental equipment, and he tells the story of tracking them down:[34]

After perusing Hughes's notebooks, it occurred to me that at some time or other he must have possessed a quantity of apparatus, so I enquired as to where these notebooks had been found. I was shown a fearful mass of rubbish in a pantechnicon off the Tottenham Court Road. There were two roomfuls of old clothes, old boots and umbrellas and masses of books and old newspapers. I went to Colonel (now Sir Henry) Lyons, the

Professor David Edward Hughes, FRS, whose inventions, discoveries, and philanthropy are still benefiting society today.

Director of the Science Museum, South Kensington and he undertook to look through all this, provided if anything of interest was found it was to go to the Science Museum. As a result, a number of Hughes original microphones and various forms of telephone receivers evidently made with his own hands, and the apparatus with which he had conducted experiments in wireless telegraphy, all in accordance with, and all readily recognized from sketches in his notebooks, were discovered, and have now been placed in the Science Museum, where they form a most interesting exhibit.

Professor David Edward Hughes left a substantial and enduring intellectual and material legacy. At the same time, he has hitherto been something of an enigma. He and other members of his family guarded their privacy closely, perhaps a habit carried over from the "child prodigy" days. His scientific achievements are well documented, but the information has been scattered, and though articles about him are legion, he had never been the subject of a full-length biography. He certainly had not received the acknowledgement he deserved in life or death, and it is hoped that this volume has gone some way towards redressing that omission, and has shed light on the life of this remarkable man.

TECHNICAL DETAILS OF THE DEVELOPMENT OF HUGHES'S FIRST TELEGRAPH INSTRUMENT DURING THE 1850S

INTRODUCTION

This appendix details the development of David Edward Hughes's first printing telegraph, which led to his first British, French, and American patents. Subsequent improvements and modifications made to the instrument, and later patents, are covered in parts 2 and 3 of this appendix.

When Hughes invented his telegraph instrument he was teaching natural philosophy and music in Kentucky, where he had moved in 1850, and he subsequently brought his telegraph instrument into practical use while only in his mid-twenties. Electrical knowledge at that period was in its infancy, a fact that becomes immediately apparent when one thumbs through natural philosophy textbooks of the time, such as D. Olmsted's *A Compendium of Natural Philosophy*, or J.L.Comstock's *A System of Natural Philosophy*—electricity was portrayed as "A new and exciting science."[1]

Professor Hughes might have consulted these textbooks in preparing his lectures. Little was known or understood about what electricity or its twin, magnetism, really were, and they were known only for the effects they caused. Magnetism had been observed for centuries through naturally occurring lodestone; the earth was also known to have a magnetic field with a north and south magnetic pole. Frictional or static electricity had been observed, but appeared to have more novelty than practical value. It was an era of high voltage experiments at social gatherings, with spectacular spark discharges and hair-raising demonstrations. Electricity itself was described as "A single imponderable subtle fluid equally distributed throughout nature."[2]

"Voltaic" and "Galvanic" electricity became available with early forms of chemical batteries which eventually could be relied on to provide a steady supply of electricity. There were several recipes for making batteries which took on the names of their inventors, such as the "Grove cell" and the "Daniell cell."

The frontier of electrical knowledge, however, was "electro-magnetism" and "electro-dynamics," that is, the study of the link between electricity and magnetism. Electromagnets could be built from a coil of wire connected to a battery, and electricity generated by electro-dynamic induction through the movement of a magnet in and out of a coil of wire. There were no standard units for voltage, current, resistance, capacitance or inductance, and laboratory instruments were few and far between. These mainly consisted of gold leaf electrometers, which were used to detect a static electrical charge, and galvanometers, which could determine the presence or flow of electrical current. The textbooks were, of course, strikingly devoid of mathematical formulas to describe or predict the behavior of electrical circuits.

This was the knowledge base that Hughes had to work with in creating his telegraph instrument. It must also be remembered that he was without the benefit of a formal university education and had none of the apparatus that might be available to an academic. On top of this, he had little money available to buy parts or tools. He was, however, very inventive, and appears to have benefited from his home schooling, extensive travels, and time spent carrying out practical experiments. He was a gifted and creative musician, and perhaps like other inventors who had their roots in the arts, such as Morse, who was a painter, and Wheatstone, a musician, he found that this background helped him form a vision of what he wished to create.

When Hughes set about developing his telegraph instrument, the leading electrical pioneers of the day were Michael Faraday, Joseph Henry, Samuel Morse, William Cooke, and Charles Wheatstone. William Thomson (later Lord Kelvin) had taken up a position at Glasgow University as a professor of natural philosophy, and James Clerk Maxwell, who was to revolutionize thinking on the yet to be discovered electromagnetic waves, was just entering Cambridge University. Later in his career Hughes saw the rise to prominence of Thomas Edison, Nikola Tesla, Alexander Graham Bell, Oliver Heaviside, Oliver Lodge, George Francis Fitzgerald, and Heinrich Hertz.

In order to appreciate how innovative the scientists and inventors of this period were, the reader must be prepared to forget much of what he or she knows of modern electrical technology and transport him or herself back to this relatively primitive electrical age.

TELEGRAPH TECHNOLOGY IN 1850

By 1852 telegraph systems in America were dominated by the Samuel Morse system, which had approximately 80 percent of the telegraph lines.[3] The other 20 percent were split between the Royal Earl House and Alexander Bain systems. In Britain the Cooke and Wheatstone system was the most common.[4]

According to the press of that period, for a telegraph to operate successfully, it had:[5]

1. To produce or develop an electric fluid in any desired quantity, and of the necessary quantity.
2. To transmit it with celerity to any required distance without injuriously dissipating it.
3. To cause upon its arrival at any assigned point to produce some sensible effects which may serve the purpose of written or printed characters.

Hughes had first seen a Morse telegraph in operation a few years earlier, and had come to the conclusion that he could improve on it. His idea was to make an instrument on which the message could be entered using a set of alphabetical keys, and thus to do away with the necessity of learning and using a code. At the receiving station, the message would be printed out in plain English and not by coded lines on a paper strip. It was this idea that formed the basis for his telegraph instrument.

The problem Hughes had to solve would of course be simple with today's technology, but it was pioneering work back then, and he and others were essentially paving the way for future telex, teletype, and fax machines—today's modern data communications. The word "telegraph" had been coined early on to describe these early instruments "that write at a distance"; there was an attempt to introduce the word "teletype" to describe printing telegraphs that "print at a distance," but the word did not catch on until many years later.

The technology and knowledge of the period determined what was possible in telegraph systems. The parameters available for electrical signaling were limited to switching the electrical current on and off, reversing its polarity, and varying its time dimension, i.e. how long a signal was "on" or "off," as in the Morse telegraph systems, which used a series of dots and dashes. The dots were short duration electrical pulses and the dashes were longer, three times as long as a dot, so that the two signals could be easily distinguished. Other systems, such as the step-by-step systems of Royal Earl House and Gustave Froment, used a variable number of pulses of relatively constant amplitude and duration. Cooke and Wheatstone, on the other hand, used constant amplitude signals but reversed their polarity for their needle system.

Single wire operation and the use of an earth return, which had been discovered some years earlier, was standard practice: only one wire was required, which saved the cost of a separate wire return.[6] Telegraph systems such as the Morse system had to transmit sufficient power over the line to operate the receiving telegraph instrument at the other end of the telegraph line. Thus, to work over longer and longer distances

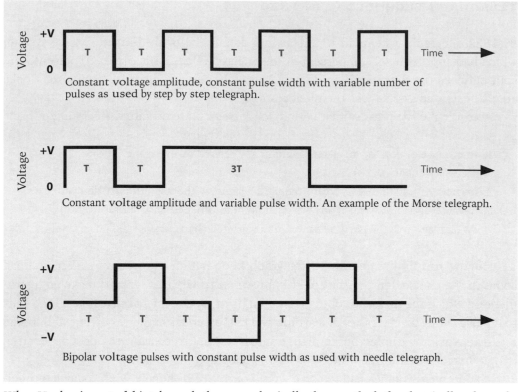

When Hughes invented his telegraph there were basically three methods for electrically telegraphing information: varying the number of pulses, varying their duration, or varying their polarity.

it was necessary to add more battery power to overcome the increased line resistance and leakage to ground, which became more pronounced in wet weather. Later, relays in conjunction with local batteries were used to boost weak signals.

THE HUGHES TYPE PRINTING TELEGRAPH

Hughes's telegraph instrument was far more ingenious than anything previously invented, both in its mechanics and in its method of transmitting information. It is these differences that allowed his machine to become so successful and to survive and dominate the market, particularly in Europe, until it was finally superseded by more modern technology, finally ending its career almost 100 years later in the 1950s.

Hughes had been mulling over his telegraph concept for a couple of years. He was intrigued by clocks and clockwork mechanisms, and spent time collecting them, examining them, and taking them apart. This obviously helped him design the mechanisms that his telegraph would have. To him, clocks represented the most precise mechanism available. Hughes was also familiar with tuning forks which vibrated at precise frequencies for tuning his harp, which had forty-odd strings. Also, he was familiar with the metronome, another clockwork device used for setting the tempo of music. This knowledge was to play a role in the design of his invention, although his personal notes do not provide many clues as to how he went about it, or the sequence of his ideas.

His challenge was to invent and construct the following:

- A method for entering the letters of the alphabet.
- A mechanism to take the entered letters and convert them into a form that could be sent electrically over a telegraph wire.
- A mechanism for capturing the electrical signals that represented the transmitted letters and passing them to a printing mechanism.
- A method for printing the letters out onto paper after they had been received.

He also had to decide what speed the instrument should operate at, and how to power the instrument. While Hughes could certainly visualize what he wanted to build, in the actual construction he was limited by some real world constraints, which were:

- He had very little money available.
- He had limited tools and what he had were all hand tools.
- Any mechanism he wanted to use would have to be scavenged from existing mechanisms such as old clocks.
- Many of the miscellaneous parts he would have to make himself, including battery cells, wire coils, relays, magnets, letter keys, a print wheel, etc.

The following is a description of each of the component parts of Hughes's telegraph instrument, although not necessarily in the order he constructed them.

The Keyboard

Hughes's idea for inputting the letters of the messages was to have a set of finger keys, one for each letter of the alphabet, somewhat similar to an early typewriter keyboard. It consisted of two rows in alphabetical order, with "A" through "N" on the top row and "O" through "Z" on the lower row, the leftmost key on the lower row being the space key (in contrast to today's three rows in QWERTY format).[7] There were twenty-seven keys and each was made out of a shirt collar stud with a letter printed on it, and was connected to a mechanical linkage. When a key was pressed, the linkage caused a spring contact arm to be moved into position so that it could make electrical contact with the mechanism responsible for transmitting the letters. The key was automatically reset after the letter had been transmitted.

There was also one extra key to the right of the keyboard, which was actually an electrical switch used in the synchronizing process described later in this section.

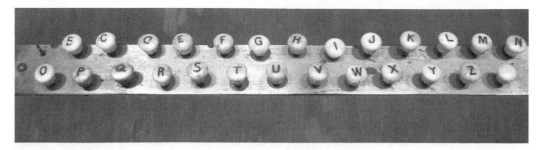

Hughes initially used collar studs to form the keys for this typewriter style keyboard, but this style did not catch on until many years later.

The Printing Mechanism

The printing mechanism was constructed by fastening the letters of a printer's set of type around the circumference of a wooden disc to form a type wheel. There were twenty-six letters followed by a gap that corresponded to the "space" character, which was followed by another gap. The second gap was where the print wheel was stopped as part of the synchronization process which will be explained shortly. Thus, in total there were twenty-eight elements on the print wheel.

An ink roller in contact with the type wheel automatically inked the letters as it rotated. When an electrical signal was received to print a letter, a platen would rapidly rise up against the print wheel, and the letter would be printed onto a paper strip. A significant difference between Hughes's printing telegraph and other systems was that the print wheel did not have to come to a stop when it printed a letter: it printed on the fly. This allowed the mechanism to run at full speed all the time and not in the stop-and-go mode of a step-by-step instrument (such as the House instrument). This method became known as "flying print." The platen action had to be exceedingly fast, and one cycle consisted of raising the paper tape via a platen and striking it against the letter on the print wheel, dropping the platen back, and advancing the paper.

The message was printed out on a paper strip from a reel on the right hand side of the instrument. The paper tape was advanced after each letter to provide the correct letter spacing, and to position the paper for the next character to be printed.

Transmission Mechanism and the "One Wave Signal"

The heart of Hughes's telegraph was his uniting of the transmitter and receiver portions of the instrument, which he designed as integral components. These elements contained a number of innovations which were unique to his instrument. One of these was a method for sending each letter using only one electrical pulse. When he devised a method for doing this he wrote the following remark:[8]

First conceived an Electric Telegraph to use but one wave to each signal.

The word "wave" was commonly used to describe what would now be called an electrical pulse. This was a radical statement, as all other systems used significantly more pulses to transmit each letter. The Morse code system, for example, used multiple pulses for each letter and also required additional time spacing between both letters and words so that the telegraph operator receiving the message would be able to distinguish them.[9] The step-by-step method of transmission that House and Froment had used involved lengthy pulse trains for each letter, which took time and limited the number of words which could be sent per minute.[10] In addition, more pulses took more electrical energy to transmit. Another factor that no doubt encouraged Hughes in his search for a new method for transmitting letters was his desire to avoid violating the patents of Morse and other inventors.

Thus Hughes devised a new way of sending information that required only a single electrical pulse for each letter. And he did this by using another dimension in the method of data transmission—that of "time division," this possibly being the first application of this technique.[11] Hughes's idea was to divide up time into equal segments. This can be referred to as the "frame time," and it was a repetitive sequence. Each of these frame times was divided into twenty-eight shorter time slices.

Each of the twenty-eight time slices was allocated to one of the twenty-six letters of the alphabet, plus a space, plus a blank used for synchronization. For example, when the letter "A" key was pressed it would complete an electrical connection between

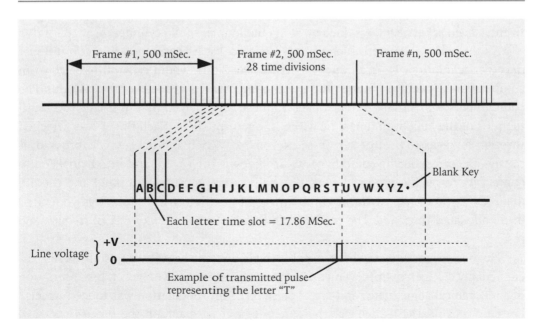

Hughes invented a unique and efficient method for transmitting information by telegraph, a form of pulse position modulation, which required only a single electrical pulse for each letter.

a battery and the telegraph line and transmit an electrical pulse in the first position of the frame, or in time slot number one; if the letter "M" was pressed, a pulse would occur in the middle of the frame, in time slot thirteen. This was in fact an early form of pulse position modulation in which one piece of binary information, a "1" or "0," was transmitted in each time slot, a "1" when a letter was transmitted, and a "0" when no letter was transmitted.

The Commutator

To create the time frame and twenty-eight individual time slots, Hughes required some sort of scanner or commutator which would maintain a steady scanning rate and repeatedly check each letter key in sequence to see if any had been selected. To create this system he turned for inspiration to an item that had been around for many years, one with which his musical background had made him familiar. This was the lowly music box, which consisted of a clockwork-driven cylinder on which there was a pattern of short pins or raised protrusions. In close proximity to the cylinder and running along its length was a metal comb whose individual fingers were tuned to a different musical note. As the cylinder rotated each protrusion on it plucked a finger on the comb and sounded a note, and thus a tune was played.

Hughes adapted this purely mechanical model to an electrical environment. Instead of the pins on the rotating cylinder plucking the fingers of the music comb to create a note, he made them electrical contacts to determine which letter key had been pressed.[12] This was done by arranging the protrusions on the cylinder into a continuous helix pattern consisting of twenty-seven pins. The metal comb was arranged to have twenty-seven separate fingers lined up along the length of the cylinder.

As the cylinder rotated, each pin on it passed by its corresponding comb finger once per revolution. Thus, in one revolution, the helix would scan all twenty-seven comb fingers. This gave a frame time equal to the rotational speed of the cylinder. The comb fingers were arranged to be offset from the cylinder, so that normally the rotating pins of the helix would pass by without touching them. Each finger was attached through linkages to a letter key on the keyboard. When a letter key was pressed, it caused its corresponding comb finger to drop down into a slot and into a position to contact its respective pin on the rotating helix. As the cylinder rotated and the pin made electrical contact with the comb fingers, a brief electrical pulse was generated in its allocated time slot. The rotating pin then lifted the finger out of its slot and reset it.

Hughes never claimed to have invented the use of the helical scan drum, as his patent actually covers his "improvements" of printing telegraphs; however, his application of a mechanical commutator and use of pulse position modulation was indeed novel.[13]

Hughes's next challenge was to figure out how to maintain the precise speed of rotation of the commutator. For this, all of his experimenting with clock mechanisms was to come in handy.

The pin barrel showing the scanning helix and the individual contacts from each letter key. The segmented wheel on the left was used for switching between transmit and receive for duplex operation.

Precision Timing

Hughes's instrument required precision timing for a number of reasons. First, for pulse position modulation to work, the electrical pulse representing a letter had to be transmitted in the correct position in time. If it was transmitted at the wrong time, then the letter would be misread by the receiving instrument, and the message would become garbled. Second, the receiving device had to be running in precise step with the transmitter so that when a pulse arrived, the correct letter was in position on the print wheel. If it was out of step, then an incorrect letter would be printed. Thus the receiver had to run in synchronism and phase with the transmitter. Hughes had to figure out how to keep these two instruments, possibly separated by tens or hundreds of miles, operating in perfect synchronization, not for a minute or two but for long periods.

Hughes also had to decide on how fast he wanted the system to operate. Certainly he wanted to be able to send messages at least as fast as the Morse system, and preferably faster. Typical speeds for Morse were in the range of twenty to thirty words per minute, or approximately two to three letters per second. Of course, this depended on a number of factors, such as how skilled the operators were at sending and receiving, the error rate, the state of the equipment and lines, etc. If Hughes was to transmit at the same rate of two to three letters per second he would have to run his scanning commutator at two to three revolutions per second, or 120 to 180 revolutions per minute. However, the differences between his system and the Morse system gave him some advantages. The letters in Morse code required up to four pulses or key presses by the operator, whereas he only required one pulse and one key press per letter. So it appeared that he could run slower and attain an equivalent transmission speed. Also, he realized he could send multiple letters per revolution of the commutator as long as they followed in alphabetical order and were not sent too close together. Hughes settled on a speed of 120 rpm, giving a frame time of 0.5 second and a letter time slot time of 17.86 milliseconds.[14]

Driving the commutator cylinder at this speed by a clockwork mechanism was quite feasible, but maintaining this speed with perfect accuracy and synchronizing it with another instrument posed a challenge.

He evidently experimented with a number of methods for regulating and controlling the timing. One thing that comes through very clearly in all of Hughes's notebooks is that he was a master experimenter, constantly trying different approaches, combinations and sequences, until he was able to arrive at a solution. His notes indicate:[15]

> Continued experimenting upon governors necessary to produce synchronous motion which was necessary to carry out the one wave system of telegraphy. Tried pendulums, combination of fans and flywheels—centrifugal force.

By examining the features found in clocks, he was able to come up with a solution. Clocks ran for extended periods of time, powered either by a coiled-up spring or a descending weight. They also operated very consistently, regulated by a pendulum, anchor, and escapement wheel that could maintain an accuracy of about one second a day.[16] This was an ingenious mechanism, the swing of the pendulum providing the precision, and the escapement wheel transferring the timing to the clock mechanism. The escapement wheel, in return, provided the small nudges required to keep the pendulum swinging, a descending weight supplying the energy to keep the mechanism running. Mechanical clocks were arranged to provide a display of seconds, minutes, and hours through various gearings from the precision swing of the pendulum. The pendulum usually swung with a period of 0.5 or 1 second (depending on the number of teeth on the escapement wheel and the follow-on gearing). Hughes, however, needed to run 120 times faster than this, and experiments with pendulums would quickly have shown that he would have needed an extremely short pendulum to run at these speeds; this was impractical, and he would have concluded that he needed an alternative to the pendulum.

Hughes turned to his musical background for a solution. He needed a frequency which was in the audio range, and he knew that tuning forks produced audible tones at a precise frequency without harmonics or overtones. However, tuning forks, after being

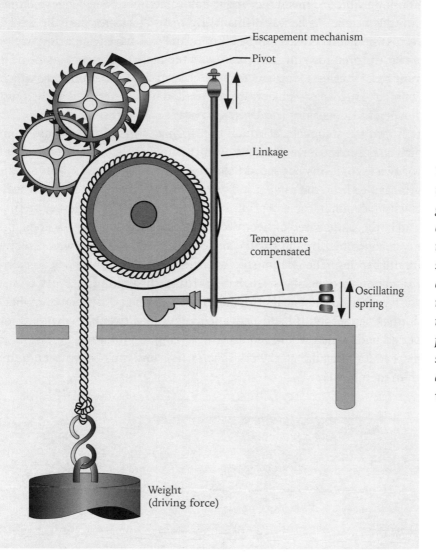

Escapement mechanism

Pivot

Linkage

Temperature
compensated

Oscillating
spring

Weight
(driving force)

The precision timing was governed by a vibrating metal spring strip driving an escapement mechanism. The power was supplied by a descending weight.

set in oscillation, soon stopped producing sound, usually within sixty seconds. So, while tuning forks were highly accurate, they would not oscillate for very long without some means of sustaining them. He was also familiar with the metronome. While less accurate than the tuning fork, as well as operating at a lower frequency, a metronome did maintain a given frequency for a longer period of time as it was operated by clock-work. Hughes probably combined these ideas, as he writes:[17]

> Discovered the application law of vibrations to the synchronizing of mechanisms. Made two instruments. Keep exact time with each other by the most simple and crude mechanism.

He first tried using a vibrating metal rod, and it has sometimes been suggested that he used a steel knitting needle. As he was dismantling many clocks for parts he would have also come across similar rods used for the chimes and may have tried using one of these. These may have proven too stiff and vibrated at too high a frequency, as he next tried a quasi tuning fork by using a single metal spring strip clamped at one end which could be set to vibrate.[18] Hughes presumably experimented until he arrived at the right frequency by adjusting its dimensions and/or its thickness.

He had determined the frequency at which the spring strip should vibrate from the speed at which he needed to have the commutator rotate. This he had determined to be 120 rpm or two revolutions per second. As the commutator had twenty-eight time slots, he arranged to have the same number of teeth on the escapement wheel. The escapement wheel, commutator, and print wheel were connected together so that they would all run at the same speed of two revolutions per second. The escapement wheel rotation was controlled by the oscillation of the anchor which was directly linked to the vibrating spring. The relationship between the escapement wheel speed and the spring vibration frequency was such that for each oscillation cycle of the spring, the escape wheel advanced one tooth. Therefore to have the escapement wheel make two revolutions per second it had to advance two times twenty-eight teeth or fifty-six teeth per second, which would require the spring to vibrate at 56 Hz. This was a very high speed for a regular clockwork mechanism and must have been quite a challenge for him to implement.[19]

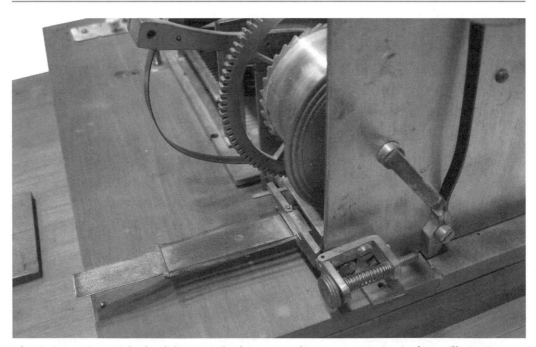

The timing spring with the sliding weight frequency adjustment. Missing is the oscillating connecting linkage to the escapement mechanism (see the left foreground).

The mode of operation was to set the spring strip vibrating; this drove the escapement wheel at a constant rate, which in turn drove the commutator at the same speed. In return, the escapement wheel provided the necessary nudges to sustain the spring in oscillation.

To adjust the frequency of oscillation, Hughes arranged a small weight which could be slid along the spring strip. Once set, the frequency would remain constant unless the temperature changed, which would affect the length of the spring and hence its frequency. The main concern would have been the frequency drift between the transmitting telegraph and the receiving telegraph, as this would manifest itself in the printing of incorrect letters. Hughes's solution to this problem was to provide a temperature compensation mechanism which is analyzed later in the appendix; in fact it was fairly easy to set the transmitting and receiving telegraphs to the same frequency and get them started in synchronism.

The Signal Detector

Hughes was not a proponent of sending high-voltage electrical signals on telegraph lines, as was required by the Morse system, where the transmitted signal had to be powerful enough to operate the receiving mechanism.[20] That method had certain limitations. One was the effect of line resistance, as iron wire was the wire of choice at the time, and it had a resistance approximately seven times higher than copper. In addition, the insulators used on telegraph poles were not entirely effective, and during wet weather and fog, signal leakage to ground increased, which reduced the energy available to operate the relay at the receiving telegraph. The receiving relay had to receive a signal of sufficient voltage to attract the armature across the air gap, overcome the armature return spring force, and actuate the inker or stylus mechanisms to print or inscribe the dots and dashes on the paper tape. Hence, the Morse telegraph needed high voltage signals, and thus required many primary battery cells (thirty to one hundred were not uncommon) to provide the necessary energy. This limited the distance over which the transmitter and receiver could operate (this problem was later overcome by the use of regeneration relays spaced along the telegraph line that repeated the messages using power supplied by a local battery).

Hughes saw two important advantages in a different approach. First, if it was possible to reduce the power required for transmission, it would cut down on the number of batteries required. Second, if it was possible to improve the reception of signals by the use of a sensitive detection device, it would be possible to communicate over longer distances and under more adverse conditions. Also, as Hughes had to make the battery cells himself, he had a good incentive to minimize the number required.

He needed a device that was:

- Capable of detecting the single transmitted pulse.
- Sensitive—he was thinking of only using one or two battery cells in the transmitter and being able to receive messages with the instruments hundreds of miles apart.

• Rapid in its response once the electrical pulse was detected so that the receiving mechanism would meet the timing constraints and print the letter within its allocated time slot.

Hughes started experimenting to see if he could come up with a method to meet these requirements, and records in his notes:[21]

Discovered the application of the holding power of natural and electro magnetism to the purpose of telegraphing—restoring the armature to its original position by means of a lever brought into play the instant the armature was set free.

This remark is a little cryptic, but it makes sense once it is understood what he had come up with. What he invented was a sensitive detector of his own design, that later became known in Europe as the "Hughes relay" and was one of the first practical applications of a polarized relay.

His detection relay consisted of a horseshoe permanent magnet with soft iron pole pieces added to its north and south poles. Two coils of wire were wound on bobbins and each was slipped over one of these pole pieces. Obtaining insulated wire for the coils was not straightforward, as it was not readily available. What was available was "bonnet wire" used in making women's hats, which was composed of iron wire with cotton thread wound around it, and he made use of this. He then set a soft iron armature on a pivot which could swing to bridge the gap between the magnet's two poles. The armature, attracted by the permanent magnet, was allowed to touch the poles. A spring was connected to this armature, arranged to pull it open and off the magnet. The tension of this spring was adjusted so that it was almost, but not quite enough to pull the armature free. The relay was activated by the reception of an electrical pulse. The coil connections were such that the electric pulse created a magnetic field opposed to that of the permanent magnet, weakening the field enough to release its hold on the armature. The armature would then fly off at a very rapid rate due to the pull of the spring. This triggered the printing mechanism into action. The beauty of this system was that once the pulse was detected, the power to drive the printing mechanism came from the spring action that was already tensioned and ready to trip, like a mousetrap that had been set. Once tripped, the weight drive system took over and momentarily drove a platen and paper strip against the inked print wheel. As part of the cycle, the relay armature was reset in preparation for receiving the next electrical pulse.

The relay that Hughes had invented required significantly less energy to activate, approximately one tenth the energy required by a conventional relay. The Hughes relay took on a life of its own in other applications and became widely adopted in European rail systems as a component in their signaling and safety systems. Further information on this relay is contained in Appendix 2.

A view of the clockwork mechanism showing the print wheel on the left and the drum onto which the drive weight cord was wound. Missing are the inking wheel and timing linkage.

The Transmitting and Receiving Mechanism

Each instrument had a transmitter and receiver which were driven by a common power source and mechanically geared together. The print wheel rotated at the same speed as the commutator and in phase with it. This ensured that when the commutator was in the letter "A" position, the same letter was in the print position on the print wheel. If the telegraph instrument's transmitter was connected to its own receiver, then the printer would print out exactly what was being typed in on the keyboard. This mode of operation was often used for demonstration purposes. In operation on telegraph lines, however, two identical instruments were required, one at each end of the line. These two instruments would have to be running at the same speed and also be in phase with each other. Note however that the print wheel in a distant receiver could also be offset by one, two, or more letters to accommodate any telegraph line transmission delays.

Weight Drive

The system to drive the various mechanisms was similar to that found on grandfather or longcase clocks. A heavy weight was suspended by a cord wound around a drum which drove the mechanisms through a series of gears, the downward force of the weight acting at the radius of the drum to produce a turning moment.

Hughes had two separate weight drives on his instruments. One was used to drive the commutator and print wheel and to provide nudges to the vibrating spring to sustain its vibration. The weight was prevented from running down at a high rate of speed by the escapement wheel, which acted as a governor. This weight was 50 pounds and acted at a radius of one inch, giving a torque of 50 inch-pounds. The second weight mechanism was used to drive the platen against the print wheel and to reset the receiving relay armature. This was a 100-pound weight wound on a drum whose radius was one inch, giving a torque of 100 inch-pounds. The weights were wound up by hand using a crank key. When the instrument was in continuous operation, the weights had to be wound up fairly frequently—every ten minutes, according to some descriptions. These weights were fairly heavy, heavier than those usually used on grandfather clocks, but the extra weight was required to drive the mechanism at a high speed and to provide the rapid response for printing. The weight was an issue, though, as together with the high speed of operation, it put significant strain on all of the mechanisms.

Battery Power

The battery was only required for the momentary transmission of the single pulses when letter keys were pressed. As Hughes used a sensitive pulse detector in the telegraph receiver, the power requirement was low. He demonstrated the instrument using only one or two Daniell cells (1.2 or 2.4 volts). This was a primary cell with copper and zinc electrodes immersed in a dilute solution of sulfuric acid. A cell was sometimes referred to as a cup. In a typical installation, the Hughes telegraph usually used five to seven cells.

Two-Way Simultaneous Communication—Duplex Operation

The Hughes telegraph was designed from the start to be able to transmit and receive at the same time, providing full duplex operation. Thus, communication in both directions could occur simultaneously between two locations: each operator could be typing in text to the other, while each instrument was printing out. This gave the Hughes system a higher productivity than the Morse system. Both systems required an operator at each location, but in the Hughes system both could be transmitting simultaneously, whereas in the Morse system only one operator could transmit on the line at any one time, the other being engaged in receiving and transcribing the message.

Duplex operation was not new: others had tried it in Europe, and Moses Farmer, in America, demonstrated a method to achieve duplex operation with the Morse system later in 1865. These methods, however, required the insertion of a piece of ancillary apparatus between the telegraph instruments and the line.

G.B. Prescott, in the 1860 edition of his book *History, Theory and Practice of the Electric Telegraph*, made the following comment in regards to Hughes's telegraph instrument and its duplex feature:[22]

> There is one more point in the splendid achievement of Mr. Hughes which should not be passed over in silence, although of no practical value; and that is his arrangement for working both ways over the same wire at the same time.

This remark was short-sighted, as within a few years, increasing the capacity of a single line became more and more important as communications traffic increased. Many schemes were developed to accomplish this, starting with duplex schemes, and including the Edison Quadruplex (1874), which allowed four messages to be transmitted over one wire at the same time. Later still came the Synchronous Multiplex Telegraph which could handle six messages simultaneously.[23]

Hughes's instrument incorporated the duplex mode as a standard feature. He accomplished this by having two rotating segmented discs mounted on the end of the rotating scanning commutator shaft. Each disc had twenty-eight segments which formed electrical contacts. The two segmented discs were displaced from each other by one half segment. The discs allowed the connection to the telegraph line to be alternated back and forth between send and receive. The inner segmented disc was in contact with the commutator and took care of the electrical path for the transmitted electrical pulse. The outer segmented disc was insulated from the commutator and took care of switching the circuit over to the receive mode and directing the incoming pulses to the receiver's detector and printer.

While it was indicated above that the time base was divided into twenty-eight time slots, each of the twenty-eight time slots was actually subdivided again into two subslots to accommodate the duplex action of transmitting and receiving a pulse within the time period. This could be viewed as a total of fifty-six time slots, where the transmitter and receiver were interleaved with each other every 8.9 milliseconds. This, of course, dictated how accurately the timing and synchronization had to be maintained between the transmitting and receiving instruments.

Starting the Instruments in Synchronism

It was necessary for the transmitting and receiving instruments to be running in synchronism and in phase with each other. These instruments were normally separated by many miles and Hughes devised the following system to accomplish this synchronization. First, before the two instruments were moved to their final locations they would be set side by side on the workbench and the vibrating springs adjusted to vibrate at the same frequency.

When the instruments were then at separate locations, they would be set in motion and latched in the blank position. This was done manually by engaging a lever that arrested the mechanism at the blank position. The transmitting instrument operator would then release the lever and press down on the blank key on the keyboard, thus sending an electrical pulse to the receiving instrument. When the receiving instrument detected the signal it unlatched its mechanism, setting both instruments to run in phase.[24] This arrangement also took care of any transmission line lags by automatically offsetting the print wheel to compensate for any time difference. As these time lags would remain constant, the instruments would remain in synchronism.

Next, to ensure that both instruments continued running at the same frequency, the following procedure was used. The transmitting instrument sent out the letter "A" several times in succession. If the receiver printed out a series of As, then they were running at the same frequency. However, if the receiver printed out letters that were later in the alphabet, say Bs, Cs, or Ds, then the receiver was running too fast; if it printed Zs, Ys, or Xs, then it was running too slow. The frequency of the receiving instrument was adjusted by moving the weight on the vibrating spring until a series of As was printed.

This may have been one of the earliest applications of "synchronous data transmission,"[25] and this was many years before the advent of digital technology, precision crystal oscillators, and self-clocking digital codes. The first models of Hughes's telegraph relied on temperature-compensated precision timing. The mechanism was self-diagnosing, in that it detected and displayed when it was either out of phase or out of synchronism by printing incorrect letters. (Later models of the instrument improved the mechanism, incorporating continuous self-correction to the timing so as to maintain tight synchronism.)

On early instruments, there was an additional feature that allowed a master transmitting instrument to selectively correspond with a particular receiving instrument. In Hughes's patent he writes:[26]

> Before transmitting a message to a distant station, it will be necessary to exclude all the other instruments which are in connection with the line wire from receiving and recording the message. For this purpose the following contrivance is provided in each instrument....

Each instrument was programmed with a letter uniquely identifying it, e.g. A for New York, B for Baltimore, C for Washington, and so on. With all instruments held in the start position (a blank), the transmitting instrument would send out the start signal to all instruments to which it was connected. Then it sent out a second signal corresponding to the letter for the station it wanted to transmit to. Only the receiving instrument with that letter was able to receive the message, while the other instruments were locked out. It is not known whether this feature was useful; perhaps not, as it was discontinued on his later models.

⋙⁓⋘

ANALYSIS OF THE PRECISION FREQUENCY SOURCE AND ITS TEMPERATURE COMPENSATION

As with any clockwork mechanism, the accuracy of Hughes's telegraph instrument was affected by temperature changes. For instance, in pendulum clocks, the pendulum lengthens or shortens by a fraction of an inch as the temperature changes, and this causes the clock to run slower or faster, respectively. A number of temperature compensation methods had been developed for pendulums which maintained them at a constant length; some of these methods were known as the gridiron, mercury, or alloy pendulum. Hughes certainly knew that his vibrating spring element would be affected by temperature changes.

The following analysis shows how Hughes's instrument would have fared without any temperature compensation, and thus indicates why such compensation was necessary. While Hughes would have carried out his evaluation by extensive experimentation, an estimate can now be arrived at by calculation. As not all the parameters are known, some assumptions must be made.

The frequency of oscillation of a spring strip is given by formula (1) below. As we know the initial frequency of vibration in Hughes's instrument, we can use this value to determine some of the unknown constants in this formula. Once these are known, the formula can be used to determine the effect of temperature changes on the frequency of oscillation, and hence their effects on the synchronization between two instruments.

The frequency of a vibrating bar clamped at one end is given by the formula:

$$f = (0.5596/L^2) \sqrt{(QK^2)/\sigma} \quad \ldots\ldots\ldots\ldots\ldots \text{(1)}$$

Where :
   f = frequency of oscillation (cycles per second)
   L = length of bar in cm.
   σ = density in grams per cubic cm of the metal.
   Q = Young's modulus in dynes per square cm.
   K = Radius of gyration; for a rectangular bar, $K = \alpha/\sqrt{12}$,
      where α is the thickness of the bar in cm in the direction of vibration.

Many of the characteristics of the spring strip Hughes used are unknown (such as σ, Q and K), and therefore some assumptions have to be made, including the assumption that the strip was made of spring steel.[27] What is known from his patent drawings are the length of the vibrating strip (three inches) and the frequency of vibration (56 Hz). These can be plugged into the formula to calculate the unknown constants by rewriting the above formula (1) as follows:

$$f(L^2) = 0.5596 \sqrt{(QK^2)/\sigma} \dots\dots\dots\dots (2)$$

$$\text{Let } Z = (0.5596 \sqrt{(QK^2)/\sigma}) \dots\dots\dots\dots (3)$$

$$\text{Then } Z = f(L^2) \dots\dots\dots\dots (4)$$

For the case where:
  f = 56 Hz
  L = 7.62 cm. (3 inches)
Then calculating Z:
  Z = 56 x (7.62²)
  Z = 3251.606 (which can be considered a constant for a particular installation)

An analysis can now be made of the effects of temperature on the frequency by calculating the length change of the vibrating spring strip and inserting these data and the values calculated for Z in formula (1) above.

The formula for linear expansion of a metal strip due to temperature change is:

$$\ell = \ell_0 (1 + \alpha\, t)$$

Where:
  ℓ = new length
  ℓ_0 = original length
  t = the rise in temperature in degrees C
  α = coefficient of linear expansion per degree C; for steel α is 0.000012

It is now possible to determine the change in frequency of the vibrating spring with temperature changes. The results are shown in the following table:

Temperature Change °C	Original spring length cm.	New spring length cm.	Oscillating frequency Hz.	Rev. per minute of print wheel	Number of rev. before wheel slip	Time in seconds until wheel slip
0	7.62	—	56.0	120.000000	—	—
1	7.62	7.6200914	55.998656	119.997112	1483.973	744
5	7.62	7.6204572	55.993281	119.985594	297.469	148
10	7.62	7.6209144	55.986562	119.971196	148.758	74

A certain amount of time slip could be tolerated between the transmitter and receiver. This tolerance amounted to the time necessary to print one character, as once the time slip exceeded this, then incorrect characters would be printed.

The time necessary to print one character was 17.86 milliseconds if the instruments were being used in the non-duplex mode, or half that if they were operating in duplex mode. This corresponds to a maximum time necessary to print a character; in practice it probably would be have been slightly less, because the printing wheel rotated continually and printed on the fly and thus did not come to rest. It is assumed that a letter printed in the middle of this period would come out perfectly, but that it might blur if it were printed too close to the period boundary.

The time that would be required for the receiver to slowly slip out of synchronism by 17.86 milliseconds can be determined by using the difference in temperature between the transmitter and receiver to calculate the difference in frequency, and then calculating how many revolutions the print wheel would make running at the slower speed in this period. Given the number of revolutions and the speed, the time can be calculated.

Let us consider a temperature difference of one degree Celsius between transmitter and receiver, with the receiver at the higher temperature. Assuming that they were running in perfect synchronism at the start, the receiver frequency would decrease from 56 Hz to 55.998656 Hz, and it would take 742 seconds (12.4 minutes) to slip out of synchronism. As can be seen from the table, this time rapidly decreases for larger temperature differences, which would probably have been unacceptable in practical applications. The slip in synchronism became noticeable when the received messages became garbled. Thus the effect would certainly have been noticeable and would have been sufficiently annoying that some form of temperature compensation was necessary. Hughes therefore added a feature to the oscillating spring to compensate for temperature changes, as he states in his patent:[28]

> ...the vibrating spring with the compensating slide or weight attached thereto, the movement of which slide or weight is effected and controlled by a lever and connecting-spring operated on by a thumb-screw, the object and effect of which are to compel a uniform movement under different temperatures.

The mechanism he incorporated for the temperature compensation was a spring that expanded and contracted with rising or falling temperature. This worked through a linkage that vibrated in sympathy with the main vibrating spring to slide a small weight up or down the vibrating spring. As the main spring lengthened with increasing temperature and thus vibrated slower, the compensator moved the weight inwards, increasing the vibrating frequency. Hughes arranged these two effects to be equal and opposite so that they would cancel each other out and thus maintain a constant frequency of oscillation. This method was very effective in keeping the length of clock pendulums constant, so it was probably effective in Hughes's instrument as well.

><~~<

PATENTS

Hughes first patented his printing type telegraph instrument in Britain in 1855, and then in France and America in 1856.

Britain: Patent No. 2058, Electro-Magnetic telegraphs, September 11, 1855, "Improvements in the Mode of and Apparatus for Transmitting Signals by the use of the Electric current, Part of which Improvements is Applicable to the Regulation Machinery Generally."

The patent covers Hughes's invention but was entered under the name of Hughes's patent agent Joseph Camp Griffith Kennedy. The eleven-page patent description is accompanied by several detailed full-scale drawings. The patent covers seven specific claims, which may be summarized as follows:

1. The Hughes relay, specifically the combination of a natural horseshoe magnet with electromagnetic coils on the pole pieces.
2. The Hughes relay, specifically the action of holding the armature closed by the permanent magnet and the adjustable spring tensioned to almost pull the armature free, plus the restoring mechanism that restores the armature to the closed position after it has been released.
3. The mechanization of the duplex operation.
4. The mechanization of receiving station selection.
5. The application of the vibrating spring timing device
6. The printing of messages from a continuously moving type wheel.
7. The commutator mechanization.

France: Patent # 25079, December 1, 1855, "Télégraph Imprimeur Électromagnétique."

Again this was filed on behalf of Hughes by his patent agent Joseph C. G. Kennedy.[29]

America: Patent # 14917, May 20, 1856, Improvement in Telegraphs. Improved Mode of Electro-Magnetic Telegraphic Communication, termed "Hughes' Compound Magnetic and Vibrating Printing Instrument."

The patent was in the name of David Edward Hughes (this is the initial patent to which the American Telegraph Company bought the rights). There are three pages of patent description which are similar to those in the British patent and three reduced-scale diagrams. There are eight claims, seven are the same as those in the British patent, while the eighth claim relates to putting a short circuit on the line at the transmitter at the same moment the main circuit is broken (there is no description of this function in the text).

I-2

Technical Details of the Development of Hughes's Improved Telegraph Instrument

Hughes's first model of the printing telegraph instrument showed the potential to improve the quality and efficiency of telegraph operations, and its design was novel enough to secure a patent. Importantly, the patent was strong enough to fend off any challenges from Samuel Morse and other inventors. The instrument became the catalyst for the formation of the American Telegraph Company, and at the same time, helped strengthen the Associated Press. Further, it provided a monetary reward for Hughes and his financial backer. However, both the American Telegraph Company and Hughes recognized that for the instrument to become a commercial success, it needed to be improved, specifically with regard to its construction. Hughes had basically constructed the model himself, with support from the watchmaker in Louisville, and while this had been a commendable effort, the instrument was somewhat delicate. For it to operate reliably over a long period of time in a business environment, it needed to be made more robust.

Hughes had used standard clock parts, which were constructed for exceedingly slow operation. These parts rarely moved any faster than one revolution per minute, but in Hughes's instrument they were operating some 120 times faster, so premature wear-out was inevitable. The descending weight drive exerted a heavy load on the gears, shafts, support bearings, and frame, and all of these needed strengthening. The keyboard and its linkages would experience heavy use by different operators, and needed to be more robust.

The instrument, therefore, went through a transformation in 1856 and the early part of 1857, and the end result was a notable improvement. Both Hughes and George Phelps of the American Telegraph Company[1] contributed to the new design. It is not clear who was responsible for what in the new machine: both claimed credit for the improvements. In the new design components were rearranged and there were changes to the way some functions were performed. The outcome was an instrument that was not only more robust, but even looked quite different from its predecessor.

The first need had been for a stout frame to support all of the components, to bear the load of the descending weight drive, and to reduce the effects of vibrations. The new frame was ornate, fashioned in brass, and embellished with the sweeping scrolls popular in many instruments of the period. All of the cogs, gearwheels, pinions, shafts, and bearings were made more substantial, or as the introduction to the patent stated in verbose Victorian prose:[2]

> My invention consists in certain improvements in printing-telegraph instruments, said improvements having for their object the rendering the instrument more certain in its action in certain particulars.

Printer's plate for image of Hughes's improved telegraph instrument used by the American Telegraph Company and tested on the Atlantic telegraph cable. The adoption of this model by the French telegraph service set Hughes on the road to success.

The Commutator

The commutator was one of the parts which was now implemented differently. It had been determined that the instrument did not give the operator enough feedback to indicate that the letter he typed had been accepted or transmitted, and this led to the transposition of letters (which was further complicated by the fact that multiple letters could be typed and sent during the same commutator scan if they followed in alphabetical order). To correct this, the rotating drum commutator with its helix pattern of pins was replaced by a rotating arm contactor. This new design used a fixed, circular, horizontally mounted plate, into which twenty-eight insulated studs were mounted. When a letter key was pressed, the corresponding stud would rise up above the surface of the plate. A rotating arm which projected from a vertical shaft swept over these studs and contacted any that had been raised by the typing of a letter. This gave the operator tactile feedback so that he knew that the letter had been transmitted, and thus could release the key. The rotating contact arm made the electrical contact with the raised stud and transmitted an electrical pulse. The contact arm then pushed the stud to reset it, pressing it back under spring pressure so that it was below the surface of the circular plate so that the rotating arm would not make contact further with the stud (until the key for that letter was

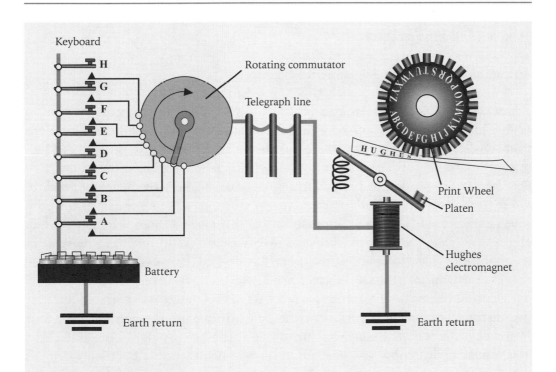

The commutator usually rotated at 120 rpm and swept over the 28 contacts linked to the keyboard. Pressing any key raised the corresponding contact which, when it touched the commutator, transmitted an electrical pulse.

pressed again). The operator could send more than one letter per contactor revolution, provided they were separated by more than a few letters and followed in alphabetical order. On average it seems that two letters were sent per revolution of the contact arm. The vertical shaft, with its rotating arm, passed through the center of the circular plate and rotated at a speed dictated by the timing mechanism, and was geared to the print wheel so that they remained synchronized.

Precision Timing

The timing spring was changed from the horizontally mounted vibrating spring strip to a vertical vibrating rod, a method Hughes had earlier explored when he experimented with vibrating knitting needles. The rod's length was nominally 22.5 cm. (8.85 inches), but the length could be adjusted to obtain the correct frequency. The rod was connected as before through a linkage to operate the anchor and the escapement wheel. The frequency of oscillation remained the same, a nominal 56 Hz. The temperature compensation linkage appears to have been removed, as it probably became unnecessary when a new type of synchronizing mechanism was incorporated (see the next section). Also, the rod may have been fabricated from an alloy with a low coefficient of expansion, which would reduce the influence of temperature changes. An arrestor linkage was added that could start or stop the rod vibrating, which started or stopped the instrument.

Automatic Synchronism Adjustment

This was an ingenious new feature, added to maintain all the instruments in synchronism. This was necessary since once the instruments (installed at different locations many miles apart) were running, there was always the potential for them to drift out of synchronization with each other, which would produce garbled messages. This new feature, in the form of a self-adjusting mechanism, kept them tightly synchronized. It was implemented by a notched wheel mounted on the same axle as the print wheel and coupled to it, so that it rotated at the same speed. Both were a friction fit on the drive axle. The notched wheel had twenty-eight "wide" notches (the same as the number of characters on the print wheel). A dog or sharp cam (Hughes referred to it as a snail due to its shape) engaged one of these notches every time an electrical pulse corresponding to a character was received. If the timing was correct, i.e. if the two instruments were in synchronism, the cam would enter the notch at its center. However, if the receiver timing was slightly slow, the cam would hit the side of the notch, pushing it forward and thus advancing the print wheel a fraction, forcing it back into synchronism. Conversely, if the receiver timing was slightly fast, the cam would hit the other side of the notch, retarding the print wheel.

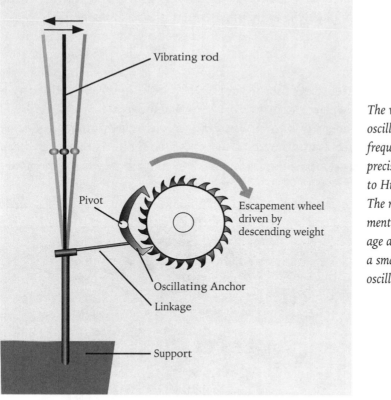

Vibrating rod

Pivot

Escapement wheel
driven by
descending weight

Oscillating Anchor

Linkage

Support

The vibrating rod oscillated at a constant frequency and provided the precision timing necessary to Hughes's instrument. The rod drove an escapement wheel through a linkage and in return received a small nudge to keep it in oscillation.

Signal Detector—The Hughes Relay

This was unchanged except for the horseshoe magnet, which instead of being of solid iron, was fabricated from five separate iron laminates to form a compound magnet. This was probably done to increase the strength of the magnet.

The Transmitting and Receiving Mechanisms

These were functionally the same, although the gear trains were rearranged. The gears, shafts, bearings, and cams were specially produced for the instrument and were much stronger, as the width of the gears had been increased by a factor of from three to five.

The Descending Weight Drive

The descending weight drive was simplified by combining the two weights used on the earlier version into a single smaller weight of 75 lbs. This drove all of the clockwork functions: the commutator, the vibrating element, the escapement, and the printing mechanism. A small removable hand crank and later a treadle was added to allow the weight to be wound up without having to interrupt the instrument's operation.

Printing Mechanism

This was essentially unchanged, except that to improve the printing speed and clarity, a roller was added to the rising platen so that the paper could move more easily with the print wheel. The feed mechanism was arranged so that at the moment the paper came in contact with the type wheel it was moved along at the same rate as the type wheel, resulting in a clean print. This mechanism was unique to the Hughes instrument and was known as "flying printing."

The power to drive the instrument derived from a descending weight of approximately 75 pounds. A chain drive and treadle mechanism allowed the weight to be wound up without stopping the instrument.

Keyboard

The keyboard was changed, and the round keys were replaced with a piano-type key-board, like that used by House and Froment.[3] This was possibly changed so that the instrument would be more similar to the House instrument, which telegraph operators were used to, and which Phelps was comfortable installing. The keys were arranged in alphabetical order. The top row of keys were black, and from left to right were A through N, while the lower row of keys were white, and from right to left were O through Z, space and "·".

Battery

The new instrument used the same battery as before, typically consisting of several individual cells connected together which provided between ten and twenty volts. Usually these were Daniell cells.

Duplex Operation

The duplex operation was retained, but was implemented differently. The alternating commutator wheel of the earlier instrument was removed, and, in its place, a better design was employed. Use was made of the dual coils which formed part of the detector of the "Hughes relay." When a letter key was pressed on the transmitting instrument, it routed the outgoing electrical pulse through one of the coils and then to the telegraph line.[4] When the pulse arrived at the receiving instrument it was routed through both detector coils (of the Hughes relay) which were connected in series so that their combined magnetic effect negated that of the permanent magnet, thus tripping the relay and activating the print mechanism. In the transmitting instrument, as the outgoing pulse went through one of the coils, it could easily trip the printing mechanism, which was undesirable. To preclude this, Hughes routed a portion of the outgoing pulse current through an adjustable retarder which consisted of a water tube resistance.[5] This was then connected to the second coil of the detector which was arranged in opposition to the first coil. Hence, by adjusting the retarder value (variable resistance), the magnetic effect could be eliminated so as to prevent the relay from tripping. This balanced the current flowing in both coils and minimized the effects of switching between transmit and receive. Thus, two instruments could be working in full duplex mode as the pulses corresponding to the letters of the messages were sent and received on the telegraph line at different points in time. For example, if station one was transmitting a letter "C" to station two while station two was transmitting letter "H" to station one, as the instruments were in synchronism, these pulses were sent at different times on the telegraph line and hence there was no conflict. If both operators sent the same letter simultaneously, the pulses on the telegraph line would occur simultaneously and would negate each other. This would unbalance the detector coils in both instruments and consequently both detector relays would trip and print the letter as required. The signal routing and switching from transmitting to receiving was done automatically by contacts activated when a letter key was pressed. This new method of duplex operation also allowed the full letter time slot of 17.86 milliseconds for each letter sent.

Synchronizing Instruments

This was basically unchanged, although the feature that allowed only one specified station to receive a message was eliminated.

MODIFICATIONS TO THE INSTRUMENT FOR USE WITH THE 1858 ATLANTIC TELEGRAPH CABLE

Hughes had to make some changes to his standard instrument to adapt it for use on the 2,000-mile-long submarine telegraph cable. These innovative changes were patented in Britain in early 1858.

The transmission of electrical signals was markedly different on submarine cables from what it was on land lines: on submarine cables they became retarded and weakened. When he began his tests with submarine cables for the American Telegraph Company, Hughes was not familiar with submarine cables and was given information that had been prepared by the Company's electrician to assist him in understanding the conditions and what transmission speeds were anticipated. This information indicated that ten words per minute was the norm and that retardation was not going to be a significant problem. This was erroneous data but Hughes had no way of knowing this at the time. Hughes therefore concentrated on two modifications. One was to slow the instrument down to be compatible with a transmission rate of ten words per minute, as the instrument usually sent and received forty words per minute over land lines when it was running at a speed of two revolutions per second (120 rpm). (An operator could send at any rate up to a maximum of forty words per minute when the instrument was running at this speed.)

What Hughes was doing when he slowed the instrument down was increasing the width of the electrical pulse transmitted as well as the time between pulses: these were both directly proportional to the speed at which he ran the instrument. Both of these changes were necessary to operate on a submarine cable. Hughes's transmitted pulse width during normal operation was 17.85 milliseconds, and assuming that two letters were transmitted per revolution, the minimum spacing of five letters between two letters transmitted during one revolution entailed that two pulses might be spaced 89.25 milliseconds apart. Pulses of this short duration would have disappeared on the submarine cable as they would have been consumed in charging the high capacitance of the cable. Pulses spaced too close together also tended to merge into each other, a smearing effect which made it impossible to distinguish between pulses. By slowing his instrument down to one revolution every two seconds (which corresponded to a transmission rate of approximately ten words per minute), he increased the pulse width to 71.42 milliseconds.

When he arrived on site in England and started experimenting, he realized that the data he had been given was erroneous, and that he needed to slow the instrument down even more, to two and a half words per minute, or one revolution every eight seconds. This gave a pulse width of 285.71 milliseconds or just over one-quarter second. The corresponding minimum pulse separation would be 1.43 seconds. At these rates Hughes was able to operate over the full length of the unsubmerged cable.

There is no record of how he modified the instrument to slow it down, but there are a number of possibilities. One was to lower the oscillation frequency of the spring rod; this would have slowed the whole mechanism down. This could have been done by lengthening the rod from 22.5 cm to 45 cm (17.7 inches), assuming that the new rod was of the same thickness and material as the old one. This however would have made the spring rod unwieldy, especially when he had to lower the speed even further, from ten to two and a half words per minute. The other possibility is that he left the spring frequency unchanged but increased the number of teeth on the escapement wheel or added a gear reduction of 4:1 between the spring timing and the commutator and print wheel. This is probably the solution he chose, and he had sufficient time before he left America for Britain to carry out this modification. In Britain of course he then had to lower the speed to two and a half words per minute, and rearranging the gearing to do so in the short time he was allotted would have been a significant challenge.

The second modification Hughes made was with respect to signal detection. He deduced that in order for his instrument to operate on the Atlantic cable, he had to increase the sensitivity of the receiver to enable it to detect the much attenuated electrical signals. He therefore added a detector based on the galvanometer (described in chapter 5 above) in front of the Hughes electromagnet. This he claimed increased the sensitivity of his instrument by 500 percent.

Hughes also made a third, relatively minor change to his instrument to operate on the transatlantic cable. It had been previously discovered that a higher number of words per minute could be sent if alternating positive and negative pulses were used for sending Morse code on submarine cables. This was called the "cable code," and on a Morse sending instrument there were two keys; one polarity was used to send dots and the other polarity to send dashes, and the keys were grounded when they were not in use. This had the effect of discharging the cable and continually returning it to a somewhat neutralized state. As Hughes's instrument normally used unipolar pulses, he had to add a mechanism to alternate the pulses sent between positive and negative. In addition, at the receiver he added a set of polarity change-over contacts. These alternated back and forth after the receipt of each signal, and were operated by a 2:1 gear from the print mechanism. These contacts ensured that the signal presented to the galvanometer detector was always of the same polarity.

⤙⤚

SUMMARY OF THE HUGHES PATENTS OF 1858 AND 1859 IN CHRONOLOGICAL ORDER

British Patent No. 938, April 27, 1858. "Improvements in the Means and Apparatus for Transmitting Signals and Electric Currents."

This patent was for the improved instrument described above in the beginning of this part of Appendix 1. The eleven-page detailed specification and description is accompanied by seven large sheets containing full-scale drawings.

The patent contains four claims, summarized as follows:

1. The use of a rotating circuit breaker (the commutator).
2. The method of frequency/timing compensation to maintain synchronization.
3. The method of implementing duplex operation.
4. The use of a combination of voltaic and induced currents for transmitting signals.

The innovation described in claim 4 was introduced when Hughes was experimenting with his instrument for use on the transatlantic telegraph cable (see chapter 5). The claim describes a method for having a constant potential on the line and to neutralize it by injecting a pulse from a magneto-induction device.

British Patent No. 1002, May 5, 1858. "Improvements in the Means of and Apparatus for Transmitting Signals and Electric Currents."

The six-page specification and detailed description is accompanied by three large sheets of full scale drawings. This patent covered the improved descending weight wind-up mechanism and also the new features implemented for operating with the transatlantic telegraph cable.

There are three claims, summarized as follows:

1. Implementation of the treadle wind-up mechanism for the drive weights without interrupting the instrument's operation.
2. Utilizing a sensitive galvanometer mechanism as a pre-detector for use on undersea telegraph cables
3. Utilizing both positive and negative transmitted currents (as used on undersea telegraph cables).

American Patent No. 22531, January 4, 1859. "Improvements in Electromagnetic Telegraphs."

David E. Hughes NY, Assignor to the American Electric Telegraph Company.

This is a two-page document with one diagram and covers the duplex operation of the telegraph. This is a companion patent to the following. There is one claim.

1. Method of implementing duplex operation.

American Patent No. 22770, January 25, 1859. "Improvements in Telegraphing Machines."

David E. Hughes, NY, Assignor to the American Electric Telegraph Company.

This is a four-page specification and description, accompanied by four pages of diagrams (significantly less detailed than those in the corresponding British patent).

There are four claims, summarized as follows:

1. Providing feedback to the operator when the typed in letter has been transmitted.
2. The method of timing compensation to maintain synchronization between instruments.
3. Method of printing in a continuous motion without stopping the print wheel.
4. Method of starting and synchronizing instruments together at different locations.

The British and American patents are similar, but there are differences. For instance, the mechanical implementations and support frame described in the two patents are different, and the American patent supplies less detail in general, and no details of the vibrating spring timing or of the descending weight drive. The British patents are far more complete, and the illustrations show multiple projections and are drawn on a 1:1 scale. Also, the British patent includes specific coverage regarding weak signal detection applicable to submarine cable operation.

⊁┉⌁⫯⫰

THE AMERICAN TELEGRAPH COMPANY MODIFIED HUGHES INSTRUMENT

Once Hughes had departed America for England, the ATC slowly changed over to a Phelps modified version of Hughes's instrument, in which Hughes's vibrating rod timing mechanism was replaced with one of George Phelps's speed governors. Unfortunately, no engravings or diagrams exist of this model. This was then superseded by the "Phelps Combination Instrument." This used elements of the Hughes and House instruments. According to George Prescott in his *History, Theory, and Practice of the Electric Telegraph*, the combination instrument took from the Hughes instrument the synchronous movement of the type wheel, the simple form of the press, the frictional movement of the cam, the correctors, and the detent. He took from the House instrument the air pump, chamber and valve, and double headed cylinder or plunger. To this he added his own electromagnetic speed governor and a different receiving relay similar to that used in Morse systems. The piano-type keyboard was retained. Phelps also used a scanning cylinder with helical pins similar to that in Hughes's first instrument, and it ran at a similar speed of 120 rpm. Phelps patented one part of this instrument,

George Phelps, the American Telegraph Company's mechanician, assisted Hughes in transforming his instrument to make it ready for production—but he and Hughes never saw eye to eye.

the electromagnetically controlled pneumatic valve (US patent No. 32452, May 28, 1861). Prescott indicates that this instrument was four years in development.

Earlier, on November 1, 1859, Phelps had obtained another patent (US No. 26003) and had assigned it to the American Telegraph Company. This patent states that it provides new and useful improvements to the Hughes Electromagnetic Telegraph that was patented in May of 1856. This patent is curious, since by that time Hughes had already obtained further patents on his new model in Britain in 1858 and in the US in January of 1859. As far as we know, this other design by Phelps never went into production and it bears little resemblance to any of Hughes's instruments or to Phelps's later combination model. One interesting quirk is that the example of printing that Phelps cited in the description of his instrument was that of the phrase "David E. Hughes Electro-Magnetic Printing Telegraph"!

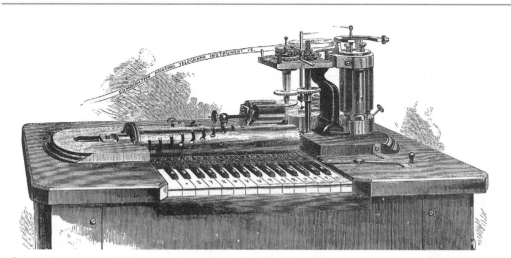

After Hughes went to Europe, George Phelps developed a new printing telegraph by combining features from the Hughes and House instruments together with some of his own ideas.

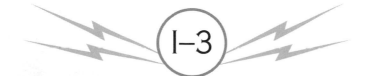

DEVELOPMENT OF HUGHES'S TELEGRAPH INSTRUMENT AFTER 1860

David Edward Hughes left America for Britain in 1858, and moved to France in 1860. It was there that his telegraph was widely adopted, and manufactured by Gustave Froment in Paris.[1] As the use of his telegraph spread throughout Europe, he entered into an additional manufacturing agreement with Siemens and Halske in Germany. Both of these manufacturers worked with Hughes to continually improve and upgrade the instrument.

The instruments that Hughes initially took to France with him were similar to the ones he had brought from America, which were described in part 2 of this Appendix. These instruments were powered by a slowly descending weight and had a piano-type keyboard, rotating commutator, and a vibrating vertical rod timing mechanism.

Froment was a skilled instrument maker with many year's experience and took the opportunity to improve the instrument by making the clockwork drive mechanism and support frame more robust. The instrument was transformed from a clockwork-looking device into a precision piece of machinery. The gears, cams, commutator, printing mechanism, and frame now looked like they were built for business. It was almost mesmerizing to watch the various components in action.

The Hughes telegraph was to have a lifetime of nearly 100 years, and naturally it underwent a number of additional

A photograph of Hughes taken around 1864–65 in Paris with one of his instruments made by Froment.

improvements and modifications during this time. Some of the principal changes and upgrades that were made over the years were the following:

1. New timing mechanism (change from the vibrating vertical rod to a conical rotating pendulum).
2. Addition of numerals and punctuation.
3. New British patent in 1863.
4. Addition of ancillary relays and switches for submarine cable operation etc.
5. Ability to accommodate different countries' alphabets and scripts (changes to keyboard and print wheel).
6. New power source (elimination of weight drive and conical rotating pendulum and replacement with a DC electric motor with a centrifugal speed governor).
7. Substitution of the electric motor for an air motor (for some applications in Britain only).
8. Manufacturing changes and general upgrades (such as refinements to governor)
9. Model manufactured in aluminum (for the French market).

1. New Timing Mechanism

Early in the 1860s, as more and more of the telegraph instruments went into service, operators discovered that although the instrument generally performed well, the vibrating rod used for the precision timing tended to break. Hughes worked with Froment to address this problem.

They implemented a new approach for the timing, using a speed governor. It consisted of a flexible rod twenty-three centimeters long, anchored at one end, with its free end inserted into a fitting on the periphery of a drive wheel which was rotated by the power of the descending weight. Mounted on the rod was a spherical weight three centimeters in diameter whose position along the rod was usually set at 17 cm from the fixed end of the rod, and whose position could be adjusted in either direction by about 5 cm. The rod and weight assembly were mounted in a horizontal plane at the rear of the instrument (though in some models it was mounted on the side). When the drive wheel rotated, the flexible rod prescribed a cone whose nominal radius was 2 cm. As the wheel speeded up, the weight was flung out by centrifugal force. This action increased the rotational radius of the rotating end of the rod. Through a crank mechanism this activated a drag brake whose friction increased with speed, which slowed the drive wheel. If the wheel slowed too much, then there was less friction from the drag brake and the wheel speeded up, the result being that the drive wheel ran at a constant speed. The speed was set by adjusting the position of the weight ball along the rod. As there was only a single weight, rather than a balanced set of weights, prescribing a circle, it probably caused some vibration. This, coupled with the fluctuating energy demands of the printer, would have required some smoothing out. Therefore, a heavy flywheel was fitted to the governor mechanism. This new timing arrangement eliminated the need for an escapement mechanism and remained in use until the next upgrade of the instrument, in which Siemens and Halske installed an electric motor and new speed governor.[2]

2. Addition of Numerals and Punctuation

To accommodate the ability to print numerals and punctuation symbols, it was decided to double the number of characters from twenty-eight to fifty-six. These were allocated to the keyboard as illustrated below, making double use of each of the white and black keys:

1	2	3	4	5	6	7	8	9	0	.	,	;	:
A	B	C	D	E	F	G	H	I	J	K	L	M	N
	"	&	)	(		=	/	X	-	+	,	!	?
*	Z	Y	X	W	*	V	U	T	S	R	Q	P	O
								**					

The keys marked with one asterisk are the Letter blank and Figure blank keys used for the shift function. On French instruments, the "X" on the key marked with two asterisks was replaced by §.

To implement the corresponding print function a system of shift keys was used to move from one character set to the other, a system later adopted for typewriters. [3] A new print wheel was designed that integrated the two character sets by alternating the alphabet characters with the numerical characters to form the following sequence: A, 1, B, 2, C, 3, etc. The print wheel diameter was increased to accommodate the extra characters. Normally, the print wheel would print the alphabet characters, but, when the shift function was activated the wheel was advanced by one character so that the numerals were moved into the print position.

This new function was cleverly implemented by making the synchronizing mechanism do double duty. Synchronizing the receiving instrument to the transmitter had already been implemented by having the print wheel connected to a separate correcting gear that had twenty-eight widely spaced teeth on it. Both of these wheels were friction fitted on a common drive shaft. If the two instruments were running in synchronism, then a correcting cam which was brought into action each time a character was received would rotate into the middle of the gap between the teeth of the correcting wheel. However, if the timing was slightly off, the cam would hit one or the other side of the teeth on the correcting gear, nudging the gear forwards or backwards to keep the timing between the transmitting and receiving instruments in tight lock.

It was also necessary to "nudge" the print wheel in order to implement the shift function, but by a set radial shift of one character (1/56). The shift function, which was termed the "Hughes radial inversion device," was controlled by two white keys on the keyboard called "letter blank key" and "figure blank key" (these keys had no markings). When the operator wanted to shift from transmitting letters to transmitting figures, he or she pressed the figure shift key, and to switch back, the letter shift key.

The print wheel actually only had fifty-four characters on it, with two gaps, each two characters wide. These gaps were separated by eight characters on the print wheel. One gap came into print position when the letter blank key was pressed, and the other when the figure blank key was depressed. As there was no character on the print wheel in these locations, nothing would be printed and a space would appear on the printed paper tape.

The gap positions, however, did double duty and played a part in the shift function. For instance, if the print wheel was printing alphabet characters and the operator wanted to switch to transmitting and printing figures, then the "figure blank key" was depressed. When the print wheel rotated into the figure blank position, the correcting cam, instead of meshing with the correcting gear teeth, found its way blocked by a toggle lever which it pushed out of the way, and this toggle lever displaced the print wheel by one character. The print wheel was now shifted and in a position to print figures. As its name implied, this lever could be toggled back and forth between the two blank positions on the print wheel/correcting gear. The toggle lever had now moved into position ready to be activated by the letter blank key. To switch back to transmitting and print-

The commutator showing the circular mounting plate with its 28 contacts. The rotating contactor (chariot) swept over these contacts twice per second to determine if any had been raised by a key press. Also visible is the print wheel and behind it the synchronizing wheel with its widely spaced teeth.

ing letters, the operator pressed the letter blank key and the correcting cam forced the toggle lever to move the print wheel back one character.

This method of enabling the telegraph instrument to send and receive fifty-six characters had the advantage of not requiring a new commutator, keyboard, or number of timeslots.

3. British Patent #241, January 27, 1863

Improvements in Means or Apparatus for Effective Telegraph Comunications.
The patent was for:

1. The conical pendulum timing mechanism.
2. The method of changing from one character set to another
3. The method for restoring the receiving electromagnet as soon as it had received an electrical pulse from the telegraph wire and triggered the armature. This was done by having a local battery switched to the contacts of the electromagnet coil but in opposite polarity to the received pulse. This had two effects: it reinforced the permanent magnet (or as Hughes put it, it restored it) and allowed a faster reset of the receiving electromagnet. This was probably more important for transmitting on long lines where the electrical pulse had been lengthened. In these cases the electromagnet could still have been energized by the telegraph line when the mechanism was trying to reset it, which might have caused the receiving electromagnet not to latch. This change prevented that from happening.
4. The method of extending the dwell time of the contactor by a factor of three or more. This involved a change to the rotating contactor to increase the width of

the electrical pulse transmitted for each letter, in order to facilitate the operation of the telegraph instrument on very long lines.

The rotating contactor or chariot, as it was sometimes called, also performed another function. This was to ensure that electrical pulses would remain distinct and not meld into each other on the telegraph line. To accomplish this Hughes limited the minimum spacing between characters to a time interval equal to the duration of five pulses. The component of the chariot called a rejecter ensured this by preventing the characters from being typed too close together.

For example if the six-letter word "CLUTCH" was to be transmitted it could be done in four revolutions of the chariot/print wheel. On the first revolution "C," "L," and "U" could be sent (as these letters are spaced more than five alphabetical characters away from each other), on the second revolution "T," on the third revolution "C," and on the fourth revolution "H." Thus, the speed of sending messages was somewhat dependent on how an operator could mentally decompose the words into combinations of letters which followed each other in alphabetical order and were spaced more than five letters apart in the alphabet.

4. Ancillary Relays and Circuits

During their many years of service Hughes's instruments had to evolve to meet the changing demands of various telegraph companies and communications networks. Some of the more important requirements were long distance operation, increasing the capacity of the telegraph lines (more words per minute), and submarine cable operation.

To transmit and receive over long distances it was often necessary to boost the strength of the electrical signals along the way by the use of automatic repeaters. This could be done by the use of repeater relays. These were known as Hughes repeaters, or if they could accommodate duplex signals, as Hughes duplex repeaters. This function could also be implemented by the Hughes instrument itself with the addition of relay contacts. This allowed an instrument to not only receive a signal but also to amplify it and retransmit it. This was done on the line from London to Rome, which had repeaters in Paris, Lyons, Turin, and Florence.

Hughes's instrument could run in a number of different modes depending on the operation it was to perform. In the simplex mode the instrument was either sending or receiving, but not both at the same time. This mode was used for communicating in a foreign language or in code; in these cases the instrument was configured to print out the message that the operator was typing as well as transmitting it over the telegraph line so that the operator could check for errors in the outgoing message. The other main mode of operation was duplex. This enabled a single telegraph line to be twice as productive by allowing its simultaneous use by two operators. As telegraph lines were often shared between Hughes equipment and Morse equipment (though they were not used on the same line at the same time) there was a need to ensure compatibility when the operator switched from one instrument to the other. Morse equipment for instance required added interfacing components to ensure that the transmitting and receiving signals did not interfere with each other during duplex operation. The two methods in use for coupling onto and off the telegraph line were the differential and bridge methods. These duplex balance circuits also helped in minimizing impedance fluctuations during sending and receiving transitions, as well as in reducing static charge build up on long lines. The Hughes instruments also made use of these circuits to interface with the telegraph line.[4]

To meet the continued demand for more capacity on the telegraph lines a Hughes quadruplex system was implemented which quadrupled the throughput on a telegraph wire. This system used time division multiplexing in combination with a duplex balance. In this arrangement, two transmitting and two receiving instruments, that is a pair at each end of the line, were used. Each pair of instruments were coupled together by gearing and driven from a single power source and governor as if they were a single instrument. This simplified the synchronizing as well as keeping the instruments in time with the time sequencing commutator.[5]

When the telephone was introduced it made new demands for capacity on available lines, and in some cases the lines were used for both telegraph and telephone simultaneously. This was possible because the telegraph signal was a quasi DC signal while the telephone signal was an AC signal, and thus the two signals could be superimposed onto the same wire. Then by the use of a suitable electrical filter, the two signals could be separated out at the receiving end.[6]

Hughes's instruments were used on a number of submarine cables across the English Channel (England to France, Belgium, Holland and Germany) and in the Mediterranean, such as the Marseilles to Algeria and Rome to Cagliari cable.[7] For operation on submarine cables it had been found that signal pulses which alternated in polarity could be transmitted faster. There were a number of schemes which could be used to accomplish this on the Hughes instrument, and the French telegraph engineer Pierre Picard appeared to have been prominent in their design. One of his schemes added additional relays that took the unipolar pulses required by the Hughes instrument and alternated them between positive and negative. Another scheme used on the Rome to Cagliari cable was to send a negative pulse preceding and following the normal positive pulse.[8] One book on telegraphy indicated that the Hughes instrument required only one half milliamp of current to operate, and therefore the voltage needed to operate on submarine cables was not unduly high, always a concern after the early submarine cable failures attributed to high voltage operation.[9]

On the Anglo-German cable, which was composed of four separate telegraph wires, it was found that electrical interference could occur between these wires, especially during duplex operation (this occurred with both the Morse and the Hughes instruments). The problem was that signals on one wire were inducing interfering signals on the three adjacent wires and visa versa, a problem Hughes had investigated and provided a solution to many years earlier. Thus a circuit was added at the submarine cable terminuses that took a fraction of the disturbing signal and sent it on the other three wires in opposition to the interfering signal, thus canceling it out.

5. Ability to Accommodate Different Countries' Alphabets

The first time Hughes had to adapt his instrument to deal with a different character set was when he tackled the Cyrillic script for Russia. As the instrument had already been upgraded to accommodate fifty-six characters, the job of handling other alphabets was easier, even if they had more than twenty-six letters.

For his Russian project, Hughes made a note that it had been agreed to use thirty characters, of which the following were the most important:

А Б В Г Д Е Ж З И К Л М Н О П Р С Т У Х Ч Ъ Ь Ы Ь Ю Я Й

Pressing the shift key would bring the following characters into operation.

1 2 3 4 5 6 7 8 9 0 Ф Ц Ш Щ . , : ? ! / È -) (" '

The special version of the instrument for Russia had the ability to communicate either in Roman or Cyrillic characters. The keyboard had both character sets engraved on it. The standard characters were in white and the Cyrillic characters in red (which were slightly different from the character set illustrated above). Two different print wheels were used that were coaxial with each other on the same shaft, one for the Roman and one for Cyrillic characters. The transmitter operated normally; that is, it transmitted a pulse based on the key depressed. However, as each could key could be used for a character in two different alphabets, the receiver and printing mechanism needed to know which character set to print. It is not known if the switch from one character set to the other was automatic based on sending a control or shift identifier character, or was manually done by the operator sliding the type wheel over. This combination model precluded the need for separate models for domestic and international use.

His next challenge was with the instruments to be supplied to Turkey, which required the use of an Arabic-based script. In the 1860s, when Hughes was involved with this project, Turkish was written in a version of Perso-Arabic also known as Ottoman Turkish script (in 1928 the country adopted a modified Latin alphabet). His contract with Turkey came about rather quickly while he was visiting Austria, and as a result he had to scramble to find detailed information on the script. The only book that could be found on the subject described the Turkish script in German, probably further complicating his task. Below is a sample of the characters of the script; the text was written and read from right to left.

As can be seen, some of the characters occupied more width and length than Latin characters. Hughes, therefore, had to widen the print wheel and also determine where

One of Hughes's Russian machines, showing two print wheels, one for Cyrillic characters, the other for Latin characters.

to locate the longer characters that he referred to as double wide. At these locations, the interleaved characters (such as numerals invoked by the shift key) had to be omitted, as there would have been interference. Also, the longer characters had to be built up rather than curve with the circumference of the print wheel so that they would print well and not blur at their edges.

The next challenge was to produce a printed script that read from right to left—the standard instrument printed for reading from left to right. He did this by printing the characters upside down; then when the message was complete, the paper strip was torn off and turned around so that it could then be read right to left.

Perso-Arabic Script (this is only an approximate sample, as it is not quite clear from Hughes notebooks which characters he used):

ذ د خ ح چ ج ت ب ء ا

ف غ ع ظ ط ض ص ش س ژ ز ر

ى ة ه و ن م ل گ ك ق

Numerals

١ ٢ ٣ ٤ ٥ ٦ ٧ ٨ ٩ ٠

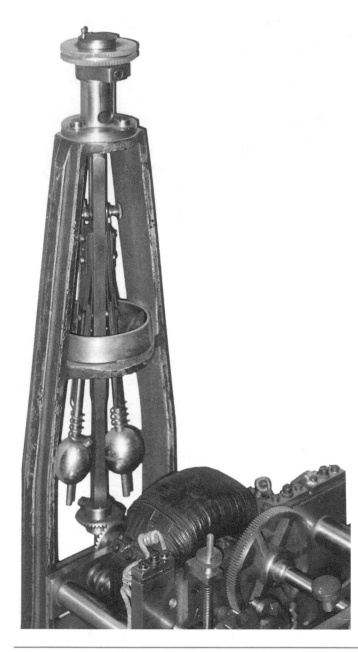

The rotating governor, with the speed adjustment at the top, the speed activated friction brake midway down, the fly-balls, and the driving gears.

6. Upgrade to Electric Motor Drive with Centrifugal Speed Governor

This upgrade was introduced by Siemens and Halske around 1880, and the electric motor replaced both the governor described in (1) and the descending weight drive. This change was implemented when electrical motors had become more reliable and centralized DC power sources more readily available. Typically, the motor was a DC series wound, two-pole type that drew about 300 milliamps. The motor speed could be adjusted by a rheostat, but to ensure a constant speed, a speed governor was added.

The governor used a centrally rotating shaft mounted vertically in a support frame. Two slim rods were suspended from the shaft by flat springs at their tops with the bottom of the rods free. Two balls were mounted on the rods so that they could slide up and down. The balls were suspended by coiled wires loosely wrapped around the rods; the wires were connected to the central shaft near its top. The rods' function was basically to guide the balls. Attached to the rods were two friction pads that could rub on a circular surface mounted on the frame. As the shaft rotated, the balls moved outward by centrifugal force and caused the friction pads to rub on the inside of a drum, slowing the rotation. If they slowed it too much, the friction decreased and the speed increased again. The speed eventually became constant. The speed could be set by means of a screw on top of the frame which altered the height of the balls. The geometric arrangement of this governor was such that it was isochronous. Over the years a number of changes were made to the governor by Daumarie in 1902, Ouvriers Mécaniciens in 1903, and Koch in 1908.

An electrically powered version of Hughes's instrument used in the UK until the 1920s; it is much more compact than the earlier mechanically powered models.

The older timing and descending weight drive was replaced by these new components, but on some models the weight drive was retained so that if the DC supply or the motor failed it could be engaged as a backup.

7. Modifications to Enable the Instrument to be Powered by an Air Motor

This was an alternate method of powering the telegraph instrument used in Britain by the Post Office. The motor was a Willmot's Air Motor (UK patent # 23001, November, 1894) and contained a small air turbine. This was probably used at specific locations where an air or pneumatic tube installation was present. This model probably used the same speed governor as used for the electric motor.

8. Later Changes and Improvements

Over the years various changes were made to the mechanism. The descending weight support cords were replaced by an endless chain, and an alarm was added to alert the operator when to wind up the weight. Pumping the treadle used to wind up the weight was quite strenuous work, and an electric motor drive was added to some models that automatically engaged when the weight descended too low. This was supposedly added to instruments that were to be operated by women; the treadle mechanism was still retained as a backup.

9. Model Manufactured in Aluminum for Reduced Weight

This was a model manufactured in France in 1911 in which many of the components were made in aluminum, with a resultant weight of nineteen kilograms. It is unknown how many of this model were made.

THE HUGHES
ELECTROMAGNET

Professor Silvanus P. Thompson was giving one of the popular Cantor Lectures in London before the Society of Arts in early 1890, on the topic of "The Electromagnet." During his discussion of the "Hughes Electromagnet" he referred to it as "the well-known Hughes Electromagnet," but then he apologized:[1]

> I feel almost ashamed to say those words "well-known," because although on the Continent everybody knows what you mean by an electromagnet, in England scarcely any one knows what you mean. Englishmen do not even know that Professor Hughes has invented a special form of electromagnet.

Hughes did not invent the electromagnet, but he did invent a particularly sensitive electromagnetic relay. The invention was part of the development of his printing telegraph instrument in 1855–56: in order to make the instrument operate as he wished, he needed an electromagnetic relay which was sensitive, required minimum current to operate, and had a rapid response.

What he invented was the antithesis of the electromagnetic relays which were being used in other telegraph instruments. These were operated by sending a current through a coil of wire wound around a soft iron core, which attracted an armature. The armature was used to activate an inker or scriber to mark a paper tape. These devices tended to be bulky and heavy, and required a relatively high current to operate.

With a traditional relay, enough electrical energy had to be sent over the telegraph line to energize the relay coils and create an electromagnetic field strong enough to attract an armature. The magnetic pull had to bridge the air gap and also overcome the return spring tension used to hold the armature open. If the telegraph line current decreased due to low battery voltage, high line resistance, or excessive leakage to ground (due to wet insulators), the relay had to be adjusted by reducing the spring tension or reducing the stroke of the armature. The situation was still worse if the relay had to perform work by actuating a mechanism rather than just closing an electrical contact. In such instances, it might not be possible to adjust the equipment enough to be able to continue operating under adverse conditions.

Hughes did not want to use a standard type relay as it did not meet his criteria for the operation of his instrument. Thompson described Hughes's unique approach:[2]

> At first sight it is not very apparent why putting a permanent magnet into a thing should make it any more sensitive. Why should permanent magnetism secure rapidity of working? Without knowing anything more, inventors will tell you that the presence of a permanent magnet increases the rapidity with which it will work. You might suppose that permanent magnetism is something to be avoided in the cores of your working electromagnets, otherwise the armatures would remain stuck to the poles when once they had been attracted up. Residual magnetism would, indeed, hinder the working unless you have so arranged matters that it shall be actually helpful to you. Now for many years it was supposed that permanent magnetism in the electromagnet was anything but a source of help. It was supposed to be an unmitigated nuisance, to be got rid of by all available means, until, in 1855, Hughes showed us how very advantageous it was to have permanent magnetism in the cores of the electromagnet.

What Hughes did was to construct an electromagnetic relay based on a permanent horseshoe magnet. To the ends of its two poles were affixed soft iron pole pieces. Wire coils were then wound onto these pole pieces to form an electromagnet. A short soft iron armature was set on a pivot so that it could either close across the pole pieces or open to be clear of them. A counteracting spring was attached to the armature in order to hold it open. The device functioned as follows. The armature was first closed and held in place by the attraction of the permanent magnet. The spring attached to the armature was fitted with an adjustment that could increase or decrease the tension. With the armature closed and held by the magnet, the spring tension was increased to the point where it almost overcame the magnet's attraction

With these two forces balanced, if an electric current was passed through the coils, and if the current was directed so that the magnetic field it produced in the coils was opposite to that of the permanent magnet, it would weaken the field of the permanent

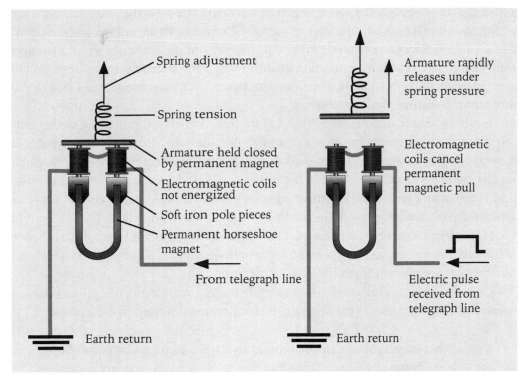

Spring adjustment

Spring tension

Armature held closed
by permanent magnet

Electromagnetic coils
not energized

Soft iron pole pieces

Permanent horseshoe
magnet

From telegraph line

Earth return

Armature rapidly
releases under
spring pressure

Electromagnetic
coils cancel
permanent
magnetic pull

Electric pulse
received from
telegraph line

Earth return

Diagram showing the operation of Hughes's electromagnetic relay. Hughes developed this new type of electromagnetic relay in 1854 as part of a sensitive receiver for his telegraph instrument.

magnet enough so that the spring could overcome the holding power of the magnet, and the armature would be rapidly released by the tension of the spring. This device was capable of responding to extremely small currents.

The following description given by T.E. Herbert, telegraph engineer for the British Post Office, gives some idea of the sensitivity of the Hughes relay:[3]

> If for example, the force of attraction is 100 units and the upward pull of the spring is 92, the armature is held down by a force of 8 units. The passage of a current through the coils in such a direction as to oppose the magnetism of the cores will cause the armature to be released immediately the attraction is reduced below 92 units. The armature will then fly off with the full force of the spring, i.e. with a force of 92 units. In this way the reduction of the attraction by anything over 8 units brings into full force the spring.

The armature was reset automatically and the attraction of the permanent magnet held it ready to receive the next signal. To ensure that the armature released quickly, it was necessary to insert a thin spacer the thickness of a sheet of paper between it and the relay pole pieces to prevent the armature from being affected by what was known as "magnetic sticking." The speed of action was important, as the relay had to react within the time it took to print one character, which was 17.85 milliseconds, assuming a rotational speed of two revolutions per second of the print wheel and twenty-eight characters. This time remained unchanged when the instrument was upgraded to accommodate numerals and punctuation in addition to the standard letters due to the way the shift feature was implemented.

Hughes's electromagnet, though, was more than a mere relay: it was a device that could control a large force by means of a much smaller one. It was a sensitive signal detector, able to control the force provided by a descending weight drive system which was in the receiver, and which could be made as powerful as was necessary and practical. Thus, a relatively small electrical signal sent over the telegraph wire was able to activate the relatively heavy printing and paper motion mechanisms.

Hughes found other ways to have a small force control a much larger force in some of his later inventions, such as his carbon microphone, in which a small acoustic signal was able to control a much larger electrical current.

Over the life of his telegraph, Hughes made many experiments to optimize and to improve the performance of the instrument, as Thompson related in his lecture:[4]

> If you wish a magnet to work rapidly, you will secure the most rapid action not when the coils are distributed all along but when they are heaped up near, not necessarily entirely on, the poles. Hughes made a number of researches to find out what the right length and thickness of these pole-pieces should be. It was found an advantage not to use too thin pole-pieces, otherwise the magnetism from the permanent magnet did not pass through the iron without considerable reluctance, being choked by insufficiency of section; also not to use too thick pieces otherwise they presented too much surface for leakage across from one to the other.

While the function of the electromagnet remained unchanged over the years, it did undergo some changes to fit in with the other modifications of the instrument.

Henry Lartigue of the French railway system used Hughes's electromagnet in his railway block safety system in 1874, and earlier it had been used by Tyer in 1872.[5] In the UK, the Hughes electromagnet was used in the Sykes railway block safety system.[6]

Hughes's electromagnet also served as inspiration to Thomas Watson, Alexander Graham Bell's assistant, during the development of the telephone, in November, 1876. In his autobiography, Watson relates how he and Bell had become stuck for weeks, unable to improve the operation of Bell's telephone. Watson went to seek inspiration at the public library by poring over technical books. There he came across a book on the electric telegraph that described Hughes's printing telegraph instrument, including its quick-acting electromagnet. Watson realized that the electromagnet configuration that Hughes had used was directly applicable to their problem. He rushed back to the laboratory and put together "a permanent magnet made up of four hardened steel

An early version (January 1877) of Bell's telephone showing the permanent horseshoe magnet with coils wound on iron pole pieces, which according to Watson was inspired by Hughes's "quick acting" magnet.

horseshoe plates bolted together, with a small soft iron core, to carry the coils, clamped to each pole of the magnet." He mounted this up to a diaphragm and mouthpiece and indicated "To my great joy the thing talked much better than any other telephone we had tried up to that time."[7]

It is important to note that the use of a permanent magnet in conjunction with the electromagnetic coils was essential to the operation of the telephone. Without the permanent magnet, the receiver diaphragm would be attracted on each half cycle of the voice frequency current, and thus the sound output would be double the frequency of the applied speech current. The addition of a permanent magnet created a constant pull on the diaphragm. During the first half cycle of the applied speech current the electromagnetic coils pulled together with the permanent magnet on the diaphragm, while during the next half cycle the force generated by the coils was opposed to that of the permanent magnet, and the diaphragm returned to a neutral position. The diaphragm thus only flexed once in each direction for each cycle of the applied speech current. The use of a magnet also tended to improve the output amplitude.

When Hughes later had to construct his own sensitive telephone receiver similar to Bell's for use with his induction balance and wireless experiments, it was relatively easy for him to do. The main components used in its construction were readily available from his telegraph instruments.

III

THE HUGHES FAMILY
IN AMERICA FROM 1860

After David Hughes left America in 1858 he only returned once for a visit. His father, brother, and sister, however, initially remained in Kentucky, all surviving the Civil War, which broke out after David had left.

While most states had taken sides in the dispute between the Northern and Southern States, Kentucky was trying to stay neutral in the conflict.[1] The Unionists from the North, however, started to set up recruitment camps in Kentucky and to ship in arms. The Confederates from the Southern States, meanwhile, moved over the state line from Tennessee and up into Bowling Green and initiated their own recruitment drive. The Confederates made a move to occupy the state in the summer of 1862, but the Unionists prevented them and forced them to retreat. Kentucky was put under martial law by the Unionists, and the Confederates considered it an "occupied Southern State." Soldiers recruited from the state, however, fought on both sides in the war, sometimes splitting families. Unfortunately at the end of the war some returning soldiers formed bands of marauders under the guise of a "Home Guard," plundering, robbing, killing and burning.

It has been possible to piece together the plight of the Hughes family in America during the Civil War due to a fortuitous meeting in New York City just after the war ended in 1865. This chance meeting occurred when John Griffith, known as the "Gohebydd," the London reporter for the Welsh newspaper *Baner ac Amserau Cymru*, who was in America on assignment, met Professor David Edward Hughes's father, Dafydd Hughes, in the lobby of the Cambria Hotel, New York in August of 1865.[2]

About nine days or a fortnight ago, I happened to be sitting in the hall of the Cambria Hotel in Chatham Street, having a look at the newspapers. I intend sometime to write a piece about the American Hotels, in that the hotel system in America is very different to the way hotels are run in our country. On entering the majority of them, there is a large hall or lobby; in one end there will be a clerk at a desk or counter taking the names of guests and taking all payments. In the middle, there is usually a table for anyone who wishes to write, and on the table a number of newspapers, railway guides, directories, etc. And along the walls can be seen the railway bills of the various companies, together with notices regarding steamboats from one port of the country to another. Around the sides of the hall will be a bench or rather a kind of sofa, and this divided into individual seats in the same manner as in a first class railway carriage. In this hall can be seen on any evening, dozens, sometimes scores, as it happens—some sitting on the sofa by the wall, others on chairs in the middle of the floor, frequently with their feet on another chair, one reading the news, the other smoking his cigar and the next in conversation with his friend.

One afternoon, about a fortnight ago, as I mentioned, I happened to sit by the side of the table; sitting, to be honest, not that it matters, as is commonly the fashion here, on a chair, with my feet on another, reading the *Tribune*. An old fellow happened to enter, went to enquire with the clerk, then sat at the other side of the table to take a look at the newspapers. There happened to be several papers from the old country on the table at the time, and I noticed that it was these which took most of his attention.

We all of us when sitting in such a place, tend to take stock to ourselves of those we see around us. I had formed the opinion that the old fellow was one of the "hangers-on" of New York City, fond of a drink, and living the best he could on his wits, in the habit of calling in the hotel in the hope of bumping into some of his old acquaintances. His clothes were rather shabby, the trousers of some material made from linen, cross bar and washed and having lost some of its colour; a waistcoat that had once been black but that was now more the brownish hue of the sheep, and a coat of brown holland that had not seen water for some time. But everything about him—his dress and manner—left the impression of one who had known better days.

He rose after a while from the table, without speaking to anyone, or anyone speaking to him. He then went over to the desk to ask the clerk something and they were in conversation for some time. The clerk came over to me and said, "This is an old Welshman who has been living in the Southern states the past fifteen years. Come and have a bit of a chat with him."

"A Welshman, are you?" I asked.

"Yes," he replied, "a pure Welshman, who has been living in the Southern States!"

"Yes—Kentucky last of all, then Tennessee before that after travelling through every state in America: through all the important towns of Upper and Lower Canada, Nova Scotia. New Brunswick, the West Indies and through every town of any note in England, Wales and Ireland."

What on earth, I thought to myself, could the old fellow be? So, to get a bit of his story, we went to sit together on the sofa bench along the wall.

"From what part of Wales?"

"From Bala," was the reply.

"Indeed—from Bala?"

Yes, he had been born and raised in Bala—but had left the town of Bala whilst quite young. After this, he was in Liverpool—in London after that—and after that, travelling around all parts of the British Isles before going to America: "But," said the old fellow, "if I started to tell you my life story, if you did not know something about me already, I am fairly sure you would not believe half my story."

"And where else did you know in Merionethshire, apart from Bala?"

"Oh, I went to Dolgellau many times, and to Barmouth, Towyn and so on."

"Who did you know in Barmouth?"

"I knew old Barnet as he used to be called, who kept the Corsygedol Arms, well, and Evan Jones, the old harpist who used to play there during the summer."

"Old Barnet," said I, "God rest his soul, died many years ago but the old Harpist Evan Jones was still alive quite recently, but very old by now."

The old fellow had cheered up by now, talking about those he knew many years past, and he started to enquire about Barnet's family and about Captain Williams of Gellfawr, and others of his acquaintance. By this time, we were becoming more confident with each other and he started to pour out his story, like water from a pitcher—some Welsh and some English—the Welsh rather rusty, through not having heard much Welsh, nor having met, as far as he knew, any Welshmen during the last fifteen or twenty years. He said he was a musician by profession and that he was the father of the *Welsh Prodigy*, taking for granted that because I knew a certain amount about Wales, and Merionethshire in particular, I was bound to know everything about the "Welsh Prodigy"—that he was also the father of Professor Hughes, the electrician—and on he went with his story, hither and thither, so that there was nothing for me to do except sit there and listen to him, and marvel. He also mentioned the huge losses that he had suffered during the war—losing horses, losing all his livestock off the farm, and losing also a large amount of money, and that he had just arrived in New York the day before with the intention of going over to the old country.

There were so many things in the old fellow's story which seemed to me to be so unlike the truth—so many things that I felt contradicted each other, so many things that seemed improbable, that I came to the conclusion, after listening to his story, that it was lies and deception from beginning to end, made up to try to beg the odd shilling here and there, either that or the old fellow was off his head.

Amidst all this talk, however, he mentioned that, in the midst of the trouble of the war, he had managed to save some money that he had in the house when the rebellion broke out—that he had managed to save it in spite of the efforts of the looters, enough, if he decided to stay in his old birthplace, to live quite comfortably for the remainder of his life; and he pulled out of his notebook a note containing a receipt showing that he had that day deposited in a New York bank, a sum, in gold, amounting to several thousand dollars.

I was surprised by the sight of the bank document. This was proof in itself of one thing—proof that however much truth or lies there was in his story, it had not been made up, as I had supposed, to gain sympathy from his fellow countrymen and extract a few shillings from their pockets. When we parted, we arranged to meet again two or three days later, and after hearing of the Aberystwyth Eisteddfod, he seemed determined, if he could get himself ready, to leave New York so as to arrive in Liverpool in time for the Eisteddfod.

After David Edward Hughes had finally completed his first telegraph models back in 1855–56, his father Dafydd Hughes decided to leave the music store of Peters and Webb in Louisville, Kentucky, where he had been employed for a few years, and open a store of his own. He first moved to Bowling Green, where his son John was living. It appears that he learned that there was a need for a good music store in the town of Clarksville, just across the border in Tennessee, approximately sixty miles from Bowling Green. He opened his store in 1858 in the town square and it appears to have been very successful, and soon John moved down to join him there. They advertised in the local newspaper: "Pianos, Guitars, Violins, Flutes, Clarinets, Accordions, Tambourines, Banjos and brass instruments as well as a large assortment of sheet music of all the favorite songs and pieces for the ladies."[3] They also offered instrument repairs done on short notice. However, when the Civil War erupted, they had to close up shop and they returned to Kentucky, losing a significant part of their investment, and also money that had been owed to them. John Griffith, the reporter, continues the story:

By now there was very little demand for pianos; it ruined not only the trade in pianos but all other trade of any kind, and the town was left to the ghosts. He returned to Kentucky and there rented a large farm of a thousand acres with eighty niggers [sic] on it. There he sheltered throughout the war; for the first year or two he was left to live in peace. In 1862, the government in Washington took possession of the farm and auctioned it to the highest bidder except that no one was to have it unless he was an "Union Man." It was taken by Hughes. By the time the rebels realized that Hughes was a Unionist, there was no mercy for him any more. Over a period, everything that could be moved was stolen—his horses, cattle, corn, hay, money—in fact everything, and he was lucky to escape with his life. They had their revolvers to his head tens of times, threatening to blow his brains out if he dared utter a word against them. During these four years, he lost between twenty five and thirty thousand dollars, apart from thousands of dollars owing to him on the books of the piano store in Clarksville, from which he is unlikely to see a dollar on a thousand.

Three months ago, he left the farm and the niggers [sic] on it completely to the overseer. He heard since then that the previous owner had sworn the oath of allegiance to the Union and that the government had given it back to him. First of all, Mr. Hughes paid a visit to his daughter who is married to a merchant in Louisville, Kentucky then his son John, who is living in Cincinnati, and after this came to New York, on his way to visit Wales—the land of his birth; and the first time we happened to meet, he had just arrived, after travelling six hundred miles, and weary from the heat. By now (it is a fortnight since then) he has revived and is a new man.

Dafydd Hughes was lucky to have escaped with his life during the war, and although he appeared at first to be financially ruined, he had somehow managed to hide some money, and had deposited $5,000 in gold in the Nassau Bank in New York. This was the same bank at which David Hughes had an account, and the bank manager wrote to Hughes telling him of the deposit his father had made. The letter went on to say that his father was asking David Hughes's advice on where he should invest it.[4]

It is not known whether Dafydd Hughes ever made it back to Wales. If he did, he did not stay and spend the rest of his days in Bala, as he had indicated he would. Sometime after the end of the Civil War, probably in 1866, he joined his son John and his family, who were now resident in Chicago and had set up an insurance agency. It was at this time that Dafydd met his long-lost younger brother, Hugh R. Hughes from Judson, Minnesota, whom he had not seen for forty years and who had also emigrated to America.[5] The meeting came about as described in the *Cenhadwr Americanaidd* (The American Missionary, published in Utica) for 1869, page 16, as follows:

Correspondence from Minnesota: Mr. Editor.... Another matter of special interest in connection with the Welsh Establishment here is the coming of the famous old Welsh harpist, D. R. Hughes, amongst us. The old fellow was once very well-known amongst the Welsh Americans and had won considerable fame for himself and his family throughout our country as skilful musicians.

David Hughes, the "electrician," as he is called, is a son of his, who by his intelligence and observation, brought out a printing telegraph, and on account of that was made a knight by the French Emperor.

Living in Judson (Minnesota) is a brother to the old man, by name of H. R. Hughes. He had not seen his brother nor heard much about him for almost 40 years. But quite providentially, the London Correspondent of *Y Faner* when on his travels in America, happened to go to Chicago, and there got hold of the old harpist, and that on the occasion when the old man was holding a supper to celebrate his son David's elevation.

The "Gohebydd" (John Griffith) had sent the story of the old harpist and his supper to his newspaper and that article happened to come to the attention of H. R. Hughes in Judson. Well, the consequence was that through that article, the two brothers got in touch with each other and your present reporter kept up a correspondence between them until the old harpist came here, and enjoyed a great deal of his company after that.

It was fortunate that they were able to meet up after all that time, as Dafydd Hughes's days were coming to an end: he passed away in 1868 in Chicago.

><del>~<del>x

In 1857, John Arthur Hughes, David Hughes's brother, was living in Bowling Green, Kentucky, while David Hughes was busy promoting his telegraph instrument. John had continued his career as a music teacher and had married Miss Fanny C. Porter in the March of that year, against her father's wishes. Her father, Dr. Lemuel C. Porter, a prominent physician in the city, was reputed to have commented:[6]

The idea of one of his children marrying a damned fiddler....

This parental disapproval may account for the order of the family's entry in the September 1860 census, where, unusually, John is listed last in his household, after his wife and their daughters Blanche and Zerelda (named after her maternal grandmother), aged two years and ten months respectively. Both John and Blanche were described as music teachers.[7]

John, possibly trying to shake off his "fiddler" image and live up to the greater expectations of his father-in-law, became the proprietor of a whisky distillery near Bowling Green and also of another distillery over the state line in Memphis, Tennessee.[8] Unfortunately John never seemed to have much luck in his business ventures, and he soon became embroiled in a lawsuit over the Bowling Green distillery, while the one in Memphis burned down under rather dubious circumstances, and the insurers pursued him. It was left to his father-in-law Dr. Porter to settle with the creditors.[9] To help him get back on his feet, his father Dafydd had John and his wife move to Clarksville, Tennessee, so that he could work in the music store with him. This lasted up until the Civil War broke out, at which time he moved back to Bowling Green, taking up residence in a house next door to his father-in-law. The Civil War wrenched families apart especially in Kentucky, which was caught between the North and South and where sympathies were divided. John's sympathies lay with the South and he enlisted in the Confederate Army.[10]

After the war, John, like his father, had had enough of the turmoil and carnage, and also of Kentucky, which was to remain occupied until the fall of 1865. John moved to Chicago, where he opened up an insurance agency as an agent for the Phoenix Insurance Co., and his father joined him there. Sadly his father lived only three more years before passing away in 1868. It is believed that John took his family with him to Chicago, but by the time of the June 1870 census, they were back in Bowling Green, living with Dr. Porter, although John was not present, and neither was their daughter Zerelda, but another daughter, Lilly, aged nine, was listed.[11] It seems likely that Fanny and the children initially went with John to Chicago, where Zerelda died and was buried, as she is not in the Porter family plot in Bowling Green with her parents and grandparents.

Following her death, Fanny may have decided to return to Bowling Green, leaving John to continue with his insurance agency in Chicago.

Bad luck and business problems seemed to follow John everywhere, as yet another catastrophe befell him in 1871, in the form of the Great Chicago Fire. This tragic event took a heavy toll on insurance companies and wiped many of them out, including John's.

He next moved to Cincinnati and tried his hand at shoe manufacturing. Unfortunately, the one person who could have advised him about boot and shoe making—his father—was no longer around to offer advice. By 1876 John's health had started to deteriorate and he was diagnosed with Bright's disease, a kidney ailment. He had to stop working and rest, but after a while, he seemed to improve and he joined his friend J.S. Zerbe in his patent agency, and became editor of their publication the *American Inventor*. It was during this period (1877–78) that the great argument broke out between Thomas Edison and John's brother Professor David Edward Hughes over the invention of the carbon microphone. John became upset over all of the false accusations leveled at his brother by Edison, and attempted to defend his brother in his publication and in the American press. John's wife Fanny died in Bowling Green in November of 1879, and John followed her to the grave within weeks, dying in January of 1880.[12]

Their youngest daughter Lilly, following the death of her parents, continued to live with Dr. Porter and his sister until November 24, 1886, when she eloped with a James Lucas and went to live in Cerrillos, New Mexico, subsequently moving to Albuquerque, New Mexico, where she died, apparently without issue, on February 3, 1939. Lilly was a prolific letter writer, and corresponded with her uncle, David Edward Hughes. She received a substantial bequest in his will, while her sister Blanche's family received nothing.

John and Fanny's eldest daughter, Blanche, had married Major David Shelby Barriger at Dr. Porter's residence on December 12, 1877, her grandfather and father acting as witnesses.[13] Major Barriger was posted to Fort Omaha, Nebraska where he and his wife went on to have four children: Shelly, Zerelda Courrts (Zizzie), Elizabeth Stanley, and a fourth sister, Eugenie, who died in infancy. Blanche, like her father, died quite young of Bright's disease on March 7, 1893, and is buried with her husband, who survived her by thirty-three years, in Omaha's Forest Lawn Cemetery.[14] After leaving the military, David Barriger appears to have been successful in business, and David Edward Hughes was under the impression that they were fairly wealthy, which was perhaps why he did not bequeath them anything in his will. Unfortunately, in 1893 David Barriger's business interests suffered a reversal and the family fell on hard times.

Their daughter Zerelda married Alfred Bowie and they had one daughter, Allene, born in 1905, but unfortunately Alfred passed away before she was born, and Zerelda was remarried to Alvin E. Hart. Her daughter Allene Hart, who had taken her stepfather's surname, married Bill Michaels in 1926, and they had two children: Nancy, who died in 2008, and William Barriger Michaels, who continues to take a keen interest in the family's history.

All three of the Barriger sisters married, and at the time of their father's death in 1926, they were identified as Mrs. A. E. Hart and Mrs. Walter Hayes of Kansas City, Missouri, and Mrs. W.R. Bascomb of New York.[15]

⤝⤜⤛

Professor David Edward Hughes's youngest sibling, Margaret, had become acquainted with a young salesman by the name of Robert Steele Millar, who worked at the music store of Peters and Webb in Louisville. Margaret's friendship with Robert blossomed and they married in 1859. They seem to have had a more stable existence than John, and went on to have four children: Katharine Douglas (Katy), Edward, Graham, and Daisy. They lived in the Louisville area for some years and then moved to Cincinnati, Ohio. David Hughes kept in touch with his sister on a regular basis and also sent her money to help out with their finances. Maggie's husband died in 1898 and Maggie moved to live with her daughter Katy and her husband in Buffalo, New York.[16] In 1910 she was living in New York, but nothing further is known of her.

Very little is known about Margaret's four children, apart from Katy, who married Edwin Jones Burrows in Wyoming, a suburb of Cincinnati, Ohio, on March 14, 1888. Katy died in 1907 in Buffalo, NY. They had three sons: Millar (1889–1980); Edwin Grant (1891–1958) and Robert Douglas (1897–1982). Millar was one of the first to study the Dead Sea Scrolls and gave them their popular name. He also took a prominent part in the production of the Revised Standard Version of the Bible. His grandson, Edwin Gwynne Burrows, is co-author of *Gotham*, the best-selling history of New York up to 1898.[17]

As for Katy's brothers, Edward became an officer in the U.S. Army and by 1907 was a major at Fort Leavenworth, Kansas, having earlier been stationed in the Philippines and Newport, Kentucky.

We have no knowledge of Graham's life or occupation, except that in 1901 he was married and living in New York. His mother may well have joined him following Katy's death and the re-marriage of Edwin Jones Burrows, which could account for her New York address in 1910.

All that is known of Daisy, the youngest, is from Lilly Hughes Lucas's letter of January 26, 1907, in which she states of her Aunt Margaret Millar: "All her children are married, Daisy the youngest in St. Louis."[18]

⤝⤜⤛

After David Edward Hughes died, his wife, Anna Chadbourne Hughes, continued to live in London for a few years; she returned to the Boston area of Massachusetts around 1910, and remained in America until her death in Cambridge, Massachusetts on July 22, 1919, at the age of 94. She was interred with her husband in the family mausoleum in Highgate Cemetery, London.

Anna generously distributed her estate among many relatives, but it is for her judicious bequest to her sister Clara Chadbourne Berry's daughter, Anna Berry, that we have particular reason to be thankful, since Anna Berry received David Edward Hughes's papers. These were carefully preserved and passed on from generation to generation, and for this, historians will always be grateful.

Anna Berry married Huntington Porter Smith and they had two children, Winifred Porter Smith and Charles Porter Smith. Winifred married Richard Mather. Their granddaughter, Diane, used to accompany her cousin Don Smith on trips to research the family's history.

Charles Porter Smith actually met David Edward Hughes shortly before he passed away in London in 1900. Charles's marriage resulted in three children, Bertha, Lawrence, and Donald McEwen Smith, and it is to Donald Smith that this book is dedicated. As the Hughes papers were passed down, he ensured that they remained safe, the current custodian being his granddaughter Donna. Donald was the catalyst and the persuading force that finally gave David Edward Hughes his time in the limelight and his long overdue biography.

NOTES

In compiling this biography the authors have made extensive use of Hughes's own papers as well as of contemporary historical documents. The sources most frequently cited are abbreviated as follows:

DEHP refers to the David Edward Hughes papers, a microfiche archive organized by J.O. Marsh and R.G. Roberts and held at the National Library of Wales as NLW Fiche no. 6 under the title *David Edward Hughes (1831–1900) F.R.S. Inventor of the microphone, papers and correspondence 1850s–90s.*

DEH I&D refers to David Edward Hughes's personal notebook titled "Inventions and Discoveries of David Edward Hughes." The notebook is among his private papers which are owned by the family, and are not part of DEHP.

DEH NPC refers to David Edward Hughes's collection of newspaper clippings among his private papers which are owned by the family, and are not part of DEHP. Hughes employed a clipping service to send him newspaper stories about himself and his discoveries.

Baner ac Amserau Cymru. Refers to the weekly newspaper *Baner ac Amserau Cymru* (The Welsh Standard and Times), which was published in Welsh in Denbigh, Wales, specifically to the section "Digwyddiadau yr Wythnos" ("The Week's Events") and the two articles titled "Gohebydd Llundain yn America" ("Our London Correspondent in America"), published September 13, 1865, pp. 3–4, and September 20, 1865, pp. 6–7.

Many of the documents cited in Chapter 5 associated with the Atlantic Telegraph cable are accessible through Bill Burns's web site "History of the Atlantic Cable and Undersea Communications" at http://atlantic-cable.com

EP = The Thomas Edison Papers, Rutgers University, New Jersey. Available at http://edison.rutgers.edu/digital.htm.

IET = Institution of Engineering and Technology Archives, London, UK.

WT BIO refers to Silvanus P. Thompson, *The Life of William Thomson, Baron Kelvin of Largs* (London: Macmillan and Co. Ltd., 1910), Chapter 8, "Failure of the Atlantic Telegraph Cable."

CHAPTER 1

1 See the article on the history of the Hughes musical career that appeared in the London Welsh magazine *Y Ddolen* ("The Link") 7.7 (July, 1932), pp. 5–6, and 7.8 (August, 1932), pp. 3–4.

2 In the Welsh name "Dafydd" the "f" is sounded as a "v" and the "dd" as a "vv." The vowels are pronounced as in "davit," so the name is pronounced "Davivv."

3 The Hughes family's early life is chronicled in two articles that appeared in the Welsh newspaper *Baner ac Amserau Cymru* (The Welsh Standard and Times), which was published in Welsh in Denbigh, Wales, specifically in the two articles titled "Gohebydd Llundain yn America" ("Our London Correspondent in America"), published September 13, 1865, pp. 3–4, and September 20, 1865, pp. 6–7. These articles are based on comprehensive interviews which were conducted by correspondent John Griffith "Y Gohebydd." Griffith personally interviewed Dafydd Hughes and a family friend from Bala by the name of Gwilym ap Ioan. This took place in 1865, many years after Dafydd Hughes had left Britain and taken up residence in America, when Griffith happened to be in New York just after the end of the American Civil War.

4 The town of Bala was founded by Roger de Mortimer circa 1310 and was granted a charter in 1324, during the reign of Edward II, when it was created a free borough. Over the centuries, it has been noted for its fairs and markets, which are held to this day along the wide High Street. In the early nineteenth century it was best known for the production of knitted woolen stockings and gloves, and the weaving of woolen cloth, flannel and linsey (a coarse cloth woven on a cotton warp). It was also a stronghold of Welsh Non-conformism, and the home of Thomas Charles (1755–1814), who was instrumental in the foundation of the British and Foreign Bible Society. Bala with its rivers and lake is a popular tourist destination and a center for white-water canoeing and sailing. The town of Corwen, which is situated on the River Dee twelve miles from Bala, was a market town. Its importance increased when the route to Ireland became established through the Dee Valley as it was on the main London-to-Holyhead route and was one of the stage coach stops and exchanges. The route basically followed the Roman road often referred to as Watling Street. In 1829 there was a daily Royal Mail coach that arrived every evening from London and left every morning to return to London. This road had been improved by Thomas Telford, who among other things completed the suspension bridge over the Menai Straits in 1826.

5 The two eldest brothers Dafydd and Hugh were baptized at Llancil Church, just outside Bala, on January 25, 1803, and September 16, 1804, respectively. Gwynedd Archives Services, Meirionnydd Record Office, Dolgellau, Parish Registers, Baptisms and Burials 1772–1812, Ref. Z/PE/10/100. While they were baptized simply David and Hugh, without second names, in later years both men appear to have added their father's name "Robert" as second names, and are referred to as Dafydd R. Hughes and Hugh R. Hughes, thus using a touch of the traditional Welsh patronymic system, though not to the same degree as their father, who affected the title "Robert Hugh Dafydd Sion Rhys," an echo of the days when any Welshman worth his salt could recite his male ancestors back for a dozen generations. Both brothers emigrated to America, with Hugh R. Hughes ending up in Minnesota. The

two brothers lost touch but were reunited in Chicago shortly before Dafydd Hughes died in 1868.

6   *Baner ac Amserau Cymru*, September 13 and 20, 1865.

7   *Baner ac Amserau Cymru*, September 13 and 20, 1865.

8   Information from the Gallery on Transatlantic Slavery, Merseyside Maritime Museum, Liverpool.

9   *Baner ac Amserau Cymru*, September 13 and 20, 1865.

10   A marriage is recorded in the Register of St. Giles, Cripplegate, London on August 7, 1823, between a David (Dafydd) Hughes, bachelor, and a Catherine Gostick, widow, both of that parish. This is the right area of London and also fits with Dafydd Hughes's claim that he married at the age of about twenty. In DEHP Section 1.7, Biographical Notes and Memos, in notes made by his wife, Hughes records that his mother was from Ware in Hertfordshire and that she often mentioned that place and the Duke of Bedford (Woburn Abbey). Gostick is an extremely uncommon name, originating in the Baronetcy of Gostwyck, not far from Woburn, where to this day there remains a small cluster of families with that name.

11   See Robert (Bob) Owen, "Hughes, Joseph Tudor," in *The Dictionary of Welsh Biography Down to 1940* (London: Honourable Society of Cymmrodorion, 1959), p. 386. Unfortunately, no source is quoted, and the author of this entry, who considered himself something of an authority on the Hughes family, admits elsewhere that he could find no baptismal entry for him in the area. Subsequent searches have also drawn a blank in Bala, London and elsewhere.

12   DEHP, Section 1.6, Autobiographical Letters. As we shall see later, it was to the family's advantage as musical performers to understate the children's age as it made their performance as "child prodigies" that much more impressive.

13   The on-line version of the *Oxford Dictionary of National Biography* gives his date of birth as "either on 18th. June 1829 or on 16th. May 1831 at Corwen, near Bala, Merioneth or Holborn, London."

14   Although this entry is two years earlier than the date of birth usually cited, it is reasonable to believe that it relates to Hughes. This conclusion is corroborated by one of the many little notes which his wife made of his reminiscences (DEHP, Section 1.7 Biographical Notes and Memos): "Mem. St. Andrew's Church, Parish of St. Andrew, Holborn, London, where his mother had told him, David Edward Hughes, when he was a child, that he was baptized."

15   The cottage called Green-y-Ddwyryd or the "Green" as it is sometimes referred to was located at Druid, 2.5 miles from Corwen, close to the junction of the A5 and the turn off for Bala (A494), near the stream that runs past Druid and Plas Isaf before joining the river Alwen. It is identified on the tithe map of 1839 and on Colonel Colby's first edition Ordnance Survey one-inch map surveyed during the 1830s. But maps from 1870 onwards do not show it, and today there is no trace of the cottage or its foundations. There is a report by John Davies Hughes of Corwen, a descendant of the Hughes family, that there were some foundations and stones still remaining in 1931.

16   John Arthur Hughes's birth date is indicated as March 10, 1832, on his memorial inscription in the Fairview Cemetery, Bowling Green, Kentucky, USA. This tallies with his given age in the 1860 United States Census,

and if correct, reinforces the case for David having been born before 1831, as he was said to be two years older than John.

17   Margaret Hughes was born at the "Lying in Hospital," London, October 17, 1837, father David Hughes, Shoe Maker, mother Catherine Hughes, formerly Gostick, according to a certified copy of her Entry of Birth, obtained from General Register Office in Southport. This document also confirms their marriage in St. Giles, Cripplegate, in 1823.

18   *Baner ac Amserau Cymru*, September 13 and 20, 1865.

19   R. B. Jones, ed., *Anatomy of Wales* (Peterston, Glamorgan: Gwerin Publications, 1972), p. 216.

20   On Robert Nicholas Bochsa see *The New Grove Dictionary of Music and Muscians* (New York: Oxford University Press, 1995), pp. 831–832. Weippert and Chatterton were competent harpists according to Dr. Rhidian Griffiths at the National Library of Wales, Aberystwyth.

21   In about 1839 the book *British Melodies: The Compositions of Master Hughes, from the Fourth to the Ninth Year of his Age* was published in London by d'Almaine. This featured on the frontispiece an illustration of the three brothers performing on their instruments, followed by lithographic facsimiles of the autographs of the subscribers, among them the Queen Dowager (Adelaide), Princess Augusta, the Duke of Sussex, the Duchess of Kent, "and several hundreds of the Nobility, Gentry and Clergy of the United Kingdom." Joseph Hughes was also honored at the Eisteddfod at Llannerchymedd, Anglesey on June 9, 1835, by having the bardic name "Blegwryd ap Seisyllt" conferred upon him.

22   A transcript of the concert poster appeared in a London Welsh magazine *Y Ddolen* ("The Link") of July, 1932, pp. 5–6.

23   Unfortunately it has not been possible to verify through the Royal Archives that they gave this concert at Windsor Castle, as Queen Victoria's diary for that period does not note such events. However when Joseph first started his private performances, a neighbor of the family by the name of Owen, trading in New Bond Street, determined to introduce him into court circles. He was on visiting terms with some members of Princess Augusta's household and invited them to dine at his home. After the meal, he produced the young harpist, who so charmed his audience that after they returned home, they related their experience to their mistress and a royal command performance was immediately forthcoming. He went on to give performances before other members of the court, including Queen Adelaide and the then Princess Victoria. This information comes from *Baner ac Amserau Cymru*.

24   DEHP, Section 1.7, Biographical Notes and Memos, two memos written by David Edward Hughes's wife in November 1885. He mentioned that this was not long before the Queen's marriage, which took place on February 10, 1840, and also that his brother came home with his harp filled with bonbons and oranges.

25   Certainly, the conditions for the lower class were still abysmal with much poverty, city slums, and unsanitary conditions. The population lived under the constant threat of a multitude of life-threatening illnesses such as diphtheria, scarlet fever, typhoid, smallpox and typhus. The Hughes family however had been rising up the social ladder and climbing out of this abyss.

26 The suggestion that the Hughes brothers had performed at Windsor Castle on November 10, 1838 was initially regarded with some skepticism, particularly as it is generally claimed that the Hughes family had emigrated to the United States of America during the latter half of 1838. Also it is often said that they left for America when David Hughes was seven years old. However, an announcement for morning and afternoon farewell concerts on Tuesday June 4, 1839, in the rather unlikely *Sussex Agricultural Express* refers to the previous Friday's concert, corroborating the article in *Y Ddolen* and firmly placing them still in England almost a year later. David Hughes was in fact ten years old in 1839.

27 See *Lloyd's List* (London), August 4, 1840: "London August 3rd Entered Outwards. New York and Charleston. Catherine, Berry. A 458 LD Sunley." London, Saturday August 29, 1840: "London, August 28th, Cleared Outwards. New York & Charleston, Catharine, Berry. A458 LD Sunley." It may have been a coincidence or a good luck gesture on Dafydd's part to his wife Catherine that they sailed from St. Katherine's Dock on a ship named *Catharine*!

CHAPTER 2

1 The semaphore was in use before the electrical telegraph was invented. It was a visual communication system consisting of a tower with a number of protruding arms that could be manually positioned. The various positions of the arms signified letters of the alphabet or abbreviated codes, which, with the use of a telescope, could be read from a distance of several miles. For conveying messages over long distances, relays of semaphore towers were built several miles apart along the route within sight of each other. France had an extensive semaphore signaling system that covered hundreds of miles. There were also systems in operation in England and Wales. See William Maver, *American Telegraphy* (New York: Maver Publishing, 1912); and Anthony R. Michaelis, *From Semaphore to Satellite* (Geneva, 1965).

2 The Hugheses arrived in NY aboard the sailing ship *Catharine* on October 8, 1840. See US National Archives Passenger Lists, Ref. M237, Roll 4.1, record 773. The father's profession was listed as music teacher and the children as musicians.

3 The preceding portrayal of the Hughes family's arrival in New York harbor is compiled from accounts of the arrivals of other sailing ships to New York after Atlantic crossings at that period.

4 The quote is from the *Baner ac Amserau Cymru*. They had departed London on August 4, 1840, so the voyage was a fairly long one of nine weeks; the ship was listed as bound for New York and Charleston, and might have stopped in the latter city first. The mayor of New York at that time was Isaac Varian, but it had almost been Samuel F. B. Morse, who was later an American telegraph pioneer: Morse had made an unsuccessful run for mayor in 1837.

5 For coverage of the history of New York City, see Edwin G. Burrows and Mike Wallace, *Gotham: A History of New York City to 1898* (New York: Oxford University Press, 1999). It is interesting to note that the author Edwin G. Burrows's ancestry can be traced back to the Hughes family.

6 The ages given on the ship's passenger list in 1840 were Joseph, fourteen; David, nine; John, five; and Margaret, two. The father was listed as being thirty-seven and the mother as forty-two. But in fact David was closer to eleven and John to eight.

7 See *Baner ac Amserau Cymru*. The author of the two articles in the *Baner*, John Griffith, interviewed David Hughes's father and also William Williams (whose Bardic name was Gwilym ap Ioan). He too originated from Bala in Wales and had been in America for some forty years as a merchant in New York, and was secretary of the St. David's Charitable Society. He had become one of the respected elder citizens of the city, and kept a scrap book of newspaper cuttings about Welshmen of note either in America or the Old Country from both English and Welsh newspapers.

8 Joseph Tudor Hughes drowned May 12, 1841, at the age of fourteen. He was buried in New York City at the Welsh Baptist Chapel in Amity Street. Note that the article in the *Baner* says that the Chapel was on Enmity Street, but this is believed to have been an error for Amity Street.

9 See *Baner ac Amserau Cymru*.

10 Scarlet fever, once the scourge of young children, is a strep infection; in the 1800s it could be fatal, but nowadays it is better known in its early stages as "strep throat" and is easily treated with antibiotics. Because of the illness, David and John were unable to attend Joseph's funeral, but several weeks later did visit their brother's grave at the Baptist Church in New York City.

11 Ole Bull, the Norwegian violinist and composer. See *The New Grove Dictionary of Music and Musicians* (New York: Oxford University Press, 1995), pp. 445–448.

12 Charles Dickens landed in Boston in January of 1842 and toured extensively, appearing in theaters in New York, Washington, Philadelphia, Richmond, Louisville, St. Louis, Montreal and Quebec. He published his *American Notes* on his return and then his novel *Martin Chuzzlewit* about a young man who came to America.

13 Dan Worrall, "David Edward Hughes: Concertinist and Inventor," *Papers of the International Concertina Association* 4 (2007), pp. 41-50, and available at **www.concertina.org/pica/index.htm**. Worrall cites articles in *The Southern Patriot* (Charleston, North Carolina) from May 9, 12, and 15 of 1845. The comments here are from his summary of those articles. According to Worrall the concertina used by the young Hughes marks the earliest documented appearance of the concertina in American music circles. It is believed that it was the one purchased from Charles Wheatstone's music store in London in 1836 by David Hughes's father when the family resided in London (see London, Horniman Museum, Wayne Archive, Wheatstone Sales Ledger 104a, p. 5, item 100). Charles Wheatstone, besides being the inventor of the English concertina, was also the inventor, along with William Fothergill Cooke, of a needle telegraph instrument used in England. David Hughes, later in his life, would meet these gentlemen, who came to view him as a competitor in the telegraph business.

14 See *Baner ac Amserau Cymru*.

15 The dangers of handling mercury were not recognized or understood at this time. Indeed, it is amazing, considering its widespread use by scientists, that so many of them survived long enough to make their discoveries! Makers of felt hats (i.e. top hats), however, did not fare so well, and the saying "Mad as a Hatter" was not without foundation. Unbeknownst to the workers in this trade at the time, the mercury that they used

extensively in the preparation of the fur and felt for hats was slowly accumulating in their bodies, finally exhibiting its toxic effects in the form of "Hatters' Shakes" and "Hatters' Syndrome," an early example of an occupational disease.

16 DEH I&D.

17 DEH I&D.

18 *Baner ac Amserau Cymru.*

19 DEH I&D.

20 DEHP, Section 1.7, Biographical Notes and Memos. The portable laboratory was made by Eccles of London and presented to him by Dr. Nathanial Brewer, a wholesale druggist of Boston.

21 See Palmer C. Sweet, *Gold in Virginia* (Charlottesville, VA: Commonwealth of Virginia, Dept. of Conservation and Economic Development, Division of Mineral Resources, 1980).

22 Roger G. Ward, *Land Tax Summaries & Implied Deeds* (Athens, GA: Iberian Publications, 1993–95), Vol. 3 (1841–1870). The land records for Buckingham County show that in 1849 the Hugheses purchased 597 acres located five miles southeast of the Court House. However, accounts from the various Hughes personal notes indicate that the farm was over one thousand acres. It is assumed that it was leased for the first few years before the purchase in 1849. Unfortunately, the Buckingham Court House designed by Thomas Jefferson burnt down in 1869, taking with it virtually all of the county records. The courthouse was rebuilt, but the loss of records was a major catastrophe, and of course, has made tracing land records and the exact location of the Hughes family farm difficult. The farm was still there in 1890 according to D.E. Hughes's sister Margaret, who paid a return visit to the area.

23 DEHP, Section 1.7, Biographical Notes and Memos, memo by Anna C. Hughes dated October 17, 1890.

24 St. David is the patron saint of Wales.

25 Steven Taber, *Geology of the Gold Belt in the James River Basin Virginia* (Charlottesville: University of Virginia, 1913).

26 DEH I&D.

27 DEH I&D.

28 DEHP, Section 1.7, Biographical Notes and Memos, memos by Anna C. Hughes dated October 6, 1885, and October 17, 1890.

29 Hughes's notes indicate that they had a number of slaves working on the farm and in the gold mine. Virginia had a high population of slaves, and in Buckingham County alone there were 8,000 black slaves out of a total population of 13,800. See Eugene A. Maloney, *A History of Buckingham County* (Dillwyn, VA: Buckingham County Bicentennial Commission, 1976), pp. 37–43. Also see *Historical, Demographic, Economic, and Social Data: The United States, 1790–1970* (Ann Arbor, MI: Institute for Social Research, University of Michigan, 1984).

30 See Eugene A. Maloney, *A History of Buckingham County* (Dillwyn, VA: Buckingham County Bicentennial Commission, 1976), pp. 37–43.

31 DEH I&D.

32 DEH I&D.

33 *Baner ac Amserau Cymru.*

34 The "electric telegraph" transported signals from one place to another over telegraph wires almost instantaneously. The technology of that period was such that all that could be sent on the wires were electrical signals that were either "on" or "off" for "short" or "longer" periods of time as in the Morse system (the luxury of a voice telephone was not to appear for another thirty years). Each letter of the alphabet was allocated a distinct code made up of various combinations of on/off signals of short and long duration, the familiar dots and dashes of the Morse code. An operator tapped these out with a Morse key (an electrical switch). At the receiving station the Morse codes were received as a series of electrical pulses. An electromagnet responded to these and moved a pen or stylus over a moving paper tape, recording the short and long signals. The operator then read the tape and translated the code back into English.

35 DEHP, Section 1.6, Autobiographical Letters, letter from David Edward Hughes to his sister Maggie, sent from London in May of 1892.

36 Various accounts of David Hughes's early teaching posts have incorrectly identified various colleges as that where he first taught. J. O. Marsh and R. G. Roberts corrected this in 1979 in their study "David Edward Hughes: Inventor, Engineer and Scientist," *Proceedings of the Institution of Electrical Engineers* 126.9 (September, 1979), pp. 929–935, where they identified the college as the "Presbyterian Female Seminary, founded in 1838, in Bardstown Kentucky, and later named Roseland Academy, under the principalship of the Reverend J. V. Cosby."

CHAPTER 3

1 Bardstown dates from 1780 and became the county seat of Nelson County in 1785. Situated forty-five miles southeast of Louisville, it took its name from one of its early settlers, David Bard. Bardstown grew and prospered and this was reflected in the many fine buildings of Greek Revival, Federal and Georgian architecture, with 300 buildings still listed on the National Register of Historic Places. Bardstown is also the location of the St. Joseph Proto-Cathedral which was the first Catholic cathedral west of the Allegheny Mountains and the home of the Sisters of Charity of Nazareth. Besides Bardstown Female Academy (Roseland Academy), where David Hughes was a professor, the town was also home to St. Joseph's College, a Catholic boys' college (located next to St. Joseph Proto-Cathedral) and The Sisters of Charity of Nazareth girls' school. Many of the streets were renamed in the 1930s, and Chestnut St. became Brashear, and Main St. is also known as Third St. With many distilleries in the vicinity, Bardstown now calls itself the Bourbon Capital of the World. See Dixie Hibbs, *Bardstown* (Charlestown: Arcadia Publishing, 1998), and Sarah B. Smith, *Historic Nelson County* (Louisville: Gateway Press, 1971).

2 The Academy, a fine colonial building, was erected by Colonel James Browne, who also was the builder of the St. Joseph Proto-Cathedral and several other residences in Bardstown. Originally the building had two large wings off the side of the main house. The building continued to house a school until the early 1900s; later it became a private residence, the side wings were removed, and a front porch added. The building still has its original interior and is now a private residence in the possession of the Jim Beam family of bourbon whiskey fame. See Sarah B. Smith, *Historic Nelson*

County (Louisville: Gateway Press, 1971), pp. 80–81. The author has personally visited this lovely house.

3 Presbyterian Historical Society Archives, Philadelphia. Rev Dr. Jouett Vernon Cosby was a Presbyterian minister and became the principal of the Bardstown Female Academy in 1847. The school was started in 1830. In 1836 the Rev. Nathan Rice, a Protestant zealot concerned about Catholic influence in the community, was instrumental in promoting this school, which was the first Protestant girls' school. It went on to earn a reputation as one of the most distinguished schools in the South in the antebellum period. Rev. Cosby was born in Staunton, Virginia, in 1816. He trained at the Union Theological Seminary at Prince Edward and Princeton Seminary and took up his duties in Kentucky in 1847. The town of Staunton was approximately forty miles from Buckingham, so there is a possibility that the Hughes and Cosby families' paths crossed in Virginia. Bardstown Female Academy was also known as Roseland Academy, a name given to it by Rev. Cosby. The Cosby residence was believed to be located further up the road on the opposite side.

4 This was his first post as a Professor of Natural Philosophy and Music, and it was a title that he maintained throughout his life.

5 Herr Hast, a musician, is often mentioned in works about Hughes as having introduced Hughes to Bardstown and as having helped him to obtain his teaching position. However, Hughes makes no mention of having received such help in his papers. The only reference Hughes makes to a Herr Hast is to a man who lived in the same rooming house and was in the room opposite to his. Hast let Hughes use his piano, although some jealousy arose and Hast then kept the piano locked up. There is also a reference indicating that Hughes met Hast through the music store Peters and Webb in Louisville. In the Bardstown historical archives there is a record of a Jacob Hast who was a painter and teacher and who was of similar age to Hughes, but died at the age of twenty-four in 1854. The famous songwriter Stephen Foster visited relatives at the John Rowen plantation at Federal Hill in Bardstown during the period Hughes was in Bardstown, although it is not known whether they ever met. Foster is remembered for his songs such as Oh! Susanna, Camptown Races and My Old Kentucky Home.

6 Hughes's invention of his telegraph has often been incorrectly attributed to his endeavor "to contrive a machine for copying extempore music, so that his melodious improvisations might not be lost." This idea first appeared in an article in The Telegrapher and was subsequently reported in the Telegraph Journal 2.51 (December 17, 1864), p. 299. This article contained many other incorrect comments as well as some derogatory remarks on Hughes's personality, such as the suggestion that he was "apparently lacking in mental power." Hughes replied in the next issue of the Telegraph Journal 2.52 (December 24, 1864), p. 307, where he writes that "I am sorry to say the article in question is without the slightest foundation of truth."

7 Alvin F. Harlow, Old Wires and New Waves (New York and London: D. Appleton-Century, 1936), pp. 153–54.

8 The Bain telegraph instrument came into use in America in 1847, introduced from England. Messages were sent in quasi-Morse code, and the receiver printed the dots and dashes on a chemically treated paper strip, directly from the line via electrochemical action. Unlike the Morse system, it did not require any electromagnetic device. The House system, invented by Royal Earl House (born in Vermont in 1814), came into use in 1849. This was a "type printing telegraph" with a keyboard resembling a piano for typing in letters directly, and was able to print the corresponding letters at the receiving station on a paper strip. House's instrument operated on the step-by-step principle, signaling over the telegraph line via multiple electrical pulses. The mechanism of the instrument was powered pneumatically, requiring two operators; the one operating the air pump was often referred to as the organ grinder. "Type printing" was a term commonly used to describe telegraph systems that printed directly in Roman letters, and House's was the first "type printing" telegraph in operational use in America. It is not known whether Hughes was aware of the House telegraph, which was operational on a few lines in the early 1850s and tended to be associated with the northeastern and western states. Hughes's telegraph instruments, however, had little in common with the House instrument. When House introduced his instrument on the New York to Boston line, the Morse Company filed for an injunction to stop it. Up to that time many suits had gone in Morse's favor, but in this case the judge ruled in House's favor. See Scientific American, December 22, 1888; this article was reprinted in the Electrical Review, January 4, 1889, pp. 17–18.

9 See Bardstown Herald, December, 1851 and August 1852, advertisement for Bardstown Female Academy.

10 DEHP, Section 1.6, Autobiographical Letters, letter from D.E. Hughes to his sister Maggie, dated May 27, 1892.

11 DEH I&D. One piece of sheet music composed by Hughes and titled Lizzie Polka has been located in the archives of the music library of Louisville University, and a second piece titled Damen Polka was published in Waltzes and Polkas (Louisville: GW Brainard & Co, 1852). Also see Marion Korda, Louisville Music Publications of the 19th Century (Louisville: University of Louisville Kentucky, 1991). At this period, polkas, marches, quick-steps and waltzes were very much in vogue and played an important role in family life; they were often performed in family drawing rooms or parlors, and also at social dances.

12 DEHP, Section 1.6, Autobiographical Letters, letter from D.E. Hughes to his sister Maggie, dated May 27, 1892.

13 DEHP, Section 1.7, Biographical Notes and Memos, the document titled "Fifteen page account of Hughes's magnet and his early years as a music teacher," referred to hereafter as the "15 page account of Hughes's early years."

14 A reference in an undated clipping from a Bowling Green newspaper (probably 1870–80) indicates that he took up residence in rooms in the back portion of Briggs and Wright, near the Arl House, and "where stand stately silver-leafed poplars on the west side of the public square." It has also been suggested that he stayed at the Potter House.

15 The Green River flowed into the Ohio River which flowed into the major waterway, the Mississippi.

16 DEHP, Section 1.7, Biographical Notes and Memos, the "15 page account of Hughes's early years." The Russellville Female Academy was first located in a building originally built for use by the Masons on

the northeast corner of Seventh and Summer Streets. It grew into an important institution and in 1867 its name was changed to Logan Female College and it was relocated to a new larger building across the street with over a hundred students. See Logan County Public Library Archives, and E. Coffman, *The Story of Logan County* (Nashville: The Parthenon Press, 1962), p. 103.

17 See DEH I&D; the 15 page account of Hughes's early years; and DEHP, Section 1.6, Autobiographical Letters, letter from D.E. Hughes to his sister Maggie, dated May 27, 1892.

18 DEHP, Section 1.7, Biographical Notes and Memos, 15 page account of Hughes's early years.

19 Catherine Hughes died at age 55 and Hughes's papers indicate that she was buried in Maysville, Virginia, but her grave has not been located.

20 Buckingham County Court House, records of land deeds, Book 4, p. 178, and Book 5, p. 491.

21 It seems reasonable to assume that the whole family became citizens. Hughes certainly traveled on an American passport (issued in 1860 and 1888). There is an article in Hughes's collection of newspaper cuttings, without date, which is a letter to the editor of the *Herald* (believed to be the *New York Herald*) by a person using the nom de plume of "Cambro American." The letter, which contains a number of verifiable facts, states: "The father with his family subsequently removed to Kentucky, where young Hughes resided when he made his invention. Though not natives of this country, both father and son became naturalized citizens." Naturalization during the 1840–50s could have been obtained individually or automatically for a family through the naturalization of the father. In order to become a citizen a foreigner had to be a free white male and over twenty-one years of age, resident in America for five years and resident in the state where naturalized for one year. An individual could file in any local, state or federal court, and at that period, each had its own procedure. No naturalization papers have been uncovered for the family, however. The newspaper cuttings cited are in Hughes's private papers, which are not part of DEHP.

22 DEH I&D.

23 DEH I&D. It is interesting to note that at the time, the major source of insulated electrical wire was bonnet wire used in making large brimmed women's hats and poke bonnets. This wire, usually of iron or copper, was over-wound with cotton or silk thread. It was designed to stiffen or add shape to women's bonnets. Also as Hughes had limited resources he had to make his own battery cells. He constructed electrical cells using pieces of sheet zinc from the roof and copper used for photographic plates.

24 DEHP, Section 1.8, Speeches, Awards of Medals and Other Honors, Bowling Green newspaper cutting of unspecified date, deduced to be 1876. This article presumably relates to the period (in 1854) when he was working on his invention while residing in Bowling Green "in rooms he occupied in the back portion in the offices of Briggs & Wright where the Arl House is now."

25 The newspaper article was written in March of 1942 by A.L. Dorsey, an attorney in Springfield, who was an avid historian and wrote frequently for the Robertson County Times. The article came to light in 2005 through research by Mr. W.B. Jones, who contributes to the "Then and Now" series in the Robertson County

Times. He republished and updated the Dorsey article in the June 29, 2005 issue of the Robertson County Times. Dorsey stated that Hughes boarded at the hotel that then stood on the south side of the Public Square which in 1942 was where The First Federal Bank and Dr. Wilkinson and Charles Willett had their offices. Dorsey indicated that Hughes was also teaching in Adairville, about ten miles from Springfield.

26 DEHP, Section 1.6, Autobiographical Letters, letter from D.E. Hughes to his sister Maggie, dated May 27, 1892.

27 David Hughes never forgot Mr. Hirschbuhl, who later in life returned to Germany. When traveling on the Continent he always paid a visit to the suburbs of Baden in Germany to put flowers on the grave of his old friend. This information comes from a biographical sketch of D.E. Hughes by J. Munro in the Hughes private papers.

28 The letter was published in *The Electrical Review* 6 (1878), p. 498 under the heading: "The First Hughes' Type Printer" and begins: "*Apropos* of Prof. Hughes' portrait biography in our issue for Nov 15th, we have received an interesting letter from Mr. Louis Schaefer, mechanician to the Eastern Telegraph Company (Malta). Schaefer had previously been employed by Siemens & Halske in Germany before he went to Louisville in America."

29 A caveat was filed to establish the date and time of an invention and was a way to establish priority and intent to follow with a formal patent application. It should be mentioned that in America, the inventor had to file for the patent in person, and that during that part of the 1800s, the inventor had also to provide a working model of the patented item with the application. The patent office kept these models. This was fortuitous, as Hughes's patented printing telegraph model has survived. The patent office later discontinued this policy, but many of these early patent models were preserved by the Smithsonian Institute in Washington DC.

30 The sequence of events during this period is sketchy: it is unclear whether they intended to obtain a patent first in America and then in England, or vice versa. Samuel Morse, for instance, reasoned that he might have a technical advantage in Europe if he did not first secure a patent elsewhere. See C. Mabee, *The American Leonardo: A Life of Samuel F.B. Morse* (New York: Alfred A. Knopf, 1943), p. 212 and Chapter XVIII. Events are further muddied by the fact that other references indicate that Hughes and Dr. Brodnax had already obtained an American patent when they were contacted by D.H. Craig and urged to go to New York. However, this cannot be the case, as Hughes did not apply for or receive his American patent until 1856, while the meeting with Craig and the subsequent business deal took place in the fall of 1855—these two dates are well documented.

31 James D. Reid, *The Telegraph in America and Morse Memorial* (New York: John Polhemus, 1886), pp. 405–407.

32 It should be noted that if they had filed for the American patent first they would have had to give up their only good model of the telegraph instrument, as the patent office at that time required a working model to be submitted along with the specifications and claims. This would have left them without a good working instrument for demonstration.

33 The rules governing the filing of a patent in England at that time were different from those in America.

In England, a patent could be applied for by the first person to introduce the product or process into the country; this of course may or may not have been the inventor! Thus, it was possible to secure a patent by having an agent such as Kennedy apply instead of the inventor, and Kennedy's name would appear on the patent. Kennedy probably took one of Hughes's prototype telegraphs with him to be on the safe side, so that they could say that it was the first to be introduced into the country. The rules required that a preliminary specification be filed first; then within six months a final specification was to be filed; this included the necessary explanatory drawings and the claims for the invention. It is not known who exactly Joseph Camp Griffith Kennedy was, aside from the fact that he is referred to as a patent agent who filed for the patent on behalf of Hughes. The patent did appear in Kennedy's name. The patent number is 2058, for an Electromagnetic Telegraph, granted on September 11, 1855.

34 T. Tate, *An Elementary Course of Natural and Experimental Philosophy* (Boston: Hickling, Swan and Brewer, 1858), pp. 206–275.

35 Batteries at that period were primary cells, that is, they were not rechargeable. They generated electricity by a chemical reaction that consumed the metallic electrodes. These batteries, unlike today's primary batteries, which are discarded when spent, could be rejuvenated by replacing the electrodes and restoring the acid to the right specific gravity.

36 There were a number of slightly different versions of the Morse code. There was the American Morse Code which was used on the American systems; the Continental, which became the basis for the International Morse Code; and another version that was used by the Bain telegraph system.

CHAPTER 4

1 An interesting comment on the changes in the American telegraph industry was made in a footnote to article # 240 in Dionysius Lardner, *The Electric Telegraph* (London: Walton and Maberly, 1855): "The American Telegraph Companies are subject to such constant change that it may be necessary to state here, once and for all, that the names and denominations to which we refer are those that were current in 1853–4, but which may be changed before these sheets come into the hands of the reader."

2 D. H. Craig, in his earlier days, was always one step ahead of his rivals to get the latest news to his clients, particularly European news. In the 1840s he had set up a carrier pigeon service between Halifax, Nova Scotia and Boston (telegraph service had not reached Nova Scotia at that time). Ships crossing the Atlantic stopped at Halifax en route to Boston or New York. Craig would board the ship, pick up copies of the English newspapers, and proceed to his cabin. He then quickly read and summarized the news and printed it by assembling the characters of a small type set in a frame and making an impression on tissue paper which he then attached to the leg of a carrier pigeon. The pigeon was launched out of a porthole and sent on its way to the city, easily beating the ship to its destination. His methods and practices often landed him in controversy, especially when it was thought that he was contributing to "speculation," a dirty word in those days. The speculation referred to might consist in buying or selling commodities on the basis of information about price changes in Europe obtained before others had access to it. There is a good account of Craig, the AP, and the rivalry among the various telegraph companies, in A. F. Harlow, *Old Wires and New Waves* (New York: Appleton-Century, 1936).

3 Samuel Morse, Smith and Kendall were worried that a news monopoly would mean a decrease in their revenues. Of course it actually worked the other way. This came about because of the way the news was sent over the telegraph. In the early days the news sent over the telegraph was highly abbreviated. Newspaper editors would then take these basic facts about a story and embellish them, using their own imaginations. Later, the AP started sending out the news in full, which was nothing less than revolutionary. This, of course, significantly increased the traffic on the telegraph system.

4 Cyrus West Field was born in 1819.

5 This description of Daniel Craig appeared in James Reid, *The Telegraph in America* (New York: Polhemus, 1886), p. 362.

6 Peter Cooper was a self-made industrialist who earned his fortune in the iron industry. He later founded the educational institute "Cooper Union." He was also next-door neighbor to Cyrus Field. James Eddy was the head of the Maine Telegraph Company, Abram Hewitt was an ironmaster, and Moses Taylor a banker and capitalist.

7 DEHP, Section 1.6, Autobiographical Letters, letter from D. E. Hughes to his sister Maggie dated May 27, 1892.

8 The principals of the company were Cyrus Field, Peter Cooper (President), Chandler White (Vice President) and Moses Taylor (Treasurer).

9 The Morse telegraph used a single telegraph wire with an earth return for communicating between locations. As Hughes's instruments were compatible with this system, it was simple to disconnect the Morse equipment and substitute Hughes's instruments.

10 DEHP, Section 1.6, Autobiographical Letters, letter from D. E. Hughes to his sister Maggie dated May 27, 1892.

11 Op. cit.

12 George M. Phelps, born 1820 in Troy, New York, grew up to be a skilled instrument maker in that same city. See John Casale, "George M. Phelps. Instrument Maker," *The Old Timer's Bulletin* 40.2 (May, 1999), pp. 21–23, and 40.3 (August, 1999), pp. 41–43.

13 The city of Troy where G. M. Phelps had his workshop was situated 150 miles north of New York City up the Hudson River.

14 Jame Reid, *The Telegraph in America* (New York: Polhemus, 1886), p. 406.

15 DEHP, Section 1.6, Autobiographical Letters, letter from D. E. Hughes to his sister Maggie dated May 27, 1892.

16 DEHP, Section 1.10, Secondary Material. A pencil note scribbled under the poem says: "probably by Dickerson Troy NY where Edward was boarding 1856 or (1857)." This note was probably added later by Hughes's wife Anna, but it is not known who Dickerson was.

17 Henry Field, *History of the Atlantic Telegraph* (New York: Charles Scribner, 1866), p. 61. In August and September of 1855 there had been an unsuccessful attempt to link Newfoundland to Cape Breton, Nova Scotia with an undersea telegraph cable. Cyrus Field consequently returned to England to order a new length of cable late in 1855.

18 Charles Bright, *The Story of the Atlantic Telegraph* (New York: D. Appleton and Co., 1903), p. 35; and Samuel Carter III, *Cyrus Field: Man of Two Worlds* (New York: Putnam's Sons, 1968), p. 121.

19 DEHP, Section 1.6, Autobiographical Letters, letter from D. E. Hughes to his sister Maggie dated May 27, 1892.

20 In Hughes's private papers, letter from Cyrus Field (from a London hotel) to Hughes (in Paris), dated February 15, 1856.

21 DEHP, Section 1.6, Autobiographical Letters, letter from D. E. Hughes to his sister Maggie dated May 27, 1892.

22 Op. cit.

23 DEH I&D.

24 DEHP, Section 1.6, Autobiographical Letters, letter from D. E. Hughes to his sister Maggie dated May 27, 1892.

25 Hughes appears never to have mentioned Phelps in subsequent years or to have acknowledged his contribution. Phelps, probably working in all good faith, seems to have been put out by Hughes's treatment. Phelps later related this to one Henry Bentley, and Bentley, discussing the Hughes microphone affair in a letter to Thomas Edison dated June 6, 1878, writes: "Phelps told me yesterday how Hughes treated him some years since in Printing Telegraph matter." See the Edison papers D7838ZCP and TAEM 19:719, cited in *The Papers of Thomas A. Edison*, ed. Reese V. Jenkins et al. (Baltimore: Johns Hopkins University Press, 1989–), vol. 4, p. 296. Phelps went on make a number of other printing telegraph instruments and to have a very successful career.

26 As neither Hughes nor Phelps recorded in detail who did what, one must refer to other observers of the period who provide some documentation on this subject. In the first edition (1860) of his book *History, Theory and Practice of the Telegraph*, George G. Prescott describes Hughes's instrument in Chapter 9 but there is no mention of G. Phelps's involvement in it at all. However, in Chapter 10, Prescott does describe the telegraph instrument known as the "Phelps Combination Instrument." Phelps developed this instrument sometime after he and Hughes parted ways in March 1857. Phelps took features from both the House and Hughes instruments as well as adding some of his own features to create this "combination instrument." On p. 145 Prescott states that Phelps used the following features of the original Hughes instrument: synchronous movement of the type wheel, the simple form of the press, the frictional movement of the cam, the correctors, and the detent. In the revised 1877 edition of his book Prescott changed how he reported the development of the Hughes instrument. This time he states that "During the greater portion of the years 1855–56 Mr. Hughes, in conjunction with Mr. George M. Phelps, an accomplished mechanician, residing at the time in Troy, N.Y., was engaged in perfecting the instrument, with a view to its practical introduction upon the lines of the American Telegraphic Company…. During this time two important and in fact essential improvements were made in the invention." He goes on to describe these improvements. The first improvement was the mechanism to readjust the synchronization, that is, to keep the transmitting and receiving instruments locked in synchronism; the second improvement was to consolidate the weight drive mechanism and thus run the transmitting and receiving mechanism from the same power source. Prescott indicated that "This important improvement is entirely due to the ingenuity of Mr. Phelps." James Reid in his book *The Telegraph in America* (1886) indicates on p. 853 when talking about Phelps's contribution to Hughes's instrument that "This resulted in the addition of two most important features by which the Hughes apparatus became thoroughly effective and useful." Unfortunately, Reid does not say what these features were.

27 DEHP, Section 1.2, Hughes's Business Papers, letter from Daniel Craig to Amos Kendall dated March 1, 1856. This letter was neatly printed in small type on very thin paper, and Craig probably composed it using the miniature print block set that he also used to send his dispatches by carrier pigeon.

28 *New York Daily Tribune*, Friday, March 13, 1857.

29 UK Patent #2058 granted to Kennedy and dated September 11, 1855; the date is actually when the patent was initially filed rather than when it was granted. While it was Hughes's invention, the patent was under Kennedy's name, who was acting as his agent, which was allowable at that time under English patent law.

30 Joseph Henry (1797–1878) was one of the most noted American physicists, known for his work in electromagnetism and development of the electromagnet. He demonstrated a rudimentary telegraph before Morse, although Morse never acknowledged this. Henry taught at Albany Academy, where he was professor of mathematics and natural philosophy. He then went on to teach at Princeton before being appointed as the first secretary and director of the Smithsonian Institute.

31 DEHP, Section 1.6, Autobiographical Letters, letter from D. E. Hughes to his sister Maggie dated May 27, 1892.

32 Op. cit.

33 US Patent # 14917, May 20, 1856, granted to David Edward Hughes for his printing telegraph, or as he liked to call it "An Improved Mode of Electro-Magnetic Telegraphic Communications which I term or designate Hughes' Compound Magnetic and Vibrating Printing Instrument." The model that accompanied his application is now in the Smithsonian Institution.

34 DEHP, Section 1.6, Autobiographical Letters, letter from D. E. Hughes to his sister Maggie dated May 27, 1892.

35 DEH I&D.

36 Op. cit.

37 The transition to the disc and rotating contactor may have been Hughes's contribution, as Phelps appeared to favor the scheme used in Hughes's original instrument, i.e. the rotating drum. The House instrument with which Phelps was more familiar also used a form of rotating drum, and when Phelps later completed his "combination instrument" he retained the rotating drum. The new synchronization mechanism may have been either Hughes's or Phelps's contribution, although novel mechanisms were more in Phelps's domain. While Hughes's instrument and other printing telegraphs continued to use the piano-style keyboard, the typewriter-style keyboard Hughes had initially used was to come back into vogue some years later, popularized by the typewriter in the 1880s and later by teletype instruments.

38 DEHP, Section 1.6, Autobiographical Letters, letter from D. E. Hughes to his sister Maggie dated May 27, 1892.

39 As David Hughes had by this point obtained a patent, it would have been more difficult for Phelps and the American Telegraph Company to obtain one based on his design.

40 DEHP, Section 1.6, Autobiographical Letters, letter to Maggie dated May 27, 1892.

41 $50,000 would be worth approximately $1,000,000 in today's dollars, and $12,500 would be worth approximately $263,000.

42 G. P. Oslin, *The Story of Telecommunications* (Macon, GA: Mercer University Press, 1992), p. 84.

43 A copy of the "Treaty of the Six Nations" can be found in Robert L. Thompson, *Wiring a Continent* (Princeton: Princeton University Press, 1947), Appendix 14. The five companies involved besides the American Telegraph Company were: The New York, Albany and Buffalo Electro-magnetic Telegraph Company; The Atlantic and Ohio Telegraph Company and the Pennsylvania Telegraph Company acting together; The Western Union Telegraph Company; The New Orleans and Ohio Telegraph Lessees; and The Illinois and Mississippi Telegraph Company and the Chicago and Mississippi Telegraph Company acting together.

44 Robert L. Thompson, *Wiring a Continent* (Princeton: Princeton University Press, 1947), p. 333.

45 Thompson, *Wiring a Continent*, p. 336.

46 DEHP, Section 1.6, Autobiographical Letters, letter to Maggie dated May 27, 1892.

47 Edwin G. Burrows and Mike Wallace, *Gotham: A History of New York City to 1898* (New York: Oxford University Press, 1999), p. 842.

48 *The Journal of Commerce*, January 19, 1858.

49 George B. Prescott, *History, Theory and Practice of the Electric Telegraph* (Boston: Ticknor and Fields, 1866), p. 142.

50 *The New York Daily Tribune*, Saturday, January 30, 1858. The article describes the operation and the function of the various components. It includes the Hughes electromagnet, the vertical vibrating steel rod for precision timing, the rotating contactor and horizontally mounted disc through which the letter key contacts protrude, the synchronizer, the printing mechanism and the weight drive mechanism. The story was also printed in the *New York Daily News* for January 19, 1858.

51 George G. Prescott, *History, Theory and Practice of the Electric Telegraph* (Boston: Ticknor and Fields, 1860), p. 143.

52 *Albany Express*, Tuesday, June 8, 1858.

53 DEHP, Section 1.2, Hughes's Business Papers, letter from A.A. Lovett, Secretary and General Superintendent of the American Telegraph Company to D.E. Hughes, dated May 23, 1859.

54 See James Reid, *The Telegraph in America* (New York: Polhemus, 1886), p. 853; and George G. Prescott, *History, Theory and Practice of the Telegraph* (Boston: Ticknor and Fields, 1860), pp. 151 and 154.

55 New York Public Library Manuscripts and Archives Division, Accession number 48 M 49, Box # 3 Business Papers Atlantic cable/Atlantic Telegraph Co. Correspondence 1858–1873, Items 1 and 2, letter from D.E. Hughes to C. Field November 22, 1858; and letter from D. Craig to C. Field, December 13, 1858.

CHAPTER 5

1 A visual semaphore telegraph had operated between Holyhead and Liverpool from the 1820s until approximately 1856 and consisted of eight line-of-sight semaphore stations. After 1856 the electric telegraph was used.

2 This was a point a couple of miles out in the River Mersey estuary. Ships would wait here for the pilot to board and for the high tide, or to be quarantined.

3 UK patent # 938, April 27, 1858. "Letters Patent to David Edward Hughes of New York, in the United States of America (but now residing in London), Telegraphic Engineer. For the invention of 'Improvements in the Means of and Apparatus for Transmitting Signals and Electric Currents'." This is the second of his English patents and references his earlier patent of September 11, 1855. The several patent drawings are full scale and highly detailed.

4 The Atlantic Telegraph Company, registered in London in October of 1856 and located at 22 Old Bond Street.

5 The gutta percha tree produces a sap which, when collected and exposed to the air to allow volatiles to evaporate, takes the form of malleable latex. When warmed to the temperature of hot water this latex becomes soft and moldable, and when cooled, hard but not brittle. It is an excellent electrical insulator and as such was used as a coating or sheath on the copper wire in undersea cables and the Atlantic telegraph cable. The tree grows in Southeastern Asia, and as Britain had a colony in Malaya, it had ready access to the substance. It should be noted that gutta percha latex is different from India rubber, another form of latex extracted from sap that had been discovered earlier.

6 The chairman of the Atlantic Telegraph Company was John Watkins Brett; vice chairman, Cyrus Field; chief engineer, Charles Tilston Bright; secretary, George Saward; and electrician, E.O.W. Whitehouse. The company had eighteen directors. John Watkins Brett had previously been head of the Magnetic Telegraph Company and had already laid cables under the English Channel (1851) and been the promoter of the Genoa-Corsica cable (1854) and of the Cape Breton-Newfoundland cable with C. Field (1855). Charles Tilston Bright, who was twenty-six at the time and who held five UK patents by 1858, was to obtain a total of eighteen UK patents during his lifetime. He had been chief engineer of the English and Irish Telegraph Company and had laid the first deep water submarine telegraph cable between England and Ireland; he had also been responsible for laying many underground telegraph cables. He was to be knighted by Queen Victoria after laying the first successful telegraph cable across the Atlantic in 1858, one of the youngest persons to receive this honor. William Thomson (later Lord Kelvin) at age thirty-four was professor of natural philosophy (i.e. physics) at Glasgow University (to which he had been appointed while only twenty-two); he was a brilliant and talented man who was not only able to develop theories to explain phenomena but was also at home with practical applications. Thomson was a director of the Atlantic Telegraph Company but not an employee; he acted a number of times as a consultant electrician but received no pay. He had determined how signals traveled through a cable and why they became retarded. He was the inventor of the mirror galvanometer and later the siphon recorder, an instrument used exclusively for receiving signals on long undersea

cables. Dr. Edward O.W. Whitehouse was a surgeon by profession who had taken up electrical experimentation. Mr. C.V. de Sauty, engineer, had played a major part in the laying of the Black Sea telegraph cable from Varna to Balaklava during the Crimean War. He also worked on the ill-fated Mediterranean cable between Marseilles and Algiers. He would go on to be the electrician for the 1866 Atlantic cable.

7   The company may have been aware by this time of a competing project to span the gap between America and Britain by an alternate route that to some seemed more practical. Another American, Col. Tal P. Shaffner was proposing a route from Newfoundland via Greenland, Iceland and the Faeroe Isles to Scotland. This proposal gained momentum in 1860, supported by the Magnetic Telegraph Company in America and Field's old rivals Amos Kendal and Francis Smith, associates of Samuel Morse.

8   The cable specifications were as follows. The core consisted of seven No. 22 BWG copper wires covered by three coatings of gutta percha insulation for a diameter of 3/8 in. It was manufactured by the Gutta-Percha Company of London. A protective outer sheathing of eighteen strands of iron wire was added over this core by two companies which were originally manufacturers of wire rope for coal mines: Glass Eliot & Co. of Greenwich and R.S. Newall & Co. of Birkenhead. There were also layers of hemp and tar involved in the construction. The final diameter of the cable was only 5/8 in. The weight was 2,000 lbs per nautical mile in air and 1,340 lbs per nautical mile in water. The cost of the cable was £225,000 (equivalent to $1,263,250 in the money of the period). To be sure that the cable was long enough to cover the full distance, including irregularities in the sea bed, the company manufactured 2,500 miles of cable. The cable, however, was not manufactured in one continuous piece, but in 1,200 pieces, each about two miles long, which were spliced together. See Bern Dibner, *Atlantic Cable* (New York: Blaisdell Publishing Co., 1959), pp. 20–25.

9   See E.O.W. Whitehouse, "Reply to the Statement of the Directors of the Atlantic Telegraph Company," London *Times*, September 22, 1858. In this article Whitehouse stated that Hughes had been given the report prepared by Samuel Morse and himself, who estimated that ten words a minute were feasible, and that based on this information Hughes modified his instrument to run much slower.

10 It had become apparent that submarine cables consisting of a central copper wire surrounded by an insulating layer of gutta percha surrounded by an outer protective layer of steel wires, when submerged in sea water, acted very differently than landlines (which were uninsulated and mounted high above the ground on poles). With submarine cables, the electrical signal that went into the cable was not what came out. For example, a voltage pulse such as a Morse code DOT or DASH slowed down and was delayed in its passage through the cable. This was referred to as the "retardation" of the cable. In addition, if a series of pulses was sent too rapidly, i.e. too close together, they seemed to pile up in the cable and the pulses coming out at the receiving end were smeared together and indistinguishable. The retardation was due to the high capacitance of these cables. Landlines, on the other hand, which also used the earth as a return, were carried high above the ground and exhibited very little capacitance, so telegraph signals appeared to travel instan-

taneously. Subterranean cables such as those used in the UK consisted of a copper core covered with a thick cotton webbing, often coated in tar. These were laid in iron pipes or wooden troughs in the ground. As they were surrounded by the ground (the return conductor) they exhibited a higher capacitance than telegraph wires strung on poles and thus exhibited some retardation, but not as much as submarine cables.

11 When the instrument was set at its normal speed of 120 revolutions per minute (rpm), an operator was able to send at a rate of thirty-five to forty words per minute. This was the maximum rate at which an operator could send, but it was always possible to send at a slower rate. When the instrument was running at 120 rpm, the duration of the pulses generated was 17.86 milliseconds. These were far too brief for operation with the submarine cable. When the instrument was slowed down, the commutator revolved more slowly, remaining on each contact for a longer period and thus increasing the duration of the pulses. Hughes's first adjustment to his instrument was to slow it down to a speed of 30 rpm. At this speed a maximum of around ten words per minute could be transmitted. This speed would have produced a pulse duration of around 72 milliseconds. However, these still proved too brief and he had to slow his instrument down even further by lowering the speed to 7.5 rpm, which gave a pulse duration of 286 milliseconds. At this speed a maximum of around two and a half words per minute could be transmitted.

12 British Patent # 1002, May 5, 1858, David Edward Hughes, Apparatus for Transmitting Signals and Electric Currents. The addition of a more sensitive galvanometer receiver was by far the most important component of this patent. As he already had the details when he filed the patent claim in early May, it can be assumed that he had conceived of the idea much earlier, possibly before he left America or while sailing across the Atlantic.

13 See appendix 2. Hughes's unique detector was to later become known as the "Hughes electromagnet" and was used by other inventors in their products.

14 The galvanometer was a very sensitive device based on H.C. Oersted's discovery of the deflection of a compass needle by current in a wire, and was first developed by André Marie Ampère in 1824, whose galvanometer used a compass needle surrounded by a coil of wire.

15 DEH I&D.

16 See Bruce J. Hunt, "Scientists, Engineers and Wildman Whitehouse: Measurement and Credibility in Early Cable Telegraphy," *British Journal for the History of Science* 29.2 (1966), pp. 155–169.

17 Whitehouse reported his results, and described his magneto-electrometer, at the British Association meetings in Glasgow in 1855 and in Cheltenham in 1856. See the reports in the volumes of the *Engineer* dated September 26, 1856 and January 23, 1857.

18 For these tests Whitehouse used a moving strip of paper on which a time base trace was printed. A trace was printed on this paper when a pulse was transmitted into the cable, and another trace recorded when it emerged. It was from these traces that he deduced the delay of the pulses sent through the cable.

19 Whitehouse used this instrument to measure the strength of electrical pulses sent over the telegraph wire. It consisted of an electromagnet with a soft iron

core that could attract a delicately balanced armature. The instrument resembled a larger version of an electromagnetic relay. However, unlike a relay, in which the armature was normally held open by a spring, Whitehouse's instrument used balance weights which resembled the balance bar on older platform weighing machines. By adding weights or sliding them along the bar he could measure the strength of the pull of the electromagnet which was proportional to the strength of the pulses.

20 It is possible that Whitehouse obtained some of his ideas from Henley's apparatus, which was a magneto-electric needle instrument and was used by the Magnetic Company and the Bright brothers. This was a device for transmitting telegraph signals which had the advantages of not needing batteries, and was claimed to have lower maintenance costs. The transmitting voltage was generated by a magneto-electric device. Whitehouse was familiar with Henley as he used Henley's company to manufacture his instruments. See T.P. Shaffner, *Telegraph Manual* (New York: Pudney & Russell, 1859), chapter 19.

21 On subterranean cables see note 10.

22 For the full contents see Bern Dibner, *Atlantic Cable* (New York: Blaisdell Publishing Co., 1959), pp. 20–21.

23 Morse had indicated that by using the Nautical Code or Cable Code (whereby dots are represented by one polarity and dashes by the reverse polarity of the battery), the transmission speed could be doubled.

24 Atlantic Telegraph Company prospectus issued in England on November 1, 1856, by Cyrus Field as vice president of the New York, Newfoundland and London Telegraph Company, titled The Atlantic Telegraph (Whitefriars: Bradbury and Evans, 1856). See Bill Burns's web site http://atlantic-cable.com/Books/1856Field/index.htm

25 This is Thomson's Square Law. The law states that an electrical signal such as a voltage pulse applied to the end of a long submarine cable becomes retarded as it travels down the cable and therefore takes time to reach the far end. This retardation is significant on long submarine cables and is caused by the resistance and capacitance exhibited by the cable. The capacitor is formed by the central copper conductor acting as one plate and the conductive sea water (the return path) acting as the other, with the gutta percha insulation forming the dielectric. Thus, if a voltage pulse is applied to one end of the cable it has to first charge up this distributed capacitor, and this retards the arrival of the voltage at the other end of the cable. The output from the cable rises gradually to a maximum and then gradually dies away. Thus pulses have to be of sufficient duration and amplitude to be able to contend with the cable capacitance. Pulses of too brief a duration are basically absorbed by the cable capacitance (which acts as a low pass filter). Thomson presented a paper on this subject to the Royal Society on May 3, 1855, titled "On the Theory of the Electric Telegraph," but he had done most of the work in 1854. The paper was published in the *Proceedings of the Royal Society of London* 7 (1854–1855), pp. 382–399.

26 While Whitehouse's instrument appeared to work on subterranean lines as well as submarine lines that were not submerged, Thomson was of the opinion that it would not have the sensitivity to work on the submerged 2,000-mile-long Atlantic cable. Thomson had actually written on his copy of one of Whitehouse's

papers that it was "The best account of what is good in Whitehouse's experiments and instruments. The conclusions however are fallacious in almost every point." At various times Thomson had remarked that Whitehouse's instruments' electromagnetic action was sluggish and had inertia that masked the results, and that the heavy electromagnetic relays introduced retardation of their own. See WT BIO, p. 332.

27 In December of 1856 Thomson wrote to Hermann von Helmholtz in Germany to inquire about his galvanometer and its technical specifications. See WT BIO, p. 335.

28 When Thomson connected his mirror galvanometer to the end of the cable it successfully detected the weak signals. Thomson patented the instrument in the spring of 1858. Thomson's original idea, which he subsequently abandoned, was to use a scale of thirteen graduations on the right hand side and thirteen graduations on the left hand side of the scale, with the left and right sides indicating the positive or negative polarity of the signal. Thus, the combination of the polarity and strength of the signal would indicate one of the twenty-six letters of the alphabet. In the end, however, he abandoned this approach in favor of a much simpler one. Thomson laid out his ideas on the use of the galvanometer in a presentation to the Royal Society in November 1856 which was published as "On Practical Methods for Rapid Signalling by the Electric Telegraph," *Proceedings of the Royal Society of London* 8 (1856–1857), pp. 299–303.

29 William Thomson, patent # 329, 1858, February 20. He patented the invention in his name and not the Atlantic Telegraph Company's. This was a shrewd move, as his instrument was to eventually play an important role in the success of the cable and was to bring him significant financial rewards.

30 In July of 1857, a 69-page pamphlet was published by the Atlantic Telegraph Company that discredited the galvanometer approach in favor of Whitehouse's approach; the title of the pamphlet is *The Atlantic Telegraph: A History of Preliminary Experimental Proceedings and a Descriptive Account of the Present State and Prospects of the Undertaking, Published by the Order of the Directors of the Company*. Bern Dibner in his book *The Atlantic Cable* (New York: Blaisdell Publishing Co., 1964), p. 177, identified the author as R.J. Mann, an associate of Whitehouse.

31 *The Family Herald*, May 26, 1858. As this story ran in a New York paper, the events described must have happened at least two weeks earlier, i.e. in early May, as news from London took approximately two weeks to reach New York by Atlantic steamer. A similar story ran in the *New York Herald*, September 1858; this appears to be a recap of a report that had run earlier that year. See DEH NPC.

32 Whitehouse admitted that he could have made a further improvement to his instruments that he claimed would have increased their speed by 70 or 80 percent, thus indicating that the instruments were not yet optimized or fully developed. See Whitehouse's "Reply to the Statement of the Directors of the Atlantic Telegraph Company," London *Times*, September, 22, 1858. It is also possible that Field was at least considering the idea of standardizing his network around Hughes's instrument. The instruments were being used by his American Telegraph Company in America and he may have considered expanding their use to cover his whole network, including in Britain.

33 See "A report by special correspondent for the Herald from Plymouth England May 3, 1858," *The Family Herald*, Wednesday, May 26, 1858, in DEH NPC.

34 Whitehouse was examined by members of the Board of Trade on Thursday, December 15, 1859; see the *Report of the Joint Committee Appointed by the Lords of the Privy Council for Trade and the Atlantic Telegraph Company to Inquire into the Construction of Submarine Telegraph Cables* (April, 1861), p. 69, item 1674. He was questioned about whether he had tested the cable after it was returned following the failed 1857 expedition. Whitehouse replied that he had suggested that the cable be stored under water. Large tanks were built for this purpose but when the cable was coiled into them and water poured in they leaked so badly that they could not retain the water. He stated that it was thus impossible to test the cable underwater. In a pamphlet that he issued in September of 1858 Whitehouse gave a brief history of his work on the Atlantic cable. One thing he said that he had been anxious to examine was the giant helix formed by the 2,150 miles of coiled up of cable: he was interested to see whether this configuration of the cable would influence (either by aiding or impeding) the transmission of signals on the cable. He reported that every electric pulse transmitted on the cable was preceded by a smaller wave of opposite polarity, inductively excited by the adjacent helical turns. It is assumed that when tests were conducted on the cable the various electricians connected their transmitting instruments to the central copper conductor at one end of the cable and their receiving instrument to the other end of the cable. As the cable was in storage and coiled up the two ends were probably only meters apart. For the return path they probably used a short connecting wire between the instruments and battery. That is, there was no electrical connection made to the outer steel protective wires that were wrapped around the copper and gutta percha insulation. The end result was that the coiled cable in dry storage exhibited different characteristics than a straight submerged cable. It had a much smaller capacitive component but a higher inductive component. Also, as no actual earth-ground path was included, they would not have experienced any effects from ground currents. Therefore tests on the stored cable did not give results that reflected conditions on the submerged cable, and probably gave overly optimistic results.

35 See "A Report by Special Correspondent for the Herald from Plymouth England May 3, 1858," *The Family Herald*, Wednesday May 28, 1858, in DEH NPC.

36 DEH I&D.

37 See Whitehouse's "Reply to the Statement of the Directors of the Atlantic Telegraph Company," London *Times*, September, 22, 1858.

38 It was reported in the *New York Herald* of September 1858 that Whitehouse was to receive a £10,000 ($50,000) salary upon the successful functioning of the cable with his instruments. Payment was to commence on the date the cable was laid and was of course contingent on perfect transmission of messages after it had been submerged. Before this he was to receive from the founding of the company to August 5 a yearly salary of £1000 ($5000).

39 WT BIO, p. 352, a letter from William Thomson to his brother James dated April 19, 1858.

40 DEH I&D.

41 Hughes would have had to change the frequency of his oscillating timing spring rod and/or change the gear ratios of his mechanism to run at two to three words per minute instead of the ten words per minute the instruments were set at. Presumably in the first trials he was able to slow the instrument down manually by adding some drag to the mechanism with his hand. Whitehouse also claimed that Hughes abandoned the letter printing function of his instrument and instead used a five-digit code to represent the letters, and also that he (Hughes) made use of his (Whitehouse's) induction coils. He further claimed that Hughes was unable to send any signals through the cable. There is no record in Hughes's notes of these changes or this failure. See Whitehouse's "Reply to the Statement of the Directors of the Atlantic Telegraph Company," London *Times*, September 22, 1858.

42 DEHP, Section 2.2, The Letters and Papers of David Edward Hughes, letter from Cyrus Field to David Hughes dated May 12, 1858, from the Atlantic Telegraph Office London. Hughes's reply, now in his private papers, is dated May 13, 1858. In his reply Hughes answered question 1 saying he had attained two and a half words per minute. In reply to question 2 he stated that as time was short he could not modify an instrument to increase its speed. To question 3 he answered three words per minute. He also stated that all experiments had stopped as all connections with the cable aboard the ship had now been broken.

43 The letter was published in the *New York Herald*. The letter was dated May 13, 1858 from H. Hyde to the Atlantic Telegraph Company.

44 DEH I&D.

45 Dr. Whitehouse had pleaded illness each time the ships were ready to sail, including in the 1857 expedition, leaving the unpaid Thomson to take his place.

46 WT BIO, p. 356.

47 Pamphlet published privately by W. Whitehouse in September 1858; it was titled *The Atlantic Telegraph: The Rise, Progress, and Development of its Electrical Department*.

48 The cable was at a depth of two miles (10,560 ft). At these depths the deep ocean water is at a temperature of 0 to 3 degrees Celsius (32 to 37.5 degrees Fahrenheit). The pressure at that depth is 320 atmospheres or 4,718.7 lb. per sq. in.

49 It appears there were a number of galvanometers used besides the oft-mentioned Thomson mirror galvanometer. A letter from Henry Moore published in the *Journal of the Society of Arts*, April 15, 1859, p. 342, states that all the signals sent from the *Agamemnon* to the *Niagara* and from Valentia to Newfoundland were received and indicated on one of his galvanometers. This was "a single needle made very delicate and exceedingly sensitive." Moore states that this was reported to him by Mr. Charles Victor de Sauty, chief electrical superintendent at Newfoundland. This galvanometer was subsequently presented to de Sauty by the Directors of the Atlantic Telegraph Company. In addition, there is a galvanometer manufactured by Henley in the London Science Museum with a plaque on its base plate stating that it is the galvanometer used at Valentia, Ireland to receive the first words transmitted over the Atlantic Cable in August of 1858. The galvanometer was presented to George Saward, Esq., secretary of the Atlantic Telegraph Company.

50 See Charles Bright, *The Story of the Atlantic Cable* (New York: D. Appleton and Co., 1903), p. 154. It was also reported that Whitehouse was using silver/zinc primary batteries, each of which had a total metal surface area of 36,000 sq. in. The induction coils were of separable helices of great length capable of creating a spark or flame of one inch length for one second. See the *New York Herald*, August 21, 1857.

51 See the transcripts of the various messages and the telegrapher's log which are reproduced in George G. Prescott, *History, Theory and Practice of the Electric Telegraph* (Boston: Ticknor and Fields, 1866), pp. 188–205.

52 Records in DEHP, Section 2.2, indicate that on August 25 or 26, Cyrus Field sent a telegraph message to Hughes and Hyde from New York via the Nova Scotia Electric Telegraph Company. The telegraph message was sent from New York to Halifax, Nova Scotia. As it was unlikely that it could have been sent over the transatlantic telegraph cable, it was probably sent aboard one of the Liverpool-bound steamers that called at Halifax.

53 Letter from Mr. S. E. Phillips, who was an assistant to Whitehouse, published in *The Mechanic's Magazine*, November 27, 1858, p. 508

54 When the cable failed, it had been in operation for about three weeks and 400 messages had been sent over it. However, a large majority of them were of no interest to the general public as they were technical messages passed between the electricians.

55 DEH NPC.

56 It is possible that the company viewed Thomson's mirror galvanometer more in the category of a testing device, which had been the usual function of galvanometers. Certainly in Field's dispatch it appeared that there was some skepticism regarding his instrument, for Field wrote that "his system was regarded by all practical telegraphers in England as perfectly childish." While an elegant instrument, its appearance, with its oil lamp flame and screen, could certainly be categorized as childish by less technical members of the company or its board. Also, Thomson had developed the instrument somewhat quickly in the preceding months, and mostly at his own expense. On the other hand, Hughes's instrument looked and operated as a telegraph instrument was expected to look and operate, and it had proved its performance, albeit on landlines. However, its performance on a submarine cable that was actually submerged was, at that stage, still unknown.

57 It is known that Hughes possessed one of Henley's galvanometers although it is not known when he acquired it. This instrument is now in the London Science Museum.

58 English Patent # 84, January 11, 1859. "An Improved Mode of Insulating Electrical Conducting Wires," David Edward Hughes of New York, now residing in Northampton Square, London. The title of the patent is rather vague, no doubt on purpose, to conceal the nature of Hughes's invention. There were a number of proprietary fluids that could provide the self-healing function. One of these was based on rosin dissolved in turpentine or turpentine and rosin soap. These compounds remained fluid until they came into contact with sea water, whereupon they solidified. Hughes carried out tests on samples that were subjected to the same pres-

sures that a cable would experience at a depth of 3,000 fathoms, and the test was run over a thirteen month period. Hughes also made a trial on a two-mile length of cable manufactured by the Gutta-Percha Company, London. It would be a hundred years before fluid filled cables and semi-fluid self-sealing applications came into use, mostly in the insulation of submarine and subterranean power cables. When silicon-based oils and other proprietary insulating oils were developed they were used in fluid-filled cables in subterranean applications, mainly for high voltage/power distribution in metropolitan areas, starting in the middle of the twentieth century. Fluid insulation has also been used to rejuvenate older subterranean and submerged power cables *in situ*. Self-sealing fluids are now best known for their use in sealing punctured tires.

59 The cable manufactured for the next attempts in 1865–66 had a cross section three times that of the 1858 cable, thicker gutta percha insulation and stronger protective outer steel wires, with a total diameter of 1.1 inches and a weight of 3,575 lbs per mile in air and 1,400 lbs per mile in water. The tensile strength was significantly increased from 6,500 lbs per square inch to 15,500 lbs per square inch. The copper core consisted of seven strands of 18 BWG copper wires.

60 For the interested reader here follow further details on the causes contributing to the failure of the cable: 1) In 1857 cable manufacturing techniques were in their embryonic stage, and this had a major effect on the design and quality of the cable. Further, the design was the result of a compromise between conflicting opinions, and the manufacturing had to be accomplished in the relatively short time of four months. Faraday, Morse and Whitehouse had recommended thin copper wire as they reasoned it took less current to "fill it up," whereas Thomson advocated a thicker copper core and insulation based on his research in devising his "square law." The thinner wire won out. Also, there was no consistency in the quality of the copper used, and so its purity and therefore its electrical resistance varied over a wide range (it is believed the average conductivity was as low as 50 percent). There also had to be some compromise with regard to the weight of the cable per mile. First, it was essential that when it was paid out it should not sink so rapidly as to overload the paying-out gear, nor should it sink so slowly that it became kinked. Second, the total tonnage of the cable had to be low enough that it could be transported in ships and laid at sea. 2) The cable had experienced degradation between the time it was manufactured and when it finally came to rest on the ocean floor. It had been exposed to the weather and sun, it had been wound and unwound into tanks and loaded on and off the ships, and it had suffered abuse and kinking during the storm in 1858. The exposure of the cable to the sun was a particularly important source of damage: this would have softened the insulation which resulted in the copper conductor becoming off-center and hence much closer to the outer layer of iron wires, increasing the chance of an electrical short or breakdown. 3) There seemed to be universal agreement that the high voltages used by Whitehouse were the final nail in the cable's coffin. Experiments showed that small defects in the insulation could be punched through by the high voltages used by Whitehouse. This would have allowed the conductive seawater to penetrate through to the copper core, thus causing a short circuit from the copper core to earth. As Charles Bright wrote in *The Story*

of the Atlantic Cable (New York: Appleton and Company New York, 1903), p. 158, it was as if "high pressure steam had been got up in a low pressure boiler."

61 DEHP, Section 1.6, Autobiographical Letters, letter Hughes wrote to his sister Maggie later in May of 1892.

62 The Atlantic Telegraph Company issued a statement as to why it had relieved Dr. Whitehouse of his duties, which was published in The Morning Chronicle, September 20, 1858; and the London Times, September 22, 1858. This article indicated that Whitehouse had failed in his duty and did not accompany the fleet as the electrician in charge; that his apparatus was faulty and that he had deceived the company by using Thomson's; that he had kept the Board in ignorance; and that he had refused assistance from other experienced submarine cable electricians. Whitehouse fought back, defending himself and his equipment in the press and repudiating the Atlantic Telegraph Company's accusations (see The Morning Chronicle of Tuesday, September 28). He also took a potshot at Hughes, saying he was not qualified to take charge of the electrical department. He went on to say that he doubted that Hughes's instrument had actually worked at Plymouth and that Hughes had depended on his relay and induction coils for actuating his instrument. And finally, he attacked the American press for being biased against him. The Atlantic Telegraph Company responded to all the accusations made by Whitehouse, pointing out that he had received compensation of £12,000, plus a salary, and that he had spent £20,000 on his electrical department, all to no avail. (His compensation of £12,000 was equivalent to $60,000, and the £20,000 to $100,000.)

CHAPTER 6

1 The author John Munro wrote about this incident in both *Heroes of the Telegraph* (London: J. Munro, 1891), p. 255; and *The Telegraphist*, August 2, 1886. Munro was the author of several other books including *The Wire and the Wave, Electricity and its Uses*, and *Pioneers of Electricity*. He was a friend of Hughes, and made a number of notes on Hughes's life and experiences which he wrote up in the form of a biographical sketch which is included among Hughes's private papers.

2 Hughes had written to Peter Cooper, president of the American Telegraph Company, to inquire how his telegraph instruments were performing, and we gather that he posed several questions. The reply was dated May 23, 1859, and the questions were answered by A.A. Lovell, the general superintendent. He stated that Hughes's instruments were used on the New York, Boston, Washington, Richmond, Albany, and Troy telegraph lines. There were thirty in use and they were being manufactured at the rate of four per month. Some of these were the "combination" model (this was a model developed by Phelps that used a combination of Hughes's, House's, and his own ideas). Some had been in use for two years. The cost of each instrument was estimated at $100.

3 The paper was published in the *Journal of the Society of Arts* 7 (April 15, 1859), pp. 334–340. The Royal Society of Arts had been established in 1754 to provide a forum for new ideas and debate in the areas of arts, manufacturing, and commerce. The paper was reprinted in the *Journal of the Franklin Institute* 68.1 (July, 1859), pp. 44–51 and 125–131.

4 See the journal *Engineer*, May 6, 1859. By implication the authors were the Electric & International Telegraph Company, which was the only company using both the double needle and Morse instruments in Britain. They used the needle telegraph in their domestic service and the dot-and-dash Morse type inker in their international service to Europe, so the mock title would make some sense to the telegraph insiders of the time. Our nineteenth-century ancestors were fond of their anonymity, which is frustrating when we seek to verify sources.

5 Clayton Mabee, *The American Leonardo: A Life of Samuel F. B. Morse* (New York: Alfred Knoff, 1943), pp. 214 ff. This later allowed Morse's system to be exploited and widely used without payment to the inventor.

6 See the *Report of the Joint Committee Appointed by the Lords of the Privy Council for Trade and the Atlantic Telegraph Company to Inquire into the Construction of Submarine Telegraph Cables* (April, 1861), p. 82.

7 These pages are in D. E. Hughes's notebook, London, British Library, Add. MS 40641.

8 If the speed of the instrument was the normal 120 rpm with 28 time slots, each letter delay was equal to 17.86 milliseconds. On the 462-mile cable Hughes was printing the letter "J," indicating a delay of 160.74 milliseconds.

9 The problem can be appreciated from the following example: if a battery is connected to one end of the cable with the other end open circuit, the cable would acquire a charge from the battery. If the battery were then removed after a period of time, it would be found that the cable had taken on the same polarity and voltage as the battery, and that it had in fact stored a certain amount of energy. This state would continue until the charge leaked away or the cable was grounded to discharge it. This charge had to be removed or neutralized in order to be able to send continuous signals down the cable. In these tests Hughes made use of carbon resistance tubes, a gold-leaf electrometer, a torsion balance, Daniell cells, Leyden jars and an influence machine (a static electricity generator). Curiously, he also carried out an experiment to determine whether a wire became longer when a current passed through it. This change would be miniscule, if it occurred, and he used an interesting method of measurement. He stretched a wire over two frets mounted on a sounding board and set it into vibration; the vibration was audible. He then passed various levels of current through the wire. If it changed length, then the tension would change, and the sound would consequently change pitch. Since Hughes had a remarkable gift for distinguishing pitches, he would be able to hear the difference. He was not able to prove that any change took place, though. These tests and devices would resurface many years later in experiments in his microphone research. Presumably the current was kept low enough so as to not heat the wire.

10 David Edward Hughes's notebook, London, British Library, Add. MS 40642, folio 15.

11 Hughes's notebook, British Library, Add. MS 40642, folio 25.

12 American passport #7381 issued in London on May 19, 1860 in DEHP. Hughes stated his age as twenty-nine when he was in fact thirty-one years of age, thus continuing the uncertainty about his exact age.

13 The French railways used a telegraph system different from the state-run system. This was called a "letter or

alphabetic telegraph" and it was a step-by-step instrument invented by Louis-Clément Bréguet. Gustave Froment had also devised a version of the alphabetical telegraph that used the same receiver device but a piano-type keyboard for inputting the letters to transmit. See Dr. D. Lardner, *The Electric Telegraph* (London: Walton and Maberly, 1855), chapters 8 and 9.

14 When the Hughes telegraph, which required only one wire, was adopted, it freed up the second wire for additional capacity.

15 Hughes's notebook, Add. MS 40645, folio 90, gives an example of a printout from the telegraph instrument of a message transmitted on July 4, 1862, from Lyons to Paris, a distance of 500 km.

16 Karl Eduard Zetsche, *Die Copirtelegraphen, die Typendrucktelegraphen und die Doppeltelegraphie* (Leipzig: B. G. Teubner, 1865), p. 61. This was also reported in the Welsh newspaper *Baner ac Amserau Cymru*, September 13 and 20, 1865, in an interview with David Hughes's father. At the time, one French franc was worth 10 English old pence.

17 Paul-Gustave Froment (1815–1865) was an instrument maker, telegraph inventor, and builder who worked for a number of telegraph engineers. He also assisted Caselli with his pantelegraph, a device for transmitting drawings, ideograms or facsimiles. The Emperor Napoleon III was interested in mechanisms and inventions and visited Froment's workshop occasionally. According to Hughes, Napoleon had become quite interested in his telegraph and inspected it a number of times.

18 T. P. Shaffner, *The Telegraph Manual* (New York: Pudney and Russel, 1859), chapter 28.

19 Théodose du Moncel, *Exposé des applications de l'électricité* (Paris: L. Hachette, 1872–1878), vol. 3. Also see Hughes's notebook, British Library, Add. MS 40642, folio 75, where he states he sent 332 messages in 6.5 hours on the Marseilles to Paris line.

20 Hughes received this honor on June 24, 1864.

21 Napoleon had a pact with Cavour to assist in liberating some of the northern provinces of the country (Lombardy and Venetia) from Austria to further Italy's desire for the unification of its many states. In return, France was to gain Nice and Savoy, which would help it strengthen its influence in the Mediterranean.

22 Reported in the Welsh newspaper *Baner ac Amserau Cymru*, September 13 and 20, 1865, in an interview with David Hughes's father.

23 See Steven Roberts's website "Distant Writing" at **www.distantwriting.co.uk.**

24 This was in the form of 2,400 shares valued at £5 each.

25 Karl Eduard Zetsche, *Die Copirtelegraphen, die Typendrucktelegraphen und die Doppeltelegraphie* (Leipzig: B. G. Teubner, 1865), p. 61.

26 Samuel Morse's instrument had been copied and was widely used on the continent as Morse had no patent protection—and hence no profits. However, possibly feeling some guilt over this situation, the European countries (except Britain) paid Morse Fr. 400,000 of compensation in 1858.

27 Hughes's private papers, letter from Mrs. Charles P. Smith to Museum of Fine Arts Boston, March 1, 1936.

28 Using one of the telegraph instruments as a baseline, he methodically varied many of the mechanical and electromagnetic components, changing various parameters such as the number of turns of wire and its diameter on the electromagnets, the geometry of the magnetic pole piece, and the number of battery cells. He also received advice and recommendations from his customers, especially concerning the vibrating spring (or blade as it was sometimes called), which had a tendency to break. It seems that the Italian telegraph engineers had recommended an improvement: see Hughes's private papers, letter to Hughes from the German telegraph administration dated August 2, 1869.

29 Hughes and Froment had been pondering how to add numerals to the instrument within the basic twenty-eight time periods, and Hughes had sketched out ideas in his notebook. The technique they settled on was not to use two separate print wheels as they had first thought, but to maintain the single print wheel and instead of having twenty-six alphabetical characters—note there were actually twenty-eight places on the type wheel: twenty-six letters plus a stop (dot character) plus a blank position—they would increase the number of characters to fifty-six. The sequence on the type wheel would be A, 1, B, 2, C, 3, D, 4, etc. To shift from letters to numerals the print wheel would be advanced 1/56 of a turn. This change was triggered by using the keys called the "letter" blank and "number" blank which were added to the keyboard. For example, to transmit the message "send 15 items" the following sequence of keys would be pressed: S, E, N, D, (NUMBER KEY), 1, 5, (LETTER KEY), I, T, E, M, S.

30 The first entry that appears to be associated with a new timing mechanism appears in 1863 in Hughes's notebook British Library Add. MS 40642, folio 63. Further entries are to be found in Add. MS 40643, folios 23, 32, and 34; Add. MS 40646, folios 10, 18, 26, and 27; and Add. MS 40645, folios 43 and 44. The new timing mechanism consisted of a horizontal rod clamped at one end. The other end was connected to a short crank mounted to a small flywheel. As this flywheel rotated the rod prescribed a circular motion. On the rod was mounted a weight in the form of a ball that swung out due to centrifugal action and the diameter of the circle prescribed was related to the speed of rotation. As the speed increased, the diameter prescribed by the crank would increase, which activated a friction brake, thus slowing the speed of rotation. Thus, by this feedback mechanism the speed of rotation was kept constant. The location of the ball on the rod could be adjusted to set the required speed. Hughes had tried this version and found that the rod had a tendency to break at the clamped end. This was solved by incorporating a spring of several loops in line with the rod to isolate the rotating portion from the clamped end.

31 British Patent # 241, January 27, 1863, "Telegraph Apparatus, Improvements in Means or Apparatus for Effective Telegraph Communications." This model is fully described in G. Miriel, *Télégraphe Hughes, album de 22 planches in-quarto, contenant 79 figures* (Brest: Impr. de J.-P. Gadreau, 1873). This book was written by a member of the French Telegraph Administration between 1866 and 1869, and its publication was delayed by the Franco-Prussian war of 1870. The book has marvelous detailed drawings of Hughes's telegraph down to the component level.

32 DEHP, Section 1.2, Hughes's Business Papers, letter from the American Telegraph Company in reply to Hughes's enquiry of December 29, 1863.

33 S. P. Thompson, *The Electromagnet* (London and New York: E. & F. N. Spon, 1891), p. 69; and *The Telegraphic Journal*, December 24, 1864, p. 302.

34 Letter from Government of India to D. E. Hughes, September, 4 1863 in the Hughes private family papers. Also see "Remunerative Speed on Submarine Cables," *Telegraphic Journal* 1.14 (April 12, 1864), p. 157; and "Mr. Sabin on Telegraphy" in *Reports on the Paris Universal Exhibition, 1867* (London: Printed by George E. Eyre and William Spottiswoode for H.M.S.O., 1868), pp. 548–549.

35 Gen. Guerhardt was involved with the existing telegraph system and long distance lines and their interface with other countries. It is assumed that he had dealt with the electrical instrument supply company Siemens and Halske, which had a subsidiary in St. Petersburg and whose main operation was in Berlin. His contact with General Guerhardt would be important to Hughes later on.

36 Hughes's notebook, Add. MS 40643, folio 62, entry dated April 12, 1865.

37 Hughes's notebook, Add. MS 40643, folios 69 and 73, includes sketches of part of the mechanism.

38 Hughes's notebook, Add. MS 40645, folio 90, gives an example of the Russian character set as printed out by the telegraph instrument.

39 Note that in Hughes's notebook, all of the measurements are given in Verst units. This is a measurement of linear length used in Imperial Russia at the time; one verst was equal to 3,500 ft.

40 Hughes's notebook, Add. MS 40643, folio 82.

41 Op. cit., folio 83.

42 Op. cit., folio 85.

43 Gustave Froment's workshop continued in opeation after his death under the name Dumoulin-Froment, though in Hughes's notes he always referred to it as Froment's workshop.

44 Siemens and Halske's main base was in Berlin, Prussia, with a division in St. Petersburg, Russia. The company was founded in 1847 as "Telegraphen-Bau-Anstalt Siemens und Halske" by the engineers Werner Siemens and Johann G. Halske in Berlin. By 1870 they had 1,000 employees.

45 DEHP, Section 1.2, Hughes's Business Papers, Siemens and Halske's contract with David Edward Hughes, signed in St. Petersburg, November 10, 1865. The contract only allowed them to make changes or modifications to the instrument that had been authorized by Hughes.

46 The lecture Hughes gave is detailed in Hughes's notebook, Add. MS 40644, folios 2–6. He demonstrated some thirty experiments and covered the history of electricity, influence machines, Leyden jars, electrometers, the first telegraph based on static electricity, the discovery of galvanism, Volta's battery, Oersted's discovery of electrical influence on a magnet, electromagnetism, Schilling's (Russian) telegraph experiments, Wheatstone's telegraph, Morse's telegraph, the invention of the relay, Hughes's telegraph, the challenges of telegraph operation, the earth as a conductor, the uses of electricity, the electric motor, Ruhmkorff's induction coil, Geissler tubes, ignition of magnesium, and the explosion of gases by electricity. In later reminiscences, Hughes also indicated that

47 Hughes's notebook, Add. MS 40643, folio 75.

48 Op. cit., folio 58.

49 Op. cit., folio 58. Hughes was listing his address as 85, Rue Notre Dame des Champs, Paris, at this time.

50 Hughes's private papers, letter of introduction from General Guerhardt, Director General of the Russian Telegraph Administration, to Colonel de Chauvin, Director of the Prussian Telegraph Administration, December ,1865.

51 Hughes's notebook, Add. MS 40644, folio 24.

52 Op. cit., folio 25.

53 Op. cit., folio 28. The entry is dated June 16, 1866. He reported that the two new instruments, when they arrived, were badly made and that he had to make several alterations. It seems that after Froment's passing the new owner was either not fully trained or was less meticulous than Froment.

54 Prussia also made use of a new type of breech-loading gun called the needle gun which provided them with a significant advantage over their enemies. Hughes must have been intrigued by the mechanism and operation as he made several sketches of it in his notebook Add. MS 40644, folio 39.

55 Major General Weber in London related many years later that he had been present in Berlin when Hughes received his payment from General von Chauvin, the Director of Telegraphs, and Hughes did, in fact, have all of the cash in a bag. It is not specified what the denominations of the coins were, but it would have been interesting to see how Hughes managed the sheer weight and security of his treasure.

56 DEHP, Section 1.2, Hughes's Business Papers, letter from George Saward of the Atlantic Telegraph Company, dated December 22, 1865. The success of the 1866 cable was followed by the laying of a French cable from Brest to the Island of St. Pierre off the coast of Newfoundland in 1869. Hughes had received an enquiry in June of 1867 from the French Telegraph Administration seeking information on the British-American transatlantic cable and the instruments used for sending and receiving the messages on it. The French transatlantic cable increased communications traffic into and out of France as well as acting as a funnel for other continental countries wishing to communicate with America. The use of Hughes's instrument on the in-country trunk lines and international lines helped to process the dispatches rapidly.

57 Dr. D. Lardner, *The Electric Telegraph* (London: Walter and Maberly, 1855), chapters 9 and 10.

58 Hughes's notebook, Add. MS 40645, folio 5.

59 This resembled the early facsimile machines (fax) of the 1960s and 70s. The image was electrically conductive and its background non-conductive, or vice versa. The receiver used a sheet of chemically treated paper to reproduce the image (providing the receiver was in synchronism and phase with the transmitter). The paper was electrically conductive and when an electrical current was passed through, it would change color, typically to blue or brown.

60 Bernhard Meyers made experiments with his model of an autographic telegraph a few years later in 1869 but seems also to have given up on the idea.

61 This occurred on May 27, 1867.

62 Hughes's notebook, Add. MS 40645, folios 34, 35, and 36.

63 Cyrus Field of the Atlantic Telegraph Company was one of the other recipients of the award.

64 Hughes indicates that he was using a Siemens relay on this route.

65 Hughes's notebook, Add. MS 40646, folios 31, 32, and 33.

66 Op. cit., folio 39.

67 Hughes's private papers contain documentation of many of the honors bestowed on him.

68 The English census of 1871 lists Hughes's wife as Maria N. Hughes, age 38. Very little is known of her and it is assumed that he had met and married her at some point on the Continent. He makes a reference to her in later correspondence, putting off some friends' visit to his house due to his wife being an invalid.

69 DEHP, Section 1.2, Hughes's Business Papers, letter issued by United Kingdom Telegraph Company Limited, July 3, 1868.

70 See *Telegraphs: Report by Mr. Scudamore on the Re-Organization of the Telegraph System of the United Kingdom, Presented to the House of Commons by Command of Her Majesty* (London: Printed by George Edward Eyre and William Spottiswoode for H.M.S.O., 1871). It also appeared that because of the war quite a few of the instruments which had been intended for use in Britain were tied up at the manufacturers in France and Germany.

71 Hughes's notebook, Add. MS 40646, folios 56, 57, and 58.

72 DEHP, Section 1.2, Hughes's Business Papers, contract between Hughes and the Submarine Telegraph Company. According to the contract, Hughes was to provide instruction to the operators of the instruments in the transmission of messages and in the adjustment, maintenance, and repair of the instruments. Hughes required the instruments to have a name plate on them which read "Telegraph Hughes, Submarine Telegraph Company." Hughes had also requested a license for the use of his instrument with the Submarine Telegraph Company (letter from the Post Office, July 19, 1871). The Post Office reminded Hughes that as they had acquired the United Kingdom Electric Telegraph Company they had inherited the patent rights to his telegraph and therefore if he sent them £200 they would grant him a license!

73 *The Telegraphist*, August 2, 1886, p. 115.

74 The Scottish papers, however, had been using the Hughes telegraph for their London feeds on the United Kingdom Electric Telegraph Company circuits for some time.

75 *The Electrician*, October 23, 1891, p. 691.

76 G. Miriel, *Télégraphe Hughes*, p. 5, indicated that in 1871, Peru and Buenos Aires, Argentina had Hughes telegraph instruments. Victor Berthold, *A History of the Telephone and Telegraph in Brazil 1851–1921* (New York: n.p., 1922), p. 22, indicated that Brazil also had Hughes telegraph instruments. It is possible that once Spain and Portugal had installed Hughes instruments, they were then introduced in Argentina and Brazil. Hughes, however, had received enquiries from the Brazilian legation in Paris in 1866 discussing terms; these letters are preserved among Hughes's private papers.

77 Eric Hausman, *Telegraph Engineering* (New York: Van Nostrad, 1915), p. 133.

78 Fons Vanden Berghen, *Classics of Communication* (Brussels: Telindus, 1999), with information extracted from the archives of the Postal, Telegraph and Telephone Service.

79 The German physicist Augustus Rape, an employee of Siemens and Halske, was responsible for a number of improvements to the Hughes instrument towards the end of the 1800s. See Anton A. Huurdeman, *The Worldwide History of Telecommunications* (Hoboken, NJ: John Wiley and Sons, 2003), p. 104.

80 Hughes was aware of a system being developed by Baudot in the mid-1870s as it was made in the same workshop of Dumoulin-Froment that made his instruments. Baudot had joined the French Telegraph Service in 1870 and became familiar with Hughes's instrument as well as with the multiplex system of Meyer. From these, he conceived a new instrument based on using a five unit code (from Gauss and Weber). Baudot had the usual problems with obtaining funding and acceptance. However, he was successful in patenting it and bringing the instrument into service in the late 1880s. From then on it was progressively adopted, becoming one of the dominant printing telegraphs by the 1900s. See E. Montoriol, "Baudot et son oeuvre," *Annales des Postes, Telegraphes, et Telephones* 5.4 (December, 1916), pp. 367–403. An English translation by Eric Fisher titled "Baudot and his Works" is available at www.transbay.net/~enf/baudot/son-oeuvre.html.

81 Passport application of July 21, 1888, at United States of America Legation in London states that Hughes had last left America on October 14, 1876. Also, a reference is made to Hughes's visit in a legal brief filed by David S. Barriger on July 26, 1905, challenging Hughes's will. Hughes's notebooks also have a gap in their entries during 1876.

CHAPTER 7

1 Paul Israel, *Edison: A Life of Invention* (New York: John Wiley, 1998), pp. 156–160.

2 Edison had spent several of his early years as a telegraph operator.

3 Thomson was knighted in 1866 for his contribution to the success of the transatlantic telegraph cable, and was later ennobled, assuming the title of Lord Kelvin.

4 The press had given Edison many nicknames such as "The Wizard of Menlo Park" for his inventiveness.

5 DEHP, Section 1.4, letter from Preece to Hughes dated June 5, 1878.

6 *New York Daily Tribune*, June 8, 1878. A copy is in the Thomas Edison Papers.

7 *New York Herald*, June 4, 1878.

8 IET, letter from Hughes to Preece dated the evening of June 5, 1878.

9 IET, letter from Hughes to Preece dated June 29, 1878.

10 EP, letter from Adams to Batchelor dated July 6, 1878.

11 The newspaper industry had exploded with the advent of the telegraph and its ability to quickly disseminate the news. The introduction of the steam engine powered rotary printing press enabled the mass production

of newspapers, which could then be widely distributed by rail.

12 After A. G. Bell launched the telephone industry it attracted many other inventors and also brought to light other experimenters such as P. Reis, T. A. Edison, E. Gray, A. Dolbear, F. Blake, and E. Berliner, to name just a few. However, this chapter will confine itself to discussing scientists with whom Hughes interacted

13 Catherine Mackenzie, *Alexander Graham Bell* (New York: Grosset and Dunlap, 1928), p. 200, quoting from William Preece's address to the Royal Institution in February, 1878.

14 The fact that these telephone models failed to work turned out to be significant when later there was a patent dispute.

15 Ronald W. Clark, *Edison: The Man Who Made the Future* (New York: Putnam, 1977), pp. 60 and 70.

16 Ronald W. Clark, *Edison: The Man Who Made the Future* (New York: Putnam, 1977), pp. 60 and 70.

17 Francis Jehl, *Menlo Park Reminiscences* (Dearborn, MI: Edison Institute, 1937), vol. 1, p. 105. Jehl was a laboratory assistant to Thomas A. Edison.

18 Sir William Thomson had noted in 1876 that in America there was a more aggressive drive to patent inventions. He criticized the British patent system and predicted with some foresight that unless the British system was reformed, America would speedily become the nursery of useful inventions for the world.

19 In the nineteenth century the scientific community was much broader than it is today, and included many people who were not professional scientists. Among these we may number Hughes and William Preece, who had earned their acceptance through their practical knowledge and accomplishments rather than through academic achievements.

20 David Edward Hughes's notebook, British Library Add. MS 40648A, folio 80.

21 See the *Report of the 47th Meeting of the British Association*, which was held at Plymouth in August, 1877. Preece's presentation was also published in *Nature* (September 6, 1877), a journal which was widely read by the scientific community. At this time Hughes was in the process of moving from Paris to London, so he may not have seen the paper in *Nature*. He makes no mention of Preece's paper in his notebook.

22 Catherine Mackenzie, *Alexander Graham Bell* (New York: Grosset and Dunlap, 1928), p. 186, indicated that although William Thomson had taken a pair of Bell telephones back from America after the Philadelphia exhibition, they were damaged in transit, and his attempt to demonstrate them in Britain failed.

23 At this time, iron telegraph wires were used for telephone transmissions, which led to many of the problems with early telephones, such as interference and noisy operation. The use of a ground return only added to the difficulties, especially in city areas, where there was a great deal of ground current activity. There was also a big difference in the frequency ranges of telegraph and telephone signals. Telegraph signals required a very low frequency response (quasi DC). Speech, on the other hand, required a frequency response of up to a thousand cycles per second, and later, up to three thousand, a fact that was poorly understood at the time. The later introduction of copper wire, separate wire pairs, and twisted pairs

significantly improved the telephone's range and audibility.

24 It is interesting to note how David Edward Hughes played a hidden role in the development of Bell's telephone: see Thomas Watson, *Exploring Life: The Autobiography of Thomas A. Watson* (New York: D. Appleton and Co., 1926), pp. 100–101, and also Appendix 2 here.

25 Thomas Watson, *Exploring Life: The Autobiography of Thomas A. Watson* (New York: D. Appleton and Co., 1926). Watson indicated (p. 134) that by November of 1877 Bell had 3,000 telephones under lease.

26 Bell's telephone operated by converting acoustic energy at the speaking end into electrical energy, transmitting this along the wires, and then converting the electrical energy back into acoustic energy at the listening end. The loss from this conversion from the speaking end to the hearing end was approximately 40db.

27 Both Bell and Edison had started by reviewing Reis's experiments and apparatus in their work on the telephone.

28 Hughes was in Russia in 1865 to fulfill a contract to install his printing telegraph, and while there he was asked to give a lecture on electricity and the telegraph by the Emperor Alexander II. He gave the lecture to his Majesty, the Empress, and their court at Czarskoizelo Palace.

29 D.E. Hughes, "The Early History of Telephony," *Electrical Engineer* 15 (March 22, 1895), p. 334. Significant debate has occurred over the years as to whether Reis's apparatus could actually transmit speech. It is doubtful that it could have done so with Reis's magnetostriction receiver. However, a carefully adjusted Reis transmitter connected to an electromagnetic receiver has been shown to transmit intelligible speech: see Basilio Cantania, "The 'Telephon' of Philipp Reis," *Antenna: Newsletter of the Mercurians* 17.1 (October, 2004), pp. 3–8.

30 David Edward Hughes's notebook, British Library Add. MS 40648A, folio 80.

31 Hughes had carried out similar tests in 1860; see chapter 6, note 9.

32 See Hughes's opening statement in D. E. Hughes, "On the Action of Sonorous Vibrations in Varying the Force of an Electric Current," *Proceedings of the Royal Society of London* 27 (1878), pp. 362–369.

33 These were obtained from a Mr. Lax according to Hughes's notes.

34 D. E. Hughes, "On the Action of Sonorous Vibrations in Varying the Force of an Electric Current," *Proceedings of the Royal Society of London* 27 (1878), pp. 362–369.

35 In fact Hughes was probably hearing mechanical disturbances, but the noises proved to be a stepping stone towards his goal of an acoustic detector.

36 D. E. Hughes, "On the Action of Sonorous Vibrations in Varying the Force of an Electric Current," *Proceedings of the Royal Society of London* 27 (1878), pp. 362–369. Hughes described making a telephone receiver in his paper to the Royal Society as follows: "I made a rough-and-ready telephone with a small bar magnet four inches long, half the coil of an ordinary electromagnet and a square piece of ferro type iron, three inches square and clamped rigidly in front of one pole of the magnet between two pieces of board." Hughes would

have had no trouble with the construction as Bell and Watson had used his quick-acting electromagnet as inspiration in the development of their telephone: see note 24.

37 Sealing wax usually came in the form of a hard red stick that could be melted by holding it in a candle flame. It then could be dribbled or applied to paper or parchment and imprinted with a seal, which is how it is best known. However, its ability to harden and stick to paper, wood, or wire made it a very useful glue. Its basic constituents were shellac, turpentine, resin, chalk, and coloring.

38 Hughes described his experimental arrangement in his paper to the Royal Society "On the Action of Sonorous Vibrations in Varying the Force of an Electric Current," published in the *Proceedings of the Royal Society of London* 27 (1878), pp. 362–369. He made his own Daniell cells based on the Minotto form, placing a spiral piece of copper wire at the bottom of a glass tumbler and covered the wire with copper sulfate. The glass was then filled with well moistened clay and water. A piece of zinc was placed on the top of the clay which was the positive terminal. Each cell yielded approx. 1.1 volt, giving 3.3 volts in total from the three cells.

39 Many of the experiments he carried out are easier to follow in his accounts in the technical journals, such as "The Hughes Telephone" in *Engineering*, May 10, 1878, pp. 369–371. Glass tubes packed with various mixtures of metallic filings, with metallic plugs sealing the ends, would become important during the wireless period: they were used as wireless detectors and became known as "coherers."

40 Henry Hunnings later expanded on Hughes's experiments by using carbon granules in the construction of a microphone.

41 *Engineering*, May 10, 1878, p. 370

42 David Edward Hughes's notebook, British Library, Add. MS 40648A, folio 84.

43 D. E. Hughes, "On the Action of Sonorous Vibrations in Varying the Force of an Electric Current," *Proceedings of the Royal Society of London* 27 (1878), pp. 362–369. Also see his paper "On the Physical Action of the Microphone," read before the Physical Society on June 8, 1878, and published in the *Philosophical Magazine*, Series 5, 6.34 (1878), pp. 44–50.

44 There was more to the explanation, as Hughes went into the effects of the molecules neutralizing each other, the effect of vertical and horizontal components, and the role played by the segmentation of a solid used as the contact.

45 David Edward Hughes's notebook, British Library, Add. MS 40648A, folios 85 and 86, dated March 6.

46 Preece had made a presentation on Edison's "phonograph" and Hughes sent a letter to him dated April 8, 1878, which is preserved in IET.

47 IET, letter from Hughes to Preece dated April 8, 1878.

48 David Edward Hughes's notebook, British Library, Add. MS 40648A, folio 87.

49 IET, letter from Hughes to Preece dated April 18, 1878.

50 Op. cit.

51 William Preece, "The Microphone," a lecture given to the Society of Telegraph Engineers on May 23, 1878; see *Nature* 18 (May 30, 1878), p. 129.

52 Hughes first called his discovery a microphone in a letter he sent to Preece on April 30. Wheatstone first used the word microphone to describe a stethoscope in 1827: see *Nature* 18 (August 1, 1878), p. 356.

53 The article in the *Times* cites the journal *Nature*; this is believed to be a reference to the short notice which was to appear in vol. 18 of that journal, in the number for May 2, 1878, on p. 20. A follow-up article appeared in the May 16 issue of *Nature*, on pp. 57–58.

54 DEHP Section 1.4, letter from Preece to Hughes dated April 30, 1878.

55 IET, letter from Hughes to Preece dated May 3, 1878.

56 See *Proceedings of the Royal Society of London* 27 (1878), pp. 362–369. Huxley stated that Hughes and his microphone were his (Huxley's) greatest discovery.

57 This explanation was contained in a subsequent paper Prof. D.E. Hughes read to the Physical Society on June 8, 1878, titled "On the Physical Action of the Microphone," which was published in the *Philosophical Magazine*, Series 5, 6.34 (1878), pp. 44–50.

58 DEHP, Section 1.4, letter from A.G. Bell to D.E. Hughes dated May 11, 1878. Bell gave his residence as 57 West Cromwell Road.

59 DEHP, Section 1.4, letter from A.G. Bell to D.E. Hughes dated May 14, 1878.

60 DEHP, Section 1.4, letter from Preece to Hughes dated May 15, 1878. Unfortunately there is no record of the letter Hughes must have sent to Preece that prompted this reply. We can only speculate that Hughes was worried that Preece might include Bell and Edison in the presentation of what Hughes considered his discovery.

61 EP, letter from Edison to Preece dated May 19, 1878; published in *The Papers of Thomas A. Edison*, ed. Reese V. Jenkins et al. (Baltimore: Johns Hopkins University Press, 1989–), vol. 4, p. 287.

62 D. E. Hughes, "On the Physical Action of the Microphone," a paper read before the Physical Society on June 8, 1878 and published in the *Philosophical Magazine*, Series 5, 6.34 (1878), pp. 44–50.

63 Edwin J. Houston and Elihu Thomson, "The Microphone Relay," *The Telegraphic Journal* 7 (August 15, 1878), pp. 343–346. This type of device, also called a sound intensifier, continued to be used into the 1920s, where it found a use as an amplifier for the early crystal sets. Beginning in 1905 a device called a "Shreeve repeater," which was based on the same principle employed by Houston and Thomson, was used on telephone lines by the Bell Company until the vacuum tube supplanted it. Edison had also invented a device called a pressure relay for translating a signal of variable strength from one circuit to another.

64 H.C. Fischer was the controller of the Central Telegraph Office in St. Martin's-le-Grand. The Post Office had a monopoly on the telegraph in England following the passage of the 1863 Telegraph Act. Two further related acts were passed in 1868 and 1869.

65 E.C. Baker, *Sir William Preece, F.R.S.: Victorian Engineer Extraordinary* (London: Hutchinson, 1976), p. 153.

66 Quadruplex telegraph was a means for sending four messages simultaneously on the same wires.

67 E.C. Baker, *Sir William Preece, F.R.S.* (London: Hutchinson, 1976), p. 157. William Orton was the president of Western Union who had been offered Bell's patents for $100,000 but turned down the offer.

68 Op. cit., p. 162.

69 Edison's telephone receiver was still under development at this time. While he had settled on plumbago as the active element, they were still struggling with improving the fidelity of the speech reproduction.

70 Paul Israel, *Edison: A Life of Invention* (New York: John Wiley, 1998), pp. 158–159.

71 See the *Report of the 47th Meeting of the British Association*, which was held at Plymouth in August, 1877.

72 Edison was granted British patent # 2909 in July, 1877, for "Controlling by Sound the Transmission of Electrical Currents and the Reproduction of Corresponding Sounds at a Distance."

73 EP, letter from Edison to Preece dated September 3, 1877.

74 EP, letter from Preece to Edison dated September 28, 1877. Edison was using a version of Bell's receiver. Hence Preece was only interested in obtaining Edison's transmitter if it had the potential to perform better than Bell's.

75 EP, letter from Preece to Edison dated October 3, 1877.

76 EP, letter from Edison to Preece dated November 25, 1877.

77 EP, letter from Preece to Edison dated December 24, 1877.

78 Paul Israel, *Edison: A Life of Invention* (New York: John Wiley, 1998), p. 154.

79 EP, letter from Edison to Preece dated February 11, 1878; published in *The Papers of Thomas A. Edison*, ed. Reese V. Jenkins et al. (Baltimore: Johns Hopkins University Press, 1989–), vol. 4, p. 77.

80 In April, Preece and Theodore Puskas, Edison's representative, exhibited the phonograph to the Society of Telegraph Engineers.

81 Telephones were being tested on existing telegraph lines, and it was quickly determined that while the lines were fine for the on/off signals used by the telegraph, they were far from ideal for transmitting speech. When speech is transformed into an electrical signal it is modulated in both its amplitude and frequency, that is, a voltage whose level and frequency change in accordance with the sounds of the words spoken. Further, telegraph circuits used only one wire, employing the earth as a return path, and this contributed noise into the telephone circuit. There was also a difference between American and British telegraph installations. American wires were carried on poles above the ground, whereas British wires in suburban areas were subterranean, which gave them different characteristics, though the long intercity lines were usually above ground and pole mounted. At the time, the theory of transmitting speech on wires was not well understood, and solutions were derived through experimentation.

82 EP; the reference to Preece as Edison's agent appears in the letter from Edison to Preece dated February 19, 1878. The telegram from Edison to Preece is dated March 15, 1878.

83 EP, letter from Edison to Preece dated March 18, 1878; published in *The Papers of Thomas A. Edison*, ed. Reese V. Jenkins et al. (Baltimore: Johns Hopkins University Press, 1989–), vol. 4, p. 182.

84 Paul Israel, *Edison: A Life of Invention* (New York: John Wiley, 1998), pp. 139–140.

85 EP, correspondence from Henry Bently to Edison, March–April 1878, and letter from H. Johnson to Uriah Painter dated March 15, 1878.

86 EP, letter from Edison to Preece dated May 5, 1878; published in *The Papers of Thomas A. Edison*, ed. Reese V. Jenkins et al. (Baltimore: Johns Hopkins University Press, 1989–), vol. 4, p. 273.

87 It is believed that here he was referring to the phonograph and his telephone.

88 EP, letter from Edison to Preece dated May 4, 1878; published in *The Papers of Thomas A. Edison*, ed. Reese V. Jenkins et al. (Baltimore: Johns Hopkins University Press, 1989–), vol. 4, p. 273.

89 Paul Israel, *Edison: A Life of Invention* (New York: John Wiley, 1998), p. 66.

90 EP, letter from Gouraud to Edison dated May 7, 1878.

91 The demonstration took place in May and was reported in *The Telegraph Journal*, July 1, 1878, p. 267. The report was a letter submitted by D.E. Hughes.

92 J.E. Kingsbury, *The Telephone and Telephone Exchanges* (London and New York: Longmans Green and Co., 1915), p. 124.

93 It was unfortunate the test was not successful as Edison's transmitter with the induction coil would prove that transmission was possibly over long distances as well as being less susceptible to line interference. The Western Union receiver however was a rather obvious copy of Bell's receiver made by George Phelps, and worked on the same principle. The main difference was in the number and arrangement of the permanent magnets. One arrangement was called the crown as the magnets formed six loops on the back.

94 EP, letter from Edison to Preece dated May 19, 1878.

95 DEHP, Section 1.4, letter from Preece to Edison dated May 22, 1878.

96 EP, letter from Preece to Edison dated May 27, 1878. Adams died the following year (1879).

97 DEHP, letter from Preece to Hughes dated May 27, 1878.

98 This would lead to the formation of the first telephone company in Great Britain in June of 1878 and to the entrance of the Post Office into an agreement to use Bell telephones by August.

99 Robert V. Bruce, *Bell: Alexander Graham Bell and the Conquest of Solitude* (Boston: Little, Brown and Company, 1973), p. 245.

100 *Nature*, June 20, 1878, p. 207.

101 IET, letter from Hughes to Preece dated May 24, 1878.

102 See *Proceedings of the Institution of Electrical Engineers* 7 (1878), p. 282. This passage is quoted in a six-penny pamphlet preserved in DEHP, Section 1.4, D. E. Hughes, *The Microphone by Professor Hughes*, p. 22.

103 DEHP, Section 1.4, letter from Preece to Edison dated May 27, 1878.

104 Paul Israel, *Edison: A Life of Invention* (New York: John Wiley, 1998), p. 158.

105 See *Engineering*, May 10, 1878, pp. 369–371.

106 D. E. Hughes, "On the Action of Sonorous Vibrations

in Varying the Force of an Electric Current," *Proceedings of the Royal Society of London* 27 (1878), pp. 362–369.

107 IET, telegraph messages from Edison to Preece and Thomson dated June 4, 1878.

108 The "heat measurer" Edison referred to in the telegraph messages was a sensitive device for measuring very small changes in temperature and called a "tasimeter," a device Edison had indeed invented some time earlier and which was based on a carbon button that could be compressed when a heat source was focused on to it. However, Hughes laid no claim to such a device, only mentioning that in his experiments he had observed that one of his arrangements was very sensitive to temperature. The press (*The Electrician*, May 25, 1878, pp. 3–4) unfortunately misinterpreted or misunderstood Hughes's presentation. First they titled their article on the presentation "Professor Hughes's Telephone, Microphone and Thermopile," and then they went on to report:

> ...this discovery of Professor Hughes will place in the hands of the physicist an extremely sensitive thermo-pile. Instead of the glass tube, as described in Fig. 2 Professor Hughes was experimenting with a quill tube, Fig. 8, and found that the instrument was exceedingly sensitive to heat. On the approach of a warm hand the galvanometer needle swings violently in one direction; on cooling the tube it swings in the other. We have seen Professor Hughes place a small French clock near the apparatus and the motion of the clock generated heat sufficient to cause the swinging of the needle, and allowing the small bell of the clock to strike, the needle swung violently as far as it could go.

The reporter had got hold of the wrong end of the stick, using the word thermopile in the title, which was incorrect, and then reporting that the heat created by the ticking from a clock was measured: quite an accomplishment! The quill tube was sensitive to heat but the tube and its contents (a powder of tin and zinc) was also sensitive to sound, which led to the confusion. Unfortunately, this caused Edison to believe that Hughes had stolen another of his inventions.

109 EP, letter from Edison to Henry Edmunds dated May 26, 1878; published in *The Papers of Thomas A. Edison*, ed. Reese V. Jenkins et al. (Baltimore: Johns Hopkins University Press, 1989–), vol. 4, p. 294. With regard to the reference to Phelps and the Hughes printing telegraph see chapter 4. While Phelps had helped Hughes early on at the American Telegraph Company, he was not the inventor of the Hughes printing telegraph.

110 *Nature*, June 20, 1878, p. 207.

111 DEHP, Section 1.4, letter from Preece to Hughes dated June 5, 1878.

112 EP, article from the *New York Daily Tribune*, June 8, 1878.

113 IET, letter from Hughes to Preece dated June 5, 1878.

114 IET, letter from Hughes to Preece dated June 24, 1878.

115 Op. cit.

116 IET, letter from Hughes to Preece dated June 29, 1878.

117 DEHP, Section 1.4, letter from Preece to Hughes dated July 1, 1878.

118 DEHP, Section 1.4, letter from Preece to Hughes dated July 13, 1878.

119 EP, letter from Sir William Thompson to Preece dated June 12, 1878.

120 DEHP, Section 1.4, letter from Preece to Hughes dated July 13, 1878.

121 EP, letter from Gouraud to Edison dated July 18, 1878, published in *The Papers of Thomas A. Edison*, ed. Reese V. Jenkins et al. (Baltimore: Johns Hopkins University Press, 1989–), vol. 4, p. 397.

122 DEHP, Section 1.4, letter from Thomson to Hughes dated July 16, 1878.

123 DEHP, Section 1.4, letter from Preece to Hughes dated July 21, 1878.

124 IET, letter from Thomson to Preece dated July 27, 1878.

125 IET, letter from Thomson to Preece dated July 30, 1878.

126 Letter from Thomson published in *Nature*, July 30, 1878.

127 EP, letter from Edison to William Barrett dated October 7, 1878, published in *The Papers of Thomas A. Edison*, ed. Reese V. Jenkins et al. (Baltimore: Johns Hopkins University Press, 1989–), vol. 4, p. 569.

128 EP, letter from Thomson to Preece dated November 5, 1878.

129 Henry Hunnings, taking as his point of departure Hughes's experiments with carbon pieces, went on to patent the carbon granule microphone with British Patent # 3647, September 16, 1878. Edison made further experiments with anthracite carbon granules in 1884 for the American Bell Company.

130 Crossley had his telephones manufactured in Bradford, Yorkshire, by Emmott and Blakeley.

131 J.H. Robertson, *The Story of the Telephone* (London: The Scientific Book Club, 1948), p. 19.

CHAPTER 8

1 DEHP, Section 2.2, The Letters and Papers of David Edward Hughes, letter from Alexander Graham Bell to Professor David Edward Hughes dated April 14, 1879. Bell was at this time working in Washington DC and gave his address as 1509 Rhode Island Ave.

2 DEHP, Section 2.4, W. H. Preece correspondence.

3 The telegraph message refers to a letter with diagrams sent separately by express mail and is a reply from Preece to Bell via W. Green, President of Western Union Telegraph Company, printed in Alexander Graham Bell, *Upon the Electrical Experiments to Determine the Location of the Bullet in the Body of the Late President Garfield; and Upon a Successful Form of Induction Balance for the Painless Detection of Metallic Masses in the Human Body* (Washington, DC: Gibson Brothers, Printers, 1882) (A Paper Read before the American Association for the Advancement of Science, At the Montreal Meeting, August 1882), p. 200. See also *The Electrician*, August 27, 1881, p. 237; *Engineering*, August 5, 1881; and *The Globe*, August 5, 1881.

4 The full letter is printed in Bell, *Upon the Electrical Experiments*, pp. 200–202.

5 Catherine Mackenzie, *Alexander Graham Bell* (New York: Grosset & Dunlap, 1928), p. 235.

6 Op. cit., p. 238.

7   Bell stated that he did not think that the cause of the failure was the metal bedsprings, and his final conclusion was that the bullet was too deep to detect: see Bell, *Upon the Electrical Experiments*, pp. 181–182.

8   *Engineering*, March 14, 1879.

9   *Telegraph Journal*, March 15, 1879.

10 There were sensitive galvanometers but these were only good for measuring direct current signals.

11 David Edward Hughes's notebook, London, British Library, Add. MS 40161, folio 67.

12 The scheme did require all of the lines in a particular group to be dedicated transmitting lines.

13 Hughes read the paper on March 12, 1879; it was published as David Hughes, "Experimental Researches into Means of Preventing Induction upon Lateral Wires," *Journal of the Society of Telegraph Engineers* 8.27 (1879), pp. 163–177. Also see British Library, Add. MS 40161, folio 56.

14 *Electrical Review*, May 22, 1891, p. 643.

15 DEH NPC, *The Morning Post*, May 26, 1892.

16 *Engineering*, April 4, 1879, pp. 280–282. Also see *Telegraphic Journal*, April 13, 1879, p. 179.

17 *Engineering*, April 4, 1879, pp. 282–283.

18 "On the Induction-Currents Balance and Experimental Researches Made Therewith," paper read to the Royal Society May 15, 1879, and published in the *Proceedings of the Royal Society of London* 29 (1879), pp. 56–65.

19 Hughes gave credit to others who had investigated forms of induction balance before him such as Charles Babbage, Sir John Herschel and Prof. Dove in Germany, as detailed by Auguste de la Rive, *Treatise on Electricity* (London: Longman, Brown, Green, and Longmans, 1853–1858), vol. 1, pp. 418–433. Dove had experimented with two coils, calling them "differential inductors," but he did not have the sensitive instruments that Hughes had invented, and it was those instruments which made the device into a practical detection device.

20 D. E. Hughes, "Induction Balance and Experimental Researches Therewith," *Philosophical Magazine* Series 5, 8.46 (July, 1879), pp. 50–56.

21 See Hughes's papers "On the Induction-Currents Balance and Experimental Researches Made Therewith," *Proceedings of the Royal Society of London* 29 (1879), pp. 56–65; and "Induction Balance and Experimental Researches Therewith," *Philosophical Magazine* Series 5, 8.46 (July, 1879), pp. 50–56.

22 D. E. Hughes, "Assaying by Induction," *The Telegraphic Journal*, June 15, 1879, p. 192.

23 Benjamin Ward Richardson, "Some Researches with Professor Hughes' New Instrument for the Measurement of Hearing; the Audiometer," *Proceedings of the Royal Society of London* 29 (1879), pp. 65–70.

24 See S.D.G. Stevens, "David Edward Hughes and his Audiometer," *The Journal of Laryngology and Otology*, 93 (January, 1979), pp. 1–6; J.E.J. John, "David Edward Hughes, FRS," *British Journal of Audiology* 13, Supplement 2 (1979), pp. 5–10; and Philip Stoney and Michael Hawk, "The First Audiometer: A Welsh Connection," *The Journal of Otolaryngology* 20.2 (1991), p. 144. The University Hospital of Wales founded the D.E. Hughes Lectures series dedicated to the furtherance of audiology in Wales; the lectures were orga-

25 nized by Professor S.D.G. (Dafydd) Stephens, and ran from 1988 to 2004.

25 The letter from Hughes to Bell via Preece is reproduced in Bell, *Upon the Electrical Experiments*, pp. 201–202.

26 *The Electrical Review* 7 (1879), p. 200.

CHAPTER 9

1   On February 4, 2008, 7:00 p.m. EST, NASA's Deep Space Network beamed the Beatles's recording of "Across the Universe" towards the North Star Polaris, 431 light years distant.

2   London, British Library, Add. MS 40161, folio 156. Hughes found that he had to press the particles together to obtain a reading on the induction balance. His continued interest in metals in a finely divided state contained in a glass tube is important as it was the basis of what later was to be called a coherer, which was used for detecting electromagnetic waves. He had used this device during his research on the microphone. Some of these devices are now in the collection of the Science Museum in London. Later in 1890 Edouard Branly discovered the cohesion of iron filings in a tube when exposed to spark discharges.

3   The "clock-microphone" was what Hughes used to create electrical pulses. It consisted of a mechanical clock on which one of his carbon microphones was mounted. The mechanical ticking was amplified by the microphone and transmitted as pulses of electrical current in the circuit. These electrical pulses surging through the coils created a rising and falling magnetic field. A second set of coils in close proximity to the first set of coils was influenced by this fluctuating magnetic field and formed a secondary circuit which was normally connected to a telephone receiver as a detector.

4   London, British Library Add. MS 40161, folio 162.

5   See the letter from D.E. Hughes to J.J. Fahie dated April 29, 1899, published in J.J. Fahie, *A History of Wireless Telegraphy* (London: William Blackwood and Sons, 1899), Appendix D, p. 290.

6   Hughes had spent a couple of days experimenting with various batteries, mentioning manganese, sal-ammoniac, and Grove batteries, and using the sonometer and clock-microphone to make some relative measurements. He tried a much higher voltage in some tests, using a battery of 40 Grove elements (approximately 44 volts). His knowledge of batteries would come in useful later when he required a small portable low-voltage cell.

7   London, British Library, Add. MS 40161, folio 167.

8   Op. cit., folio 168.

9   Thomas Edison had noticed a similar effect in 1875.

10 Other investigators who had made experiments with "extra current" but had been unable to make substantial progress with it included Thomas Edison, Elihu Thomson and Edwin Houston, and Silvanus P. Thompson.

11 London, British Library, Add. MS 40161, folio 173.

12 Hughes had experimented with what he called thermo loops quite often. While he was aware that dissimilar metals which were joined together and heated produced a small voltage, he sometimes used similar metals and still referred to them as a thermo joint. This could have been due to the fact that they were or had been heated and oxidized.

13 London, British Library, Add. MS 40161, folio 176. Hughes writes that "The sounds seem to come entirely of molecular character not undulating but sharp clicks of making and breaking of innumerable contacts." So it is probably at this time that he switched over to using the clockwork-driven circuit interrupter. He does refer later to the clockwork-driven interrupter supplied by his friend and instrument maker Augustus Stroh. He recommends that the clockwork-driven cam should have a great many teeth and produce a distinct make and break, and that it should be oiled each day. He also notes that metal contacts were better than carbon contacts. Hughes made a visit to the Royal Mint at this time (see folio 177) and mentions that the Mint was using a large version of his induction balance whose secondary coils could give a painful shock. It is likely this induction balance was being excited by a clock-work-driven interrupter.

14 Edison had observed that when he had an electrical buzzer (a coil with a self-oscillating armature) operating, he could draw sparks not only from the armature associated with the coils but also from other metal objects in the room such as gas pipes. See "The Discovery of Another Form of Electricity," *Scientific American* 33 (December 25, 1875), pp. 400–401; and "The New Phase of Electric Force," *Scientific American* 33 (December 25, 1875), p. 401. On Hughes's awareness of Edison's experiments see London, British Library, Add. MS 40161, folio 181.

15 Unfortunately Edison first publicized his results in the popular press (he repeated the same mistake in the microphone affair). The newspapers decided that Edison's "etheric" force sounded much the same as the "Odic" force of the German chemist Carl Reichenbach, who had claimed that he had discovered an unknown force, a "psychic force," responsible for spiritual and occult phenomena. It was downhill after this for Edison. His work was further discredited by an article by Elihu Thomson and Edwin Houston, who indicated that what Edison had discovered was not a new force but simply the effect of "induction currents." See Edwin J. Houston and Elihu Thomson, "Electrical Phenomena: The Alleged Etheric Force: Test Experiments as to Its Identity with Induced Electricity," *Journal of the Franklin Institute* 101 (April, 1876), pp. 173–174. For discussion of this episode in Edison's career see Ian Wills, "Edison and Science: A Curious Result," *Studies in History and Philosophy of Science*, Part A, 40.2 (2009), pp. 157–166.

16 Thompson's article is "On Some Phenomena of Induced Electric Sparks," *Philosophical Magazine* 2 (September, 1876), pp.191–198.

17 While it would be simpler to call these two parts a transmitter and receiver, I have avoided using these names until the point in time when Hughes himself introduced these terms.

18 A condenser is known today as an electrical capacitor.

19 London, British Library, Add. MS 40161, folio 196.

20 Op. cit., folios 196 and 197.

21 This is important, as later experimenters would concentrate on detecting single events via a coherer that had to be continually reset.

22 It should be pointed out that these junctions of the microphonic joint were usually formed by two metals simply resting on each other, and as a result if they were mechanically jarred they caused a disturbance in

the telephone receiver—in effect they were acting as a loose joint microphone.

23 London, British Library, Add. MS 40161, folio 200.

24 Despointes was superintendent-in-chief at the Submarine Telegraph Company and was later employed by the Post Office. The reference to Depointes occurs in London, British Library, Add. MS 40161, on a page pasted in between folios 229 and 230 which is dated November 4, 1879.

25 London, British Library, Add. MS 40161, folio 212.

26 The word "thermo" figures throughout Hughes's notes over the years and he evidently believed that many of the phenomena he observed were due to some thermo-couple action.

27 The water pipe was lead or iron, as was the gas pipe, and the connecting wires either copper or iron, so that there were connections between a few different metals.

28 London, British Library, Add. MS 40161, folio 215. Hughes's battery, along with a small chloride of silver battery contained in an ebonite case made by Adolphe Gaiffe of Paris, are now in the collection of the Science Museum, London.

29 Letter from D.E. Hughes to J. J. Fahie dated April 29, 1899, published in J.J. Fahie, *A History of Wireless Telegraphy* (London: William Blackwood and Sons, 1899), Appendix D, p. 290.

30 The fender of a stove was a decorative protective surrounding usually made of brass, averaging twelve inches high, several inches deep and as wide as the stove it was protecting, typically four to five feet.

31 London, British Library, Add. MS 40161, folio 218.

32 The Clerac tube, named after its French inventor, consisted of a tube filled with powdered carbon that had a screw adjustment that could compress the carbon powder. The electrical resistance decreased with increased pressure.

33 London, British Library, Add. MS 40161, folios 223 and 224.

34 Op. cit., folios 224 and 225.

35 To Victorian scientists the space surrounding them was not just air as we know it today but a complex medium that they termed the ether. This idea derived from attempts to explain how light could possibly travel, whether as vibratory energy, a periodic disturbance in space and time, or a wave motion: "Waves we cannot have unless they be waving in something," as the scientist Oliver Lodge had said. The ether was the hypothetical medium that electromagnetic waves could travel in; Victorian scientists believed that matter and the ether were fundamentally mechanical in nature. The ether took on new forms as time progressed as it was adapted to each new discovery or theory. When light was shown to be a transverse wave, with the medium waving in a direction perpendicular to the direction of wave propagation, the ether became an elastic jelly. Over time it progressed from being an invisible "elastic solid" to a "jelly" to "molecular vortices" and a "vortex sponge." The mechanical models that were proposed to try to explain the operation of the ether were just as varied: they ranged from cog wheels to rack and pinion gears and idler wheels.

36 London, British Library, Add. MS 40161, folio 226.

37 Op. cit., folio 236.

38 What was happening was that Hughes's transmitter was sending out a series of electromagnetic waves which were created by the action of his circuit interrupter switching on and off the battery to a coil. When the circuit was broken it created a spark across its contacts due to the collapse of the coil's magnetic field. The spark discharge kicked the circuit into oscillation at a frequency determined by the circuit parameters (inductance, capacitance, and resistance). This was probably a fairly high frequency that decayed fairly rapidly, and was constantly renewed by the clock interrupter. It would have appeared as a damped sine wave. The crude aerial and a connection to ground completed the circuit for transmitting electromagnetic waves. In the receiver these electromagnetic waves excited the aerial wire but were at too high a frequency to actuate the telephone receiver and were also beyond the range of human hearing. However, they were detected by the microphonic joint which acted as a rectifier. This rectification transformed the sine waves into half sine wave cycles or pulsed DC. These pulses were smoothed out by the inductance of the telephone receiver. Thus each burst of high frequency radio waves, transmitted at the slow rate of the interrupter, produced a single pulse in the telephone which was in the audible range. The high frequency waves acted as a carrier for the pulses which occurred at the circuit interruption rate. Additional voltage increased current flow in the detector and resulted in better sensitivity, and it seems that Hughes recognized this and added a small DC voltage in series with the detector to achieve this result.

39 London, British Library, Add. MS 40161, folio 242.

40 Michael Faraday had visualized electric lines of force surrounding electrically charged objects and magnetic lines of force surrounding magnets. These invisible lines can be made to reveal themselves by placing a piece of paper over a bar magnet and then sprinkling iron filings onto the paper. The filings will form a pattern of curved lines which emanate from the magnet's north pole and loop round to the south pole, the concentration being highest in the vicinity of the poles and diminishing with distance from them. While this demonstration reveals the lines in two dimensions, the effect actual takes place in three dimensions. Hughes certainly looked up to Faraday, and in fact had his engraved portrait adorning the flysheet of one of his record books. Faraday's papers were widely available and Hughes was probably aware of Faraday's theories; the fact that the papers were devoid of mathematical formulas makes it more likely that Hughes would have studied them.

41 London, British Library, Add. MS 40161, folio 246.

42 The microphone/telephone receiver amplifier was constructed by attaching a microphone directly to a telephone receiver. Thus a weak signal heard in the telephone receiver activated the microphone which boosted the signal. This was a very successful product and was used well into the crystal set era of the 1900s.

43 London, British Library, Add. MS 40161, folio 249.

44 Op. cit., folio 230; and letter from D.E. Hughes to J.J. Fahie dated April 29, 1899, published in J.J. Fahie, A History of Wireless Telegraphy (London: William Blackwood and Sons, London, 1899), Appendix D, p. 290.

45 William Preece was later to conduct his own experiments on induction. However it was he who gave Marconi a start with his wireless experiments many years later.

46 London, British Library, Add. MS 40161, folio 255.

47 Letter from D.E. Hughes to J.J. Fahie dated April 29, 1899, and published in Fahie, A History of Wireless Telegraphy, Appendix D, p. 290

48 Hughes invited several persons to witness his experiment: see London, British Library, Add. MS 40161, folio 230.

49 Letter from Spottiswoode to Hughes dated February 14, 1880, in Hughes's private papers.

50 London, British Library, Add. MS 40161, folios 262 and 263.

51 Op. cit., folio 263.

52 DEHP, Section 1.5, letter from Spottiswoode to D. E. Hughes dated February 22, 1880.

53 This was not the first time that Stokes had demolished new theories—he had unfortunately done the same to James MacCullagh's optical theories in 1862. See Bruce J. Hunt, The Maxwellians (Ithaca, NY: Cornell University Press, 1991), p. 10. Oliver Lodge in his book Talks About Wireless (London: Cassell and Company Ltd., 1925), p. 21, indicates that Sir William Crookes had had a similar experience, for Stokes had told him that according to recognized principles, the phenomena that Crookes described could not happen.

54 Michael Faraday for all his brilliance had suffered the same problem, for his writings and explanations were not always easy to follow, and as a self-taught experimenter he lacked the mathematical background to express his theories in precise mathematical formulas. His work was often frowned upon by university scientists.

55 The proposers of Hughes's membership included William Thomson, W. Grylls Adams, who had also seen his experiments, and Warren de la Rue.

56 Alan Campell-Swinton, "Some Early Electrical Reminiscences," Journal of the Institution of Electrical Engineers 60 (1922), pp. 492–496.

57 See J. Munro's biographical sketch of Hughes in Hughes's private papers.

58 The references of these papers are William Thomson "On the Mathematical Theory of Electricity in Equlibrium," Cambridge and Dublin Mathematical Journal 1 (1846), pp. 75–95; 3 (1848), pp. 131–140, 141–148, and 266–274; 4 (1849), pp. 276–284; and 5 (1850), pp. 1–9; James Clerk Maxwell, "On Faraday's Lines of Force," Transactions of the Cambridge Philosophical Society 10 (1855–56), pp. 27–83; and James Clerk Maxwell, "On Physical Lines of Force," The London, Edinburgh, and Dublin Philosophical Magazine and Journal of Science 21 (January–June, 1861), pp. 161–175, 281–291, and 338–348.

59 In the preface to his Treatise on Electricty and Magnetism Maxwell states that the physical hypotheses that he put forward are entirely different from those used by mathematicians and physicists on the Continent (they were based on the principle of action at a distance). He says that the two approaches should be compared as both have succeeded in explaining the principle electromagnetic phenomena and both have attempted to explain the propagation of light as an electromagnetic phenomenon.

60 George Francis FitzGerald, "On the Possibility of Originating Wave Disturbances in the Ether by Means

of Electric Forces," paper read at the Royal Society, Dublin, in two parts on November 17, 1879, and May 19, 1880, and published in *The Scientific Writings of the Late George Francis Fitzgerald*, ed. Joseph Larmor (Dublin: Hodges, Figgis & Co., Ltd., 1902). Oliver Lodge, *Talks About Wireless* (London: Cassell and Company Ltd., 1925), pp. 26–27.

61 See Bruce J. Hunt, *The Maxwellians* (Ithaca, NY: Cornell University Press, 1991), p. 35.

62 See *Fortnightly Review* 51 (February, 1892), p. 173.

63 J.J. Fahie, *A History of Wireless Telegraphy* (London: William Blackwood and Sons,, 1899), Appendix D.

64 Op. cit., Appendix D.

65 Oliver Lodge, *Talks About Wireless* (London: Cassell and Company Ltd., 1925), pp. 20–21.

66 Letter from D.E. Hughes to Latimer Clark, dated May 18 (believed to have been written 1880 or thereabout), sold at Christie's and now in a private collection.

67 See W.K.E. Geddes, "Hughes' Place in the History of Radio," *British Journal of Audiology* 13, Supplement No. 2 (1979), pp 13–16. Geddes cites Sir Joseph Larmor, "Precursors of Wireless Telegraphy," *Nature* 109 (April 1, 1922), p. 410.

68 E.P. Wenaas, "From Coherers to Crystal Rectifiers," *Antique Wireless Association Review* 22 (2009), pp. 147–232. See also T. M. Cuff, "Coherers, A Review," MSc Thesis, Temple University, Pennsylvania, 1993 (3 vols.).

69 Edouard Branly is usually noted for discovering two devices in 1890. One was a cylinder filled with iron filings whose resistance dropped significantly when exposed to electromagnetic radiation. This was similar to what Hughes had used in his microphone experiments and later in his wireless experiments. However as the particles cohered and needed to be constantly mechanically reset, Hughes abandoned the device. The second item was a point contact devise consisting of two rods either of iron or copper that were lightly oxidized and rested upon each other.

70 L. Austin, "Some Contact Rectifiers of Electrical Currents," *Bulletin of the Bureau of Standards* 5 (August, 1908), p. 138.

71 US Patent #707266, June 2, 1902.

72 G.F. Pickard, "How I Invented the Crystal Detector," *Electrical Experimenter* 7.4 (August, 1919), p. 325.

73 Walter Massie, Oscillaphone detector, US Patent #819779, August 18, 1905. The Massie detector consisted of a single steel needle resting horizontally across two beveled carbon blocks and was almost identical to one of Hughes's originals.

74 Other minerals used as crystal detectors were iron pyrites, hematite, graphite, and carborundum (manmade). Ferdinand Braun in Germany had actually observed the conduction of electricity in one direction in various metal sulfides during the 1870s, although the significance of his discovery was not understood until many years later. Crystal detectors operate as semiconductors that exhibit a P-N junction at various points on their surface and pass a current only in one direction. Man-made semiconductors can be created to exhibit the same effects by adding impurities in minute quantities (a process known as doping) to substances such as silicon or germanium to create electron-rich N (negative) type or electron-poor P (positive) type regions.

75 The explanation at the time for the thermo-electric mechanism was that the radio frequency signal detected caused a current to flow across the detector junction, which resulted in a heating of the junction. This heating induced a thermoelectric voltage due to the dissimilar materials of the junction. The polarity of this voltage then aided current flow in one direction and opposed it in the opposite direction. This resulted in the asymmetrical voltage-current characteristic typical of a diode.

76 George Pierce, "Crystal Rectifiers for Electric Currents and Electric Oscillations: Part 1: Carborundum," *Physical Review* 25.1 (July, 1907), pp. 31–60. Pierce was actually preceded by the work of Hermann Brandes in Germany. See also G. Pierce, *Principles of Wireless Telegraphy* (New York: McGraw Hill Book Co. 1910), p. 171.

77 E.P. Wenaas and J. Bryars, "Experiments with Mock Ups of the Italian Navy Coherer," *Antique Wireless Association Review* 21 (2008), pp. 45–68.

78 London, British Library, Add. MS 40161, folio 230. Several of Hughes's notebooks were bound together to form MS 40161. This note was pasted in onto a blank page at the front of this notebook and reads:

> Mr. F. Despoints at my rooms Nov 4th 1979.
>
> Nov 12, 1879. Tried the Experiments between the Public Baths Tottenham Court Road and Gt. Portland Street no one present.
>
> -----
>
> Dec 15, 1879
>
> Tried these effects between Mr. Grove house Bolsover Street and Portland road—with no good results.
>
> -----
>
> Feb 20, 1880 Mr. Spottiswoode President of Royal Society and Prof. Stokes and Prof. Huxley—visited me to see these aerial experiments Prof Stokes contested that results were due to Induction and not conduction through air as I supposed.
>
> -----
>
> Mr. Preece saw these experiments about the same time Prof. W. Grylls Adams Prof. Austin Roberts—also Prof W. Crooks saw these shortly afterwards.

79 "Wireless Telegraphy," *Electrician* 39 (October 1, 1897), p. 736.

80 George G. Blake, *History of Radio Telegraphy and Telephony* (London: Chapman and Hall Ltd., 1928), p. 45. Also see *The Telegraph and Telephone Journal* (March, 1923), pp. 96, 102, and 107.

CHAPTER 10

1 David Edward Hughes was elected to the Royal Society on June 3, 1880. Two of Hughes's several sponsors were William Thomson (later Lord Kelvin) and Walter de la Rue. Fellows are selected on the basis of individual research achievements from among those who have made distinctive and original contribution to science. It is interesting to note that William Preece was on the list but missed out. He was elected the following year (1881).

2 Little is known about Hughes's first wife Maria. She was listed as David Hughes's wife in the 1871 census

in London. In a letter Hughes wrote in 1878 he refers to her as being an invalid. No death certificate has been located. She may have been from the Continent, possibly Paris, and this may have been where she died and was laid to rest.

3 E.C. Baker, *Sir William Preece, F.R.S.: Victorian Engineer Extraordinary* (London: Hutchinson, 1976), pp. 116–117.

4 J. Munro, *The Romance of Electricity* (London: The Religious Tract Society, 1893), p. 291.

5 Sir Charles Bright had become friends with Hughes earlier in 1858 when they were working on the transatlantic telegraph cable project.

6 The French General Post Office in Paris had a hundred Hughes printing telegraph instruments in operation at that time, manufactured by M. Froment's workshop, as reported by the Comte du Moncel in his lecture on "The Telegraph" given during the exhibition. Reported in the London *Times*, September 15, 1881.

7 See the London *Times* report on the exhibition in its issue of September 15, 1881. The polarized relay used by the railways was based on the one that Hughes used in his printing telegraph.

8 *Scientific American*, December 31, 1881, pp. 422–423.

9 Ibid. The Ader microphone, which was based on Hughes's carbon pencil design, consisted of two rows of five small carbon pencils supported on three carbon crosspieces. These were mounted to a small pine board which vibrated in sympathy with the sound waves. There were five microphones covering the left hand side of the stage and five covering the right hand side. The microphones were isolated from the vibrations of the stage floor by large blocks of lead which were supported on rubber feet. The microphones were excited from a Leclanche battery and connected to an induction coil to give the signals a boost prior to the transmission over double wires to the exhibition hall. The receivers were arranged so that at each listening position the listener had a left and right ear receiver, these corresponding to left and right hand stage microphones. In total there were eighty receivers serving forty listeners. The microphones could be switched between three rooms. The receivers were of Ader's design based on Bell's telephone receiver. As the batteries became rapidly polarized, two sets were provided for each microphone and the batteries switched over every fifteen minutes by a commutator.

10 J. Munro, *The Romance of Electricity* (London: The Religious Tract Society, 1893), p. 288.

11 M. Cochery was the Minister of Posts and Telegraphs for France.

12 DEHP, Section 1.6, Autobiographical letters, letter from D.E. Hughes to his sister Maggie written from Paris on August 18, 1882.

13 Anna was actually three years older than him.

14 This is based on D.E. Hughes's letter to his sister Maggie in America dated August 18, 1882, just cited. In it he talks of receiving many congratulatory letters regarding his forthcoming marriage, which implies that he had been publicizing it prior to this date.

15 David Hughes had changed his address at about that time from 94 Great Portland Street to 108 Great Portland Street; this is confirmed by various letters that show his new address.

16 The following is taken from Marie de Mare, *G.P.A. Healy, American Artist* (New York: David McKay Co. Inc., 1954), pp. 176–178. George Healy was a famous American painter of the nineteenth century and was known as the "Painter of Presidents."

17 George Peter Alexander Healy's portrait of Anna Chadbourne Morey (Hughes) is now in the Museum of Fine Arts, Boston. It is oil on canvas, 61 x 44 inches, Accession Number 21.2232.

18 Letter from Anna Chadbourne to her brother, February 23, 1849, in Hughes's private papers.

19 Associated with Dodge, Bacon & Co., London.

20 Goodyear patented his rubber vulcanization process in 1844. India rubber in its natural form melted in hot weather and froze or cracked in cold weather, and had thus found limited application. Goodyear discovered how to stabilize rubber by heating and mixing it with sulfur; this process strengthened it and allowed it to be made into a range of consistencies from flexible membranes to hard but resilient solids. It was applied to products such as waterproof raincoats and shoes, and eventually to automobile tires. The Goodyear Rubber company was named after him but not started by him. The boats exhibited evidently bore a striking resemblance to today's inflatable craft.

21 Rev. Bradford Peirce, *Trials of an Inventor: Life and Discoveries of Charles Goodyear* (New York: Carlton and Porter, 1866), p. 177.

22 Reported in a letter concerning Charles Morey's death which appeared in the *Boston Journal*, January 28, 1857

23 Rev. Bradford Peirce, *Trials of an Inventor: Life and Discoveries of Charles Goodyear* (New York: Carlton and Porter, 1866), p. 179.

24 He patented hair combs, knife handles, women's corset spring strips (previously they had been made from whale bone). Manufactured goods included picture frames, hardware, musical instruments, fans, buttons, etc. This information comes from a brochure published in French in 1854 by Charles Morey: Charles Morey, *Caoutchouc durci* (Paris: Imprimerie d'Aubusson et Kugelmann, 1854).

25 The famous American artist G.P.A. Healy, who had a studio in Paris at the time, painted portraits for Goodyear on his rubber panels.

26 It seems that quite a few respectable persons had found themselves locked up in French debtors' prison, including Horace Greeley, editor of the *New York Tribune*, and the banker John Abel Smith.

27 *Boston Journal*, January 28, 1857. Clipping in Hughes's private papers.

28 Reported in the *New York Daily Times* from their Paris correspondent on July 23, 1857.

29 DEHP, Section 1.6, Autobiographical Letters, letter from Hughes to his sister Maggie dated August 18, 1882.

30 DEHP, Section 1.6, Autobiographical Letters, letter from Hughes to his sister Maggie dated August 18, 1882.

31 Hughes was fairly wealthy by this time but he was not extravagant. He certainly had more than this available in his savings.

32 Neither David nor Anna Hughes ever mentioned an

apartment in Richmond again so it is not clear whether they ever took up residence there.

CHAPTER 11

1   See *Journal of the Society of Telegraph-Engineers and Electricians* 15.60 (January 28, 1886), p. 3.

2   Dr. Warren de la Rue proposed D.E. Hughes for the Royal Medal for his discoveries of the microphone, induction balance, and sonometer.

3   Prof. D.E. Hughes, "Inaugural Address [including comments and minutes]," *Journal of the Society of Telegraph-Engineers and Electricians* 15.60 (January 28, 1886), pp. 6–26, esp. p. 6.

4   Self-induction can be described as follows. If a magnet is thrust into a coil of wire it creates a moving magnetic field and induces a current in the conductors (of the coil) that are cut by the moving field (but only while the magnet is in motion). This was discovered by Faraday and Henry. A moving magnetic field can be created in another way. When a current rises and falls in a conductor or a coil of wire (such as by switching a current on and off or by a pulse on a telegraph line) it creates a magnetic field that also rises and falls. As the current rises, the magnetic field expands outwards from the conductor, and when the current decreases, the magnetic field collapses. As the magnetic field expands and collapses, it is effectively in motion and will induce a voltage in any conductor that is exposed to it; this also includes the conductor that is creating it. This ability of a conductor to induce a voltage in itself (self-induced voltage) when the current is changing is known as "self-inductance." If there is another wire or coil close by that is exposed to the rising and collapsing field, it too will experience an induced voltage, and this is one of the causes of electrical interference.

5   See the detailed discussions of this subject and time period in D. W. Jordan, "The Adoption of Self-Induction by Telephony, 1886–1889," *Annals of Science* 39 (1982), pp. 433–461, and D. W. Jordan, "D. E. Hughes Self-Induction and the Skin Effect," *Centaurus* 26 (1982), pp. 123–153.

6   J. O. Marsh and R. G. Roberts made this observation in their paper "David Edward Hughes: Inventor, Engineer and Scientist," *Proceedings of the Institution of Electrical Engineers* 126 9 (September, 1979), pp. 929–935. They indicated that his transition had started earlier with his investigation into interference on telegraph lines in 1879.

7   Hughes produced ten papers on magnetism and magnetic properties of metals between 1880 and 1884.

8   The term "Hertz" did not come into use until much later.

9   William Thomson saw a similarity between the way heat propagated along a solid metallic rod and the way an electrical pulse propagated along a submarine cable, and found this analogy helpful in deriving his cable formula.

10   Thomson of course eventually got round the roadblock by inventing his own equipment to work successfully with submarine cables, first his mirror galvanometer and later the siphon recorder.

11   See D. W. Jordan, "D. E. Hughes Self-Induction and the Skin Effect," *Centaurus* 26 (1982), pp. 123–153.

12   Hughes had read a paper titled "Preventing Induction upon Lateral Wires" at the Royal Society in March of 1879; the paper was published as "Experimental Researches into Means of Preventing Induction upon Lateral Wires," *Journal of the Society of Telegraph Engineers* 8.27 (1879), pp. 163–177.

13   D. E. Hughes, "On an Induction-Currents Balance and Experimental Researches Made Therewith," *Proceedings of the Royal Society* 29 (1879), pp. 56–65.

14   See Oliver Heaviside, *Electrical Papers* (New York and London: Macmillan and Co., 1894). Heaviside had published a number of papers relating to telegraph problems and telegraph lines. See vol. 1, Art. 13, "On Telegraphic Signaling with Condensers"; Art. 14, "On the Extra Current"; Art. 15, "On the Speed of Signaling through Heterogeneous Telegraph Circuits"; and Art 19, "On Induction Between Parallel Wires."

15   Institution of Engineering and Technology Archives, letter from Hughes to Heaviside dated January 18, 1889. In the letter Hughes stated "I have for some years past read your papers and cut them out of the "Electrician" Etc. in order to preserve them together in book form...." Hughes also thanked Heaviside for the copy of his book *Electromagnetic Waves* that he had sent him. Hughes, in fact, was a great collector of articles from various sources and employed a newspaper clipping service to keep up with the news, etc., especially with reference to himself.

16   Prof. D. E. Hughes, "Inaugural Address," *The Journal of the Society of Telegraph-Engineers and Electricians* 15.60 (January 28, 1886), p. 6. Hughes's reference to his previous articles are to "Induction-Currents Balance," *Proceedings of the Royal Society* 29 (1879), p. 56; and "Molecular Electro-magnetic Induction," *Proceedings of the Royal Society* 31 (1880–1881), pp. 525–536.

17   Hughes's "Inaugural Address," p. 20. Hughes's reference to his study of 1883 is to the discussions on the paper of W. H. Preece on electrical conductors in *Proceedings of the Institute of Civil Engineers* 75 (1883).

18   Hughes's "Inaugural Address," p. 18.

19   A Wheatstone bridge was a piece of test equipment used for measuring and determining an unknown electrical resistance value.

20   Similar variable induction coils were to appear later in early wireless sets for tuning and were called variometers.

21   Hughes's "Inaugural Address," p. 20.

22   The self-inductance of iron is approximately a thousand times that of copper.

23   Hughes's "Inaugural Address," p. 11. See also Paul J. Nahin, *Oliver Heaviside, Sage in Solitude* (New York: IEEE Press, 1987), p. 142.

24   Lord Rayleigh, a brilliant mathematician and physicist, was awarded the Nobel Prize for physics in 1904.

25   See Paul J. Nahin, *Oliver Heaviside, Sage in Solitude* (New York: IEEE Press, 1987), and also B.J. Hunt, *The Maxwellians* (Cornell University Press, 1991). Oliver Heaviside, a scientist and mathematician, was considered one of the Maxwellians, for he interpreted the work of James Clerk Maxwell and recast Maxwell's many equations into the now familiar four vector equations in 1884–5. He helped establish the basis of modern electrical theory and developed the "distortionless circuit" and operational calculus. His work in wireless and his theory relating to the reflectivity of the ionosphere led to one of these layers being named the Heaviside layer.

26 Skin effect: a DC current flowing in a wire is distributed uniformly over its cross section. However, when the current is alternating the distribution is no longer uniform. As the frequency of the alternating current increases the current moves to the outer layers of the wire, and at very high frequency it is almost entirely concentrated in the surface layer or "skin." Thus, the effective resistance of the wire is greatly increased. The effect is created by the rapid reversals of the current which induce longitudinal voltage loops in the wire and these in turn create eddy currents. The eddy currents flow around the boundary of these voltage loops in the same direction as the main current at the surface of the conductor and in the opposite direction in the center of the conductor.

27 Oliver Heaviside, *Electrical Papers* (New York and London: Macmillan and Co., 1894), vol. 1, preface.

28 Professor D. E. Hughes F.R.S., "Researches upon the Self-Induction of an Electric Current," *Proceedings of the Royal Society* 40 (1886), pp. 450–469.

29 *Journal of the Society of Telegraph-Engineers and Electricians* 15 (1886), p. 28.

30 Institution of Engineering and Technology Archives, letter from D.E. Hughes to William Preece dated February 22, 1886.

31 *Journal of the Society of Telegraph-Engineers and Electricians* 15 (1886), pp. 27 ff.

32 *Journal of the Society of Telegraph-Engineers and Electricians* 15 (1886), p. 55.

33 *Journal of the Society of Telegraph-Engineers and Electricians* 15 (1886), p. 64.

34 S.P. Thompson, author of the successful book *Dynamo Electric Machinery*, was principal of the Finsbury Technical College, London, which was part of the City & Guilds of London. The college was a prototype for the great London polytechnic universities.

35 During the 1870s Professor Heinrich Fredrich Weber was an assistant to Hermann von Helmholtz in Germany.

36 Paul J. Nahin, *Oliver Heaviside, Sage in Solitude* (New York: IEEE Press, 1987), p. 154.

37 Oliver Heaviside, *Electrical Papers* (New York and London: Macmillan and Co., 1894), vol. 2, p. 488.

38 Heaviside, *Electrical Papers*, vol. 2, p. 28; also see *The Electrician* April 23, 1886, p. 471.

39 Heaviside, *Electrical Papers*, vol. 2, pp. 33 and 35, "On the Use of the Bridge as an Induction Balance." Also published in *The Electrician*, April 30, 1886.

40 Heaviside, *Electrical Papers*, vol. 2, p. 170

41 Heaviside, *Electrical Papers*, vol. 2, p. 170. See *The Electrician* January 10, 1885, also published in Heaviside, *Electrical Papers*, vol. 1, Section XXX/II p. 434, "On the Transmission of Energy through Wires by Electric Current." Also see vol. 1, Section XXVIII, #20, p. 378.

42 See *The Electrician*, April 30, 1886.

43 Heaviside, *Electrical Papers*, vol. 2, p. 100.

44 D. E. Hughes, "Researches upon the Self-Induction of an Electric Current," *Proceedings of the Royal Society* 40 (1886), pp. 450–469.

45 "Litz" wire, which was stranded insulated wire woven together to effectively increase the surface area, was later introduced to mitigate the skin effect in applications using higher frequencies.

46 Maxwell, *Treatise of Electricity and Magnetism*, vol. 2, p. 291.

47 D. E. Hughes, "Researches upon the Self-Induction of an Electric Current," *Proceedings of the Royal Society* 40 (1886), pp. 450–469.

48 Institution of Engineering and Technology Archives, letters from Hughes to Heaviside, SC MSS 1/6/21/01–08

49 Paul J. Nahin, *Oliver Heaviside, Sage in Solitude* (New York: IEEE Press, 1987), p. 145. Nahin added the indication that the mathematician was Heaviside.

50 Distortionless line: Oliver Heaviside had worked out a theory and equation which indicated how telephone speech signals could be transmitted over long lines without them becoming distorted. He suggested that the line parameters be adjusted to satisfy the equation L/R = S/K, where L was the inductance, R the resistance, S the capacitance, and K the leakage conductance of the line. When the parameters met this criterion, a distortionless telephone line would be obtained. For overhead copper telephone lines, the parameter in this equation that could be easily adjusted was the inductance. Heaviside advocated the introduction of loading coils along the telephone wire, among other practical solutions, to achieve this goal. This technique was rejected by the Post Office, which delayed its introduction for many years. In the USA Micheal Pupin patented the same idea and its introduction significantly improved long distance telephony.

51 Heaviside, *Electrical Papers*, vol. 1, preface.

52 Oliver Lodge was professor of physics at Liverpool University. At the time he had just been elected to the Royal Society in 1887; one of his proposers had been D. E. Hughes.

53 For an account of Lodge's experiments see Peter Rowlands and J. Patrick Wilson (eds.), *Oliver Lodge and the Invention of Radio* (Liverpool: PD Publications, 1994).

54 A lightning strike is not oscillatory. It is caused when the build-up of a static electrical charge in the clouds reaches a potential that is sufficient to break down the air and flashes down to the ground to equalize the potential. In the argument between Preece and Lodge, Preece was actually right in believing that lighting was like a high voltage DC discharge.

55 Oliver Lodge, *Lightning Conductors and Lightning Guards* (London: Whittaker and Co. 1892).

56 Ibid., pp. 74–86.

57 Ibid., p. 60.

58 John Henry Poynting was professor of physics at Mason College, Birmingham. He produced this equation, which is normally referred to as the Poynting Vector, in 1884. See Peter Rowlands and J. Patrick Wilson (eds.), *Oliver Lodge and the Invention of Radio* (Liverpool: PD Publications, 1994), p. 51.

59 B. J. Hunt, *The Maxwellians* (Cornell University Press, 1991), p. 149.

60 George Francis FitzGerald was professor of natural philosophy at Trinity College, Dublin.

CHAPTER 12

1 Letter from D.E. Hughes to Hugh Hughes, Corwen, one of David Hughes's cousins, dated February 14, 1896. He also corresponded with Hugh's nephew, John Davies Hughes, who once visited him in London.

Transcripts of these letters are in the Bob Owen Croesor Collection, National Library of Wales, Aberystwyth.

2 This short biography of Hughes was compiled from notes and biographical material compiled by John Munro, a writer friend of Hughes, and is now part of Hughes's private papers. Munro was the author of *Heroes of the Telegraph*, *Pioneers of Electricity*, and *The Wire and the Wave*. It seems that Hughes's wife Anna was hoping to have J. Munro publish a biography of Hughes in 1901 with Macmillan in London, but this never came to pass.

3 Frascati's restaurant was at 26–32 Oxford Street and Great Portland Street, where Hughes lived. The street ran into Oxford Street.

4 Hughes had an interesting remedy for a sore throat, which was to take one of his Caporal cigarettes and soak it in a mixture of petroleum and Vaseline. Presumably he allowed it to dry before smoking it. This detail is recorded in J. Munro's notes.

5 Pagani's Restaurant was located close by, on the corner of Great Portland street and Little Portland street.

6 *Tit-Bits* was a weekly British paper billed as "Tit-Bits from all the interesting books, periodicals and contributors in the world."

7 D. E. Hughes, "Note on Some Effects Produced by the Immersion of Steel and Iron Wires in Acidulated Water," *Journal of the Society Telegraph Engineers* 9.32 (1880), pp. 163–167, with a summary in *Nature* 21 (April 22, 1880), pp. 602–603; "On the Molecular Rigidity of Tempered Steel," *Proceedings of the Institution of Mechanical Engineers* (January, 1883), pp. 72–79; and "On the Physical Condition of Iron and Steel," *Proceedings of the Institution of Mechanical Engineers* (1884), pp. 36–60.

8 D. E. Hughes, "Molecular Magnetism," *Proceedings of the Royal Society of London* 32 (1881), pp. 213–225; "Theory of Magnetism Based upon New Experimental Researches," *Proceedings of the Royal Society of London* 35 (1883), pp. 178–202; and "Magnetic Polarity and Neutrality," *Proceedings of the Royal Society of London* 36, (1883–1884), pp. 404–417.

9 According to the domain theory of magnetism, large groups of atoms stick together and loosely orient themselves in the same direction to form domains that act like very small permanent magnets. In an unmagnetized piece of iron, these domains may be randomly oriented such that the net magnetic effect is zero. When subjected to a magnetic field, the domain boundaries move so as to align with the magnetic field and grow and dominate the material so that it takes on a strong polarity, i.e. it acquires a north pole and a south pole.

10 Hughes's last notebook of the series in the British library is Add MS 40163 and covers the period from May 1883 to January 1886. It is unknown whether Hughes compiled any later notebooks.

11 See "The Royal Institution and the Late Prof. Hughes," *Electrical Review*, February 9, 1900.

12 Paul Tunbridge, *Lord Kelvin: His Influence on Electrical Measurements and Units* (London: P. Peregrinus, 1992), p. 72. Also see Paul Nahin, *Oliver Heaviside, Sage in Solitude* (New York: IEEE Press, 2003), p. 103.

13 Anton A. Huurdeman, *The Worldwide History of Telecommunications* (Hoboken, NJ: Wiley-Interscience, 2003), p. 139.

14 "The Anglo-French Telephone Line," *The Times*, January 12, 1891.

15 "Speaking to Paris," *The Times*, March 19, 1891.

16 It was becoming standard practice, especially on long routes, to use twin copper wires for telephone circuits, which were twisted as they passed from pole to pole. This method was used by the Post Office in the UK and by others on the Continent such as L. M. Ericsson on their Stockholm to Gothenburg line of 285 miles. See *Electrical Review*, September 20, 1889.

17 J. J. Fahie, *A History of Wireless Telegraphy 1838–1899* (New York: Dodd, Mead and Co., 1899), Appendix. Also see *The Electrician*, May 5, 1899.

18 Munro's biographical sketch of D. E. Hughes, in Hughes's private papers.

19 The letter was printed in the *Electrical Review* 7 (1879), p. 200.

20 The Albert Medal was awarded to such notables as Michael Faraday in 1866, Fothergill and Cooke in 1867, and Sir William Thomson (Lord Kelvin) in 1872. There were often suggestions in some of the technical journals that Hughes should be honored with a knighthood as some of his colleagues had been. Hughes was, however, an American citizen which made him ineligible, although many people thought he was British—which he was by birth.

21 J. Munro, "The Late Professor Hughes," *The Electrical Review* 46.1158 (1900), pp. 185–187.

22 J. Munro's biographical sketch of D.E. Hughes, in Hughes's private papers.

23 *Proceedings of the Institute of Electrical Engineers* 29.146 (1900), p. 951.

24 The exchange rate in 1900 was £1 = $4.8. Comparison of monetary values from different eras is difficult, but in today's money this would probably be in the range of £13 million, or $20 million. Hughes's money was almost all invested in a diverse portfolio of international stocks and bonds, in industries such as railroads, gas and electricity companies, banks, breweries, waterworks, and flour mills. He also owned stock in Frascati's restaurant, which he frequented.

25 Information supplied by Mr. Phillip Boyes, Operational Director, University College London Hospitals Charities, December 11, 2008.

26 Information supplied by Mr. John W. Collinson, Director, King's College Hospital Charity, March 29, 2010.

27 Information supplied by Ms. Jane Miles, Chief Executive, Imperial College Healthcare Charity (which embraces the Charing Cross Hospital).

28 Information supplied by Mr. Jonathan Evans, Trust Archivist, Barts and the London NHS Trust.

29 This account of her journey and the quotations are taken from four letters she sent to her sister Clara while she was traveling, dated April 1, May 10, May 11, and June 9, 1903. The letters were very faded and partly illegible and were transcribed, probably in the

1930s, and these copies are now among Hughes's private papers. The whereabouts of the original letters is unknown.

30 Bombay is now known as Mumbai and Calcutta as Kolkata.

31 Letter from Anna C. Hughes to her sister Clara in America dated June 9, 1903, in Hughes's private papers.

32 Letter from Anna C. Hughes to her sister Clara in America dated April 1, 1903, in Hughes's private papers.

33 Letter from Anna C. Hughes to her sister Clara in America dated May 10, 1903, in Hughes's private papers.

34 Alan A. Campbell Swinton, *Autobiographical and Other Writings* (London: Longmans Green and Co, 1930). See also *Nature*, April 15, 1922, p. 485.

APPENDIX I-1

1 D. Olmsted, *A Compendium of Natural Philosophy* (New Haven: Babcock, 1842); J.L. Comstock, *A System of Natural Philosophy* (New York: Robinson, Pratt & Co., 1839).

2 D.E. Wells, *Familiar Science, or, The Scientific Explanation of the Principles of Natural and Physical Science* (Philadelphia: Childs & Peterson, 1856), p. 319.

3 R.L. Thompson, *Wiring a Continent* (Princeton: Princeton University Press, 1947), p. 241.

4 The Morse system was patented in America on June 20, 1840, as patent #1647. Initially the Morse system's receivers were recording devices: the receiver had an inker or stylus that printed out or inscribed the received Morse code pulses on a moving paper strip. The inker or stylus was operated by an electromagnetic relay directly off the line and the paper movement was driven by clockwork. The sender was a Morse key that switched the electrical current to the line on and off in accordance with the dots and dashes to be sent. It was not until later (particularly in America) that the recording was dropped in favor of just listening to the sound of the receiving relay and decoding the dots and dashes. When Morse tried to patent his telegraph in England his application was denied partly because of the challenge put up by Cooke and Wheatstone, and also by Davy. The Bain system, which was introduced from England (UK patent # 6328, 1849), used a code similar to that of Morse and transmitted via a similar sending key that switched the current on and off. The receiver, however, used the signaling current from the telegraph line to print the coded message directly on a chemically treated paper strip. The paper strip was moved along at a constant rate by clockwork. A stylus (receiving the current from the line) which rode on the paper passed the current through the paper to a grounded (earth) backing plate. The paper was conductive as it was treated with one of a number of chemical solutions, such as prussiate of potash, to which a little nitric and hydrochloric acid had been added. When a current was applied, it decomposed at the point of contact, leaving a blue or brown mark. The House system was invented by the American Royal E. House, American patent # 4464, 1846. This transmitted and received Roman letters, rather than code, and printed them out on a paper strip. It was, however, a two man operation, one to type in the letters and another to crank a wheel to provide the pneumatic power; the latter operator was called the organ grinder, after the street musicians who cranked a handle on their portable organs. Letters were typed in on a keyboard that resembled a piano keyboard, and scanned mechanically by a rotating cylinder with a helical pattern of pins. Letters were sent to the line as a variable number of pulses (see the explanation of step-by-step systems). The pneumatic supply was used to drive the rotating cylinder that both detected which key was pressed and provided the interrupter to generate the pulses. The receiving telegraph used the pulses to operate an electromagnetic solenoid valve which in turn controlled the pneumatic air supply to step the letter type escapement wheel, move the paper, and type the letters. In this system the type wheel came to a stop when it was necessary to print a letter. The House system may have been one of the first applications of a solenoid valve. The Cooke and Wheatstone telegraph was patented # 7390 in Britain in 1837, and in America, in 1840, ten days before Morse obtained his patent. Unlike the Morse system, which was a recording telegraph, the Cooke and Wheatstone was a needle telegraph. This relied on the operator to decode each letter by reading the direction (left or right) of five center-biased needles. It also required five telegraph wires with an earth return for operation, unlike the majority of telegraphs, which used a single wire and earth return. There were later models that used two needles and an ABC system that used a dial to display the letters of the message transmitted. This was essentially a step-by-step system and was used in Britain but was not adopted in America.

5 *Harpers Weekly*, Telegraph Supplement, September 4, 1858.

6 The earliest Cooke and Wheatstone needle telegraph required five wires.

7 The typewriter, though patented earlier, did not really make its debut in America until about 1867. Hughes's style of keyboard was, however, ahead of its time. Existing telegraph systems (such as those of House and Froment) favored the piano-style keyboard. Hughes's later models also switched to this style. Of course, many years later the typewriter keyboard came back into fashion.

8 DEH I & D.

9 For instance, the Morse code for the letter "E" was a single pulse, a DOT, and the letter "X," was four pulses, DOT, DASH, DOT, DOT. In terms of time units, if we count a dot as a single unit, a dash was three times longer, or three units. Further, the spacing between pulses was equivalent to one unit, and the spacing between letters was equal to three units. Therefore it took four time units to transmit the letter "E" and twelve time units for the letter "X." Additional time intervals equivalent to six time units were required to separate words.

10 The step-by-step telegraph used a method whereby the transmitter and receiver instrument were started at the same letter (usually a blank or space character). Communication from the transmitter consisted of a variable series of unipolar pulses. The number of pulses used to transmit a letter depended on the previous letter sent. For example, to send the letters A, G, S, the transmitter would send:

1st letter A = 1 pulse
2nd letter G = 6 pulses (6 letters on from A)
3rd letter S = 12 pulses (12 letters on from G)

If the receiving system missed a pulse then the message became garbled.

11 This type of modulation was the forerunner of Time Division Multiplexing (TDM). Today TDM is best known as a method of sending information from multiple data sources as a single composite signal for transmission over a cable or wireless link. This is accomplished at the transmitting end by selecting the multiple inputs via a multiplexer (sequencer switch) in a repeating sequence. Each of the multiplexed signals is assigned a specific time slot or segment in the composite signal that is to be transmitted. To recover the original individual signals, the receiver must be in both synchronism and phase with the transmitter. Then, via a demultiplexer, each of them can be extracted from the composite signal.

12 See Taliaffero Preston Shaffner, *The Telegraph Manual* (New York: Pudney & Russell, 1859). Other electricians had also built mechanisms inspired by the musical box. Cooke had started with a mechanism of this type but later abandoned it (see p. 185 of Shaffner's book); also see p. 373 on Froment's use of this type of device, and p. 391 on House.

13 Digital Pulse Modulation finally came into its own in the 1900s. As there were a number of different modulation techniques they were rigorously categorized. Pulse Position Modulation became defined as a series of pulses whose width and amplitude remained unaltered but the pulse occurrence was delayed or advanced in accordance with the input signal. See M. Schwartz, *Information Transmission, Modulation, and Noise* (New York: McGraw-Hill, 1959).

14 0.5 seconds divided by twenty-eight time slots.

15 DEH I & D.

16 The operation of the pendulum and escapement wheel was as follows. The escapement wheel was constructed with longish pointed teeth over which sat a curved device called the anchor, which straddled several teeth. The anchor pivoted at its center and each of its ends had a hook that could engage with the teeth of the escapement wheel. The pendulum was attached to the anchor so that as it swung, it rocked the anchor back and forth and could thus engage the teeth of the escapement wheel. As the pendulum swung to the right, a tooth on the right side escaped, but the wheel was not free to turn rapidly, as the hook on the left end of the anchor caught a tooth on the left side of the wheel and arrested it. As the pendulum swung over to the left, that tooth was released, but now a hook on the right end of the anchor caught a tooth on the right side of the wheel. The anchor allowed only one tooth of the gear to escape at a time, with each swing of the pendulum giving the familiar "tick, tock." The rotation of the escapement wheel was powered by a falling weight held on a cord (or alternately by a wound-up spring). The cord was wound onto a drum that through a series of gears drove the escapement wheel. As the pendulum would eventually stop swinging due to friction, it was necessary to give it a nudge on each swing to sustain the oscillations. The shape of the teeth on the escapement wheel accomplished this, giving it a little push as the tooth escaped from the anchor. While the speed of a clock was one revolution per minute, the pendulum was usually swinging much faster, depending on the number of teeth on the escapement wheel and the gearing involved. A typical pendulum might swing at a rate of once or twice per second.

17 DEH I & D.

18 The electrically driven tuning fork was introduced some years later in such items as the Delaney Synchronous Multiplex telegraph, and still later as a constant frequency source for watches and chronometers. Many years later the quartz crystal oscillator made it all easy.

19 The vibrating spring strip proved to be an accurate frequency source and was often referred to as running isochronous, that is, maintaining a constant frequency regardless of the arc through which it vibrated.

20 The first Morse relay weighed in at 300 lbs, and it was thought that the height of improvement had been reached when a relay was made that weighed 70 lbs. But in 1892 the Morse relay weighed only 3.5 lbs. See W.J. Maver, *American Telegraphy* (New York: Maver Publishing Company, 1903), Introduction.

21 DEH I & D. Hughes often used the word "discovered" when he discovered or found out something for himself for the first time, without the implication that it had not been discovered by someone else.

22 George B. Prescott, *History, Theory and Practice of the Electric Telegraph* (Boston: Ticknor and Fields, 1860), p. 142.

23 The Synchronous Multiplex Telegraph used a mechanical scanning device that sequentially scanned the several input circuits and sent the composite signal to the line. To maintain an accurate speed of rotation so that the instruments at both ends of the line could remain in synchronism, use was made of electric motors that received electrical pulses from tuning forks or vibrating reeds which were kept in a state of oscillation electrically.

24 The explanation given here is the best interpretation that can be deduced from the text and drawings in the patent, but while the description of the device's functioning is believed to be correct, the exact mechanisms that Hughes used may have been different. We do know that the print wheel was a friction fit on its arbor so that it could be stopped at the blank position as well as offset to compensate for line delays. It is assumed that the commutator was also a friction fit or could be declutched so that it could also be stopped at the blank position. After the synchronization process was started by releasing the arresting lever on the transmitting instrument, it is not known with 100% certainty whether an electrical pulse was transmitted automatically or whether the operator had to use the separate key to the right of the keyboard.

25 It has been stated that Moses Farmer had one of the first synchronous systems. See patent US #9634, 1853, "Improvement in Electric Telegraphs." He called his instrument a Synchronous Telegraph. This system was actually a sequencer that allowed two of Farmer's devices to share the line simultaneously. In addition to the regular telegraph line, his system required a second wire for control. The system consisted of a commutator rotated by a step-by-step method that oscillated back and forth between the two devices. The commutator rotated at a fairly fast rate of 150 revolutions per minute, thus allowing adequate time to sample each of the four inputs many times. Once started in sequence the two devices maintained synchronism as the control oscillated back and forth between them.

26 British Patent #2058.

27 Examination of the patent model now in the Smithsonian confirms that it was steel.

28 United States Patent #14,917, May 20, 1856. Improvements in Telegraphs, David E. Hughes.

29 This patent has not been examined but is assumed to be similar to his English patent.

APPENDIX I-2

1 George Phelps had become a partner in the company "House's Printing Telegraph Instrument Manufacturer" in Troy, New York. Phelps, who had fine mechanical abilities, had been manufacturing these instruments for about four years. He then worked for the American Telegraph Company when it was formed, and worked on the Hughes instrument. See John Casale, "George M. Phelps: Instrument Maker," *The Old Timer's Bulletin* 40.2 (May, 1999), pp. 21–23, and 40.3 (August, 1999), pp. 41–43.

2 American Patent No. 22770

3 It appears that a piano-type keyboard had been used as far back as 1832 by P.L. Schilling: see K. Beauchamp, *History of Telegraphy* (London: Institution of Electrical Engineers, 2001), p. 28. The industry stuck with the piano-style keyboards for quite some time and it remained the standard on the Hughes instrument. The typewriter-style keyboard came back into vogue much later in the 1800s, and the now familiar "QWERTY" key arrangement came to dominate.

4 Each station had its own battery with one terminal connected to ground.

5 The water retarder, as Hughes called it, was adjustable. The water, with an additive to make it slightly conductive, was contained in a glass tube stoppered at both ends. The connecting wires were slid through the stoppers. The amount of wire exposed to the water and the gap between them could be adjusted, with Hughes recommending that the gap be set at 1 inch for every 100 miles of telegraph cable.

APPENDIX I-3

1 The company was known as Dumoulin-Froment. Other nameplates also appeared on the instruments, such as "ADMINISTRATION des POSTES TELEGRAPHES HUGHES a CDE Directe L. DOIGNON, INGR CONSTR MALAKOFF (SEIGN) No 9."

2 E. E. Blavier, *Nouveau traité de télégraphie électrique* (Paris: Lacroix, 1867), pp. 237–269.

3 The shift principle on typewriters was not introduced and patented until 1875 by B.A. Brooks at the Remington typewriter factory. See Michael H. Adler, *The Writing Machine: A History of the Typewriter* (London: G. Allen and Unwin Ltd., 1973).

4 T.E. Herbert, *Telegraphy: A Detailed Exposition of the Telegraph System of the British Post Office* (London: Whittaker & Co., 1916), p. 450.

5 H.H. Harrison, *Printing Telegraph Systems and Mechanisms* (London: Longmans, Green and Co., 1923), p. 120.

6 H.H. Harrison, *Printing Telegraph Systems and Mechanisms* (London: Longmans, Green and Co., 1923), p. 119.

7 It was also reported that his instruments were in use on the Persian Gulf cable which was part of the cable to India.

8 H.H. Harrison, *Printing Telegraph Systems and Mechanisms* (London: Longmans, Green and Co., 1923), pp. 122–123.

9 T.E. Herbert, *Telegraphy: A Detailed Exposition of the Telegraph System of the British Post Office* (London: Whittaker & Co., 1916), p. 427. See also E. Buels, *Consideration sur le travail en duplex par appareil Hughes sur les lignes sous-marines* (Brussels: Imprimerie des Travaux Publics, 1891), first published in the *Bulletin de la Société Belge d'Électriciens*.

APPENDIX II

1 Silvanus Phillips Thompson, *The Electromagnet, and Electromagnetic Mechanism* (London and New York: E. & F.N. Spon, 1891), p. 186.

2 Thompson, *The Electromagnet, and Electromagnetic Mechanism*, p. 295.

3 T.E. Herbert, *Telegraphy* (London: Whittaker and Co., 1906), p. 431.

4 Thompson, *The Electromagnet, and Electromagnetic Mechanism*, pp. 186–187.

5 Alain Gernigon, *Histoire de la signalisation ferroviaire française* (Paris: La Vie du rail & des transports, 1998), p. 134; and A. L. Ternant, *Les télégraphes* (Paris: Hachette, 1887), p. 338.

6 Leonard P. Lewis, *Railway Signal Engineering* (New York: Van Nostrand, 1912; third edition J. H. Fraser, 1932). Republished in 1995 by Peter Kay, Orchard Gardens, Teignmouth, Devon, UK.

7 Thomas Watson, *Exploring Life: The Autobiography of Thomas A. Watson* (New York: D. Appleton and Co., 1926), pp. 99–101.

APPENDIX III

1 Dixie Hibbs, *Nelson County: A Portrait of the Civil War* (Charleston: Tempus Pub., 1999).

2 *Baner ac Amserau Cymru*, September 13 and 20, 1865. National Library of Wales, Aberystwyth.

3 *The Clarksville Jeffersonian* (Clarksville, Tennessee), April 27, 1859, and July 9, 1859.

4 Letter from the Nassau Bank, New York, to D.E. Hughes, dated September 15, 1865, in Hughes's private papers.

5 " In Search of Welsh Roots," *Y Drych*, October, 1963. *Y Drych* was the oldest North American Welsh newspaper; it has now merged with *Ninnau*, a monthly Welsh newspaper.

6 Martha Jackson reminiscences (MS 73, Clarence McElroy Collection, Library of Western Kentucky University, Bowling Green). On John and Fanny's marriage see Kentucky Marriage Bond 349 BKD, March 11, 1857.

7 See USA 1860 Census, Roll 398, Kentucky, vol. 24 (323–871), Union and Warren Counties.

8 Warren Co. Deed Book No. 28, pp. 182–183 (1861), and common law suit No.11323 in 1859—Samuel Putnam & G.W. Crook (Pl.) vs. John A. Hughes (Def.) at Bowling Green Courthouse.

9 Warren Co. Deed Book No. 29, pp. 242–243 (1861) at Bowling Green Courthouse.

10 He enlisted in Lexington, KY, on September 10, 1862, with Company C of the 3rd Kentucky Cavalry Regiment, which was consolidated with the 1st Kentucky Cavalry Regiment in 1863. Both units list him as a private and two record cards show him as AWOL. The CSA marker placed on his grave in Bowling Green's Fairfield Cemetery by the United Daughters of the Confederacy refers only to Company C of the 3rd Cavalry.

11 See USA 1870 Census, Roll 502, Kentucky, vol. 32 (1–442), Warren and Washington Counties.

12 Both John A. Hughes (1832–1880) and Fanny Hughes (1838–1979) are buried in Fairview Cemetery in Bowling Green, section A, plot 25.

13 See the Marriage Bond and Marriage Certificate dated March 12, 1877, Warren County, Kentucky.

~~...........l P....l, O....l., N.l....l.., ...~~

16 Edwin Gladding Burrows (Maggie's grandson), *The Cup & the Unicorn: Episodes From a Life. Millar Burrows 1889–1980* (privately printed, 1981).

17 Edwin G. Burrows and Mike Wallace, *Gotham: A History of New York to 1898* (New York: Oxford University Press, 1998).

18 Letters of Lilly Hughes Lucas (D.E. Hughes's brother John's youngest daughter) to Dr. John E. Younglove of ~~.........~~ ~~.......~~ ~~...~~ ~~.l...~~ ~~.....l......~~ ~~.l......l......~~

CORRIGENDUM AND ADDENDA

In Picture Credits and Sources on page 373, for "Pages 110, 120, 139, 145, 199, 200, 203, 206, 260: British Library, London" substitute

"Pages 110 - Add Ms 40643 Folio 71; 120 - Add Ms 40645 Folio 34; 139 - Add Ms 40648A Folio 80; 145 - Add Ms 40648A Folio 85; 199 – Add Ms 40161 Folio 192; 200 – Add Ms 40161 Folio 196; 203 – Add Ms 40161 Folio 220; 206 - Add Ms 40161 Folio 226; 260 – 3687.75 © The British Library Board"

PICTURE CREDITS AND SOURCES

Pages 3, 20–21, 51, 54–55, 64, 67, 131, 145, 186, 189, 195, 215, 244, 245, 256, 275, 276, 278, 314: David E. Hughes Papers

Page 4: Dolgellau Library, Wales

Page 7: Thomas Dugdale, *England And Wales Delineated* (London, 1846)

Page 9: National Library of Wales

Page 11: William H. Prior, *Old and New London* (London: 1873–1878)

Page 14: Museum of the City of New York

Pages 15, 44–45, 49, 98, 112–113, 130, 176, 180–181: Library of Congress

Pages 24–25, 284, 287, 290, 293, 329: Author photo. Division of Work and Industry, National Museum of American History, Smithsonian Institution, Washington, DC

Page 28: Dixie P. Hibbs, Bardstown, KY

Page 29: Mrs. Booker Noe, Bardstown, KY

Page 36: Division of Work and Industry, National Museum of American History, Smithsonian Institution, Washington, DC

Pages 40, 41, 78, 249, 282, 285, 289, 303, 305, 327: Technical Illustrator Carole Ruzicka

Page 46: James Reid, *The Telegraph in America* (New York: 1887), p. 363

Page 48: Bill Burns, www.Atlantic-Cable.com

Page 72: *Encyclopaedia Britannica*, 1911 edition

Pages 74–75, 86, 88: Bill Burns, www.Atlantic-Cable.com, from *Frank Leslie's Illustrated Newspaper*, June 26, 1858

Page 76: Bill Burns, www.Atlantic-Cable.com, from Louis Figuier, *Les Merveilles de la Science* (Paris, 1868)

Page 77: Bill Burns, www.Atlantic-Cable.com, from Science Museum, London

Page 105: A.L. Ternant, *Les Télégraphes* (Paris: Librarie Hachette et Cie, 1887), pp. 186–187

Pages 109, 317: Author photo, Musée des Arts et Métiers, Paris

Pages 110, 120, 139, 145, 199, 200, 203, 206, 259: British Library, London

Pages 115, 321: The A.S. Popov Central Museum of Communications, St. Petersburg, Russia

Pages 121, 127: France Télécon/APH, France

Pages 123, 306: Fons Vanden Berghen, Halle, Belgium

Page 137: Count du Moncel, *The Telephone* (New York: Harper Brothers, 1879), pp. 66–67

Pages 141, 142, 143, 146, 191, 204, 210: Author photo, Science Museum, London

Pages 171, 173, 273, 302, 322, 323: Author photo

Page 179: Alexander Graham Bell, *Upon the Electrical Experiment to Determine the Location of the Bullet in the Body of the late President Garfield* (Washington, DC: Gibson Brothers, Printers, 1882)

Page 184: Henry Collins Brown, *Book of Old New York* (New York: privately printed, 1913), p. 285

Page 209: *The Children's Encyclopedia*, edited by Arthur Mee (London, 1922), vol. 5, p. 3361

Page 221: Eric P. Wenaas

Page 222: Eric P. Wenaas, sketch from Pickard's personal notebook

Page 228: *Nature*, October 20, 1881, p. 587

Pages 229, 230: *Scientific American*, December 31, 1881

Page 232: George Peter Alexander Healy. *Mrs. Charles Morey (Anna Chadbourne, later Mrs. David E. Hughes)*, 1855, oil on canvas, Museum of Fine Arts, Boston, Ellen Kelleran Gardner Fund, 21 2232

Page 246: Robert John Strutt Rayleigh, *John William Strutt, Third Baron Rayleigh* (New York: Longmans, Green & Co.; London: E. Arnold & Co., 1924)

Page 247: Institution of Engineering and Technology, London

Page 268: *Illustrated London News*, March 28, 1891

Page 274: Royal Society, London

Page 312 (top): James Reid, *The Telegraph in America* (New York: 1887), p. 853

Page 312 (bottom): George B. Prescott, *History and Practice of the Electric Telegraph* (Boston: Ticknor and Fields, 1860)

THE AUTHORS

Ivor Hughes received his B.Sc. degree in Electrical Engineering from Bradford University in the UK where he worked in the telecommunications and aerospace industry. He was lured to the USA by the cutting edge technology being developed there, and holds patents on several electronic systems he designed. His background in electrical engineering proved invaluable in understanding Professor Hughes's notebooks and investigating his technical discoveries.

Hughes is a member of the Antique Wireless Association and has written a number of articles on wireless and telegraph history, as well as given lectures on Professor Hughes. Recently retired, he lives with his wife in Monkton, Vermont

David Ellis Evans was born in North Wales and received his education at Bala Boys' Grammar School. He is recently retired, having worked locally throughout his career, mostly in purchasing and material management in an engineering environment. His overriding passion has been cars and motorsport, both as a spectator and a competitor in cars of his own construction.

Evans has a strong interest in local and family history and is a first language Welsh speaker, which was very useful in the research for this book. He lives with his wife Joan in the house where he was born in Druid, near Corwen, in North Wales, a mere stone's throw from the spot where Professor Hughes is said to have been born.

INDEX

Hughes electromagnet
perpetual maintenance battery, 80
Perso-Arabic script telegraph, 320, 321
Phelps combination telegraph, 58–59, 68, 108–9, 311, *312*
Phelps, George M., 52–53, 56–59, 69, 157, 162–63, 302, 311, *312*
Phelps magneto receiver, 172
Philadelphia Centennial Exhibition, 132
Philadelphia Local Telegraph Company, 157
phonograph, 155–56, 159, 160
piano-type keyboard, 58, 63, 105, 307, 311, *312*, 315–17, *323*
Picard, Pierre, 319
Pickard, Greenleaf Whittier, 220, 221
Pierce, George, 221
Pilkington, James, 106
plucked wire experiments, 139, 140
plumbago, 150, 151, 153, 155
polarity, 122–23, 281, 309, 310, 319
polarity change-over contacts, 309
polarized relay, 292
Pope, Frank L., 250
Post Office. *See* British Post Office
Post Office insert #13 microphone, 172
Poynting, John Henry, 252, 261
practical men *vs.*
theoreticians
debate, 194, 239–62
drawbacks of practical approach, 240
electromagnetic wave research, 214–16
misunderstanding terms, 211–12, 219, 242, 247
precision oscillator, 101
Preece, William, 152, 267
accused by Edison, 129–35, 150–70
Garfield bullet, 177–78
Post Office positions, *131,*

135, 152–53, 156, 164, 226, 251
professional relationships, 147, 154, 159, 260
self-induction debate, 238, 251, 259
telephone, 136, 144, 146, 149–50
views on wireless apparatus, 207
Prescott, George B., 58, 67, 68, 295, 311, 312
press and the telegraph. *See* news industry and telegraph
Printing Telegraph. *See* Hughes printing telegraph
print wheel, *36, 42,* 112, 284, *293, 303,* 304, 316–17, *321*
Projector of the Atlantic Telegraph Cable. *See* Field, Cyrus West
Protestant Female College Bardstown. *See* Roseland Academy
Prussia, 114, 117–18, 119, 124
pulse. *See* electrical pulse
pulse position modulation, 285–86, 287–91

Q

Queen Victoria, 11, 90
quill tubes, *142*

R

radiotelegraphy, 223
rail systems and Hughes technology, 127, 227, 292
recorder-repeater, 153
rectifiers. *See* detectors (rectifiers)
Red Sea Company, 102
regeneration relays. *See* repeater relays
Reid, James D., 37, 52, 58, 68
Reis, Prof. Philipp, 136, 138, 148
rejecter, 318
relay receiver, Whitehouse, 79–80
repeater relays, 68, 112, 116, 282, 291, 318
reputation and standing, Hughes's, 33–34, 128, 135, 149–50, 160–61, 170, 209,

226, 236–38, 257, 258
retardation effect, 77–86, 94, 101–2, 308
rheotome. *See* interrupter (rheotome)
right-to-left print adaptations, 120, 321
Roberts-Austin, Sir William, FRS, 207
Roberts, Chandler, FRS, 190
Roman-Cyrillic telegraph, 112
Roseland Academy, 25–30
rotating arm contactor, 63, 303, 317–18
rotating commutator, 286, 303–4, 310, 317
rotating drum scanner. *See* helical scan drum
rotating pendulum. *See* conical rotating timing pendulum
rotating speed governor, 58–59, 68, *123,* 315, *322, 323*
rotonome, *244*
Royal Institution, 149, 155–56, 267
Royal Society, 147–49, 161–62, 190, 209–13, 211, 219, 225, 274
Russia, 110–16, 138, 320, *321*

S

Sanders, Thomas, 172
Saward, George, 87, 118
scanner. *See* rotating commutator
scanning helix. *See* helical scan drum
Schaefer, Louis, 37
Schiffler, Mr., 122
Scientific American, 176, 198
scientific community, 131, 135
scientific freedom of Bell and Hughes, 182
scientific interests, 17–19, 28–29, 109, 128, 151, 182, 265
scientific scandals, 50, 56–60, 84, 148–70, 163
scrounged and homemade apparatus, 34, *36,* 141, 197,